Introducing Transformational Grammar

From Rules to Principles and Parameters

Jamal Ouhalla

Queen Mary and Westfield College
University of London

Edward Arnold

A member of the Hodder Headline Group
LONDON   NEW YORK   SYDNEY   AUCKLAND

Edward Arnold is a division of Hodder Headline PLC
338 Euston Road, London NW1 3BH

© 1994 Jamal Ouhalla

First published in the United Kingdom 1994

2 4 6 7 5 3
95 97 99 98 96

Distributed exclusively in the USA by St Martin's Press Inc.
175 Fifth Avenue, New York, NY 10010, USA

British Library Cataloguing in Publication Data
Available on request

ISBN 0-340-55630-7

Typeset in Monotype Times by
Hewer Text Composition Services, Edinburgh
Printed and bound in the United Kingdom by
St Edmundsbury Press Ltd, Bury St Edmunds, Suffolk and
J W Arrowsmith Ltd, Bristol

Contents

For Sima

Acknowledgements

I owe a debt of gratitude to the individuals listed below. The list includes former and current students, former and current teachers, former and current colleagues, and friends who have contributed directly or indirectly:

Vanessa Barker, Imogen Bell, Abderrafi Benhallam, Misi Brody, Patrizia Brown, Ben Cavanagh, Deborah Cawkwell, Kate Chase, Stephen Daly, Afif El Amrani, Pablo Farba, Robert Gilles, Julia Gold, Marcus Haas, Sibylle Hallik, Eszter Havas, Nick Hodder, Wilf Hodges, Dick Hudson, Abderrahim Jamari, Stephen Jennings, Rosetta Jolley, Alex Kalaitzis, Tom Keenan, Ruth Kempson, Bettina Knipschild, Andrea Krunovar, Aleksandra Kucera, Kweiki Kwapong, Rita Manzini, Ibrahim Mohammed, Isabelle Moran, Ida Ofori, Ralph Penny, Jose Pita, Ian Press, James Prosser, Lucy Reid, Neil Smith, Susan Teuteberg, Ianthi Tsimpli, Debra Vincent, Chris Wilder, Caroline Wills, Deirdre Wilson, Hilary Wise, Helen Yeh, and Ayham Zikra.

I am also indebted to the editorial team of Edward Arnold, in particular Lesley Riddle and Naomi Meredith. Special thanks to Sarah Barrett for being an excellent editor.

Cover illustration: Detail from *Hillside in Provence* by Paul Cezanne. Reproduced by courtesy of the Trustees, National Gallery, London.

1

Language and Linguistic Theory

Contents

1.1 *Language and Mind*

1.1.1 Knowledge of Language

Linguistics is usually defined as the discipline which concerns itself with the study of language, although what language is taken to be may differ from one school to another. In the Generative Grammar tradition, language is understood to refer to the knowledge that native speakers have which, together with their other faculties, enables them to communicate, express their thoughts, and perform various other linguistic functions. Accordingly, the task of the linguist is to characterize, in one form or another, the knowledge that native speakers have of their language. Let us take Chris to be a native speaker of English and review certain 'things' that Chris knows by virtue of being a native speaker of English.

Obviously, Chris knows the words of the English language, that is, the way they are pronounced and what they denote or refer to. The word *pin*, for example, is pronounced in a particular way, and refers to a particular entity in the world. Words are basically sound symbols which bear an arbitrary relationship to whatever they refer to. As a matter of fact, Chris's knowledge of the words of the English language involves much more subtle information than simply the ability to pair sound symbols with meanings. For example, the word *pin* is made up of discrete sound units, so that the initial sound /p/ can be replaced with the minimally different sound /b/ to obtain the different word *bin*.

Chris also knows that the word *unhappy*, for example, is made up of two smaller meaningful units (**morphemes**), the negative **prefix** *un-* and the adjective *happy* which together convey the meaning 'not happy'. The negative prefix can be attached to various other adjectives, such as *kind* and *sympathetic*, to derive the complex negative adjectives *unkind*, with the meaning 'not kind', and *unsympathetic*, with the meaning 'not sympathetic'. Interestingly, Chris knows that the negative prefix *un-* is different in meaning from the homophonous prefix found with complex verbs such as *unpack* and *unbutton*. The verb *unpack*, for example, does not mean 'not pack', but means roughly 'reverse the action of packing'. Somehow Chris knows that the negative prefix can only attach to adjectives, so that if one comes across a complex verb which includes the prefix *un-*, this prefix must be the 'reversative' one.

In addition to knowledge of words, Chris knows that words can be arranged together to form meaningful sentences, and that different arrangements of words (word orders) give rise to different meanings. Consider the following examples:

1. The the likes boy girl
2. The boy likes the girl
3. The girl likes the boy
4. The girl is liked by the boy

If the words in these sentences are arranged as in (1) they do not make a meaningful sentence, but if arranged as in (2), (3), and (4) they make meaningful sentences. (2) means that *the boy* experiences a certain feeling towards *the girl*, and that this feeling is not necessarily shared by *the girl*. (3) has the (opposite) meaning, whereby *the girl* experiences a certain feeling towards *the boy*, and that this feeling is not necessarily shared by *the boy*. Finally, (4) has a meaning which is similar to that of (2), rather than that of (3), even though it has a word order which is similar to that of (3), rather than that of (2).

As with knowledge of words, Chris's knowledge of sentences involves some quite subtle aspects of language:

6a. The girl asked the boy to leave
6b. The girl asked the boy to be allowed to leave

7a. The boy is too stubborn to talk to the girl
7b. The boy is too stubborn to talk to

(6a) can have the meaning whereby *the boy* is supposed to leave (the girl ordered the boy to leave) or the (more subtle) meaning whereby *the girl* is supposed to leave (the girl asked permission from the boy to leave). However, if *to leave* is replaced with *to be allowed to leave*, as in (6b), only the meaning whereby *the girl* is supposed to leave is accessible. On the other hand, (7a) has the meaning whereby *the boy* is supposed to do the talking to somebody else. However, if *the girl* is dropped from the sentence, as in (7b), *the boy* changes from being the individual who is supposed to do the talking (to somebody else) to becoming the individual who is supposed to be talked to (by somebody else).

Chris also knows that sentences can convey different messages in different contexts. Consider the following brief dialogue from Sperber and Wilson (1986):

8a. *The boy*: Do you want some coffee?
8b. *The girl*: Coffee keeps me awake

The girl's answer to *the boy*'s offer can mean 'yes, please' (acceptance) or 'no, thank you' (decline), depending on *the girl*'s intentions and plans and the time in which the dialogue takes place. If *the girl* intends to stay up late at night, then (8b) is likely to convey an acceptance of the offer. But if *the girl* intends to have a good night's sleep to be able to wake up early the next morning, then (8b) is likely to convey a decline of the offer. Presumably, these two possibilities presuppose that the dialogue in (8a and b) takes place some time in the evening. If it is assumed to take place early in the morning, a different message might be deduced from *the girl*'s answer.

Thus, the ability to infer the right message from *the girl*'s answer depends on knowledge of contextual information relating to the time at which the dialogue takes place and the intentions and plans of *the girl*, as well as encyclopedic knowledge relating to the fact that coffee contains a substance which can cause one to be awake. There is a clear sense in which this kind of knowledge is not of the same order as the formal knowledge of how to derive complex words from simpler units and how to arrange words together to form sentences with particular meanings. For example, it is possible that a native speaker of English will fail to infer the right message from *the girl*'s answer in (8b), for lack of the right background information. However, it is unlikely that the native speaker will fail to realize that *keeps* consists of the verb *keep* and the third-person singular marker *-s*.

We can make a distinction between Chris's knowledge of the English language and Chris's ability to use this knowledge properly in various situations. The former includes knowledge of words and the rules which govern pronunciation, word-formation, and sentence-formation, among other aspects of language. The latter, on the other hand, includes knowledge of language, as defined, in addition to knowledge relating to people's beliefs, the rules that govern social behaviour, and encyclopedic knowledge, as well as rules of inference which enable people to interpret utterances in relation to a given context. We have now narrowed down the expression 'knowledge of language' to mean knowledge of the rules which affect various aspects of language, in addition to words. It is this specific definition of (knowledge of) language we are interested in here, and which we will assume in the rest of the discussion.

1.1.2   Language and Other Faculties

The Chris we have been assuming so far could be a normal person with an average intelligence. Now, Jane may be more skilful than Chris at knowing how to manipulate language to persuade, give good speeches, write detective stories, and so on. However, there is no sense at all in which Jane could be said to be more skilful than Chris at knowing, for example, that in (7a) above *the boy* is the individual who is supposed to do the talking to somebody else, whereas in (7b) *the boy* is the individual who is supposed to be talked to by somebody else. This kind of knowledge is common to all normal speakers of English, irrespective of their other abilities and skills.

Now take Chris to be an adult with the mental age of a young child. Chris may have many problems grasping the rules which govern social behaviour in relation to adults, and may also have difficulties with problem-solving tasks which are otherwise not supposed to be taxing for people of a similar biological age. However, it is quite possible that Chris knows, much as (skilful) Jane does, that sentence (4) above has a meaning which is similar to that of (2), rather than that of (3), even though (4) has a word order which is similar to that of (3) rather than that of (2).

Smith and Tsimpli (1991: 316–17) have reported the case of a '29-year-old man . . . whose non-verbal IQ averages between 60 and 70, who is institutionalised because he is unable to look after himself'. However, this man has a perfectly normal mastery of his native language, English; more spectacularly, 'when given a passage written in any of some 15 or 16 languages simply translates it into English at about the speed one would normally read aloud a piece written in English'. Other cases have been reported in the literature of people of varying ages who display a sharp discrepancy between their general cognitive abilities, including communicative skills, and their linguistic abilities (knowledge of language) (see Curtiss (1977; 1981; 1982; 1988) Yamada (1990)).

Finally, take Chris to be somebody who, as a result of an accident or a stroke, has received physical damage to certain areas of the left hemisphere of the brain, and consequently is suffering from what is clinically known as Aphasia, more precisely, Agrammatism in Broca's Aphasia. Chris may not have lost the ability to pick up cues from contexts to interpret sentences, and may not have lost the ability to solve taxing problems, and so on. But it is quite possible that Chris may have lost the basic ability to interpret sentence (4) as having a meaning similar to that of (2) rather than that of (3). Numerous studies have reported cases of aphasic patients who have difficulties interpreting sentences of the type in (4), but not necessarily sentences of the type in (2) and (3) (see Caplan (1987) and references therein).

Interestingly, the difficulties mostly arise in relation to a specific class of these sentences. Compare the following examples:

9a. The boy is kicked by the girl
9b. The door is kicked by the girl

(9a) is called a 'reversible passive', where either of the two individuals involved can in principle perform the action described by the verb (kicking), so that 'The girl is kicked by the boy' is also a meaningful sentence. (9b), on the other hand, is a 'non-reversible passive', where only *the girl* can perform the action described by the verb, so that 'The girl is kicked by the door' does not 'make sense'. The patients reported in the studies cited are likely to misinterpret (9a) as meaning 'the boy kicks the girl', but are not likely to misinterpret (9b) as meaning 'the door kicks the girl'. Presumably, this is because their knowledge of the world and their ability to reason (intact) enables them to exclude the unacceptable interpretation of (9b) whereby 'the door kicks the girl'.

The discussion here should lead to the conclusion that knowledge of language is quite independent of the other faculties of the mind/brain. It is independent of intelligence, can remain intact when other faculties are impaired, and can itself be impaired when other faculties are intact. The human mind/brain is said to have a **modular** structure, where each faculty has an autonomous existence from the others, although the ability of humans to use their language normally in general involves an interaction between each of these autonomous modules. Having said that, because knowledge of language forms an autonomous module it is possible to study it separately from the other faculties of the mind/brain, a point which we will come back to later in this chapter.

1.1.3   Grammar and Universal Grammar

We have defined knowledge of language as knowledge of words, and knowledge of rules dealing with various aspects of the language. Let us now classify this knowledge into identifiably distinct categories. Knowledge of words can be characterized in terms of an open-ended mental dictionary, called the **Lexicon**. Like a dictionary, the Lexicon can be considered to consist of **lexical entries** for words, where each lexical entry specifies various types of information necessary for the proper use of the word. Knowledge of rules can, on the other hand, be characterized in terms of the notion **Grammar**, so that we can say that Chris knows the grammar of the English language to mean that Chris knows the rules of the English language.

The term 'Grammar' is understood here to refer to all aspects of language, pronunciation, word-formation, sentence-formation, among others. The aspect of language relating to pronunciation is called **Phonology**, and the aspect of language relating to word-formation is called **Morphology**. Finally, the aspect of language relating to sentence-formation is called **Syntax**. These terms are also used by linguists to refer to the sub-disciplines of linguistics which correspond to each of these aspects of language, a point to which we will come back later on. Here, these terms are understood to refer to aspects of Chris's knowledge of English, and therefore are components of Chris's mind. Thus, knowledge of the grammar of English consists of an amalgam of more specialized types of knowledge which, together with the English Lexicon, form knowledge of the English language.

Restricting our attention to grammar, let us now ask the following question: how did Chris come to have this intricate and highly specialized system of rules which we call knowledge of English? It is very unlikely that Chris was taught this knowledge. It is quite possible that, at an early age, Chris was told to say *brought* instead of *bringed* and *mice* instead of *mouses*, and, at a later age, to try to speak 'proper English' instead of 'teenage gibberish'. However, it is highly unlikely that Chris was taught that, if one substitutes *to be allowed to leave* for *to leave* in (6) above, the meaning whereby *the boy* is supposed to leave disappears. This type of knowledge is subconscious, in the sense that, although native speakers possess it and use it, they do not have direct access to it, and therefore cannot teach it.

It is also highly unlikely, in fact practically impossible, that Chris came to know English by memorizing all the sentences that exist in the English language, simply because the number of such sentences is infinite. An important property of human languages is that a substantial number of sentences produced by native speakers are **novel**, meaning they are uttered for the first time. Human languages are said to be **creative**, insofar as there is no limit to the number of novel sentences that can be produced by native speakers. This creative aspect of human languages provides the strongest evidence that knowledge of language is essentially knowledge of rules, that is, a computational system which, together with the Lexicon, makes it possible to **generate** an infinite number of sentences from a finite number of rules.

A somewhat more plausible answer to the question raised above is that Chris came to know English by observing others speaking it, deriving the rules from their speech, and then **internalizing** those rules, all at a subconscious level. Having said that, one cannot help the feeling that there is something miraculous about this great achievement. The examples discussed above give us only a glimpse of the highly complex nature of human languages, a fact which is all too clear to linguists, but not necessarily to people who do not undertake the task of analysing languages in search of rules and generalizations. Yet Chris managed to master English at an age when certain much simpler tasks are beyond the reach of most children at a similar age. As a matter of fact, the complexity of human languages is such that learning them from scratch must surely be beyond the reach of any living organism which does not have some kind of special predisposition, that is, an **innate** ability of some sort.

Let us see what the nature of this predisposition or innate ability is likely to be. We have seen that knowledge of language is independent of the other faculties of the mind/brain. Therefore, it is unlikely that this predisposition is common to all faculties of the human mind/brain; if it were, we would not expect the kind of selective impairment of faculties reported to exist. Rather, the predisposition in question must be a specialized one, in the sense that it is unique to language. It is plausible to argue that to determine the nature of this predisposition we must look at the nature of language itself, the idea being that the nature of the predisposition to develop language must somehow be reflected in the properties of language itself. We have seen that language basically consists of rules of various types which, in combination with the Lexicon, make it possible for native speakers to produce an infinite number of sentences. On this basis, we can plausibly conclude that the innate predisposition to master language basically consists of a set of rules, i.e. a grammar.

Once we accept this conclusion, Chris's achievement in mastering the English language becomes amenable to a more rational explanation. Chris approached the task of mastering English already equipped with a rich system of rules, so that the learning process amounts to the comparatively more manageable task of learning certain aspects of the English Lexicon, and certain rules specific to the English language, as opposed to Berber, for example. Much of what remains of what we have been calling Chris's knowledge of English was there right from the beginning, and could not possibly be said to have been learned in the way one learns how to drive or play chess, for example.

The grammar which characterizes the innate predisposition to learn language is called **Universal Grammar (UG)**, where the term 'universal' is understood in terms of biological necessity. This is to say that UG is the set of rules that all humans possess by virtue of having certain common genetic features which distinguish them from other organisms. Consequently, UG rules are to be found in English, Berber, and, indeed, any human language, and form part of the knowledge that native speakers have of their language. This means that Chris's knowledge of English consists of the rules of UG and certain rules specific to the English language, in addition to the English Lexicon. Likewise, Idir's knowledge of Berber consists of the rules of UG and certain rules specific to the Berber language, in addition to the Berber Lexicon.

1.2   *Language and the Linguist*

1.2.1   The Task of the Linguist

Assuming that there are good reasons to study human languages, not least the prospect of learning something about the distinctive properties of the human mind/brain, the task of the linguist can be described as an attempt to characterize, in formal terms, the knowledge that humans have of their language. Notice that the task involved is essentially one of reconstruction: the linguist tries to reconstruct, via the process of analysing data, knowledge that exists in the mind/brain of the speakers. In other words, the task of the linguist is to formulate a theory (or a model) of language, in so far as theories of natural phenomena in general are attempts at reconstructing the mechanisms underlying those phenomena. Needless to say, such theories and models are meant as approximations of the reality, supported by the evidence available, rather than exact replicas.

Obviously, it is quite possible that the theories (approximations of knowledge of language) produced by the linguist may at some stage be off the mark, and even completely misguided. However, this is in the nature of scientific inquiry in general. The process of building a theory of language (or any other natural phenomenon, for that matter) is a constant process of revising one's ideas to accommodate new data, thereby broadening the empirical base of the theory. In view of this, it is quite possible that, over the years, the (many times) revised version of a given theory may bear little resemblance to its earlier self. At the same time, it is also possible that a revised version might reintroduce an idea that was previously rejected on the grounds that there was not enough evidence to support it. Newly discovered evidence might support an idea for which there was little evidence at an earlier stage in investigation, thereby justifying its resurrection.

We have characterized knowledge of language as involving, in addition to the Lexicon, knowledge of universal and language-specific rules, i.e. knowledge of a grammar. This means that a given theory of language is itself a grammar, in so far as it incorporates the (reconstructed) rules which govern the various aspects of language. It is for this reason that the term 'grammar' is sometimes said to be used by (some) linguists with 'systematic ambiguity'. It is used to refer to the knowledge that native speakers have as a component of their mind/brain, as well as to the theory constructed by the linguist as an approximation of that knowledge.

The grammar constructed by the linguist should be able to distinguish the language-specific rules from the rules of UG, so that it is possible to have theories of particular languages and a theory of language or universal grammar. Obviously, sentences of particular languages do not come wearing on their sleeves the rules involved in generating them. These rules can only be arrived at through rigorous analysis. Moreover, once these rules have been identified they are not likely to be wearing labels which identify them as either universal or language-specific. The task of identifying a given rule as a rule of UG must take the form of a hypothesis to be tested against further data from the same language, and ultimately against data from other languages.

A grammar which correctly describes a native speaker's knowledge of her/his language (i.e. a theory of a particular language) is said to meet the condition of **descriptive adequacy**. On the other hand, a grammar which correctly describes UG (i.e. a theory of UG), where UG is understood to be the set of rules which define human languages, is said to meet the condition of **explanatory adequacy**. Note that the goal of achieving explanatory adequacy is very much tied to the question of how native speakers acquire their language. Recall that we came to the conclusion that Chris must have been born with a predisposition to learn language on the basis of the fact that the knowledge Chris has is highly complex and cannot reasonably be said to be learned. A theory which describes accurately the predisposition in question (i.e. UG), and explains how the knowledge that Chris currently has follows from this predisposition, can be said to meet the condition of explanatory adequacy.

A distant, and somewhat less realistic, goal is to construct a theory of language use, that is, a theory which will characterize how knowledge of language interacts with other components of the human cognitive system in performing various functions. Notice that this theory entails individual theories which characterize the properties of the various interacting systems, including a theory of language. Because very little is known about the properties of some of these systems, the prospect of arriving at a theory of language use seems less realistic, for the time being.

1.2.2 Some Necessary Idealizations

We have seen that the ability to use language properly, for communication and other purposes, is the result of an interaction between different faculties of the mind/brain, including, of course, the language faculty. This means that the speech produced by native speakers is likely to contain a jumble of information not all of which reflects their knowledge of language. Now, a linguist who is interested in studying native speakers' knowledge of their language faces an obvious dilemma: basically, to ensure that conclusions reached on the basis of an analysis of the speech produced reflects accurately and solely native speakers' knowledge of their language.

In view of this, the linguist has to take certain steps to avoid drawing misguided conclusions on the basis of tainted speech. One such step, mentioned above, is to make a clear distinction between knowledge of language, that is, knowledge of rules, and the use of language in particular situations, which involves other faculties of the mind/brain. This is the distinction between what Chomsky calls in earlier work (*Aspects of the Theory of Syntax*, 1965) **competence** (knowledge of language) and **performance** ('the actual use of language in concrete situations'). Having made the distinction, the linguist is then in a position to work out which properties of speech should be attributed to competence and which to performance, although sometimes this may not be an easy task.

Chomsky explains that speech is usually affected by performance factors such as false starts, hesitation, or memory lapses, all of which are extraneous to language itself and should, therefore, be purged from the data to be analysed. In other words, the linguist should deal with an idealized form of speech hypothetically produced by an 'ideal speaker-listener', that is, a speaker-listener who is not affected by the performance factors mentioned. It is hardly worth emphasizing that this is not a claim about reality (there is no such thing as an ideal speaker-listener) but a necessary idealization designed to isolate for investigation only those properties of speech which reflect language.

Another idealization relates to the notion of the 'homogeneous speech community', that is, a community where there are no individual or other types of variation. Here again, it is hardly worth emphasizing that this is not a claim about reality (there is no such thing as a homogenous speech community) but a necessary idealization designed to ensure that we identify properties which are common to all speakers of a given language. As a matter of fact, this abstraction from individual or larger differences is routinely assumed in everyday situations when people use the expression 'the English language', for example. There exists no 'pure instantiation' of the English language. Rather, English exists in the form of a collection of dialects (American English, British English, Australian English are just a few of the larger categories) which are collectively referred to as 'the English language'. Presumably, the underlying assumption is that speakers of all these dialects have certain properties in common that make them speakers of English and not, say, Berber.

Just as English, or any other language for that matter, has no 'pure instantiation', UG also has no 'pure instantiation'. UG is instantiated as a component of larger systems of rules which include language-specific rules. In other words, UG is instantiated as part of English, Berber, Japanese, etc. Thus, to be able to isolate the properties of UG when analysing data from individual languages (the only route), the linguist has to abstract away from the properties of those individual languages. Like the previous idealizations, this one is also a necessary procedural move, designed to isolate for investigation a specific component of language.

It is interesting to note that the data the linguist initially has to deal with, which, as we have seen, is generally 'degraded' in nature, is precisely the kind of data that the child is faced with when acquiring a language. Yet, on the basis of this 'poor evidence' the child succeeds in developing a rich and highly complex system of knowledge only fragmentarily illustrated in the examples above. This is one of the major arguments, usually known as the 'poverty of stimulus' argument, for the innateness hypothesis. Only if humans are assumed to be genetically predisposed in terms of a rich system of knowledge can this otherwise impossible achievement be rationally explained. Presumably, in acquiring a language the child undertakes a series of idealizations, abstractions away from the non-pertinent properties of speech, similar in principle to the idealizations the linguist has to undertake. The difference, of course, is that in doing so the child is guided by UG (the innate predisposition), whereas for the linguist UG forms part of the object of investigation.

1.2.3   Speakers' Judgements: The 'little experiments'

Another source of data which the linguist can – in fact must – rely on is called **native speakers' judgements**, that is, the **intuitions** native speakers have about sentences of their language. Consider the following examples:

10a. I think (that) John fixed the car with a crowbar
10b. What do you think John fixed with a crowbar?
10c. How do you think John fixed the car?

11a. I wonder whether John fixed the car with a crowbar
11b. ?What do you wonder whether John fixed with a crowbar?
11c. *How do you wonder whether John fixed the car?

Native speakers of English are likely to judge the questions in (10b) and (10c) as 'good' or, to use a more technical term, **grammatical**. They are also likely to judge (11b) as being slightly deviant, that is, not as 'good' as its counterpart in (10b), but, at the same time, not as 'bad' as (11c), with *how* understood to modify the verb *fix*. The latter sentence is technically said to be **ungrammatical**. These subtle judgements surely reveal crucial information about native speakers' knowledge of English, and therefore must be taken into consideration by the linguist.

Although these 'grammaticality judgements' may in certain cases be affected by certain irrelevant factors, there is a sense in which they are a reliable source of data. It is possible to think of 'grammaticality judgements' as the result of 'little experiments', whereby native speakers subject the sentences they are presented with to the test of whether they are generated by the speakers' mental grammar or not. A sentence is judged grammatical if it is generated by the mental grammar of the native speaker, and ungrammatical if it is not.

Now, since the grammar constructed by the linguist (the linguist's grammar) is intended to be a model of the mental grammar, we should expect the linguist's grammar not to generate a sentence that is not generated by the mental grammar. This means that the expression 'grammaticality judgement' is also systematically ambiguous, in so far as it relates to the linguist's grammar and (by transitivity) to the mental grammar. If the expected parallelism (or extensional equivalence) between the linguist's grammar and the mental grammar does not hold with respect to a given sentence or set of sentences, the linguist will have to revise the linguist's grammar to accommodate that particular sentence or set of sentences.

Notice that a linguist who is working on a language of which she/he is a native speaker, can rely on her/his own judgements of sentences. In this case the linguist is said to engage in the process of gathering data by **introspection**. Although in principle introspection should be sufficient, it is sometimes useful and instructive to compare one's own judgements to those of other native speakers of the same language. However, by and large this would only be necessary in situations involving so-called borderline cases, as opposed to clear-cut cases. For example, it is possible that some native speakers of English would find (11b) above as being 'good' (grammatical), on a par with its counterpart in (10b). However, this is less likely to be the case with (11c), with *how* understood to modify the verb *fix*. (11b) is a borderline case, but (11c) is a clear-cut case of an ungrammatical (or ill-formed) sentence, and (10b) and (10c) are clear-cut cases of grammatical (or well-formed) sentences.

Borderline cases and clear-cut cases generally tend to elicit the same type of reaction across speakers: repeating the sentence to oneself a few times before giving a 'yes' or 'no' answer (borderline cases), as opposed to an instantaneous and dry 'yes' or 'no' answer (clear-cut cases). Notice that, to the extent that this is generally true for certain sentences, it implies a pattern, and therefore a piece of data which should be taken into consideration by the linguist. This is to say that we should expect an adequate theory of language (the linguist's grammar) to be able to distinguish between borderline cases and clear-cut cases: to explain why native speakers are clear-cut in their judgements about certain particular cases, but tend to be hesitant about others.

Given the fact that native speakers can be hesitant in relation to some (borderline) sentences, what might sometimes look like 'conflicts of judgements' or 'disagreements on data' between native speakers may well be in actual fact no more than a reflection of the borderline status of the sentences in question assigned to them by the (mental) grammar. Needless to say, clear-cut cases are not expected to, and usually do not, give rise to 'conflicts of judgements' or 'disagreements on data'.

1.3   The Principles and Parameters Theory

1.3.1   A Brief Historical Overview

The Principles and Parameters Theory is the current version of a larger set of different versions of modern Generative Grammar. The latter developed in the 1950s in the context of what came to be known as 'the cognitive revolution' which marked a shift – more accurately, a return – to a focus on the mental processes underlying human behaviour, from a mere concern with human behaviour for its own sake. As far as language is concerned, it marked a shift from a concern with the mechanics of certain limited aspects of particular human languages (mostly, morphophonemics) to a concern with the mental processes underlying a broader range of the properties of language. This change led to the articulation of certain ideas about the mental processes underlying language, some of which have been mentioned above. Here we will limit ourselves to a brief and broad description of the evolution of some of the major ideas which have influenced the development of the Principles and Parameters Theory. Inevitably, some of the specialized terminology used will not be transparent to the uninitiated reader; but I hope that it will be once the content of this book is covered.

Initially, Grammar was considered to consist of a set of Phrase Structure (PS) rules which generate Phrase Markers (Deep Structures), and a set of transformational rules which perform various types of operation (movement, insertion, deletion, etc.) on these Phrase Markers to derive appropriately modified Phrase Markers (Surface Structures). PS rules are 'rewrite' rules of basically two types: the 'context-free' type of the form $X \rightarrow Y$, and the 'context-sensitive' type of the form $X \rightarrow YXZ$, where Y and Z represent the context for X. The former type generate phrasal categories such as NP, VP, S, and the latter introduce lexical items into appropriate contexts in Phrase Markers. For example, a transitive verb is inserted into a transitive VP structure, and an intransitive verb is inserted into an intransitive VP structure, and so on. Transformations were largely construction-specific, so that there was a transformation for passives, a transformation for yes/no questions, and so on. UG was considered to contain a kind of blueprint which prescribes the types of possible rule system, and an evaluation metric which restricts the range of possible grammars to the ones (ideally, one) compatible with the data available to the child.

At a later stage it became clear that there was a conflict between the desire to provide a description of further phenomena – i.e. the desire to achieve descriptive adequacy, which resulted in the proliferation of rule systems – and the need to constrain this proliferation – i.e. the desire to achieve explanatory adequacy. The initial reaction to this conflict marked the beginning of what in later years developed into the much more sophisticated model now called the Principles and Parameters Theory, going through intermediate models called the Standard Theory, the Extended Standard Theory, and Government-Binding Theory. The reaction was basically to derive general principles from the existing range of rules and attribute them to UG. These principles would then serve as conditions on representations, or perform a restricted range of (linking) operations. As components of UG these general principles also serve to define the notion 'possible human language'.

Thus, PS rules were replaced with a limited set of conditions on the structural representation of categories, largely derived from the PS rules themselves (X-bar Theory). On the other hand, the ever-increasing number of construction-specific transformations was reduced to a few, and later on to a single general principle (Move/Affect-alpha), applying across construction types. The conditions on transformations, previously built into the transformational rules themselves to prevent them from overgenerating, were also reduced to a few general conditions on the application of Move-alpha or its output. Increasingly, the model acquired a modular structure, whereby different sub-theories deal with different aspects of language, the result being the consequence of an interaction between the principles of the various sub-theories.

As the theory was developing, its empirical range was widening, eventually to include a fairly broad range of diverse languages. This led to the sharpening of some of the existing ideas, but most prominently to the formulation of clear ideas about the principles responsible for linguistic variation. It turned out that some of the major aspects of linguistic variation can be accounted for in terms of simple and well-defined sets of options (parameters), largely determined by the lexical properties of categories. The comparative work carried out within this framework has been largely successful in identifying common underlying properties of superficially different languages, so much so that it has led to the realization that even 'Chinese is like English', albeit at a different level of representation.

1.3.2 About this Book

Although this book is intended as an introduction to the Principles and Parameters Theory, it also incorporates an attempt to explain some of the fundamental shifts of perspective which have shaped its development. These include the shift from a model of grammar based on category-specific and construction-specific rules to one which is based on general principles with a broader empirical range; the shift from a model of grammar with a minimal (or no) internal structure to one which is highly structured in terms of modules or sub-theories dealing with various aspects of language; and the shift from a model of grammar whose main focus was to provide an in-depth description of the grammars of a few individual languages to one which combines the task of describing the grammars of a broader range of individual languages with an attempt to account for linguistic variation in terms of parameters which define and set the limits on linguistic variation.

The task of presenting and illustrating these major shifts of perspective which have taken place over a substantial period of time will inevitably involve a process of selection of issues, data, hypotheses, opinions, bibliographical sources, and so on. Combining this task with that of providing an introduction to the formal mechanisms of the Principles and Parameters Theory will also inevitably involve a process of adapting ideas from previous frameworks in ways that affect the format of their presentation and sometimes also their content. For example, in Chapter 3 the construction-specific transformations of the previous frameworks are not presented in the format in which they were originally presented (SD and SC), although the reader is given an idea about the original format in relation to one transformational rule at the beginning of the chapter. Moreover, the task of justifying the eventual reduction of most transformations to the more general principle Move-alpha (in Chapter 8) has meant that the definitions of the relevant individual transformations (in Chapter 2) must emphasize their aspect as movement transformations, while at the same time emphasizing their other aspect as construction-specific rules.

Chapters 2 and 3 deal with the category-specific (PS) rules and the construction-specific (transformational) rules respectively. Chapters 4, 5, 6, 7, and 8 deal with each of the major sub-theories of the Principles and Parameters Theory, and the way each principle accounts for the relevant aspects of the derivation and representation of sentences. Up to this stage in the book the data discussed are exclusively from English, even though on occasions the purpose would be better served in terms of data from other languages. The point is to drive home the message that it is possible to formulate hypotheses relating to the universal character of some deep and abstract principles on the basis of an in-depth study of a single language.

This goal partly determines the content and organization of Chapter 9, which deals with cross-linguistic variation (i.e. the parameters side of the Principles and Parameters Theory). Some of the major principles established on the basis of English in the previous chapters are shown to hold for other languages, although sometimes this may not seem to be the case initially. Various parameters are discussed which deal with certain major aspects of cross-linguistic (and cross-dialectal) variation extensively discussed in the literature.

Note on Further Reading. The information included in the Further Reading section at the end of each chapter is by no means exhaustive. Moreover, some of the ideas discussed in various parts of the book are presented in an adapted form for reasons having to do with consistency in presentation and other considerations. The reader is strongly advised to consult the original sources.

Further Reading

Discussions of the philosophical and methodological foundations of linguistic theory in general and Generative Grammar in particular can be found in Chomsky (1957; 1965; 1966; 1968; 1975b; 1980a; 1986a; 1987a, b; 1988; 1991a, b), and Chomsky *et al.* (1982). Smith and Wilson (1979) and Newmeyer (1983) include a summary of the core ideas, discussed and explained at a fairly accessible level. An equally accessible discussion of the underpinnings of linguistic theory and related issues can be found in Smith (1989), a book described as 'popularization of science in the very best sense'.

Chomsky (1975a), based on an unpublished text written originally in 1955, includes an additional introduction which provides invaluable information relating to the earlier stages of the development of Generative Grammar. A more up-to-date account of the development of the theory and reflections about its future shape can be found in Chomsky (1987a, b). Newmeyer (1980) is an excellent historical account of the major debates and 'linguistic wars' which have shaped the evolution of the particular version of Generative Grammar outlined in this book, and which have led to the development of other distinct, but equally important, versions.

A general discussion of the shift from a rule-based grammar to a principle-based grammar can be found in Chomsky (1986a). Chomsky (1981) is a detailed and highly technical account of the attempts to replace rules with general principles, and explains cross-linguistic variation in terms of parameters. An interesting and insightful evaluation of the current state of the principle-based model and its relationship to earlier models can be found in Newmeyer (1991).

Discussions of the issue of modularity can be found in most of Chomsky's references cited above, as well as in the references cited in the main text of this chapter, in particular Curtiss (1977; 1981; 1982; 1988), Yamada (1990), and Smith and Tsimpli (1991). A general discussion of the issue of modularity can also be found in Newmeyer (1983) and Smith (1989). For a philosophical oriented discussion see Fodor (1983).

References relating to language acquisition and aphasia (Neuro(psycho)linguistics) are provided in the Further Reading section of Chapter 9.

2

A Phrase Structure Grammar

Contents

2.1 *Preliminary Remarks*

In the previous chapter we characterized the native speaker's knowledge of English as consisting of rules (a grammar) and a Lexicon (a mental dictionary). The latter consists of lexical entries for words which specify various types of information crucial for the proper use of the word. A typical entry will include information relating to (i) the pronunciation of the word (a phonetic representation), (ii) the meaning of the word (a representation of meaning), and (iii) the class of categories (the part of speech) it belongs to, i.e. whether it is a verb, a noun, an adjective, a preposition, an adverb, etc (a categorial representation). We will see later on in this chapter that additional information needs to be specified in lexical entries which is equally crucial for the proper use of the word.

So far, we have been using the term 'word' without defining it. It is hard, if not impossible, to find an accurate definition for this term. For example, *kicked* in (1) below would normally be referred to as a word, despite the fact that it consists of two smaller meaningful units (morphemes): the verb *kick* and the Tense marker *-ed*:

1. John kicked the white ball

Tense is the category which specifies the time of the event described by the sentence (past, present or future) in relation to the time when the sentence itself is uttered. For example, the event of 'kicking' described in (1) takes place in the past in relation to the time when the sentence is uttered. It is not clear whether *-ed* is a word of the same order as *kick*, since, unlike *kick*, it cannot 'stand alone'. At the same time, the Tense marker *-ed*, like *kick*, is a meaningful unit in its own right, and contributes to the overall meaning of the sentence. For this reason, among many others, we will avoid the term 'word' here, and instead use the less controversial term 'lexical item'. We will assume that *kick* and *-ed* each constitutes a lexical item.

2.2   *Constituencies and Hierarchies*

In this section we will try to determine the broad aspects of the structure of the sentence. Note that this statement includes the implicit claim that sentences have a structure. How do we know that this is the case? Our answer to this question will, for the moment, be that we simply do not know. We are using this claim as a hypothesis which we intend to verify against data. If it turns out that the data support the hypothesis, that is, if we can show that the best way to explain certain properties of sentences is by assuming that they have a structure, our hypothesis will be valid. On the other hand, if it turns out that the data do not support the hypothesis – if we fail to show that properties of sentences can be explained in terms of a structure – we will either have to modify our hypothesis or give it up altogether.

First, we need to clarify what the expression 'sentences have a structure' means. In the present context we will understand this expression to mean that the lexical items which make up a given sentence are hierarchically ordered with respect to each other, such that some are at a higher, lower, or the same level of hierarchy as other items. To illustrate, consider the abstract diagram in (2). There is an obvious sense in which A is higher than B and C, and B and C are higher than D and E. There is an equally obvious sense in which B

2.

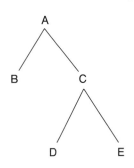

is at the same level of hierarchy as C, and D at the same level of hierarchy as E. Moreover, D and E are directly linked to C, while B and C are directly linked to A. Using more formal terminology, D and E are **constituents** (members) of C, and B and C are constituents of A. D and E, however, are not constituents of B, since they are not linked to B. It is these kinds of relation which we expect to find among lexical items which make up sentences when we say that 'sentences have a structure'.

Consider the following, simple, sentence:

3. This boy can solve the problem

We saw above that lexical items belong to different classes of categories. As a first step towards determining the structure of (3), we can specify the categorial nature of each word by using the following abbreviations: **N** for nouns, **AUX** for modal auxiliaries, **V** for verbs, and **Det** for determiners. These abbreviations are known as **categorial labels**. The categories in (3) together form the larger and more complex category **Sentence**, abbreviated as **S** (see (4)). The triangle in this diagram (and others below) is used to indicate that no specific claim is intended or made (yet) concerning the internal structure of the relevant category. On other occasions, the triangle will be used to include categories which are not directly relevant to the point being discussed.

4.

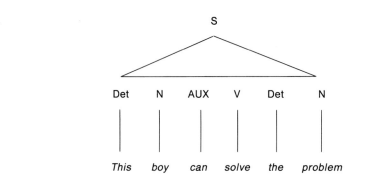

A priori, there are a number of ways the categories in (4) can be hierarchically related to each other and, ultimately, to S. (5) and (6), where the question mark stands for an unspecified categorial label, represent two arbitrarily chosen possibilities. (4) incorporates the claim that the determiner *this*, the noun *boy*, the auxiliary modal *can*, and the verb *solve* together form a constituent which excludes the determiner *the* and the noun *problem*.

5.

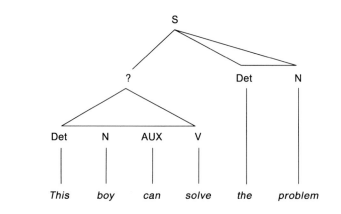

6.

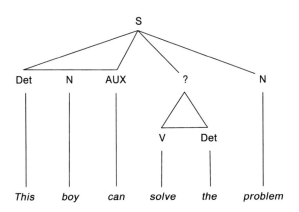

(6), on the other hand, incorporates the (different) claim that the verb *solve* and the determiner *the* together form a constituent which excludes the other categories in the sentence.

Which is the correct structure, if any, is an empirical question which can only be resolved on the basis of a proper investigation of relevant data. Our strategy will be to select strings of categories and see whether their members behave as a unit or block with respect to certain phenomena. The string of categories we will select first is *solve the problem*, which we will examine in relation to the phenomena of **displacement, deletion, co-ordination** and **replacement with a pro-form**. The latter are **constituency** criteria (or tests), used to determine whether a given string of categories forms a constituent. If the categories in the selected string can, in one block, move, delete, be co-ordinated with a similar string of categories, or replaced with an appropriate pro-form, we will conclude that they form a constituent.

Consider the following examples:

7. Displacement
   This boy is determined to solve the problem and
   [solve the problem] he will [—]

8. Deletion:
   John cannot solve the problem, but this boy can [—]

9. Co-ordination:
   This boy will [solve the problem] and [win the prize]

10. Replacement with a pro-form:
    This boy can solve the problem and [so] can the others

In (7) the string of categories we have selected (included in square brackets) has been displaced from the position marked [—], where it is 'understood', to the position preceding the pronoun *he*. In (8) the string in question has been deleted from the position immediately following the modal auxiliary *can*, i.e. the position where the deleted material is 'understood'. In (9) the same string of categories is coordinated (using *and*) with a similar string of categories, i.e. a string which also consists of a verb (*win*), a determiner (*the*), and a noun (*prize*). Finally, in (10) the string of categories chosen is replaced with the pro-form *so*. The latter is a pro-form in the sense that it stands for the string *solve the problem*.

On the basis of the facts illustrated in (7–10) we can conclude that the categories included in the string *solve the problem* together form a single, larger constituent. In other

11.

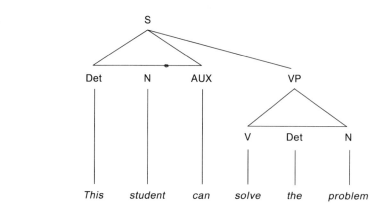

words, we can think of the facts illustrated in (7–10) as empirical evidence in favour of postulating a structure for (2) where the verb *solve*, the determiner *the,* and the noun *problem* together form a single constituent which excludes the other categories in the sentence. In diagram (11) the constituent in question is labelled **Verb Phrase (VP)**. Pending the evidence, the rest of the categories in the sentence, i.e. the determiner *this*, the noun *student*, and the Modal *can*, are linked to S in terms of a triangle. Likewise, pending the discussion of the internal structure of VP, its constituents are linked to it in terms of a triangle.

The conclusion we have reached on the basis of the facts illustrated in (7–10) already excludes both (5) and (6) as possible structures of (2). This is because neither of these structures has the verb *solve*, the determiner *the*, and the noun *problem* included under a single constituent. In other words, (5) and (6) make the wrong predictions with respect to the constituency tests discussed above. Because the categories in question are not included under a single constituent, they are not predicted to cluster together as a unit/block with respect to the phenomena of displacement, deletion, co-ordination, and replacement with a pro-form, contrary to what we saw above. Thus, structures (5) and (6), and the hypotheses they incorporate, can be dismissed on the grounds that they are empirically inadequate.

Following the same procedure, let us now select another string of categories to determine the structure of the rest of the sentence. This time we will select the string *this boy*, which consists of the determiner *the* and the noun *boy*. Consider the following examples:

12a. [This boy] and [that girl] can solve the problem
12b. [He] will solve the problem
12c. [This boy], I believe [—] can solve the problem

In (12a) the determiner and the noun are coordinated with a similar string of categories, and in (12b) they are together replaced with the pro-form (pronoun) *he*. Finally, in (12c) the determiner and the noun have been displaced to the beginning of the sentence. All these facts suggest that the determiner and the noun preceding the modal auxiliary together form a constituent. Incorporating this conclusion into diagram (11), we obtain the more articulated structure (13), where the larger category which includes the determiner and the noun is labelled **Noun Phrase (NP)**. Note that this structure also incorporates the implicit conclusion that AUX alone forms an autonomous constituent of S. Since AUX is the only category left, this conclusion seems to be warranted, if not inescapable.

To make sure that there is an empirical basis for this conclusion, we can test it in terms

13.

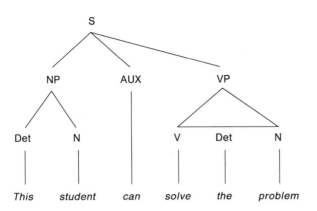

of the constituency criteria. If the conclusion is correct, we expect AUX to be able, for example, to be displaced, and to be co-ordinated with another AUX element, independently of the categories which make up NP and VP. The following examples suggest that this is indeed the case:

14a. [Can] this boy [—] solve the problem?

14b. This boy [can] and [will] solve the problem

In (14a) the modal auxiliary *can* is displaced to the front of the sentence, across the NP *this boy*. In (14b) the modal auxiliary is co-ordinated with another modal auxiliary, *will*. These facts confirm that AUX alone forms an autonomous constituent of S, as shown in (13).

Our remaining task with respect to (13) is to determine the internal structure of VP. That is, we need to determine whether each of the categories included under VP is an autonomous constituent of VP or whether some of them cluster together in the form of a larger constituent of VP. As a matter of fact, this task has already been carried out. Like their counterparts *this* and *boy*, the determiner *the* and the noun *problem* are likely to form an NP constituent too. Generalizations of this type are expected, on the grounds that categories of the same class tend to cluster together in the form of larger constituents. As it will transpire in this book, generalizations of this type form the backbone of linguistic research. On this basis alone, we can conclude that the determiner and the noun inside VP form an NP constituent of VP.

The consequence of this conclusion is that V also forms a constituent of VP. As in the previous situation, to make sure that there is an empirical basis for the conclusion that *the* and *problem* form a single constituent, we can test it in terms of relevant constituency criteria. Consider the following examples:

15a. This boy can solve [it]
15b. This boy can solve [this problem] and [that puzzle]
15c. [This problem], I believe the boy can solve [—]

In (15a) the determiner and the noun (inside VP) are replaced with the pronoun *it*, and in (15b) they are co-ordinated with a similar string of categories. Finally, in (15c) the determiner and the noun have together been displaced to the beginning of the sentence. These examples and the evidence they present confirm the conclusion that the determiner and the noun form a constituent of VP which excludes the verb.

We now have a fully articulated structure of sentence (3), shown in (16). The numbers associated with NPs have no theoretical status. They are merely convenient devices to

16.

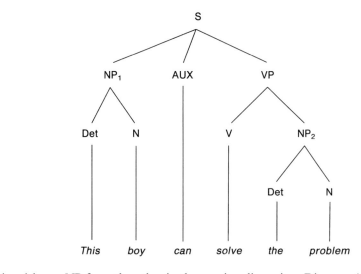

distinguish one NP from the other in the ensuing discussion. Diagram (16) is basically a graphic way of representing the conclusions we have reached concerning the constituent structure of the sentence discussed. The advantage of (16) lies in the fact that it shows clearly (in visual terms) that categories are indeed hierarchically related to each other and, ultimately, to S. For example, V and NP$_2$ are not at the same level of hierarchy as NP$_1$, AUX, and VP. This is because V and NP$_2$ are constituents of a constituent of S, whereas NP$_1$, AUX, and VP are all constituents of S. V and NP$_2$ are **immediate constituents** of VP, whereas NP$_1$, AUX and VP are immediate constituents of S. On the other hand, Det and N are immediate constituents of NP.

The hierarchical relations between categories are usually expressed in terms of the relation of **dominance**. A category is said to **immediately dominate** its immediate constituents. Thus, S immediately dominates NP$_1$, AUX, and VP; VP immediately dominates V and NP$_2$; and NP (in both occurrences) immediately dominates Det and N. Note, however, that although S does not immediately dominate V and NP$_2$, because the latter are not its immediate constituents, it does dominate them. The distinction here is between immediate dominance and (mere) dominance. A category is said to immediately dominate its immediate constituents, and to (merely) dominate the constituents of its constituents. The notion 'constituent of a constituent' is crucial in determining dominance relations. Because V and NP$_2$ are not constituents of a constituent of NP$_2$, the latter does not dominate them.

A diagram like (16) is called a **tree diagram**, by analogy with family tree diagrams. And terms used to refer to family relations, in particular **mother, daughter,** and **sister**, are also used to refer to relations between categories in a tree diagram. Immediate constituents of a category are daughters of that category. For example, Det and N are daughters of NP, and V and NP$_2$ are daughters of VP. Obviously, if Det and N are daughters of NP, then NP is their mother, and if V and NP$_2$ are daughters of VP, then VP is their mother. Also, if Det and N are daughters of the same mother, then Det and N are sisters, and if V and NP$_2$ are daughters of the same mother, then V and NP$_2$ are sisters, and so on.

Tree diagrams such as (16) are not the only means of representing structures. Another, equally frequently used, means is known as **labelled brackets**. (17) below represents exactly the same information as (16), albeit by different means:

17. [$_S$ [$_{NP1}$ [$_{Det}$ *This*] [$_N$ *boy*]] [$_{AUX}$ *can*] [$_{VP}$ [$_V$ *solve*] [$_{NP2}$ [$_{Det}$ *the*] [$_N$ *problem*]]]]

The difference between tree diagrams and labelled brackets is that in tree diagrams categories are represented in terms of labelled **nodes**, and related to each other in terms of **branches**, whereas in labelled brackets categories are represented in terms of labelled brackets, and related to each other in terms of inclusion and exclusion relations. In (17) the bracket labelled VP, for example, includes the brackets labelled V and NP_2, meaning that V and NP_2 are constituents of VP. At the same time, the bracket labelled VP excludes the brackets labelled NP_1, and AUX, meaning that the latter are not constituents of VP. As expected, the bracket labelled S includes all the other brackets, reflecting the fact that all categories in the sentence are either constituents of S or constituents of constituents of S. Depending on the issue discussed, we will be using both means of representing structures, with the choice being entirely a matter of convenience.

2.3   *Phrase Structure Rules*

2.3.1   The Nature of Phrase Structure Rules

The claims about the structure of the sentence represented by diagrams (16) and (17) above can be formulated in terms of 'rewrite rules' such as the ones in (18) (read '→' as 'rewrite as' or, less formally, 'goes to'):

18a. S → NP AUX VP
18b. NP → Det N
18c. VP → V NP

(18a-c) are **Phrase Structure (PS)** rules which incorporate claims (specified to the right of the arrow) about the constituent structures of phrases (specified to the left of the arrow). PS rules are said to **generate** categories, where 'generate' is understood to mean 'make explicit'. (18a), for example, generates the structure of S in the sense that it makes explicit the information that S consists of NP, AUX, and VP. (18b), on the other hand, generates the structure of NP in the sense that it makes explicit the information that NP consists of Det and N. Finally, (18c) generates the structure of VP in the sense that it makes explicit the information that VP consists of V and NP. Tree diagrams and labelled brackets are (visual) devices of representing claims about constituent structures made by PS rules.

   PS rules incorporate information relating not only to the number and nature of constituents a category may have but also to their linear order. Part of the information included in (18b), for example, is that Det precedes N in linear order. The opposite order, where Det follows N, illustrated in example (19a), below, is therefore excluded (the asterisk is a convention used to designate ungrammatical examples):

19a. *[NP *Boy this*] can solve [NP *problem the*]

19b.

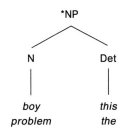

By specifying the appropriate order of constituents in the relevant PS rule, ungrammatical examples such as (19) are excluded (not generated). The argument extends to the order of constituents in the other categories as well.

The PS rules (18a–c) were based on sentence (3) in the previous section. However, their generative capacity goes well beyond this sentence, to include all possible sentences in the language with similar strings. Here are a few examples:

20a. The police will arrest the thief
20b. This girl can drive that car
20c. The President will chair the meeting
20d. The Parliament can impeach the President

These sentences are similar to (3) in that they all consist of NP, AUX, and VP, where NP consists of Det and N, and VP consists of V and NP. Therefore, like sentence (3), they, and a large number of possible sentences like them, can all be generated by the PS rules (18a–c), in combination with the Lexicon.

To generate a specific sentence of the set of sentences generated by rules (18a–c), another set of rules can be added which generates specific lexical items. Sentence (3), for example, is fully generated by the following set of rules:

21a. S → NP AUX VP
21b. NP → Det N
21c. VP → V NP

21d. AUX → *can*
21e. Det → *the, this*
21f. N → *boy, problem*
21g. V → *solve*

Any of the sentences in (20a–d) can be generated by rules (18a–c) together with a set of rules which generate the specific lexical items included in each sentence. Rules (18a–c) generate **phrasal categories**, one of whose constituents is usually a **terminal node**: AUX, Det, and V. For example, the phrasal category VP has the terminal node V as one of its constituents, and NP has the terminal node N as one of its constituents. Rules (21d–g), on the other hand, generate terminal nodes, by introducing corresponding lexical items in the sentence. The structures generated by both sets of rules are called **Phrase Markers**. Structures (16) and (17) in the previous section are examples of Phrase Markers.

Obviously, there is also an equally large number of possible sentences which PS rules (18a–c) cannot generate, mainly because they have constituency patterns which differ from the ones in sentences (3) and (20a–d). In the rest of this chapter, we will try to accommodate as many types of these sentences as possible, essentially by enriching the system of PS rules developed so far. We will discuss each of the rules in (20a–c) separately, and modify it in such a way that it can accommodate a broader range of constituency patterns, and therefore a broader range of sentences. Our first target will be AUX.

2.3.2   AUX

Consider the following examples, which differ from the ones discussed so far in that they apparently lack a (Modal) auxiliary:

22a. The boy kicked the ball
22b. The boy saw the girl

(22a and b), and a large number of similar sentences, are problematic for rule (18a) because the latter states that AUX is an obligatory constituent of S. To accommodate (i.e. to enable rule (18a) to generate) sentences such as (22a,b), as well as sentences with AUX, we need to modify rule (18a). An obvious way of achieving the desired result is, simply, to make the occurrence of AUX optional. Notationally, this can be done by including AUX between parentheses, as in (23):

23. S → NP (AUX) VP

(23) states that S consists of NP, an optional AUX, and VP. The revised version of the rule now generates the type of sentence discussed in the previous section, i.e. sentences which instantiate a Modal auxiliary, as well as the type of sentence illustrated by (22a,b), which apparently do not instantiate a Modal auxiliary.

However, there is an alternative way of accommodating sentences such as (22a,b) which, when examined carefully, turns out to be more adequate than the solution which makes the occurrence of AUX optional. Consider the following examples:

24a. *The boy* [AUX *will*] *kick the ball*
24b. *The boy* [AUX *doesn't/didn't*] *like the party*
24c. *The girl* [AUX *didn't*] *like the party, but the boy* [AUX *did*]
24d. [VP *Kick the ball*] *I wonder whether he* [AUX *will*] [—]

In (24a) Tense (which, remember, is the category which specifies the time when the event described by the verb is carried out) shows up as the Modal *will*. In (24b) Tense also shows up on the auxiliary *do*, suggesting that Tense is a constituent of AUX, rather than of VP. This is confirmed in (24c) by the fact that deletion of the verb and its complement (i.e. deletion of VP) does not affect Tense, and in (24d) by the fact that displacement of VP does not affect Tense. All in all, examples (24a–d) show clearly that Tense is a constituent of AUX, rather than of VP.

Now, given that sentences usually have a Tense category, and given that Tense is a constituent of AUX, it follows that all sentences instantiate an AUX category. Sentences differ only in that some of them instantiate a Modal auxiliary under the AUX node, in addition to Tense, as in *This boy could solve the problem*, whereas others instantiate only Tense under the AUX node, as in (22a,b) above. Thus, the optionality of AUX implied by (22a,b) is only apparent, in the sense that it only reflects the optionality of the occurrence of a modal in addition to Tense. In view of this, our initial solution, which made the occurrence of AUX optional, is inadequate. This is because it was based on the assumption that Tense is not a constituent of AUX, contrary to what examples (24a–d) indicate. The solution which is consistent with the facts illustrated in (24a–d) is one which maintains AUX as an obligatory constituent of S, on the grounds that it is the node under which Tense is located.

Having said that, what needs to be explained with respect to examples such as (22a,b) is why the Tense category shows up on the verb, despite the fact that it is generated under AUX. This question will be addressed in the next chapter. For the moment, note that a general fact about Tense elements, e.g. the past Tense marker *-ed*, is that they are morphologically dependent (**bound morphemes**). They cannot stand alone, and need to attach to (lean on) a verbal category, such as a Modal or a verb. It is for this reason that Tense in sentences such as (22a,b) appears attached to the verb. Obviously, Tense attaches to the verb only when AUX does not include a Modal category. In sentences where AUX includes a Modal category, e.g. *This boy will solve the problem*, Tense appears on the Modal category, and the main verb appears unmarked for Tense.

The possibilities relating to the constituent structure of AUX can be captured in terms

25a. Aux → Tense (Modal) (Neg)

25b.

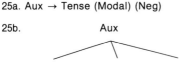

Aux

Tense   (Modal)   (Neg)

of rule (25a). (25b) is the internal structure of AUX implied by this rule. That Neg, i.e. *not* and its contracted counterpart *n't*, is also a constituent of AUX is shown by the following examples:

26a. This politician [cannot] and [will not] solve the problem
26b. [Can't] this politician [—] solve the problem?

In (26a) the Modal and Neg (as well as Tense) are co-ordinated with a similar string of categories, implying that the Modal and Neg form a constituent, namely AUX. This conclusion is confirmed in (26b), where the Modal and Neg (in its contracted form) are together displaced to the beginning of the sentence.

To summarize, the discussion in this section has led us to the conclusion that AUX is an obligatory constituent of S. The reasoning behind the conclusion goes as follows. Sentences are invariably marked for Tense, meaning they instantiate the Tense category which specifies the time frame (past, present or future) of the event described by the sentence. Tense is a constituent of AUX, as shown by the fact that it gets affected by the processes which apply to AUX. It follows that AUX is invariably present in sentences, including the ones which do not instantiate a Modal and/or Neg. In sentences which lack a Modal, Tense appears attached to the verb, as a default option. The PS rule which generates AUX has Tense as an obligatory constituent and Modal and Neg as optional constituents.

2.3.3   Verb Phrase

The PS rule which generates VP established above on the basis of example (27a) looks as in (27b):

27a. *This boy can* [$_{VP}$ [$_V$ *solve*] [$_{NP}$ *the problem*]]
27b. VP → V NP

As pointed out earlier, (27b) incorporates the claim that VP consists of V and NP. However, while this is true of (27a) and similar sentences, it is not true of sentences such as the following:

28a. The boy cried
28b. *The boy* [$_{VP}$ [$_V$ *cried*]]

29a. The girl smiled
29b. *The girl* [$_{VP}$ [$_V$ *smiled*]]

VP in these sentences, and a large number of similar ones, consists of the category V only.

To accommodate sentences such as (28) and (29), the occurrence of the NP constituent of VP can be made optional, by enclosing it within parentheses. (30) below is the revised version of the VP rule above, and (31a,b) are the two VP structures it generates:

30. VP → V (NP)

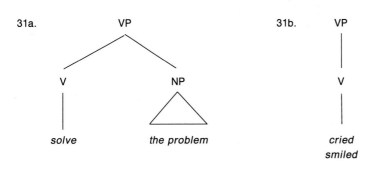

31a. VP

31b. VP

V   NP

solve   the problem

V

cried
smiled

The revised VP rule (30) now generates sentences of the type in (28) and (29), where VP consists of V only, as well as sentences of the type in (27a), where VP consists of V and NP. In (27a) the NP is said to be the **complement** of the verb *solve*, the latter being a member of the class of **transitive** verbs.

Just as there are verbs which take NP complements, there are verbs which take other categories as complement. Consider the following examples:

32a. The teacher hinted to the solution
32b. *The teacher* [VP [V *hinted*] [PP *to the solution*]]

33a. The girl knocked on the door
33b. *The girl* [VP [V *knocked*] [PP *on the door*]]

The complement of the verb in these sentences consists of a preposition (*to* in (32) and *on* in (33)) and an NP (*the solution* in (32) and *the door* in (33)). The preposition and the NP are said to form a constituent called **Preposition Phrase (PP)**, generated by rule (34a) which implies the structure shown in (34b): That P and a following NP form a (PP) constituent can be verified on the basis of some of the constituency tests discussed above. The reader can verify for herself/himself.

34a. PP → P NP

34b. PP

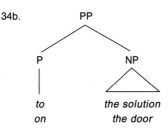

P   NP

to   the solution
on   the door

To generate sentences of the type illustrated in (32) and (33), the VP rule (30) needs to be revised to allow for the possibility that VP can consist of V and PP, in addition to the other possibilities discussed. Notationally, this can be done as in (35):

$$35.\ \text{VP} \rightarrow \text{V}\ (\begin{Bmatrix} \text{NP} \\ \text{PP} \end{Bmatrix})$$

(35) includes the information that VP can consist of V only, V and NP, or V and PP. The first two possibilities are illustrated in (31a, b) above, and the third possibility in (36). The internal structure of PP is as shown in (34b) above. The NP which follows the preposition is the complement of the preposition, just as PP itself is the complement of the verb.

36.

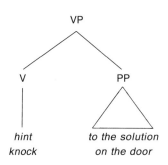

It is clear that the rule becomes increasingly complex as revisions are introduced to accommodate new types of VP, and therefore a larger number of possible sentences. Although the complexity of a given rule only reflects the complexity of the various patterns of constituency it is intended to deal with, we will avoid formulating complex rules here. Instead, we will restrict ourselves to the version of the rule which is relevant to the example being discussed. The point that a given rule can be revised (made more complex) to accommodate a larger number of data should already be clear.

Examples (37) and (38) below imply the (version of the) VP rule in (39a) and the structure in (39b):

37a. The boy sent a letter to the girl
37b. *The boy* [VP [V *sent*] [NP *a letter*] [PP *to the girl*]]
38a. The girl gave a present to the boy
38b. *The girl* [VP [V *gave*] [NP *a present*] [PP *to the boy*]]
39a. VP → V NP PP

39b.

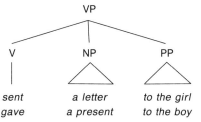

The verbs *send* and *give* belong to a group of verbs which take two complements, an NP and a PP. Therefore, the VP which includes these verbs consists of V, NP, and PP, as shown in (39a,b). By now it should be clear that complements of categories are represented as sisters to those categories, and that the constituent structure of a given phrasal category, e.g. VP, depends largely on whether the item occupying the terminal node, e.g. the verb, takes one complement, two complements, or none at all. We will come back to this point below.

The following examples, on the other hand, imply rule (42a) and structure (42b):

40a. The boy said he would send a letter to the girl
40b. *The boy* [VP *said* [S *he would send a letter to the girl*]]
41a. The girl thought she would give a present to the boy
41b. *The girl* [VP *thought* [S *she would give a present to the boy*]]
42a. VP → V S

42b.

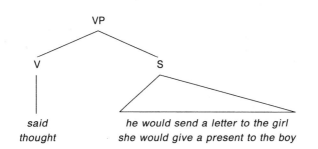

The verbs *say* and *think* take S as a complement, implying that their VP has the form shown in (42b). That the complements in (40) and (41), included under S in (42b), are of the category S is shown by the fact that each one of them can stand alone as a complete sentence: *He would send a letter to the girl* and *She would give a present to the boy*.

Now, compare examples (40) and (41) to their counterparts in (43a, b) below, which differ only in that they include the extra item *that*, called **Complementizer (COMP)**:

43a. The boy said that he would send a letter to the girl
43b. The girl thought that she would give a present to the boy

COMP has the function of introducing the S-complement of the verb. For reasons which will become clear later on, COMP is not a constituent of S, as might be thought, but a constituent of another super-category, called **S′** (read 'S-bar', not 'S-prime'). S′ is generated by rule (44a) and has the structure shown in (44b):

44a. S′ → COMP S

44b.

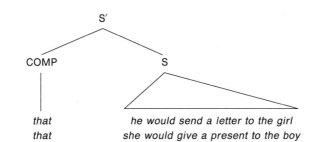

Note that, according to rule (44a), S is also a constituent of S′, represented in (44b) as a sister to COMP.

Accordingly, VP in examples (43a, b) has the structure shown in (45b), generated by rule (45a):

45a. VP → V S′

45b.

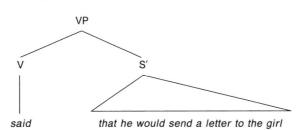

46.

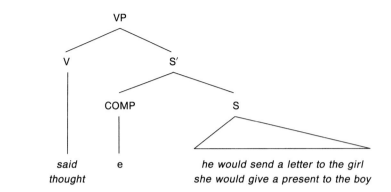

The (internal structure of the) S'-complement is generated by rule (44a), in combination with the rules which generate S and its major constituents. An S'-complement is sometimes called a **clausal complement**, or, alternatively, a **sentential complement**. The term 'clause' is sometimes used synonymously with 'sentence', so that examples such as (40), (41), and (43) are said to be bi-clausal, meaning that they consist of two clauses. The larger clause (S) which includes the complement clause is called the **main/matrix/root clause**, and the complement clause is called the **subordinate/embedded clause**.

At this stage, it seems as though the complement of the verb in examples (40) and (41) has a different categorial status from the one in examples (43a,b). In the former the complement is S, and in the latter it is S'. However, there is an alternative way of looking at the relationship between the two types of clausal complement which results in assigning both of them the same categorial status. The clausal complement in (40) and (41) can also be assumed to be S', like its counterpart in (43a,b), and to differ only in that COMP is e(mpty), i.e. not filled with the complementizer *that*. This is shown in (46). According to this analysis, the VPs in (40) and (41) are generated by the same version of the rule which generates their counterparts in (43a,b), namely (45a). Consequently, version (42a) can be dispensed with altogether, at least as far as the examples discussed are concerned. In Chapter 3 we will discuss evidence which shows clearly that sentences such as (40) and (41), which do not include the complementizer *that*, do instantiate a COMP position. Pending the discussion, we will assume the analysis outlined in (46).

To summarize, the rule which generates VP can be modified to accommodate VPs with different constituencies. The constituency of VP is to a large extent determined by the type of verb it includes, i.e. whether the verb takes a complement, what type of complement it is, and so on. Complements which can stand alone as sentences were argued to be of the category S', which consists of COMP and S. COMP is filled with the complementizer *that* in sentences which instantiate this element, and remains empty in related sentences which do not instantiate this element.

2.3.4 Noun Phrase

The PS rule which generates NP established above on the basis of example (47a) is as in (47b):

47a. [NP [Det *This*] [N *boy*]] *can solve* [NP [Det *the*] [N *problem*]]
47b. NP → Det N

We have seen that the constituent structure of VP varies depending on the type of verb it includes. The same is true of NPs; the constituent structure of NP also depends on the type of N it includes. Consider the following examples:

48a. The cancellation of the party annoyed the boys

48b. [NP *The cancellation* [PP *of the party*]] *annoyed the boys*

49a. The girl resents the claim that she likes the boy

49b. *The girl resents* [NP *the claim* [S′ *that she likes the boy*]]

The noun *cancellation* in (48) takes a PP complement, implying that the NP which contains it consists of Det, N and PP. On the other hand, the noun *claim* in (49) takes an S′-complement, implying that the NP which contains it consists of Det, N and S′.

50a. NP → Det N PP

50b.

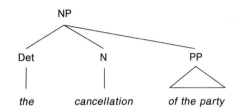

51a. NP → Det N S′

51b.

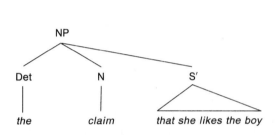

The first NP has the constituent structure shown in (50b), generated by the version of the NP rule in (50a), and the second NP has the constituent structure shown in (51b), generated by the version of the NP rule in (51a). The more general rule which generates both NPs would therefore have to include the information that PP and S′ are optional constituents of NP.

The occurrence of the category Det (preceding the noun) also needs to be made optional, as suggested by the following examples:

52a. Mary likes the film

52b. [NP *Mary*] *likes* [NP *the film*]

53a. The boy likes bananas

53b. [NP *The boy*] *likes* [NP *bananas*]

These examples include NPs which consist of Det and NP (*the film* and *the boy*) and NPs which consist of the noun only (*Mary* and *bananas*). Both types of NP are generated by rule (54a) below. (54b) is the structure of NPs which consist of the noun only. Whether a determiner can occur in an NP also depends on the noun involved, although determiners are not complements of the noun. In English, nouns such as *Mary* do not tolerate a determiner, whereas nouns such as *boy* and *cancellation* require a determiner.

Not only determiners can precede the noun in NPs but full NPs as well:

55a. John's cancellation of the party annoyed the boys

55b. [[NP *John's*] *cancellation of the party*] *annoyed the boys*

54a. NP → (Det) N

54b.

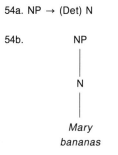

56a. The girl resents the boy's behaviour
56b. *The girl resents* [NP [NP *the boy's*] *behaviour*]

57a. NP → NP N . . .

57b.

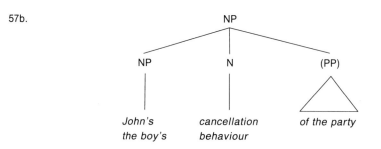

The NPs in the example above have the structure shown in (57b), generated by rule (57a). The NPs in (55) and (56), sometimes called 'pre-nominal NPs', are in complementary distribution (cannot co-occur) with determiners:

58a. *John's the cancellation of the party annoyed the boys
58b. *[NP [NP *John's*] [Det *the*] *cancellation of the party*] . . .
59a. *The girl resents the boy's the behaviour
59b. *. . . [NP [NP *the boy's*] [Det *the*] *behaviour*]

The ungrammatical status of these examples is due to the fact that the pre-nominal NP co-occurs with the determiner in the pre-N domain. The rule which generates NP would therefore have to take this restriction into consideration. This can be done by including Det and NP in curly brackets, a notation which excludes co-occurrence:

60. NP → $\left\{ \begin{array}{c} \text{NP} \\ \text{Det} \end{array} \right\}$ N . . .

This formulation guarantees that ungrammatical NPs of the type illustrated in (58) and (59) are excluded.

To summarize, the PS rule which generates NPs can be enriched, using appropriate notational devices, to accommodate additional types of constituency patterns, and therefore a larger number of sentences. As with VP, the constituent structure of NP largely depends on the type of noun it includes. This is true not only with respect to complements of nouns but also with respect to Det elements.

2.3.5   Adjectives and Adverbs

Adjectives typically occur in the positions indicated in the examples below:

61a. The boy is tall
61b. *The boy* [VP *is* [AP *tall*]]
62a. The tall boy likes the girl
62b. [NP *The* [AP *tall*] *boy*] *likes the girl*

In (61) the adjective is a constituent of VP, together with the verb *is*, whereas in (62) it is a constituent of NP, together with the noun it modifies and the determiner. In (61) the adjective is said to have a **predicative** function, for reasons which will be explained in the next section. On the other hand, in (62) the adjective is said to have an **attributive** function, in the sense that it specifies an attribute of the noun it modifies.

As is the case with verbs and nouns, some adjectives take complements while others do not. The adjective *tall*, for example, does not take a complement, whereas the adjective *suspicious* takes a PP complement, though optionally:

63a. The suspicious girl is Mary
63b. *The* [AP *suspicious*] *girl is Mary*

64a. The girl is suspicious of the boy
64b. *The girl is* [AP *suspicious* [PP *of the boy*]]

This means that the PS rule which generates the Adjectival Phrase (AP) must be as in (65a), where PP is an optional constituent.

65a. AP → A (PP)

66a. 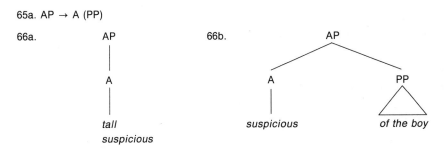 66b.

Having established the rule which generates AP, we now turn to the rules which generate the phrasal categories which contain AP in the examples above. The rule which generates VP in (61) and (64) has the form shown in (67a), and the rule which generates the NP in (62) and (63) has the form shown in (68a). (67b) and (68b) are the structures implied by these rules:

67a. VP → V AP

67b.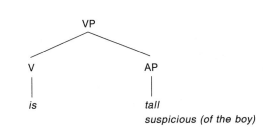

68a. NP → Det AP N

68b.

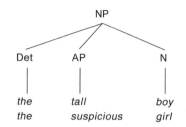

Turning now to adverbs, they typically occur in at least three major positions, depending on the category they modify:

69a. John quickly fixed the car
69b. John fixed the car quickly

70a. Evidently, John fixed the car
70b. John fixed the car, evidently

The adverb *quickly* in (69a, b) refers to the manner in which John fixed the car. Together with another group of adverbs which includes *cleverly, clumsily, deftly*, etc., *quickly* is called a **manner adverb**. Because manner adverbs modify the verb (and its complements), they are structurally represented as constituents of VP. For this reason, manner adverbs, together with others, are sometimes also called **VP-adverbs**. The adverb *evidently* in (70a, b), on the other hand, refers to a situation which suggests that John indeed fixed the car. In this case, the adverb is said to modify the whole sentence, rather than a specific constituent of the sentence. For this reason, *evidently* is classified, together with other adverbs such as *presumably, ironically, probably*, as **S(entence)-adverb**.

The assumption that manner adverbs are constituents of VP is confirmed by the fact that they can be displaced along with the constituents of VP:

71a. Fix the car quickly, I wonder whether John will
71b. [VP *Fix the car quickly*] *I wonder whether John will* [—]

Thus, manner adverbs are generated by the VP rule (72), depending on their position in relation to the other constituents of VP. (73a) is the structure of the VP in (69a), where the adverb immediately precedes the verb, and (73b) the structure of the VP in (69b), where the adverb is in the final position.

72. VP → (ADV) V (NP) (ADV)

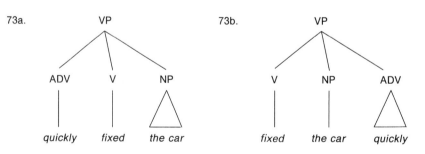

As constituents of S, S-adverbs are generated by the rule which expands S. (75a) is the structure of example (70a), where the S-adverb is in the initial position, and (75b) the structure of (70b), where the S-adverb is in the final position.

74. S → (ADV) NP Aux VP (ADV)

75a.

```
                              S
         ┌──────────┬────────┴────────┬──────────┐
        ADV         NP               AUX         VP
         │           │                │         ╱╲
     Evidently      John            Tense    fix the car
```

75b.

```
                              S
         ┌──────────┬─────────┴──────┬──────────┐
        NP         AUX              VP          ADV
         │          │              ╱╲            │
       John       Tense         fix the car  evidently
```

The adverbs discussed so far have in common the bound morpheme (or **suffix**) -*ly*, and hence the fact that they are sometimes called '*ly*-adverbs'. However, there are adverbs which do not have the suffix -*ly*, such as *hard* and *fast*:

76a. John hit the nail hard
76b. *John* [VP *hit the nail hard*]

77a. Mary ran fast
77b. *Mary* [VP *ran fast*]

Like *quickly*, these adverbs are also manner-adverbs, in that they describe the manner in which the event denoted by the verb is carried out. As such, they are constituents of VP.

   Note, finally, that in addition to the adverbs discussed, linguists also talk about other categories which have an 'adverbial function'. The most prominent examples of these adverbial functions relate to place and time. The bracketed constituents in the examples below are said to have an 'adverbial function', although as categories they are PP (78a, b) and S′ (79a, b):

78a. *John fixed the car* [PP *in the garage*]
78b. *John fixed the car* [PP *in the morning*]

79a. *John fixed the car* [S′ *where Bill had left it*]
79b. *John fixed the car* [S′ *when Bill was still sleeping*]

Whether categories with the adverbial functions of place and time are constituents of S or VP is a difficult question which we are not going to address here. This does not prevent the reader from applying suitable constituency tests to find out for herself/himself.

   To summarize, we have identified two major types of adverb: VP-adverbs and S-adverbs. VP-adverbs are generated by the PS rule which expands VP, either in the position immediately preceding the verb or the rightmost position of VD. S-adverbs, on the other hand, are generated by the PS rule which generates S, either as the leftmost or the rightmost constituents of S.

2.3.6   Summary

We have postulated a set of rewrite rules which generate ('make explicit') the structure of the sentence. A subset of these rules generate phrasal categories such as S, VP, NP, and another subset generate specific lexical items. The latter rewrite a terminal node as a corresponding lexical item. Initially, the rules which generate phrasal categories were based on a single sentence. Then, it was shown that these rules could be revised in appropriate ways to generate phrasal categories with different constituency patterns, thereby accommodating a larger number of sentences. Each revision represents a small step towards the goal of developing a model of grammar which generates all and only grammatical sentences. The task of developing a model which only generates grammatical sentences means that the model should be able to exclude ungrammatical sentences. Above, we came across a situation where the rule which generates NP had to be revised in such a way as to exclude ungrammatical NPs where a pre-nominal NP co-occurs with a Det element. Thus, the revisions introduced are motivated by the need not only to accommodate additional grammatical sentences but also to exclude ungrammatical ones. The next section is entirely devoted to (further) revisions which are specifically designed to exclude certain types of ungrammatical sentence.

2.4   *Subcategorization Rules and Selectional Restrictions*

2.4.1   The Problem of Over-generation

Although the system developed so far generates a large number of grammatical sentences, it also generates an equally large number of ungrammatical ones. In this section, we will discuss two major respects in which the system is said to **over-generate**, and then seek possible ways of constraining it so that at least certain types of ungrammatical sentence are excluded.

One respect in which the system over-generates concerns ungrammatical sentences such as (80) and (81), compared to (82):

80a. *The boy relied
80b. *The boy* [VP *relied*]

81a. *The boy relied the girl
81b. *The boy* [VP *relied* [NP *the girl*]]

82a. The boy relied on the girl
82b. *The boy* [VP *relied* [PP *on the girl*]]

(80a) is ungrammatical because the complement required by the verb is missing. (81), on the other hand, is ungrammatical because the complement of the verb, though present, is not of the type required by the verb *rely*. The latter requires a PP complement, as shown in (82).

(80) and (81), though ungrammatical, are both generated by the system as envisaged so far (we continue to ignore the question of how Tense attaches to the verb). (84a) is the structure of (80), generated by the set of rules in (83). (84b) is the structure of (81), also generated by the same set of rules. Note that the option of not having a complement or having a complement of the type NP are both allowed by rule (83b).

The other respect in which the system can be said to over-generate concerns sentences such as the ones in (85a, b), which are grammatically sound but odd as far as their interpretation is concerned (the notation ! is used here to indicate oddity of meaning, understood to be a different notion from 'ungrammaticality').

83a. S   →   NP AUX VP
83b. VP   →   V (NP) (PP)
83c. NP   →   Det N
83d. V   →   *rely*
83e. Det →   *the*
83f. N   →   *boy, girl*

84a.

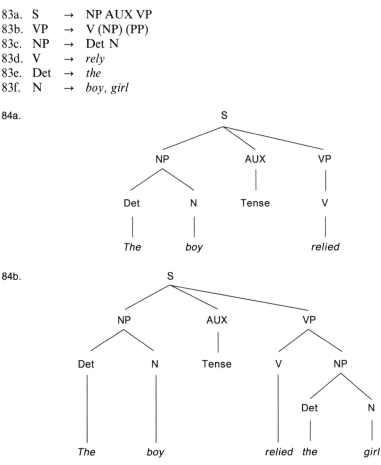

84b.

85a. !The boy frightens sincerity
85b. !Sincerity kicked the boy

86a. S   →   NP AUX VP
86b. VP   →   V (NP) (PP)
86c. NP   →   Det N
86d. V   →   *frighten, kick*
86e. Det →   *the*
86f. N   →   *boy, sincerity, girl*

The oddity of (85a, b) arises from the fact that their meaning is inconsistent with our expectations in the real world. Given our knowledge of the world, we do not expect abstract concepts such as 'sincerity' to be frightened or to perform the act of 'kicking'. Obviously, (85a, b) would be interpretable in an imaginary world (of the type found in children's books, for example) but this does not alter the fact that they are odd in the context of the real world.

87a.

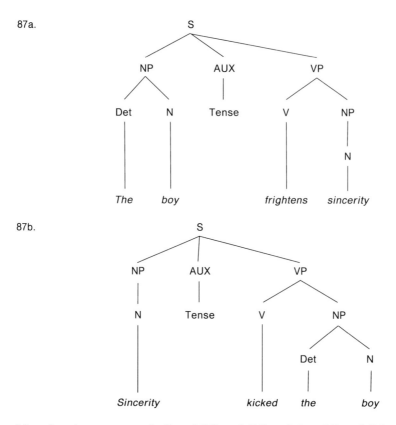

87b.

Note that the ungrammaticality of (80) and (81) and the oddity of (85a, b) both have to do with the properties of individual lexical items, in particular the verb. (80) and (81) are ungrammatical because they are inconsistent with the fact that the verb *rely* requires a complement of the type PP. On the other hand, (85a, b) are odd because they are inconsistent with the fact that the verbs *frighten* and *kick* cannot be associated with abstract nouns in certain positions. This suggests that the revisions required to exclude the examples in question are not likely to affect the PS rules which generate phrasal categories. Recall that these rules were revised earlier in this chapter with the purpose of enabling them to cater for different types of verb. Rather, the revisions required are likely to affect the rules which generate individual lexical items, that is the rules which rewrite a terminal symbol as an appropriate lexical item.

2.4.2 Subcategorization Rules

Verbs are said to **subcategorize** into various groups, depending on whether they require a complement, what type of complement they require, if any, and so on. *Kick*, for example, belongs to the group of transitive verbs, i.e. verbs which require an NP complement. *Sit*, on the other hand, belongs to the group of **intransitive** verbs, i.e. verbs which do not require an NP complement. Other groups include verbs which require a PP complement, e.g. *rely*, verbs which require both an NP and a PP complement, e.g. *put*, verbs which require an S'-complement, e.g. *think*, etc.

The subcategorization properties of verbs can be formally represented in terms of **frames** such as those in (88a–e), called **subcategorization frames**:

88a. *kick*: [V; — NP]
88b. *sit*: [V; —]
88c. *rely*: [V; — PP]
88d. *put*: [V; — NP PP]
88e. *think*: [V; — S']

These frames specify the categorial class of the lexical item, and the environment in which it can occur. For example, (88a) specifies the information that *kick* is a verb, and that it requires a complement of the type NP. This information implies that *kick* is to be inserted under a V node in a VP structure where V has an NP sister. Given that subcategorization frames specify (idiosyncratic) information relating to the properties of individual lexical items, they are associated with lexical items in their lexical entries. Thus, information concerning the subcategorization properties of lexical items, which is necessary for their proper use, as we have seen, is an additional type of information to be added to the other types of information included in lexical entries and briefly discussed in section 2.1 above. Obviously, similar subcategorization frames exist for other categories: nouns, adjectives, and prepositions. Verbs are used here merely for illustration. Moreover, (88a–e) by no means exhaust the range of possibilities relating to the subcategorization properties of all verbs.

Subcategorization frames illustrated in (88a–e) can form the basis on which a general **subcategorization rule** can be set up which would make the process of rewriting a terminal symbol as a specific lexical item sensitive to the subcategorization properties of the lexical item. More precisely, this rule would make it possible to rewrite a terminal node as a lexical item in association with its subcategorization frame. The consequence of this rule is that a given lexical item can only be associated with a phrasal structure which is consistent with its subcategorization requirements. The rule in question can be formulated as in (89):

$$
89.\ V \rightarrow Y / \left\{ \begin{array}{l} -\ NP] \\ -\ ] \\ -\ PP] \\ -\ NP\ PP] \\ -\ S'] \\ \ldots \end{array} \right\}
$$

(89) specifies the various environments in which a given verb, represented by the variable symbol *Y*, can be introduced. Which frame is chosen obviously depends on the subcategorization properties of the verb which substitutes for the variable. If the verb is *rely*, for example, the chosen subcategorization frame would be: — PP], if the verb is *think* the chosen frame would be: — S'], and so on.

With (89) incorporated into the system of rules, we guarantee that ungrammatical sentences such as (80) and (81), where the verb is associated with an inappropriate frame, are excluded. Because subcategorization frames are chosen on the basis of the subcategorization properties of the verb, we ensure that verbs are paired with appropriate frames from the set specified in (89). To illustrate how the revised system works, the grammatical sentence (90), reproduced from above, is generated by the set of rules in (91):

90. The boy relied on the girl

91a. S   →   NP AUX VP
91b. VP   →   V (NP) (PP) (S') . . .
91c. NP   →   Det N
91d. V   →   *rely*/— PP]
91e. Det →   *the*
91f. N   →   *boy, girl*

Rule (91d) is an instantiation of one of the options specified in the more general rule (89) above, where the variable *Y* is replaced by the verb *rely*. Because rule (91d) specifies the frame of the verb it generates, it ensures that the verb is associated with this frame, thereby excluding ungrammatical sentences such as (80) and (81).

Rule (89), of which (91d) is an instantiation, is a Subcategorization Rule. Unlike (91a–c), the Subcategorization Rule (91d) is 'context-sensitive', in the sense that it specifies the context in which a given category can occur. In contrast, rules (91a–c) are 'context-free', since they do not specify contexts, but merely list the constituents that a given phrasal category can include, and the order in which they occur. We now turn to examples (85a, b) and see how they too can be excluded. Since the problem they pose involves contextual information as well (i.e. which verbs can be paired with which nouns), the solution to the problem they present is likely to involve 'context-sensitive' rules as well.

2.4.3   Selectional Restrictions

As pointed out above, the odd nature of examples (92a, b) seems to have to do with the fact that the verbs *frighten* and *kick* are inappropriately associated with abstract nouns:

92a. !The boy frightened sincerity
92b. !Sincerity kicked the boy

The solution to the problem posed by these examples will, therefore, consist of ensuring that the verbs *frighten* and *kick*, among others, are not associated with abstract nouns in certain positions. More generally, the system should include a mechanism which ensures that only nouns with appropriate properties are associated with given verbs in a given context.

Features such as [+/– abstract], [+/– animate], among others, are inherent and idiosyncratic properties of nouns. Therefore, like subcategorization properties, they are specified in the lexical entries of nouns. The lexical entry of *sincerity*, for example, includes the feature [+ abstract], among other features, and the lexical entry of *boy* includes the feature [+ animate], among others. Lexical information of this type can be used to set up the following 'rewrite' rule, which specifies the contexts in which a given verb can occur:

$$93.\ [V] \rightarrow Y/ \begin{cases} \text{(i) } [+/-\ \text{abstract] AUX} — \\ \text{(ii) } — [+/-\ \text{animate}] \end{cases}$$

(93i) refers to the **subject** position, i.e. the position which immediately precedes AUX and is occupied by *the boy* in (92a) and *sincerity* in (92b). (93ii) refers to the **object** position of the verb, i.e. the position which immediately follows the verb occupied by *sincerity* in (92a) and *the boy* in (92b)). (93) is called a **selectional rule**, in the sense that it specifies certain selectional restrictions associated with verbs, and presumably other categories as well. Obviously, the version of (93) which would account for all possible combinations is much more complex, (93) being simply an illustration of the form the rule can possibly take.

With respect to the verbs *frighten* and *kick*, the corresponding selectional rules would look as in (94) and (95):

$$94.\ V \rightarrow frighten/ \begin{cases} [+/-\ \text{abstract] AUX} — \\ — [+\ \text{animate}] \end{cases}$$

95. V → *kick*/ $\left\{ \begin{array}{l} [+ \text{ animate}] \text{ AUX } - \\ - [- \text{ abstract}] \end{array} \right\}$

The verb *frighten* can take either a non-abstract subject, as in *The girl frightened the boy*, or an abstract subject, as in *Sincerity frightens the boy*. But it can only take an animate object, as in *The girl frightened the boy*. Consequently, example (92a) above is excluded, since it involves a non-animate object (i.e. *sincerity*), which is incompatible with the selectional restrictions of the verb *frighten*. The verb *kick*, on the other hand, can only take an animate subject, as in *The girl kicked the boy*, and can only take a non-abstract object, as in *The girl kicked the boy/chair*. Example (92b), therefore, is excluded, on the grounds that it involves an abstract (or non-animate) subject (i.e. *sincerity*) which is incompatible with the selectional restrictions of the verb *kick*. Like subcategorization rules, selectional rules such as (94) and (95) are 'context-sensitive', in that they specify the environment in which a given verb can occur.

Having said that, one might wonder whether the problems posed by examples such as (92a, b) are of the same order as the ones posed by examples (80) and (81). In other words, it is not clear whether selectional restrictions should be dealt with in terms of the same mechanisms (rules) which deal with subcategorization requirements. Recall that while violations of subcategorization requirements affect the grammatical status of sentences, violations of selectional restrictions do not necessarily affect the grammatical status of sentences, but, rather, their interpretation in relation to a given world. In view of this, one could argue that selectional restrictions involve an aspect of language (meaning and interpretation) which is different from the one involved in subcategorization. More precisely, selectional restrictions involve a different component of the grammar, which exists over and above the component which deals with the grammatical properties of sentences.

It seems, therefore, that we have to make a distinction between two different components of the grammar. One component comprises PS and subcategorization rules, and has the task of generating all and only grammatical sentences. We will call this component the **Syntactic Component**. The other component comprises a set of rules, whatever their nature, which assign an interpretation to sentences in relation to a possible world. For the moment, we will call the component in question the **Semantic Component**. The relationship between the two components is an input–output relationship, in the sense that sentences generated by the Syntactic Component serve as input to the Semantic Component which then assigns them an interpretation. This relationship between the two components explains the remark made earlier with respect to examples (92a, b), namely that, although they are odd as far as their interpretation is concerned, they are grammatically sound. These sentences are grammatically sound because they can be generated by the Syntactic Component.

The rules which are involved in assigning interpretations to sentences are still poorly understood, and therefore will not figure much in the rest of this book. Our concern here is with the syntactic properties of sentences, that is, the properties which can be accounted for in terms of syntactic rules. Having said that, our view of the Semantic Component will change gradually as we go along. One of the interesting conclusions which will emerge is that some of the mechanisms involved in assigning interpretations to sentences are indeed syntactic in nature, and, therefore, should be dealt with in terms of the rules of syntax. A graphic representation of the shape of the model of grammar which results from the distinction made between the Syntactic Component and the Semantic Component is given at the end of this chapter.

2.4.4   Summary

In this section we have discussed two situations in which the system of rules developed in the previous sections is said to over-generate. One situation concerns sentences where the subcategorization properties of the verb are not properly reflected. To exclude such situations, subcategorization rules were added to the existing set of rules, which rewrite a terminal node as a given lexical category in association with its subcategorization frame. These rules ensure that verbs (and other categories) are paired with appropriate subcategorization frames, thereby excluding ungrammatical sentences where verbs are associated with the wrong subcategorization frames. The other situation concerns sentences where the selectional properties of lexical items (though not necessarily their subcategorization properties) are not properly reflected. To exclude such sentences, it was initially suggested that a set of selectional rules could be included, which operate in terms of binary semantic features such as [+/− abstract], [+/− human]. These rules would ensure that lexical items such as verbs are paired with appropriate nouns in certain positions. Subsequently, it was decided that these rules do not belong to the domain of Syntax, given that the problems they are supposed to deal with are not syntactic in nature. Instead, they belong to the domain of Semantics, the component which assigns interpretations to (grammatical) sentences generated by the (rules of) Syntax.

2.5   *Separating the Lexicon from the Syntax*

2.5.1   The Lexical Insertion Rule

Most of the revisions undertaken so far have been motivated by the need to accommodate further grammatical examples, and exclude as many ungrammatical ones as possible. Each revision introduced strengthens the descriptive power of the Grammar, and therefore represents a step towards the goal of achieving descriptive adequacy (see Chapter 1). However, our success in accommodating certain types of new data required the introduction of new rule systems into the model. For example, to exclude sentences where the subcategorization properties of lexical items are not properly reflected, we had to introduce 'context-sensitive' rules, to be added to the existing set of 'context-free' PS rules. Given that the need to achieve explanatory adequacy depends on restricting the proliferation of rule systems (see Chapter 1), it seems as though some of the steps we have taken towards the goal of achieving descriptive adequacy have resulted in corresponding steps away from the goal of achieving explanatory adequacy. We seem to have a dilemma.

The way out of this dilemma is to attribute some of the functions we have been (wrongly) attributing to the Syntactic Component to other components. For example, we have seen that the function of ensuring that the selectional restrictions of lexical items are properly reflected can be attributed to the Semantic Component, i.e. the component which assigns an interpretation to sentences generated by the Syntactic Component. The consequence is that the 'context-sensitive' rules required to accomplish this function can be eliminated from the Syntactic Component. Although this move has not resulted in the total elimination of 'context-sensitive' rules from the Syntactic Component, it represents a step towards the goal of restricting the proliferation of the rule systems it includes. In view of this, it is desirable to eliminate the remaining set of 'context-sensitive' rules, i.e. Subcategorization Rules, from the Syntactic Component. Let us see how this can be done.

Given their nature as 'rewrite' rules, Subcategorization Rules have the curious effect of equating the 'rewriting' of phrasal categories into individual constituents with the 'rewriting' of terminal symbols into lexical items in association with their subcategorization properties. In other words, Subcategorization Rules are syntactic in format, in so far as they are 'rewrite' rules, even though, unlike PS rules, they make reference to lexical information. This implies a view whereby the Syntactic Component and the Lexicon are somehow merged, which does not necessarily have to be the case. It is plausible to think of the Lexicon as being independent of the Syntactic Component, in so far as it includes information which, though relevant to the syntactic representation of categories, is essentially lexical in nature. What is needed, then, is a general rule that will serve as a link between the Lexicon and the Syntactic Component, i.e. a rule which will have the function of inserting lexical items under appropriate nodes in Phrase Markers generated by the PS rules of the Syntactic Component.

Let us call the rule in question the **Lexical Insertion Rule**, and define it as in (96):

96. **Lexical Insertion Rule (LIR)**
    Insert lexical item X under terminal node Y, where Y corresponds to the categorial properties of X, and YP corresponds to the subcategorization properties of X.

LIR performs the operation of inserting lexical items under terminal nodes subject to two conditions. First, the terminal node must match the categorial class of the lexical item. This will ensure that verbs are inserted under V nodes, nouns under N nodes, and so on. The second condition is that the phrase containing the terminal node, i.e. the VP of V, the NP of N, etc., must match the subcategorization properties of the lexical item. This means that if the lexical item is a verb which subcategorizes for an NP, the VP containing V must include an NP, and if the lexical item is a verb which does not subcategorize for an NP complement, the VP containing V must not include an NP, and so on. Consequently, ungrammatical sentences where lexical items are associated with inappropriate subcategorization frames are excluded.

It should be clear that LIR performs the functions that were previously performed by Subcategorization Rules, so that the latter can be dispensed with altogether. This means that the Syntactic Component can now be thought of as consisting of one rule system, the 'context-free' PS rules. It might be argued, in view of the fact that LIR is different in nature from PS rules, that we have simply replaced one rule system with another. LIR differs from PS rules in that it performs an operation, as pointed above, whereas PS rules merely generate structures. However, we will see in the next chapter that such rules are needed in the Grammar for quite independent reasons, over and above the need for PS rules. Viewed in this wider context, the move to replace Subcategorization Rules by LIR does not, strictly speaking, amount to replacing one rule system with another, but to harnessing an independently needed rule system to perform additional tasks.

We now consider the Lexicon as being separate from the Syntactic Component. Note that the existence of separate components should, in principle, be justifiable, preferably, on the grounds that they have properties which distinguish them from other components. For example, the autonomy of the Semantic Component from the Syntactic Component is justifiable on the grounds that it includes rules which are different in nature from the rules of Syntax. Thus, we should expect the autonomy of the Lexicon to be also justifiable on similar grounds: we should expect the Lexicon to include rules which are different in nature from the rules of Syntax. We turn to this issue now.

2.5.2   Lexical Rules of Derivation

Our view of the Lexicon so far is that it is an unordered list of lexical entries, with each entry specifying a range of information necessary for the proper use of the lexical item. Part of this information relates to the categorial property of the item, whether it is a verb, a noun, etc., and another part relates to its subcategorization properties. Note that LIR makes crucial reference to both types of information in performing the operation of lexical insertion, to ensure that lexical items are paired with appropriate contexts.

With this in mind, consider the following examples (the notation *(. . .), used in (98a) and elsewhere, means that the sentence is ungrammatical if the material between parentheses is not included):

97a. *predict + ion → prediction* (Verb-to-Noun)
97b. *book + ish → bookish* (Noun-to-Adjective)
97c. *colony + ize → colonize* (Noun-to-Verb)

98a. Mary translated *(the book)
98b. The translation (of the book) was awful

Examples (97a–c) illustrate the fact that the process of forming complex 'words' from simpler lexical items can result in a change of the categorial property of the lexical item which serves as the **base** for the derivation. Thus, the **affixation** of *-ion* to a verb base results in the derivation of a noun, the affixation of *-ish* to a noun base results in the derivation of an adjective, and the affixation of *-ize* to a noun base results in the derivation of a verb. Examples (98a,b) seem to indicate that the morphological rules of word-formation affect not only the categorial nature of lexical items but also their subcategorization properties. The presence of a complement is obligatory with the verb *translate*, as shown in (98a), but apparently only optional with the noun *translation* derived from it, as shown in (98b).

Now, given that these rules affect the categorial nature and the subcategorization properties of lexical items, they must apply at a stage prior to their insertion into Phrase Markers. This is because, as pointed out above, LIR makes crucial reference to the categorial nature and the subcategorization properties of lexical items to ensure that they are inserted under appropriate nodes located in appropriate contexts. Presumably, the stage at which these rules apply is the Lexicon, so that the Lexicon is not merely a list of lexical entries but also includes rules. Assuming that the Syntax does not include rules of word-formation which affect the categorial nature and the subcategorization properties of lexical items, the autonomy of the Lexicon is justifiable on the grounds that it includes rules which are distinct in nature from the rules of Syntax.

Before we leave the discussion of the processes of affixation, let us discuss the status of affixes in comparison to base categories. Note, first of all, that not all bound morphemes change the categorial nature of the items they attach to. For example, the plural morpheme *-s* does not change the categorial nature of the nouns it attaches to, so that *book* is a noun and *books* is also a noun. Likewise, the past tense morpheme *-ed* and the third person-singular marker *-s* also do not change the categorial nature of the verbs they attach to, so that *kicked* and *kicks* are verbs. These morphemes, together with others, are called **inflectional morphemes**, as opposed to the **derivational morphemes** shown in (97a–c). It is not at all clear, however, whether the distinction between inflectional and derivational morphemes can be based solely on whether they change the category of the items they attach to. For example, the prefix *re-* in examples such as *re + write* and *re + affirm* does not change the category of the verbs it attaches itself to (prefixes in English generally do not have this effect), and yet one would be hard-pressed to call it an inflectional morpheme on a par with the plural, tense, and third person singular morphemes. We will come back to this issue briefly in the next chapter.

Affixes can be assumed to have lexical entries of their own, which specify, among other idiosyncratic properties, the categorial class they belong to and their subcategorization properties. For example, the fact that the suffix *-ion* turns the categories it attaches to into nouns can be attributed, at least in part, to the assumption that it itself is a noun. The same reasoning leads to the conclusion that *-ish* is an adjective and *-ize* a verb. Accordingly, the internal structures of the examples in (97a–c) are as in (99a–c):

99a. [$_V$ *predict*] + [$_N$ *ion*] → [$_N$ [$_V$ *predict*] [$_N$ *ion*]]
99b. [$_N$ *book*] + [$_A$ *ish*] → [$_A$ [$_N$ *book*] [$_A$ *ish*]]
99c. [$_N$ *colony*] + [$_V$ *ize*] → [$_V$ [$_N$ *colony*] + [$_V$ *ize*]]

Notice that it is the categorial class of the affix which usually determines the categorial class of the derived complex. For this reason, among others, the affix is sometimes said to be the **head** of the complex 'word'.

The subcategorization properties of affixes have to do with the fact that they tend to be selective as to the categories they can attach to. For example, we saw in the previous chapter that the negative prefix *un-* attaches to adjectives, as in *unhappy*, but not to verbs, contrary to the 'reversative' *un-* which usually attaches to verbs, as in *unpack*. Likewise, the suffix *-ion* usually attaches to verbs, whereas *-hood* can attach to nouns, as in *boyhood*, or to adjectives, as in *falsehood*. These idiosyncratic selectional properties of affixes can be captured in terms of special subcategorization frames associated with each affix. Using the suffixes *-ion* and *-hood* for illustration, their subcategorization frames can look as follows:

100a. *-ion*: [N; [V] —]

100b. *-hood*: [N; $\left\{ \begin{array}{c} [N] \\ [A] \end{array} \right\}$ —]

Notice, however, that this type of subcategorization differs from the type of subcategorization discussed above in that it operates in terms of lexical categories, V, N, etc., rather than in terms of phrasal categories, NP, PP, etc. To distinguish between the two types of subcategorization we will refer to subcategorization of lexical categories by affixes as **morphological subcategorization**, and to the subcategorization of phrasal (or syntactic) categories as **syntactic subcategorization**. The former is relevant to the rules of word-formation applying in the Lexicon and the latter to (the rules of) Syntax.

2.5.3   Categorial Features

In the previous discussion we referred to the affix *-ion* as a noun and to the affix *-ize* as a verb. This may appear strange, since it implies that we are putting these affixes at the same level as more familiar instances of nouns such as *table* and instances of verbs such as *kick*. The use of categorial terms in relation to affixes reflects a crucial assumption underlying these terms: that they are understood merely as labels for **categorial features**, and have no implication whatsoever as to whether the labelled item refers to (or names) an entity or an individual, or whether it denotes an event. Thus, *table*, for example, is a noun not because it refers to (or names) an entity but because it is specified for the categorial feature [+ N]. Likewise, *kick* is a verb not because it denotes an action (or event) but because it is specified for the categorial feature [+ V]. In this context, it is not strange at all that affixes can be called nouns or verbs, meaning they are specified for the categorial features [+ N] and [+ V].

To be more precise, categorial labels are understood as 'bundles' of categorial features, along the lines of the treatment of sound segments in feature-based Phonology as 'bundles' of distinctive features. For example, the vocalic sound /i/ is understood to be a 'bundle' of the features [+ high, – low, – back, – round], and the sound /u/ is understood to be a 'bundle' of the features [+ high, – low, + back, + round]. This decomposition of segments into features allows for the possibility of capturing certain common properties between segments which are otherwise different. For example, although /i/ differs from /u/ in terms of the values of the features [+/− back] and [+/− round], it is similar to /u/ in terms of the values of the features [+/− high] and [+/− low]. The sounds /i/ and /u/ are said to form a **natural class** with respect to their common features, but not with respect to the other features. One of the reasons underlying this view is that some of the rules of Phonology make reference to specific features of segments, so that all segments which have a given feature referred to by a given rule will be subject to that rule, although the segments may differ with respect to other features.

The view that syntactic categories are also 'bundles' of features has been motivated on similar grounds. Unfortunately, we cannot go into the details at this early stage, as we have not yet discussed the kind of rules that have been used to justify the assumption. Here, we will simply give the **feature matrix** of each categorial class, which we will assume in the rest of the book:

101a. N: [+ N, − V]
101b. V: [− N, + V]
101c. A: [+ N, + V]
101d. P: [− N, − V]

Note, first of all, that this classification assumes that nominal and verbal features are the only primitive categorial features, so that even categories such as A and P are 'bundles' of nominal and verbal features. Ns and As form a natural class in relation to the feature [+ N], and Vs and Ps form a natural class in relation to the feature [− N]. Presumably, categories which form a natural class are expected to pattern together with respect to certain syntactic phenomena.

As a final note, the idea that categories are essentially 'bundles' of features plays a crucial role in the theory discussed here. This will become clear in the subsequent chapters, where additional features are introduced that play a crucial role in the syntactic representation of categories. It is important to get used to thinking of categories as 'bundles' of features.

2.5.4   Summary

In this section we have investigated the possibility of eliminating the 'context-sensitive' subcategorization rules from the Syntactic Component. We have seen that these rules can be replaced by a single general rule, the Lexical Insertion Rule, which inserts lexical items under terminal nodes situated in contexts which are consistent with their categorial features and subcategorization properties. The consequence of this move is that the Syntactic Component now consists of 'context-free' PS rules only, and the Lexicon exists separately from the Syntactic Component. The Lexicon is not merely a list of lexical entries but includes certain morphological rules of derivation which are different in nature from the rules of Syntax. We have also seen that categorial labels are essentially bundles of categorial features, as well as other features to be discussed in subsequent chapters.

2.6   *A Note on Grammatical Functions*

The terms 'subject' and 'object' are said to refer to the **grammatical functions** of categories. They are not categorial labels, and therefore should not be confused with categorial labels

102a. The boy will kick the ball

102b.

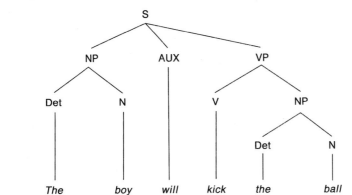

such as NP, VP, or V. In (102), for example, *the boy* is an NP category which has the grammatical function 'subject', and *the ball* is another NP which has the grammatical function 'object'. Moreover, the functions of 'subject' and 'object' are structurally based: the subject is the 'NP-daughter-of-S', and the object is the 'NP-daughter-of-VP'. Thus, in (102) *the boy* is the subject by virtue of being the 'NP-daughter of S', and *the ball* is the object by virtue of being 'the NP-daughter of VP'.

Grammatical functions such as 'subject' and 'object' are also said to be **relational**, and the expression **grammatical relations** is often used synonymously with 'grammatical functions'. The NP *the boy* in (102) is the subject of the sentence, that is, it is a subject in relation to the sentence. On the other hand, the NP *the ball* is the object of the verb, that is, it is an object in relation to the verb. Recall that objects of verbs are specified (mentioned) in the subcategorization frames of verbs, whereas subjects are not. The relational nature of grammatical functions can be captured in terms of the following representations:

103a. Subject-of-S: [NP, S]
103b. Object-of-V: [NP, VP]
103c. Predicate-of-S: [VP, S]

'Predicate' is another grammatical function which is also relational in nature. The predicate of a sentence is usually the string of categories which includes the verb and its complements, i.e. the string of categories included under the VP node. For example, the predicate in (102) above is *kick the ball*. It is for this reason that the AP in the sentence *The boy is tall* discussed earlier was said to be predicative. The term 'predicate' is also used, in a different context, to refer to certain types of lexical items to be discussed in Chapter 5.

Structural relations which determine grammatical functions are encoded in PS rules. For example, the structural relation 'NP-daughter-of-S' which underlies the grammatical function 'subject' is encoded in the PS rule which expands S (S → NP AUX VP). On the other hand, the structural relation 'NP-daughter-of-VP' which underlies the grammatical function 'object' is encoded in the PS rule which expands VP (VP → V NP). Thus, in addition to specifying the internal structures of phrasal categories, and the linear order of their constituents, PS rules also specify the grammatical functions of categories.

Note, finally, that linear-based notions such as 'precede' and 'follow' do not play a role in determining grammatical functions. Thus, 'subject' cannot be defined as the NP which precedes the verb, and 'object' cannot be defined as the NP which follows the verb, although as far as the type of sentences discussed so far are concerned these statements would not be descriptively inaccurate. In the subsequent chapters we will discuss examples where these statements are clearly descriptively inaccurate. The fact that subjects precede the verb and objects follow the verb in certain types of English sentence is a by-product of the geometrical aspects of the structures generated by PS rules. As we proceed, it will become clear that linear-based notions such as 'precede' and 'follow' do not play a major role in the grammar: grammatical relations and rules are structurally based. Having said that, because linear terms are very useful in identifying categories in discussions we will continue to use them, bearing in mind that they have no theoretical status.

2.7   *Conclusions and Revisions*

The model of Grammar we have constructed so far consists of the Lexicon, the Syntactic Component, and the Semantic Component. The Lexicon consists of an unordered list of entries, as well as morphological rules of derivation. Lexical entries specify information relating to the categorial and subcategorization properties of lexical items, among others. The subcategorization properties are represented in terms of subcategorization frames which specify information relating to the number and nature of complements, if any. The categorial properties, on the other hand, are represented in terms of complexes of categorial features.

The Syntactic Component consists of 'context-free' Phrase Structure (PS) rules, which have the role of specifying the various constituency patterns phrasal categories can have, the order of constituents, and their grammatical functions. PS rules generate Phrase Markers, whose terminal nodes are filled with items from the Lexicon in terms of a general rule called the Lexical Insertion Rule (LIR). LIR ensures that lexical items are inserted in contexts which match both their categorial features and subcategorization properties. Phrase Markers generated by PS rules in combination with LIR are fed to the Semantic Component which assigns them a semantic representation. The Semantic Component is said to be 'interpretive' in nature, in so far as it operates on Phrase Markers generated by the Syntactic Component.

The Grammar also includes another component which we have not discussed so far simply because it is somewhat irrelevant to the purpose of the book. This is the **Phonological Component** which, like the Semantic Component, is also 'interpretive' in nature. This means that it applies to Phrase Markers derived by the Syntactic Component, and assigns them a phonetic representation. The latter, presumably, operates in terms of rules which are distinct in nature from the rules of Syntax, the underlying assumption being that the autonomy of a given component is justifiable in so far as it includes rules which are distinct in nature from the rules which characterize the other components. The Semantic Component and the Phonological Component are also known as the 'interface levels', meaning that they connect the language faculty to the other faculties.

104.

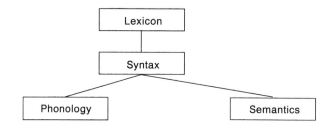

The model of Grammar just outlined can be graphically represented as in (104). The fact that the Semantic Component and the Phonological Component are not directly linked implies that there is no input-output relationship between them. While the two components both operate on representations (Phrase Markers) generated by the Syntax, the Semantic Component does not operate on representations produced by the Phonological Component, and the Phonological Component does not operate on representations produced by the Semantic Component.

Exercises

Exercise 1

Assign a structural description to each of the following sentences, using both tree diagrams and labelled brackets:

1. Mary thinks that John is clumsy
2. She cleverly avoided the question
3. Bill donated money to the charity
4. The tall building is new, obviously
5. The claim that John is a cheat is absurd

Exercise 2

Provide a formalized subcategorization frame for each word in the following list, making sure you support each decision with as many examples as necessary:

1. suggest
2. fond
3. dismissal
4. behave
5. believe
6. depend
7. suggestion

Exercise 3

In Chapter 1 we discussed one respect in which human languages are said to be creative: the ability of native speakers to produce novel sentences. Another respect in which human languages are said to be creative is the ability of native speakers to produce, in principle, indefinitely long sentences. This is illustrated in the following not so long examples ((2) is adapted from the nursery rhyme 'The Court of King Caractacus'):

1. John claims that Bill believes that Mary thinks that Jane said . . . that he is a fool
2. The boys put the powder on the noses of the faces of the ladies of the harem of the court of King Caractacus

Explain whether the system of rules discussed in this chapter accounts for this property of human languages, and if so, how.

Exercise 4

The sentences below are said to be **structurally ambiguous**, meaning that every sentence has two different interpretations (meanings), each of which implies a different structure:

1. John saw a man with binoculars
2. The boy called the girl from London

Provide the structures underlying the two interpretations of each example.

Exercise 5

Each of the examples below represents a type of sentence we have not analysed in this chapter:

1. Beans, I don't like
2. Do you like beans?
3. The ball was kicked (by the boy)
4. I wonder which ball the boy kicked

See whether these sentences can be generated in terms of the system of rules developed in this chapter. If you find out that they cannot, and that they require new rules, try to explain the nature of the rules needed, and how they can be implemented to derive sentences of the type in (1–4).

Further Reading

Chomsky (1957; 1965) include some of the early discussions of the general properties of phrase structure and the rules underlying it. The category AUX and its status in the phrase structure of the sentence has attracted a considerable amount of attention in the literature. For an overview of the major issues and views see Akmajian *et al.* (1979), Steele (1981), and Heny and Richards (1983). On the classification of adverbs and their representation see Jackendoff (1972).

The discussion of the issue of over-generation in this chapter is based on Chomsky (1965). The latter marks the first serious attempt to constrain the generative power of the theory, which led to the postulation of the Semantic Component and the separation of the Lexicon from the Syntax. The book also includes a discussion of grammatical functions/ relations.

The proposal to view categories as bundles of categorial features is outlined in Chomsky (1970). A recent evaluation of this propoal can be found in Muysken and van Riemsdijk (1985).

In addition to Chomsky (1965; 1970), a discussion of morphological derivation in relation to the Lexicon and the Syntax can be found in Aronoff (1976), Selkirk (1982), Fabb (1984), Marantz (1984), Di Sciullo and Williams (1987), Sproat (1985b), Zubizar-reta (1987), and Baker (1988). For an overview of the major opinions relating the nature of the rules of Morphology and their place in the Grammar see Scalise (1984) and Spencer (1991).

Kempson (1977) and Fodor (1982) include good overviews of the issues standardly thought to fall under the scope of Semantics.

Finally, good overviews of the major issues and theories in Phonology can be found in Hyman (1975), Kenstowicz and Kisseberth (1979), Goldsmith (1990), and Durand (1990). One of the current issues is whether Phonology operates in terms of the same formal mechanisms as Syntax, a view outlined in Kaye and Lowenstamm (1986) and defended in Kaye (1989), or involves different mechanisms, as argued in Bromberger and Halle (1991), following a long tradition.

3

Transformations

Contents

3.1 *The Nature of Transformations*

3.1.1 Topicalization

Compare the following examples:

1a. I can solve this problem
1b. *I can* [$_{VP}$ *solve* [$_{NP}$ *this problem*]]
2a. This problem, I can solve
2b. *This problem, I can* [$_{VP}$ *solve*]

The two sentences differ with respect to the position of the NP *this problem*. In (1) it is in the object position of the verb, where it is expected to be, given its function as the object of the verb *solve*. However, in (2) the NP is in the initial position of the sentence, although it is understood as the object of the verb. As shown in (3a, b) below, the verb *solve* is transitive, and therefore associated with a transitive subcategorization frame:

3a. I can solve *(this problem)
3b. *solve*: [— NP]

Sentence (1) is consistent with (3b), since the verb is associated with a transitive subcategorization frame. However, (2) apparently is not consistent with (3b). The absence of the object from the object position of the verb seems to imply an intransitive VP structure, rather than the required transitive structure. Recall (from the previous chapter) that situations where a given verb is associated with an inappropriate subcategorization frame invariably give rise to ungrammaticality, as shown in (3a). Recall also that ungrammatical sentences of this type are excluded in terms of LIR, reproduced here for reference:

4. **Lexical Insertion Rule**
   Insert item X under terminal node Y, where Y corresponds to the categorial features of X, and YP corresponds to the subcategorization properties of X.

Given the conditions encoded in this rule, sentences of the type illustrated in (3a) are predicted to be excluded.

In view of this, it seems that the model, as envisaged so far, makes the wrong predictions with respect to (2) and similar sentences. (2) is expected to be ungrammatical on the grounds that the transitive verb *solve* is inappropriately associated with an intransitive frame, on a par with (3a). We therefore have to revise the model in such a way that grammatical sentences such as (2) are not excluded, without compromising its ability to exclude ungrammatical sentences such as (3a). Obviously, there is a clear difference between (2) and (3a), which suggests that the similarity is merely superficial, though not unproblematic. In (3a) the object of the verb is missing from the sentence altogether, whereas in (2) it is only missing from the (object) position where it is expected to be by virtue of (3) in combination with LIR. Moreover, although the NP *this problem* in (2) is not situated in the object position of the verb, it is still interpreted as the object of the verb, i.e. the thing to be solved. A possible way of explaining this apparent inconsistency between the function of the NP and the position it occupies is to assume that the NP in question actually originates in the object position of the verb, and is subsequently displaced to the sentence-initial position. In other words, we could postulate the following derivation for (2) (and similar sentences) (read ⇒ as 'transform as'):

5a. *I can solve* [NP *this problem*] ⇒
5b. [NP *This problem*], *I can solve* [—]

(5a) is the underlying representation, generated by PS rules in combination with LIR. In this representation the verb *solve* is associated with a transitive frame, as specified in (3b). A rule of a different nature then applies to this underlying representation, and displaces the NP *the problem* from the object position of the verb, where it originated, to the initial position of the sentence, deriving sentence (2).

Before discussing the nature of the rule which displaces the object of the verb, it is important to see how the derivation outlined in (5a,b) solves the dilemma we faced above, i.e. the contrast between (2) and (3a). By assuming that the NP *this problem* originates in the object position of the verb in the representation generated by PS rules and LIR, the problem of the verb *solve* being associated with an inappropriate subcategorization frame ceases to exist. As shown in (5a), the verb is correctly associated with a transitive frame. The rule which displaces the NP object to the initial position applies at a later stage. When compared to (2), the ungrammatical example (3a) involves a different situation. Because the NP object is missing altogether, the analysis outlined for (2) (in terms of 'displacement') does not extend to it. In other words, (3a) represents a situation where the (transitive) verb is indeed associated with an inappropriate (intransitive) subcategorization frame, in both the underlying representation and the derived representation.

The rule which displaces the NP *this problem* to the initial position shown in (5) is called a **Transformation**. It transforms Phrase Marker (6), generated by PS rules and LIR, into the slightly different Phrase Marker (7). The displaced NP is attached to the left side of S, a structural position which corresponds to its linear position in (2) as the leftmost constituent of the sentence. The symbol *t*(*race*) in the object position of the verb in (7)

6.

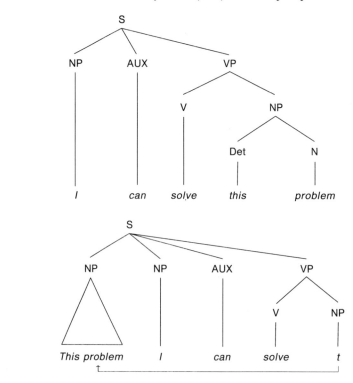

marks the position from which the NP *this problem* has been displaced. The status and function of *trace* in the structural representation of sentences will be discussed later on in detail.

The transformational rule involved in the derivation of (2) is called **Topicalization**. Its peculiar property is that it moves a category and attaches it to the left side of S. As we will see below, other transformational rules have different properties, having mainly to do with where they place the category they move. A possible way of formulating the transformational rule of Topicalization is as in (8):

8. X – NP – X (Structural Description (SD))
    1   2   3 ⇒
    2   1   3 (Structural Change (SC))

Structural Description (SD) refers to the Phrase Marker generated by PS rules and LIR, and corresponds to the underlying representation (6) above. NP is the category targeted by the transformation, and X is a variable which stands for the categories (including zero) to the left and to the right of NP. The numbers in (8) are simply devices which help us keep track of the changes which take place. Structural Change (SC), on the other hand, refers to the Phrase Marker derived by the application of Topicalization, and therefore corresponds to the derived representation (7) above. The targeted NP (designated with number 2) has been displaced (topicalized) to the initial position of the sentence.

    The format illustrated in (8) can be used to formulate all types of transformation. However, here we will define transformational rules using simple English prose. Thus, Topicalization can be defined as follows:

9. **Topicalization**
    Move XP and attach it as the leftmost constituent of S.

XP is a variable which stands for any phrasal category. This general definition of Topicalization captures the fact that not only NPs but other phrasal categories can be topicalized. In the following examples, the topicalized categories are PP and VP, respectively:

10a. To John, Mary gave the book
10b. [$_{PP}$ *To John*], *Mary gave the book* t

11a. Fix the car, I wonder whether he will
11b. [$_{VP}$ *Fix the car*], *I wonder* [$_{S'}$ *whether* [$_S$ *he will* t]]

Various other phrasal categories can also be subject to Topicalization. However, the examples discussed so far are sufficient to justify the use of the variable XP in the definition of Topicalization.

    The S category to which the topicalized XP is attached can either be the first one which contains the XP in the underlying representation or, in appropriate examples, a higher one. In (11) above, for example, the topicalized VP is attached to the root S, although it has been displaced from the embedded clause. The options of attaching the topicalized category to the embedded S or the root S are more clearly illustrated in the following examples:

12a. This problem, I believe that I can solve
12b. [$_{NP}$ *This problem*], *I believe* [$_{S'}$ *that* [$_S$ *I can solve* t]]

13a. I believe that this problem, I can solve
13b. *I believe* [S′ *that* [S [NP *this problem*], *I can solve* t]]

In (12) the topicalized NP is attached to the root S, whereas in (13) it is attached to the embedded S.

3.1.2 Traces and The Trace Convention

As pointed out above, *trace* designates the position from which the topicalized category is moved. Put differently, *trace* marks the position where the moved category is 'understood' as far as its interpretation in the sentence is concerned. With respect to example (2), reproduced below, the presence of *trace* in the object position of the verb helps explain the observation that the topicalized NP is interpreted as though it were in the object position of the verb:

14a. This problem, I can solve
14b. [NP *This problem*]ᵢ, I can [VP *solve* tᵢ]

The relation between a moved category and its trace is encoded in terms of co-indexation, as shown in (14b). The co-indexation of the topicalized NP and *trace* is intended to convey the information that the topicalized NP has the interpretation associated with the position occupied by *trace*. The moved category is said to be the **antecedent** of the *trace* it is related to (co-indexed with).

Trace is said to have a full grammatical status on a par with categories such as NP and PP. This means, first, that *trace* has categorial features, which are usually the features of the moved category it is related to. In (14), for example, *trace* is an NP, and in examples (10) and (11) above the trace is a PP and a VP, respectively. Secondly, *trace* can enter into grammatical relations, and, as we will see below, also determine certain grammatical processes. In (14), for example, *trace* has the grammatical function 'object', by virtue of the fact that it occupies the object position of the verb. Since the antecedent of *trace* is co-indexed with it, the antecedent receives the interpretation of object by inheritance from *trace*. These properties, among others which will transpire in the course of this book, all point to the conclusion that *trace* is a category in its own right. It differs from **lexical** or **overt** (i.e. pronounced) categories only in that it is **empty** or **null**, meaning it is not phonetically realized (not pronounced).

Obviously, it is preferable, if not essential, to have some clear evidence for the presence of *traces* in sentences which have undergone a movement transformation. A substantial amount of such evidence has been pointed out and evaluated in the literature, some of which is discussed in various places in this book. At this stage, we will discuss one such piece of evidence, having to do with the phenomenon of *wanna-* contraction in colloquial English. Consider the following examples:

15a. I want to read this novel
15b. I wanna read this novel

16a. I want this novel to be considered for a prize
16b. *I wanna this novel be considered for a prize

Examples (15a,b) show that (in colloquial English) *want* and *to* can contract to *wanna* when they are adjacent. (16a,b) show that *want* and *to* cannot contract to *wanna* when they are not adjacent. In this sentence the NP *this novel* intervenes between the two categories, thereby preventing them from contracting.

With this in mind, compare (15a, b) and (16a, b) with examples (17) and (18) below, which involve topicalization of the NP *this novel*:

17a. This novel, I want to read
17b. This novel, I wanna read
17c. [$_{NP}$ *This novel*]$_i$, *I want to read* t$_i$

18a. This novel, I want to be considered for a prize
18b. *This novel, I wanna be considered for a prize
18c. [$_{NP}$ *This novel*]$_i$, *I want* t$_i$ *to be considered for a prize*

In (17) *want* and *to* are adjacent, and therefore can contract to *wanna*, as shown in (17b). The trace of the topicalized NP is in the object position, following the verb, and therefore does not intervene between *want* and *to*. In (18), however, the trace of the topicalized NP intervenes between *want* and *to*, as shown in (18c). For this reason, the two categories cannot contract to *wanna*, as shown by the ungrammatical status of (18b). What this fact shows is that *trace*, though null, is visible to the grammatical rule which contracts *want* and *to*.

The presence of categories in Phrase Markers have so far been motivated on the basis of PS rules in combination with subcategorization requirements. However, the presence of *trace* cannot be motivated on similar grounds, as it arises as a result of a movement transformation applying to the Phrase Marker generated by PS rules in combination with LIR. It seems that we need a special mechanism to motivate the presence of *trace* in relevant sentences. For the moment, let us assume that the mechanism in question is simply the convention stated in (19):

19. **Trace Convention**
    Movement transformations leave a trace (in the original position of the moved category).

Ideally, the presence of *trace* should follow from some general requirements of the grammar, rather than be stipulated in terms of a convention such as (19). In the subsequent chapters we will discuss reasons to believe that the presence of *trace* does indeed follow from some general requirements of the grammar. Pending the discussion, we will continue to assume that movement transformations leave a *trace* behind, by convention.

3.1.3   Levels of Representation: D-structure and S-structure

The derivation outlined above for sentence (2) implies the existence of two representations (Phrase Markers) for the sentence: an underlying representation, where the NP *the problem* is in the object position of the verb, and a derived representation, where the NP in question is attached to S and its position in the underlying representation is filled with a trace. (20a) below corresponds to Phrase Marker (6), and (20b) to Phrase Marker (7):

20a. *I can* [$_{VP}$ *solve* [$_{NP}$ *this problem*]] ⇒
20b. [$_{NP}$ *This problem*]$_i$, *I can* [$_{VP}$ *solve* t$_i$]

(20a) is the representation generated by PS rules and LIR. (20b), on the other hand, is the representation derived by applying the transformational rule Topicalization to the underlying representation (20a).

The underlying representation (20a) is known technically as the **Deep Structure (D-structure)**, and the derived representation (20b) as the **Surface Structure (S-structure)**. The idea is that the derivation of sentences in general involves two structures (Phrase Markers): a D-structure, where all categories are in the positions where they are expected to be, by virtue of PS rules and the subcategorization requirements, and an S-structure, where categories may appear in positions other than the ones where they are expected to be. In D-structure (20a), for example, the NP *this problem* is in the object position of the verb, as expected, whereas in S-structure (20b) it occupies the initial position of the sentence. Transformational rules such as Topicalization represent the link between D-structure and S-structure representations. Transformational rules are said to map D-structure representations onto S-structure representations.

The idea that the derivation of sentences involves two levels of representation is a direct consequence of introducing transformational rules. The Syntactic Component of the Grammar now comprises two sub-components. One sub-component includes context-free PS rules, and is sometimes known as the **Base**. The other sub-component includes transformational rules, such as Topicalization and others to be discussed below. The Base generates D-structure representations, which serve as input to transformational rules. Transformational rules introduce modifications into D-structure representations, by, for example, moving a category from one position to another, and derive S-structure representations. The organization of the model implied by the revision introduced is further discussed and illustrated at the end of this chapter.

3.1.4   Summary

The major aim of this section was to argue the need for an additional set of syntactic rules to derive sentences where a given category appears in a position other than the position where it is 'understood'. The rules in question are called Transformations, and have the effect of modifying Phrase Markers generated by PS rules and LIR, and deriving modified Phrase Markers. In the case of Topicalization, the modification amounts to moving a phrasal category from the position where it originates and attaching it to the left side of S. Movement transformations are assumed to leave a trace behind, by convention. Traces are null (unpronounced) categories which have the role of linking moved categories to the positions associated with their interpretation. The consequence of introducing transformational rules means that the Syntactic Component now consists of two sub-components. The first sub-component, sometimes called the Base, consists of PS rules. Together with LIR, these rules (base-)generate D-structure representations. The second sub-component consists of transformational rules, which apply to D-structure representations and introduce certain modifications into them, deriving S-structure representations.

3.2   *Affix-Hopping, V-Raising to AUX, 'Do'-Support, and Subject–AUX Inversion*

3.2.1   Affix-Hopping: Main Verbs

In the previous chapter it was concluded that Tense is an (obligatory) constituent of AUX, and that the rule which generates AUX is as in (21):

21. AUX → Tense (Modal) (Neg)

22a. Mary will solve the problem
22b. Mary solved the problem

When AUX dominates a Modal, in addition to Tense, as in (22a), Tense appears on the Modal and the main verb is unmarked for Tense. And when AUX does not dominate a Modal, Tense appears on the main verb, as in (22b). The question as to how Tense, which is a constituent of AUX, ends up attached to the main verb in sentences such as (22b) was left open. We are now in a position to address it.

A priori, Tense and the main verb could be joined together in one of two possible ways: by moving Tense (from AUX) to V, or moving V to Tense (in AUX). The two options are outlined in (23a,b):

23a. *Mary* [$_{AUX}$ *-ed*] [VP *solve the problem*]

23b. *Mary* [$_{AUX}$ *-ed*] [VP *solve the problem*]

Which of the two options is used is an empirical question, to be settled on the basis of evidence. The evidence we will discuss here relates to the order of verbs in relation to VP-adverbs.

Recall that VP-adverbs typically occur in the leftmost or rightmost positions of VP, as indicated in rule (24):

24. VP → (ADV) V . . . (ADV)

Concentrating on the leftmost (pre-verbal) position, we find the following pattern:

25a. Mary cleverly avoided Bill
25b. John rarely visited Mary

Note that the order [ADV V + Tense NP] displayed by these examples implies that AUX moves rightward to V. In other words, the order shown in (25a, b), where the adverb precedes the complex V + Tense, implies the derivation shown in (26).

26a. *Mary* [$_{AUX}$ t$_i$] [$_{VP}$ [$_{ADV}$ *cleverly*] *avoided* + [*-ed*]$_i$ *Bill*]

26b. *John* [$_{AUX}$ t$_i$] [$_{VP}$ [$_{ADV}$ *rarely*] *visit* + [*-ed*]$_i$ *Mary*]

26c.

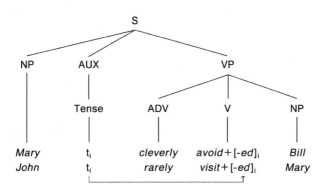

It seems, therefore, that Tense and the main verb are joined together by movement of AUX to V, rather than by movement of V to AUX. If V were to move leftward to AUX, the derived order would be [V + Tense ADV NP]. However, as shown by (27) and (28), this order is excluded:

27a. *Mary avoided cleverly Bill
27b. *Mary* [$_{AUX}$ [*avoid*]$_i$ + [*-ed*] [$_{VP}$ [$_{ADV}$ *cleverly*] t$_i$ *Bill*]

28a. *John visited rarely Mary
28b. *John* [$_{AUX}$ [*visit*]$_i$ + [*-ed*] [$_{VP}$ [$_{ADV}$ *rarely*] t$_i$ *Mary*]

These examples illustrate a general fact about English: adverbs cannot intervene between a verb and its NP object. Here, we will take this fact to mean that the verb cannot **raise** to AUX. Rather, it is AUX that **lowers** to V.

Presumably, the rule which moves AUX to V is a transformational one. To find an accurate definition of this rule, we need to take certain facts into consideration. Recall (from the previous chapter) that when AUX dominates a Modal, in addition to Tense, Tense appears on the Modal, rather than on the verb. This is shown in the following examples, where *do* is understood to be a Modal which conveys 'assertion' or 'emphasis':

29a. John did visit Mary
29b. *John do visited Mary
29c. *John* [$_{AUX}$ *do* [$_{Tense}$ t$_i$]] [$_{VP}$ *visit* + [*-ed*]$_i$ *Mary*]

Thus, the rule which moves AUX to V applies only when AUX does not dominate a Modal. Essentially, this observation amounts to a condition on the application of the rule in question, necessary to exclude ungrammatical sentences such as (29b).

Conditions on transformations such as the one illustrated in (29b) can either be incorporated into the definition of the transformation or stated separately. Here, we will adopt the strategy of incorporating conditions on transformations into their definitions. Accordingly, the rule which moves AUX to V, known as **Affix-hopping**, can be defined as follows:

30. **Affix-hopping**
    Move AUX to V, unless AUX dominates a Modal.

The *unless*-clause ensures that ungrammatical sentences such as (29b) are not derived. The past Tense morpheme is an affix which morphologically subcategorizes for V (see Chapter 2), hence the fact that it has to attach to a verb (or a Modal). Notice that Affix-hopping is basically a rule of affixation which derives a complex verb by attaching Tense to a simple verb. As such, it is not very different from the morphological rules of derivation which apply in the Lexicon (see Chapter 2), although Affix-hopping is considered to be a (transformational) rule of Syntax. It seems that, after all, not all rules of derivation are limited to the Lexicon. Notice, however, that the rule of Affix-hopping, as defined in (30), is subject to a condition which is syntactically based, i.e. a condition which refers to a node in the Phrase Marker. This property can be taken as justification for its status as a rule of Syntax, even though it is a rule of affixation. The working hypothesis we will adopt here is that rules of affixation can apply both in the Lexicon and in the Syntax, and that the ones which apply in the Syntax either make reference to syntactic information or, more generally, play a rule in the syntactic representation of sentences.

3.2.2   V-raising to AUX: Auxiliary Verbs

Compare (31) to the examples discussed above.

31a. John was rarely happy.
31b. *John* [AUX Tense + [*be*]ᵢ [VP [ADV *rarely*] tᵢ *happy*]

31c.

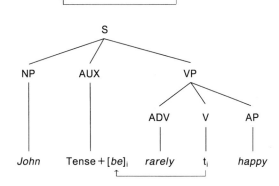

As shown in (31b, c), the derivation of (31a) involves movement of the verb *be* to AUX, rather than movement of AUX to V (Affix-hopping). This example illustrates the general fact that (auxiliary) verbs such as *be* are joined with Tense by a transformational rule which is different from the one which joins Tense with main verbs. This conclusion extends to the other auxiliary verb, *have*.

32a. Mary has cleverly avoided Bill
32b. *Mary* [AUX *Tense* + [*have*]ᵢ [VP [ADV *cleverly*] tᵢ *avoided Bill*]

32c.

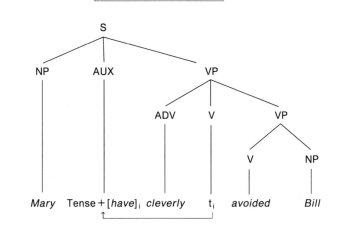

Like *be*, the auxiliary verb *have* in (32) also moves from inside VP to AUX, across the adverb. The assumption underlying this analysis is that *have* in (32), contrary to what its name might suggest, is base-generated inside VP, not under the AUX node. Moreover, we shall assume here that *have* in sentences such as (32a) has its own VP node, distinct from that of the main verb. This is shown in (32c), where the auxiliary *have* and the main verb *avoided* each has a VP node of its own, with the VP node of the main verb a sister to the auxiliary verb. Auxiliary verbs differ from main verbs in that auxiliary verbs can take VP as a complement.

To distinguish auxiliary verbs from main verbs, we will assume, for the moment, that auxiliary verbs are marked with the feature [+AUX], whereas main verbs are not. The usefulness of this feature in distinguishing between auxiliary and main verbs is that it makes it possible to provide an accurate definition of the transformational rule which moves auxiliary verbs to AUX. The rule, which we will call here **V-raising to AUX**, can be defined as in (33):

33. **V-raising to AUX**
    Move V   to AUX, unless AUX dominates a Modal.
       [+AUX]

By specifying the targeted verb with the feature [+AUX], we make sure that the rule applies only to auxiliary verbs, to the exclusion of main verbs. Note that main verbs have to be exempted from this rule, otherwise ungrammatical sentences such as (27) and (28) above, derived by raising the main verb to AUX, will not be excluded. That the condition expressed in the *unless*-clause in (33) is crucial is shown by the following examples:

34a. Mary could/should have avoided Bill
34b. John could/must be in the garden

35a. *Mary could/should has avoided Bill
35b. *John could/must is in the garden

Examples (34a, b) show that, when AUX dominates a Modal, in addition to Tense, Tense appears on the Modal, and the auxiliary verb is unmarked for Tense (non-conjugated). Examples (35a, b), on the other hand, show that applying V-raising to AUX in sentences where AUX dominates a Modal gives rise to ungrammaticality.

Note, finally, that the properties of sentences with an auxiliary verb and a main verb, in particular the fact that it is the auxiliary verb which carries Tense, implies that the rule of Affix-hopping should be prevented from taking place in these sentences. Otherwise, ungrammatical sentences such as (36) below, where Tense is carried by the main verb, rather than by the auxiliary verb, will not be excluded:

36a. *Mary have avoided+ Tense Bill*
36b. *Mary $[_{AUX}$ $t_i]$ $[_{VP}$ have avoided+ [Tense]$_i$ Bill]*

Sentences of this type can be excluded by excluding main verbs in the participle form from the set of verbs that Affix-hopping can apply to. Alternatively, a condition can be added to the definition of Affix-hopping, which will prevent it from taking place in sentences which include an auxiliary verb, in addition to the main verb. The latter solution implies the following, revised definition of Affix-hopping:

37. **Affix-hopping**
    Move AUX to V, unless

    (i) AUX dominates a Modal or
    (ii) VP dominates a V
           [+AUX]

Condition (ii) prevents Affix-hopping from applying to sentences which include an auxiliary verb in addition to the main verb, thereby excluding (36) and similar sentences.

3.2.3   *Do*-support: Negative Sentences

Consider the following negative sentences:

38a. Mary did not avoid Bill
38b. George did not answer the question

In these examples Tense appears on *do*, and the main verb is unmarked for Tense. In this respect, negative sentences such as (38a,b) differ from their affirmative counterparts, where, as we saw above, Tense appears on the main verb, and *do* is absent. Descriptively, the presence of Neg (under AUX) seems to prevent Tense from joining with the verb. In other words, Neg somehow prevents the rule of Affix-hopping from applying in negative sentences. The element *do* is said to be 'semantically empty' (a 'dummy' element), in the sense that it does not contribute to the meaning of the sentence. Its function seems to be to 'support' Tense, because Tense is prevented (by Neg) from seeking 'support' from the main verb. When AUX dominates an element which can 'support' Tense, the 'dummy' *do* does not show up:

39a. Mary must/could not avoid Bill
39b. George will/may not answer the question

Recall that Affix-hopping does not apply to sentences such as (39a,b) because AUX dominates a Modal. However, Affix-hopping is expected to apply to (38a,b), since AUX does not dominate a Modal in these examples. Yet Affix-hopping seems to be prevented by Neg from applying, resulting in the appearance of *do* to 'support' Tense.

The situation just described requires two measures. The first is to revise the definition of Affix-hopping in such a way as to prevent it from applying to negative sentences. Otherwise, ungrammatical sentences such as (40) and (41) will be derived:

40a. *Mary not avoided Bill
40b. *Mary [$_{AUX}$ t$_i$ *not*] [$_{VP}$ *avoid* + [*-ed*]$_i$ *Bill*]

41a. *George not answered the question
41b. *George [$_{AUX}$ t$_i$ *not*] [$_{VP}$ *answer* + [*-ed*]$_i$ *the question*]

The second measure is to introduce a transformational rule which inserts *do* to 'support' Tense in sentences where Affix-hopping cannot apply and consequently Tense is left 'stranded'.

A simple way of revising Affix-hopping in the required sense (i.e. to make it sensitive to the presence of Neg in AUX) is to add Neg to Modal in the *unless*-clause, as shown in (42):

42. **Affix-hopping**
    Move AUX to V, unless

    (i) AUX dominates a Modal or Neg or
    (ii) VP dominates a V
    [+AUX]

This slight revision ensures that Affix-hopping does not apply to negative sentences, and that ungrammatical sentences such as (40) and (41) are excluded. As for the rule which inserts *do* to support 'stranded' Tense, it can be defined as follows:

43. ***Do*-support**
    Insert *do* to support stranded Tense.

The word 'stranded', with the meaning specified above, encodes the condition that *Do*-support applies only when Affix-hopping fails to apply. In negative sentences, Affix-hopping fails to apply due to the presence of Neg (under AUX). Below, we will discuss another situation where Affix-hopping also fails to apply, thereby triggering *Do*-support.

Note, finally, that V-raising to AUX, unlike Affix-hopping, does not need to be revised, as Neg does not prevent auxiliary verbs from joining with Tense:

44a. John was not happy
44b. *John* [$_{AUX}$ [*be*]$_i$ + Tense *not*] [$_{VP}$ t$_i$ *happy*]

45a. Mary had not avoided Bill
45b. *Mary* [$_{AUX}$ [*have*]$_i$ + Tense *not* [$_{VP}$ t$_i$ *avoided Bill*]

Auxiliary verbs can move to AUX, irrespective of whether AUX dominates Neg. Therefore, V-raising to AUX need not be made sensitive to the presence of Neg under AUX. Moreover, given that V-Raising to AUX can usually apply in negative sentences with an auxiliary verb, Tense does not get 'stranded', and, consequently, *Do*-support fails to be triggered. This explains the fact that the 'dummy' *do* does not appear in negative sentences with an auxiliary verb.

3.2.4 Subject–AUX Inversion: Yes/No Questions

The following sentences are examples of **yes/no questions** (i.e. questions which typically require 'yes' or 'no' as an answer):

46a. Can you solve the problem?
46b. Will John fix the car?

The major characteristic of yes/no questions is that AUX and the subject appear inverted, compared to their order in declarative sentences: *You can solve the problem*, and *John will fix the car*. Presumably, yes/no questions are derived from a D-structure where AUX is to the right of the subject, as in declarative sentences. Recall that the PS rule which generates S, reproduced here, places AUX to the right of the subject:

47a. S → NP AUX VP

47b.

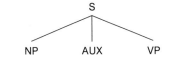

Recall also that PS rules incorporate claims about word order, so that AUX must be to the right of the subject in the D-structure representations of (46a, b). It follows that the inversion effect is the result of a transformational rule which applies in the mapping from D-structure onto S-structure.

A priori, the inversion effect can be derived from the underlying order specified in (47) either by moving AUX to the left of the subject or by moving the subject to the right of AUX. We will assume here that the inversion effect is derived by moving AUX to the left of the subject. The theoretical and empirical basis for this assumption will become clear as we go along. Accordingly, yes/no questions such as (46a, b) have the following derivation:

48a. [*Can*]$_i$ *you* [$_{AUX}$ t$_i$] [$_{VP}$ *solve the problem*]?
48b. [*Will*]$_i$ *you* [$_{AUX}$ t$_i$] [$_{VP}$ *fix the car*]?

Assuming this to be the case, the next step is to determine the position in which AUX is placed after it has been moved from its position following the subject.

In the previous chapter it was assumed that complement clauses such as the ones in (49a, b) are both of the category S′ and therefore have the structure in (50b), generated by PS rule (50a).

49a. The girl thought that she should give a present to the boy
49b. The girl thought she would give a present to the boy

50a. S′ → COMP S

50b.

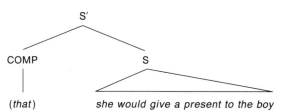

In sentences where the complementizer *that* is missing, such as (49b), the COMP node is empty. The importance of this assumption for our present discussion relates to the implication that rule (50a) has for the structure of root clauses. Given that the category S is generated by the rule which expands S′, it follows that every S implies the presence of an S′, and, consequently, a COMP position. Thus, a simple sentence such as (51a), for example, has the structure shown in (51b), where e stands for empty.

51a. The boy kicked the ball

51b.

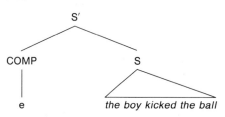

Going back to yes/no questions, the transformational rule which moves AUX to the left of the subject, outlined in (48a,b), can be said to place (the moved) AUX in the COMP position to the left of the subject. Accordingly, (48a), for example, has the structure and derivation shown in (52). The transformational rule which moves AUX to COMP in the derivation of yes/no questions is called **Subject-AUX Inversion (SAI)**.

52.

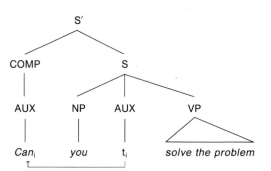

SAI is said to be a **root transformation**, meaning that it applies in root clauses only. Consider the following sentences, which include instances of so-called indirect yes/no questions:

53a. I wonder whether you can solve the problem
53b. *I wonder* [S′ *whether* [S *you can solve the problem*]]

54a. *I wonder whether can you solve the problem

54b. *I wonder [$_{S'}$ whether can$_i$ [$_S$ you t$_i$ solve the problem]]

Indirect yes/no questions are yes/no questions which appear in an embedded domain, and are usually introduced by *whether*, as in (53a,b), or *if*, as in *I wonder if this student can solve the problem*. Both these elements occur in the COMP position, and are in complementary distribution with each other: *I wonder whether if/if whether you can solve the problem*. Examples (53a,b) and (54a,b) show that SAI does not apply in embedded clauses. As shown by (53a,b), in this domain AUX remains in its D-structure position, following the subject. The status of the clause as a yes/no question is indicated by the COMP element *whether/if*. Note that it could be argued that the reason why AUX in (53a,b) and (54a,b) cannot move to COMP in the embedded clause is because COMP is already filled with *whether*. This argument would lend support to the assumption that AUX in yes/no questions does indeed move to COMP. When the latter is already filled, the movement is blocked. However, the situation is more complicated than it looks, as we will discover in the next section. Whatever the reason for the inability of AUX to move to COMP in (53a,b) & (54a,b), it remains true that SAI does not apply to embedded yes/no questions.

Following the strategy of incorporating conditions on transformations into their definition, the restriction to root clauses on the application of SAI needs to be built into the definition of SAI:

55. **Subject–AUX Inversion (SAI)**

Move AUX to Comp, unless AUX is situated in a non-root clause.

Obviously, there are various other possible ways of defining SAI in such a way that ungrammatical sentences such as (51) are excluded. As it stands, (52) achieves the desired result.

Let us now check the implications that SAI, as defined in (55), has for auxiliary verbs and main verbs. Auxiliary verbs can move to COMP (in the derivation of yes/no questions), whereas main verbs cannot:

56a. Was John happy?

56b. Has Mary avoided Bill?

57a. *Avoided Mary Bill?

57b. *Solved you the problem?

How does (55) account for the contrast between auxiliary verbs and main verbs illustrated by these examples? Recall that auxiliary verbs can move to AUX (by V-raising to AUX), whereas main verbs cannot: main verbs merge with Tense in terms of the rule of Affix-hopping. Because SAI, as defined in (55), makes reference to AUX, only elements which can occupy AUX (either by being base-generated there or moved from another position) are predicted to be affected by SAI. It follows that auxiliary verbs will be affected, since they can occupy AUX, albeit by being moved there. It also follows that main verbs, contrary to auxiliary verbs, will not be affected by SAI, since they never occupy AUX. Thus, the ungrammatical examples (57a,b) are excluded. Examples (56a,b), however, are correctly predicted to be grammatical.

The grammatical versions of (57a,b) involve the 'dummy' element *do* and therefore the rule of *Do*-support:

58a. Did Mary avoid Bill?

58b. Did you solve the problem?

Recall that *Do*-support applies when Tense is left 'stranded'. In negative sentences, Tense is left 'stranded' due to the presence of Neg under AUX, which results in blocking the rule of

Affix-hopping. The yes/no questions exemplified in (58a,b) represent another situation where Tense, apparently, is also left 'stranded', thereby triggering *Do*-support. Presumably, Tense is left 'stranded' in (58a,b) as a result of AUX moving to COMP, i.e. as a result of being 'too far away' from the main verb inside VP. This observation seems to imply the incorporation of a **locality** condition into the rule of Affix-hopping to prevent it from applying in situations such as (58a,b) where AUX is not adjacent to VP. However, we will leave the rule of *Do*-support as it is for the moment. The facts of yes/no questions discussed also seem to imply that transformational rules should perhaps be ordered with respect to each other, an issue which we will not address here (see Exercises at the end of this chapter).

3.2.5 Summary

Four different transformational rules have been identified and discussed in this section: Affix-hopping, V-raising to AUX, *Do*-support and Subject–AUX Inversion. Affix-hopping joins Tense with the main verb in sentences where AUX does not dominate a Modal and/or Neg, and VP does not dominate an auxiliary verb. V-raising to AUX joins auxiliary verbs with Tense in sentences where AUX does not dominate a Modal. *Do*-support provides morphological support for 'stranded' Tense by inserting the 'semantically empty' element *do*. Tense is 'stranded' in sentences where AUX dominates Neg (i.e. negative sentences without a Modal or an auxiliary verb), and sentences where AUX is moved to COMP (yes/no questions). Finally, SAI moves AUX to COMP in the derivation of yes/no questions. All four transformations have in common the fact that they affect non-phrasal categories, i.e. AUX and V. In this respect, they differ from Topicalization which, remember, applies to phrasal categories, NP, PP, VP, etc. In the remaining sections, we will discuss further instances of transformational rules which resemble Topicalization in that they also affect phrasal categories.

3.3 *Wh-movement*

3.3.1 *Wh-*questions

Compare the following pairs of examples:

59a. Which problem did you solve?
59b. You solved which problem!

60a. Who does the boy like?
60b. The boy likes who!

(59a) and (60a) are instances of **wh-questions**, which usually have the function of asking for (new) information. (59b) and (60b), on the other hand, are instances of so-called **echo-questions**, which are usually used to express surprise at information just made available to the speaker. As such, echo-questions are not (information-seeking) questions, although like *wh*-questions, they also include **wh-phrases** such as *which problem* in (59b) and *who* in (60b). Although we are not concerned here with (the derivation of) echo-questions, they are useful in that they give us a clue as to the derivation of *wh*-questions. In the echo-questions (59b) and (60b) the *wh*-phrase appears in the object position of the verb, a situation which is consistent with the interpretation of the *wh*-phrase as an object of the verb. In the *wh*-questions (59a) and (60a), however, the *wh*-phrase appears in the initial position of the sentence. Now, if the position occupied by the *wh*-phrase in the echo-questions is assumed to be the D-structure position of the *wh*-phrase, the *wh*-questions

(59a) and (60a) can be said to be derived by a transformational rule which moves the *wh*-phrase from the object position of the verb to the initial position of the sentence.

As a matter of fact, we do not need to appeal to echo-questions to reach this conclusion. The reasoning adopted earlier with respect to topicalized objects also applies to the *wh*-phrases in (59a) and (60a). The verbs *solve* and *like* are both transitive, and therefore associated with a transitive frame in the Lexicon and at D-structure. The verbs *solve* and *like* have the (simplified) subcategorization frame shown in (61a). Examples (61b, c) show that these verbs must take an object:

61a. solve; like: [— NP]
61b. I solved *(the problem)
61c. The boy likes *(the girl)

It follows from the information shown in (61a–c) that the verbs *solve* in (59a) and *like* in (60a), must have an object. Otherwise, the two sentences should be ungrammatical for the same reason that (61b) and (61c) are ungrammatical without an object. The object of the verb in (59a) and (60a) is the *wh*-phrase, base-generated in the object position, and subsequently moved to the initial position of the sentence. The derivation of these examples is as outlined in (62):

62a. D-structure:
You [$_{AUX}$ *Tense*] [$_{VP}$ *solve* [$_{NP}$ *which problem*]]
The boy [$_{AUX}$ *Tense*] [$_{VP}$ *like* [$_{NP}$ *who*]]

62b. S-structure:
[*Which problem*]$_i$ [*did*]$_j$ [$_S$ you [$_{AUX}$ t$_j$] [$_{VP}$ solve [$_{NP}$ t$_i$]]]?

[*Who*]$_i$ [*does*]$_j$ [$_S$ *the boy* [$_{AUX}$ t$_j$] [$_{VP}$ *like* [$_{NP}$ t$_i$]]]?

The transformation responsible for movement of the *wh*-phrase to the sentence-initial position is called **Wh-movement**.

Note that not only the *wh*-phrase moves in the derivation of (59a) and (60a), but also AUX. Movement of AUX to the left of the subject is, obviously, an instance of SAI, discussed in the previous section. Recall that SAI in sentences with a main verb only results in the 'stranding' of Tense, and the subsequent insertion of *do* (by *Do*-support) to 'support' it. This is precisely what happens in the derivation of (59a) and (60a). Wh-movement of the object of the verb (as well as other categories to be discussed below) is said to trigger SAI, just as SAI was said in the previous section to trigger *Do*-support in the absence of a Modal or an auxiliary verb. As expected, SAI does not apply in indirect (embedded) *wh*-questions, given the conclusion that SAI is a root transformation:

63a. I wonder which problem Mary solved
63b. *I wonder* [$_{S'}$ [*which problem*]$_i$ [$_S$ *Mary* AUX [$_{VP}$ *solved* t$_i$]]]

Thus, although embedded *wh*-questions involve *Wh*-movement, they do not involve SAI. Consequently, Tense does not get 'stranded', and *Do*-support fails to be triggered. Instead, Tense is joined with the main verb via Affix-hopping.

Note that *Wh*-movement of the subject in root *wh*-questions such as (64) below apparently does not trigger SAI and the subsequent insertion of *do*:

64a. Who solved the problem?
64b. *Who*$_i$ [$_S$ t$_i$ AUX [$_{VP}$ *solved the problem*]?

An alternative analysis for (64a) would be to assume that the subject *wh*-phrase remains in

65a.

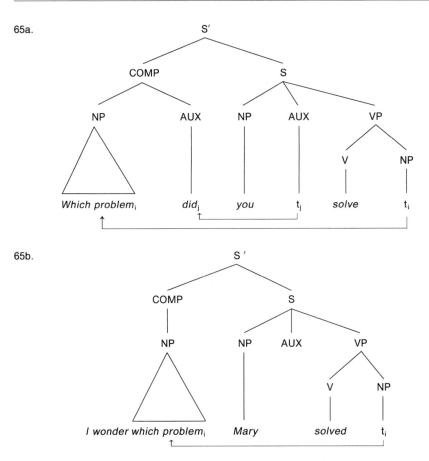

65b.

the subject position, in which case no *Wh*-movement would be involved. However, we will assume here that the analysis outlined in (64b) is the correct analysis for (64a), the underlying idea being that all *wh*-phrases in simple questions such as (64a), (59a) and (60a) are subject to *Wh*-movement. The movement in (64a) is sometimes said to be **(string) vacuous**.

In order to be able to define *Wh*-movement we need first to determine the sentence-initial position in which moved *wh*-phrases are placed. The fact that the *wh*-phrase occurs to the left of the inverted AUX in root questions such as (59a) and (60a) implies that, unlike topicalized phrases, *wh*-phrases are not attached to S. Instead, they occupy the COMP position, just like inverted AUX. Thus, a more detailed representation of the S-structure of (59a) is (65a). (65b) is the S-structure representation of the embedded *wh*-question in (63). In (65a) the COMP position is occupied by two categories, the *wh*-phrase and AUX, moved from inside S. In (65b), however, COMP is occupied by the *wh*-phrase only. The transformation responsible for attaching Tense to V in (65b) has been ignored since it is not crucial to the point of the discussion.

Having identified the position to which *wh*-phrases in *wh*-questions are moved, we are now in a position to define Wh-movement:

66. ***Wh*-movement**
     Move *wh*-XP to COMP.

The targeted COMP can either be in the root clause or an embedded clause, depending on the sentence derived. In the bi-clausal sentence (63) the *wh*-phrase is moved to the COMP of the embedded clause. In the following examples, the *wh*-phrase is moved from the embedded clause to the COMP of the root clause:

67a. Which problem do you think (that) Mary solved?
67b. [*Which problem*]ᵢ *do you think* [S′ *(that)* [S *Mary solved* tᵢ]]?

68a. Who didn't you know (that) the boy liked?
68b. [*Who*]ᵢ *didn't you know* [S′ *that* [S *the boy liked* tᵢ]]?

The use of the variable XP in the definition of *Wh*-movement is motivated by the fact that *wh*-phrases other than NP can also undergo *Wh*-movement:

69a. [AP *How difficult*] *was the problem you solved?*
69b. [ADV *When*] *did you solve the problem?*
69c. [ADV *Where*] *did you solve the problem?*

PP's can also undergo *Wh*-movement, although in English P usually has the option of staying behind:

70a. To whom did you give the book?
70b. [PP *To whom*]ᵢ *did* [S *you give the book* tᵢ]?

70c. Who did you give the book to?
70d. [NP *Who*]ᵢ *did* [S *you give the book* [PP *to* tᵢ]]?

(70c, d) is an instance of **preposition-stranding**, where the *wh*-NP complement of the preposition is *wh*-moved, and the preposition is 'stranded' behind. (70a,b), on the other hand, is an instance of **pied-piping**, where the preposition is moved (pied-piped) to COMP along with its *wh*-NP complement.

Before we move on to discuss other issues relating to Wh-movement, a word about the internal structure of *wh*-phrases. For the moment, we will assume that *wh*-phrases which consist of both a *wh*-word and a noun, e.g. *which problem*, have the structure shown in (71a), where the *wh*-word occupies the Det position. On the other hand, *wh*-phrases which apparently consist of a *wh*-word only, e.g. *who, what*, have the structure shown in (71b), where the *wh*-word is under the N node. Note that in both instances the *wh*-phrase is a phrasal category, Wh-movement being an instance of the set of transformations which affect phrasal categories.

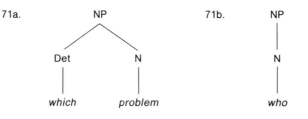

3.3.2   Conditions on 'Wh'-movement

3.3.2.1   The [+ WH]-COMP Condition   Compare the following examples:

72a. I wonder which problem Mary solved

72b. *I wonder* [$_{S'}$ *which problem*$_i$ [$_S$ *Mary* AUX [$_{VP}$ *solved* t$_i$]]]

73a. *I believe which problem Mary solved

73b. **I believe* [$_{S'}$ *which problem*$_i$ [$_S$ *Mary* AUX [$_{VP}$ *solved* t$_i$]]]

Together these examples show that *Wh*-movement cannot move a *wh*-phrase to any COMP position. While movement of the *wh*-phrase to the embedded COMP is allowed in (72), it is obviously not allowed in (73). Thus, our definition of *Wh*-movement has to be revised to take into consideration the fact that not all COMPs are legitimate targets for *Wh*-movement.

The difference between (72) and (73) lies in a difference in the subcategorization properties of the verbs in the root clause. The verb *wonder*, among others, subcategorizes for an interrogative clause, which can either be a *wh*-clause, as in (72), or a yes/no clause, as in *I wonder if/whether John solved the problem*. The verb *believe*, among many others, differs in that it does not subcategorize for an interrogative clause. Instead, it subcategorizes for a declarative clause, as in *I believe that John solved the problem*. The difference in the subcategorization properties of the two types of verb can be encoded in terms of the feature [+/− Q(uestion)] associated with the COMP of the clause they subcategorize for. Interrogative clauses are [+ Q], whereas declarative clauses are [− Q]. Accordingly, the subcategorization frames of the verbs in (72) and (73) are roughly as shown in (74):

74a. *wonder*: [— S']
          [+ Q]

  b. *believe*: [— S']
          [− Q]

To make a distinction between yes/no interrogatives and *wh*-interrogatives, let us assume the existence of another feature: [+/− WH]. Yes/no interrogatives are [+Q, − WH], whereas *wh*-interrogatives are [+Q, +WH]. Since we are concerned here with *wh*-questions, we will use the feature [+/− WH] in the discussion below. Note that [+/− WH] implies [+Q], a fact which can be encoded in terms of the rewrite rule C → [+/− Q], in combination with the rule [+Q] → [+/− WH].

With this in mind, let us now go back to examples (72) and (73). In (72) the COMP of the embedded clause is marked with the feature [+ WH] as required by the subcategorization properties of the root verb *wonder*. In (73), however, the COMP of the embedded clause is marked with the feature [− WH] as required by the subcategorization properties of the root verb *believe*. Now, if we assume that *Wh*-movement can only move *wh*-phrases to a COMP which is [+WH], (73) will be excluded on the grounds that it involves *Wh*-movement to a [− WH]-Comp. We will call the condition in question the **[+WH]-Comp Condition**, and incorporate it into the definition of *Wh*-movement as in (75):

75. **Wh-movement**
    Move *wh*-XP to a [+ WH]-COMP.

The assumption that interrogative clauses are marked with the feature [+ WH] plausibly extends to root interrogatives such as *Which problem did John solve?* Like embedded clauses, root sentences can also be interrogative or declarative, among other possiblities. It is natural to assume that root sentences are distinguished in terms of the same mechanism as subcategorized clauses, so that root *wh*-interrogatives are marked with the feature [+ WH] and root declaratives are marked with the feature [−WH]. Consequently, movement of the *wh*-phrase to COMP in root *wh*-interrogatives is also consistent with (75). Note, finally, that the feature [+/−WH] can also be used to distinguish between (genuine) *wh*-questions and echo-questions such as *John solved which problem!* Echo-questions can be said to be [–WH], meaning they are not *wh*-questions, even though they include a *wh*-phrase.

3.3.2.2   The Wh-island Condition   Compare the following examples where the *wh*-phrase *how* is understood to modify the embedded predicate:

76a. How do you think (that) Mary solved the problem?
76b. [*How*]ᵢ *do you think* [ₛ′ (*that*) [ₛ *Mary solved the problem* tᵢ]]]?

77a. *How do you wonder whether Mary solved the problem?
77b. *[*How*]ᵢ *do you wonder* [ₛ′ *whether* [ₛ *Mary solved the problem* tᵢ]]]?

In both examples the *wh*-phrase *how* is moved out of the embedded complement clause to the COMP of the root clause. However, the two complement clauses differ in that the COMP position of (77) is occupied by another *wh*-phrase, whereas the COMP position of its counterpart in (76) is not. It is plausible, therefore, to attribute the ungrammaticality of (77) to the fact that the COMP position of the clause from which the *wh*-phrase is moved (or extracted) dominates a *wh*-phrase.

The contrast between (76) and (77) illustrates the fact that it is generally more difficult to extract a *wh*-phrase out of a (complement) clause whose COMP position dominates a *wh*-phrase than it is from a clause whose COMP position does not dominate a *wh*-phrase. This fact is further illustrated in the following examples (the declarative counterpart of (79) is *I wonder why John went this way*):

78a. Which way did you think (that) John went?
78b. [*Which way*]ᵢ *did you think* [ₛ′ (*that*) [ₛ *John went* tᵢ]]?

79a. *Which way do you wonder why John went?
79b. *[*Which way*]ᵢ *do you wonder* [ₛ′ *why* [ₛ *John went* tᵢ]]?

The COMP of the embedded clause in (79) dominates a *wh*-phrase, whereas its counterpart in (78) does not. The contrast between the two examples is due precisely to this difference.

Because it is difficult for a *wh*-phrase to escape out of a clause whose COMP is filled with another *wh*-phrase, these clauses are called **wh-islands**, and the condition on *Wh*-movement they illustrate is called the **Wh-Island Condition**. Continuing the strategy of incorporating conditions on transformations into their definitions, *Wh*-movement can now be defined as in (80):

80. **Wh-movement**
   Move *wh*-XP to a [+WH]-COMP, unless *wh*-XP is included in a *wh*-island which excludes the targeted COMP.

The revised version of *Wh*-movement now excludes (77) and (79) on the grounds that they involve *wh*-movement out of a *wh*-island.

3.3.2.3   The Complex Noun Phrase Condition   The following example where the *wh*-phrase *why* is understood to modify the embedded clause *Mary bought a spacecraft*, illustrates another condition on *wh*-movement:

81a. *Why did you hear the claim that Mary bought a spacecraft?

81b. *[*Why*]$_i$ *did you hear* [$_{NP}$ *the claim* [$_{S'}$ *that Mary bought a spacecraft* t$_i$]]?

This example involves movement of a *wh*-phrase out of a clause which is included inside an NP. The NP has the complex phrase structure NP → Det N S', where S' is the complement of the noun *claim*. (81) illustrates the fact that it is generally difficult to extract a *wh*-phrase out of a complex NP, implying that, like a *wh*-clause, a complex NP is also an island for *Wh*-movement. This fact is further illustrated in the following example (the declarative counterpart is *John spread the rumour that Mary owns spacecraft*):

82a. *What did John spread the rumour that Mary owns?
82b. **What*$_i$ *did John spread* [$_{NP}$ *the rumour* [$_{S'}$ *that Mary owns* t$_i$]]?

Like *claim*, the noun *rumour* also subcategorizes for an S'-complement, so that its NP has a complex structure. (82) confirms the conclusion that complex NPs are indeed islands for *Wh*-movement.

The condition on *Wh*-movement which involves complex NPs is called the **Complex NP Condition**. The incorporation of this condition into the definition of *Wh*-movement yields the following, more complex definition:

83. ***Wh*-movement**
    Move *wh*-XP to a [+WH]-COMP, unless *wh*-XP is contained in
    (i) a *wh*-island which excludes the targeted COMP (*Wh*-Island Condition) or
    (ii) a complex NP which excludes the targeted COMP (Complex NP Condition)

This version of *Wh*-movement excludes the examples which involve a violation of the Complex NP Condition, as well as the examples which involve a violation of the *Wh*-island Condition and the [+WH]-COMP Condition.

3.3.2.4 The Cyclicity Condition   One important characteristic of *Wh*-movement is that it seems to be **unbounded**, in the sense that it can operate across any number of clausal boundaries:

84a. Which problem do you think (that) Jane believes (that) Bill claims (that) Mary solved?
84b. [*Which problem*]$_i$ *do* [$_S$ *you think* [$_{S'}$ *(that) Mary believes* [$_{S'}$ *(that) Bill claims* [$_{S'}$ *(that)*

    Mary solved t$_i$]]]]?

In this sentence, *Wh*-movement crosses at least three clausal boundaries. In this respect *Wh*-movement differs from the movement transformations which affect heads, i.e. Affix-hopping, V-raising to AUX, and Subject–AUX Inversion, discussed in the previous sections. These transformations are **local** (or bounded) in scope, in the sense that they apply inside the same clause.

Note, however, that although *Wh*-movement appears to be unbounded there are **locality conditions** on its application, i.e. conditions which restrict its scope to smaller domains. The *Wh*-island Condition and the Complex NP Condition are examples of such conditions, in so far as they specifiy certain domains over which *Wh*-movement cannot apply. In view of this, one might wonder whether *Wh*-movement does indeed operate directly in example (84), even though (84) includes neither a *wh*-island nor a complex NP island.

Consider the following examples:

85a. John knows which problem Mary solved
85b. Which problem does John know (that) Mary solved?

Although the two examples are not synonymous, let us assume that the derivation of (85b) is partially similar to that of (85a) in that the *wh*-phrase moves first to the position occupied by the *wh*-phrase in (85a), i.e. the COMP of the embedded clause, before it moves to the COMP of the root clause. The derivation implied is outlined in (86):

86. *Which problem$_i$ does* [$_S$ *John know* [$_{S'}$ t$_i'$ *(that)* [$_S$ *Mary solved* t$_i$]]]?

The trace in the embedded COMP position (t′) is called an **intermediate trace**, to distinguish it from the **initial trace** in the original position of the *wh*-phrase. Thus, just as the initial trace marks the position from which the *wh*-phrase has been extracted, the intermediate trace marks the position through which the *wh*-phrase has passed on its way to the root clause. Traces are sometimes said to encode the 'history of movement'.

So far, nothing in the system forces the *wh*-phrase in (85b) to move through the COMP position of the embedded clause. Suppose that the *wh*-phrase in this example has to move to the COMP of the embedded clause on its way to the COMP of the root clause. What we need to do is set up a condition which will force it to do so. The condition in question has to do with the notion **transformational cycle**. The latter is a domain within which a transformation can apply exhaustively. For example, S′ is a transformational cycle because *Wh*-movement can apply within it (without leaving it), as in example (85a) above where the *wh*-phrase moves to the COMP of the embedded clause, and therefore does not leave the embedded clause. Let us now assume that in sentences such as (85b), where the *wh*-phrase is moved from the embedded clause (embedded cycle) to the root clause (root cycle), *Wh*-movement has to apply within the embedded cycle before it moves to the root cycle. This means, in simpler terms, that Wh-movement has to move the *wh*-phrase to the embedded COMP first before it moves it to the root COMP. This yields the derivation outlined in (86) above.

The condition which forces *Wh*-movement out of an embedded clause to apply in **successive cyclic steps**, instead of in one step, is called the **Cyclicity Condition**. There are various ways in which this condition can be incorporated into the definition of *Wh*-movement. A simple way of achieving the desired result is simply by adding the word 'nearest' to the instruction 'Move *wh*-XP to [the nearest] [+ WH]-COMP':

87. ***Wh*-movement**
    Move *wh*-XP to the nearest [+ WH]-COMP, unless *wh*-XP is contained in
    (i) a *wh*-island which excludes the targeted COMP (*Wh*-island Condition) or
    (ii) a complex NP which excludes the targeted COMP (Complex NP Condition)

Given this definition, any derivation where a *wh*-phrase is not moved to the nearest COMP will be excluded. We have not in fact discussed ungrammatical sentences that would be excluded by the revised definition but not by the previous one. However, the need for the Cyclicity Condition on *Wh*-movement will become obvious in the subsequent chapters. The Cyclicity Condition has the effect of imposing a relatively severe locality condition on *Wh*-movement, so that *Wh*-movement is not, strictly speaking, unbounded, contrary to the impression we had from example (84). In this example, as in (86), *Wh*-movement applies in successive cyclic steps, with each step targeting the nearest COMP position.

As a final point, the revision introduced seems to create a problem relating to the condition that the targeted COMP must be [+ WH] (the [+ WH]-COMP Condition). In

(86) the embedded clause can potentially be [+WH], since the verb *know* can select a [+WH]-clause, as shown in (85a). Therefore, the embedded COMP is a legitimate target for the first step of Wh-movement in this example. However, this is not the case with the embedded COMP in the following example:

88a. Who do you believe (that) Mary saw?
88b. *Who_i do* [_S_ *you believe* [_S'_ t'_i *(that)*] [_S_ *Mary saw* t_i]]]?

89a. *I believe who Mary saw
89b. *I believe* [_S'_ *who_i* [_S_ *Mary saw* _i*]]

Recall from above that the verb *believe* does not subcategorize for a [+WH]-clause, hence the ungrammaticality of (89). This implies with respect to (88) that the first step of *Wh*-movement targets a [–WH]-COMP, apparently in violation of the [+WH]-COMP Condition. Presumably, it is possible to rephrase (87) in such a way that the requirement that the targeted COMP be of the type [+WH] applies only to the last COMP, i.e. the COMP where the *wh*-phrase surfaces. This version would allow the *wh*-phrase to pass through COMPs which are not necessarily [+WH], provided it ends up in a COMP which is [+WH]. However, we shall not undertake this revision here.

3.3.3 Summary

The derivation of *wh*-questions involves a movement transformation called *Wh*-movement. The latter performs the operation of moving a *wh*-phrase to a COMP position which is marked with the feature [+WH], i.e. the feature which designates root and embedded *wh*-clauses. In addition to the condition that the COMP targeted by *Wh*-movement must be [+WH], *Wh*-movement is also subject to three locality conditions. The *Wh*-island Condition prevents *Wh*-movement from extracting a *wh*-phrase out of a clause whose COMP dominates a *wh*-phrase. The Complex NP Condition prevents *Wh*-movement from extracting a *wh*-phrase out of a complex NP. Finally, the Cyclicity Condition forces *Wh*-movement to target the nearest COMP, so that long-distance *Wh*-movement applies in short (or successive Cyclic) steps.

3.3.4 Relatives

3.3.4.1 *Relatives with an Overt Wh-phrase*   Compare the following examples:

90a. I have heard the claim that Mary owns a spacecraft
90b. *I have heard* [_NP_ *the claim* [_S'_ *that Mary owns a spacecraft*]]

91a. I have seen the spacecraft which Mary owns
91b. *I have seen* [_NP_ *the spacecraft* [_S'_ *which Mary owns*]]

Both examples include a complex NP, which consists of Det, N, and S'. However, the S' constituent has different functions in each NP. In (90) S' is the complement of the noun *claim*, as we saw above. But, in (91) S' is not a complement of the noun. Rather, its function is to modify the noun, much as an adjective does (*the green car*), by restricting its reference to a specific entity among an existing class of similar entities. This type of S' is traditionally called a **relative clause**.

Relative clauses differ from complement clauses of nouns in one other crucial respect.

92.

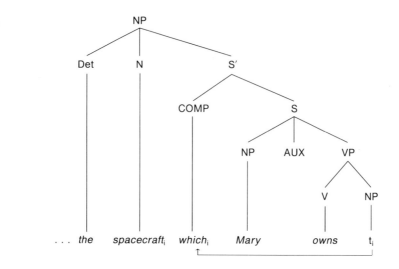

In the relative clause in (91) the object of the verb *own* appears in the form of a preposed *wh*-phrase, whereas in the complement clause in (90) the object of the same verb appears as a non-*wh*-phrase located in the object position. As in the derivation of sentences with a topicalized object and *wh*-questions with a preposed *wh*-object, the *wh*-phrase in the relative clause in (91) must have originated in the object position of the verb *own*, and subsequently moved. Presumably, the transformation responsible for this movement is *Wh*-movement, given the *wh*-nature of the category affected and, more importantly, the position to which the *wh*-phrase is moved. The derivation implied is as shown in (92). Note that, for the instance of *Wh*-movement involved to be consistent with the definition of *Wh*-movement, we have to assume that the COMP of relative clauses is [+WH], although relative clauses are not *wh*-questions.

The co-indexation of the noun *spacecraft* with the *wh*-phrase *which* and, consequently, with its trace, encodes the fact that the *wh*-phrase in (91), and in relative clauses in general, has the same reference as the noun modified by the relative clause. The noun modified by the relative clause is often called the **head** of the relative clause, but sometimes it is also referred to (somewhat misleadingly) as the 'relativised category'. The important thing to remember about relatives is that it is not the head noun which undergoes movement, but the *wh*-phrase related to it. The fact that (91/92) is interpreted as if *the spacecraft* were in the object position of the verb *own* is the consequence of the co-indexation of the *wh*-phrase with the head noun. Formally speaking, it is the *wh*-phrase which functions as the object of the verb *own*, not the noun.

Note that, since relative clauses are included inside a complex NP, we expect extraction of a *wh*-phrase out of them to give rise to a violation of the Complex NP Condition, on a par with extraction out of the similarly complex NP with a complement clause. The declarative counterpart of example (93) below is *I know a person who owns a spacecraft*, where the *wh*-phrase co-indexed with the head noun is the subject of the relative clause:

93a. *What do you know a person who owns?
93b. *What_i do you know [NP a person_j [S' who_j [S t_j owns t_i]]]?

As a matter of fact, relatives are more frequently used to illustrate the Complex NP Condition than complement clauses of nouns.

The relative clause in (91/92) is called a **restrictive relative (clause)**. This is because, as pointed out above, it restricts the reference of the head noun it modifies. There are other types of relative, illustrated in the following examples:

94a. Mary, whom you will meet soon, is our president
94b. *Mary, [$_{S'}$ whom$_i$ [$_S$ you will meet t$_i$ soon], is our president*

95a. Whatever they say, we will press ahead with the project
95b. *[$_{S'}$ Whatever$_i$ [$_S$ they say t$_i$], we will press ahead with the project*

The relative clause in (94) is called an **appositive relative**. Unlike restrictive relatives, appositive relatives do not necessarily restrict the reference of the noun they modify; they are essentially a kind of afterthought. The relative clause in (95), on the other hand, is called a **free relative**, mainly because it does not modify a noun in the sentence in which it occurs (it does not have a head). Appositive and free relatives involve *Wh*-movement just as restrictive relatives do, although they have certain peculiar properties which need not concern us here. The rest of the discussion will be restricted to restrictive relatives.

3.3.4.2 Relatives with a Null Wh-phrase Now compare the relative clause discussed, reproduced below as (96a), with its synonymous counterparts in (96b) and (96c):

96a. I have seen the spacecraft which Mary owns
96b. I have seen the spacecraft that Mary owns
96c. I have seen the spacecraft Mary owns

The relative clauses in (96b, c) differ from the one in (96a) in that they apparently do not exhibit a *wh*-phrase. (96b) exhibits the element *that* which traditionally tends to be called a relative pronoun, on a par with the *wh*-phrase in (96a). Moreover, *that* in relative clauses is considered to be different from the *that* which introduces embedded declarative clauses, as in *I know that Mary owns a spacecraft*. While acknowledging that the *that* of relative clauses may well have properties which distinguish it from the similar element which introduces declarative clauses, here we will adopt the view that the *that* of relatives is not a *wh*-phrase. Consequently, this element cannot be said to originate in the object position of *own* and subsequently to move to COMP, as we have assumed for the *wh*-phrase in (96a). Rather, it originates directly under COMP. The relative clause in (96c) differs from the ones in (96a, b) in that it apparently lacks both a *wh*-phrase and *that*.

In the discussion of (96a) above, it was pointed out that the *wh*-phrase functions as the object of the verb, meaning it originates in the object position of the verb and subsequently *wh*-moves to COMP. The *wh*-phrase is co-indexed with the head noun, hence the interpretation whereby the object of the verb *own* has the same reference as the head noun. The fact that the relatives in (96b, c) have exactly the same interpretation implies that they also include a *wh*-phrase with the same function. In other words, for the head noun to be linked to the object position of the verb *own* it needs to be co-indexed with an element which occupies the object position of the verb *own* at D-structure. Moreover, from a formal point of view, the system forces on us an analysis for (96b, c) which assumes the presence of an object for *own*. The latter is a transitive verb, and therefore requires the presence of an object. It follows that in (96b, c) the verb *own* must have an object, otherwise the sentences should be ungrammatical for the same reason that **Mary owns* is ungrammatical.

Assuming that the relative clauses in (96b, c) do include an object for the verb *own*, the category in question, presumably, is null (phonetically unrealized). Since the equivalent of this category in the synonymous relative in (96a) is a *wh*-phrase, it is plausible to conclude that the null category in (96b, c) is also a *wh*-phrase. Moreover, this null *wh*-phrase

97.

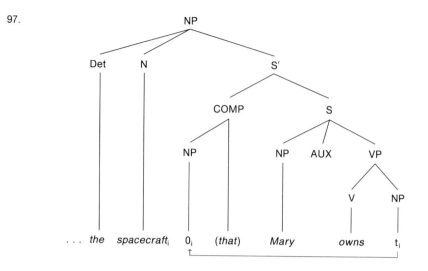

originates in the object position of *own*, and then moves to COMP via *Wh*-movement. Accordingly, the derivation of (96b, c) is as shown in (97), where the null *wh*-phrase is represented with the symbol 0. According to this analysis, relatives without an overt *wh*-phrase are identical to their counterparts with an overt *wh*-phrase. They differ only in that they instantiate a null *wh*-phrase instead of an overt one.

Although the parallelism with relatives with an overt *wh*-phrase is sufficient to justify the analysis outlined, it is desirable to seek further evidence for its viability. If relatives without an overt *wh*-phrase do indeed instantiate a null *wh*-phrase which undergoes *Wh*-movement as claimed, we expect them to show the effects of island violations, given that the latter are conditions on *Wh*-movement. To apply this test we need to embed a *wh*-island or a complex NP island inside the relative clause, as in the following examples:

98a. *I know the way (that) you wonder whether Mary solved the problem
98b. *I know [NP the way$_i$ [S' O$_i$ (that) [S you wonder [S' whether [S Mary solved the

problem t$_i$]]]]]

99a. *I know the way (that) you heard the claim that Mary solved the problem
99b. *I know [NP the way$_i$ [S' O$_i$ (that) [S you heard [NP the claim [S' (that) [S Mary

solved the problem t$_i$]]]]]]

(98) involves a *wh*-island, and (99) a complex NP island. In both examples the head noun is located outside the island but is associated with a position inside the island. The fact that this situation gives rise to ungrammaticality shows that relatives without an overt *wh*-phrase do indeed involve *Wh*-movement, and therefore a null *wh*-phrase. This is because the island conditions are conditions on *Wh*-movement. Island violations are good indicators for the presence of *Wh*-movement and are standardly used as diagnostic criteria for the presence of *Wh*-movement in the derivation of a given sentence.

3.3.4.3 Recoverability and the Doubly Filled COMP Filter   Two questions arise in relation to the analysis outlined for relatives without an overt *wh*-phrase. First, why cannot *Wh-questions instantiate null* wh-phrases on a par with relatives? In other words, why is example (100a) below ungrammatical with the analysis outlined in (100b)?

100a. *Did Mary solve? (with the meaning: What did Mary solve?)
100b. *[$_{S'}$ O$_i$ *Did* [$_S$ *Mary solve* t$_i$]?

Note that, according to the analysis outlined in (100b), the ungrammaticality of (100a) cannot be attributed to a possible violation of the subcategorization requirements of the verb. The latter are satisfied by the null wh-phrase (and its trace) for the same reason they are in the relative clause *The problem* [$_S$ 0$_i$ *Mary solved* t$_i$].

The difference between the wh-question (100a) and relatives with a null wh-phrase is that in the latter the null wh-phrase has an antecedent in the sentence, namely, the head noun it is co-indexed with. The head noun is the antecedent of the null wh-phrase in the sense that it identifies the reference of the null wh-phrase it is co-indexed with. The null wh-phrase in the wh-question (100a), however, does not have an antecedent in the sentence, and consequently the content (reference) of the null wh-phrase remains unidentified. The contrast between (100a) and relatives with a null wh-phrase illustrates a general condition on the occurrence of null categories, called the **Recoverability Condition**:

101. **Recoverability Condition**
     The content of a null category must be recoverable (from a co-indexed overt category in the sentence).

Thus, the wh-question (100a) is excluded on the grounds that it involves a violation of (101). Relatives with a null wh-phrase, however, do not involve a violation of (101), as the null wh-phrase is identified by the head noun of the relative clause. Note that (101) does not make reference to a specific class of null categories, and therefore is expected to hold all types of null categories, including traces. Traces invariably satisfy (101) by virtue of being linked to the moved category which functions as their antecedent. Traces of null wh-phrases in relatives are indirectly identified by the head noun via the null wh-phrase.

The other question which arises in relation to the analysis outlined for relatives without an overt wh-phrase is the following: If a wh-phrase can co-occur with the complementizer *that* in COMP, as shown in (97), why is the following example ungrammatical?

102a. *I know the problem which that Mary solved
102b. *I know* [$_{NP}$ *the problem*$_i$ [$_{S'}$ *which*$_i$ *that* [*Mary solved* t$_i$]]]

This example differs from (97) only in that the wh-phrase which co-occurs with *that* under COMP is overt instead of null. For some reason, an overt wh-phrase cannot co-occur with the complementizer *that* under COMP, although a null one can. There are various ways to exclude ungrammatical examples such as (102). However, imposing a condition on *Wh*-movement preventing it from placing an overt wh-phrase under a COMP filled with *that* is not one of them. This is because this measure would render *Wh*-movement sensitive to whether the wh-phrase is null or overt, and therefore would undermine the idea that null and overt categories have the same status and therefore are treated equally by grammatical rules. In other words, transformational rules are not expected to discriminate between overt and null categories.

A more plausible alternative is to formulate a condition on the co-occurrence possibilities in COMP, irrespective of whether the elements involved originate there or are moved to it. This condition will have the effect of excluding sentences where an overt wh-phrase co-occurs with *that* under COMP, that is sentences where COMP is 'doubly filled' in the intended sense. A possible way of defining the condition in question is as follows:

103. **Doubly Filled COMP Filter**
     *[COMP *wh*-XP *that*], if *wh*-XP is overt (non-null).

(103) acts as a 'filter' on (S-structure) representations derived by *Wh*-movement, and rules out sentences which include a COMP filled by an overt *wh*-phrase and *that*. Note, crucially, that (103) does not exclude sentences such as *Which problem did Mary solve*, where COMP is filled by the *wh*-phrase as well as AUX. Although COMP in this example is also 'doubly filled', it is not 'doubly filled' by the categories specified in (103).

Unlike the conditions which we have incorporated into the definitions of transformations, the Recoverability Condition and the Doubly Filled COMP Filter are not conditions on (the application of) transformations. Rather, they are conditions on representations (i.e. Phrase Markers) derived by transformations. The assumption underlying conditions on representations such as these is that transformations can be allowed to over-generate to a limited degree. The undesirable representations can then be excluded by conditions or 'filters' which apply to the output of transformational rules. Thus, the Recoverability Condition and the Doubly Filled COMP Filter are new additions to our system, which previously consisted exclusively of rules and conditions on rules. The implications that these conditions have for the model as a whole are discussed at the end of this chapter.

3.3.4.4 Summary Relatives are clauses which modify a noun with which they form a complex NP. Relatives resemble *wh*-questions in that their derivation also involves *Wh*-movement. However, they differ from *wh*-questions in that the *wh*-phrase they include can either be overt or null. This is due to the fact that the *wh*-phrase in relatives is invariably co-indexed with an overt noun which the relative clause modifies. This relationship makes it possible to recover the content of the null *wh*-phrase from the noun. The conclusion that relatives without an overt *wh*-phrase involve a null *wh*-phrase and Wh-movement was based on their similarities with relatives with an overt *wh*-phrase in interpretation. It was then confirmed on the basis of the fact that they also show the effects of island violations, just like *wh*-questions and relatives with an overt *wh*-phrase.

3.4 *NP-movement*

3.4.1 Passives

Compare the following examples:

104a. Mary solved the problem
104b. The problem was solved (by Mary)

(104a) is an **active** sentence, where the subject and the object of the verb appear where they are expected to be, given PS rules and the subcategorization requirements of the verb. (104b), on the other hand, is a **passive** sentence, where the object of the verb appears in the subject position and the subject appears, optionally, in the form of a **by-phrase** (*by Mary*) located at the end of the sentence.

The term 'subject' is used here in both its structural sense (i.e. 'NP-daughter-of-S') and its semantic sense, referring to the individual who performs the act described by the verb.

The NP *the problem* in (104b) is a subject in the structural sense, but not in the semantic sense. Conversely, the NP *Mary* is the subject in the semantic sense, but not in the structural sense, since it is not the 'NP-daughter-of-S'. The same is true of the term 'object'. The NP *the problem* in (104b) is the object of the verb in the semantic sense (i.e. it is the entity which undergoes the event described by the verb), but not in the structural sense, since it is not in the object position of the verb. Semantic subjects and objects are sometimes called **logical subjects** and **logical objects**.

Putting aside the *by*-phrase for the moment, the analysis for (104b) (and passives in general) imposed on us by the system is one where the NP *the problem* originates in the object position of the verb, and subsequently moves to the subject position of the sentence. The reasoning underlying this analysis is the same as for topicalized and *wh*-moved objects. The verb *solve* is transitive, and is therefore expected to be associated with a transitive VP at D-structure. The object position in this representation is occupied by *the problem*, which is the logical object of the verb. In the mapping from D-structure onto S-structure, a transformational rule applies to the NP in the object position and moves it to the subject position. This derivation is outlined in (105).

105a. D-structure
    [s [NP e] AUX [VP *was solved* [NP *the problem*]]]
105b. S-structure
    [s [NP *The problem*]ᵢ AUX [VP *was solved* tᵢ]]

105c.

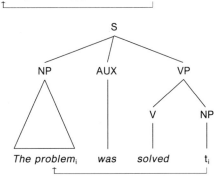

Movement of the auxiliary *be* from inside VP to AUX has been ignored, as it is not crucially relevant to the point of the discussion. However, this does not mean that the auxiliary verb *be* is not an essential property of passives. The presence of the auxiliary *be* and the participle form of the main verb are, at least superficially, some of the distinguishing properties of passives. The derivation of passive participles and their relation to the active verbs from which they derive is discussed in Chapter 5.

Another (less obvious) property of passives, according to the analysis outlined, is that their subject position is empty at D-structure, as shown in (105a). It gets filled as a result of movement of the object of the verb from the object position. The reason why the subject position of passives is empty at D-structure will also be discussed in Chapter 5. Its relevance to the current discussion lies in the fact that the definition of the rule which moves the object to the subject position makes reference to an empty subject position. The rule in question is called **NP-movement**, and can be defined as in (106):

106. **NP-movement**
    Move NP to an empty subject position.

Unlike Topicalization and *Wh*-movement, NP-movement, as its name suggests, applies only to NPs. A PP, for example, cannot be moved to the subject position in passives:

107a. *To Mary was given the book (by John)
107b. *[S [PP *To Mary*]ᵢ AUX [VP *was given the book* tᵢ]]

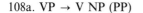

Although NP-movement applies only to NPs, the property which crucially distinguishes it from the other movement transformations, and the latter from each other, is the position to which the category affected is moved. The target of NP-movement is the subject position, whereas the target of *Wh*-movement, for example, is COMP.

Let us now turn to the *by*-phrase. Its occurrence is generally optional, and has the function of specifying the individual who performed the act undergone by the object-cum-subject. When the *by*-phrase is missing, as in *The problem was solved*, the 'implicit' logical subject is said to have an **arbitrary** interpretation, roughly paraphrasable as 'somebody'. As far as the structural status of the *by*-phrase is concerned, we will assume, for the moment, that it is represented as the rightmost constituent of VP, as shown in (108a, b).

108a. VP → V NP (PP)

108b.

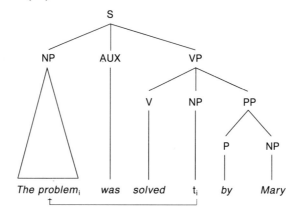

Passives which include a *by*-phrase are sometimes called **long passives**, and the ones which do not include a *by*-phrase are called **short passives**.

3.4.2 Raising Constructions

NP-movement is involved in the derivation of other constructions besides passives. Compare the following examples:

109a. It seems (that) Mary has solved the problem
109b. *It seems* [(that) *Mary has solved the problem*]

110a. Mary seems to have solved the problem
110b. *Mary seems* [*to have solved the problem*]

In (109) the NP *Mary* occupies the subject position of the embedded clause, while the subject position of the root clause is occupied by the 'semantically empty' NP *it*, known as an **expletive** or **pleonastic** element. In (110), however, *Mary* occupies the subject position of the root clause, despite the fact that it is related to the embedded clause, meaning that it is the logical subject of the embedded verb. The two examples also differ in that the verb of the embedded clause is conjugated in (109) but not in (110), a difference which will play a crucial role in the analysis to be outlined. (110) is called a **raising construction**, for reasons which will become clear shortly.

What we need to do with respect to (110) is reconcile the fact that *Mary* is the logical subject of the embedded verb with the fact that, structurally, it is in the subject position of the root clause. This situation is not radically different from the situation encountered above with respect to passives, where an NP which is the logical object of the verb functions structurally as the subject of the sentence. This property of passives was accounted for by assuming that the NP in question originates in the object position of the verb and subsequently moves to the subject position. This strategy can be extended to (110), so that *Mary* can be said to originate in the subject position of the embedded clause and subsequently move to the subject position of the root clause. The derivation implied is as follows (a tree diagram for the structure is provided in (117) below).

111a. D-structure

[$_S$ [$_{NP}$ e] *seems* [$_S$ [$_{NP}$ *Mary*] *to have solved the problem*]]
111b. S-structure

[$_S$ [$_{NP}$ *Mary*]$_i$ *seems* [$_S$ [$_{NP}$ t$_i$] *to have solved the problem*]]

The transformational rule shown in (111b) is an instance of NP-movement, given that it targets an NP and raises it to an empty subject position. It differs from the instance of NP-movement involved in passives only in that the moved NP occupies the subject position of a different clause at D-structure. The instance of NP-movement involved in raising constructions such as (111) is sometimes called **subject-to-subject raising**, and the one involved in passives **object-to-subject raising**.

Just as object-to-subject raising in passives is associated with a particular type of verb, i.e. passive verbs, subject-to-subject raising is also associated with a particular type of verb, called **raising verbs/predicates**. These include, in addition to *seem*, verbs such as *appear*, and predicates such as *be likely*:

112a. It appears (that) Mary has solved the problem
112b. Mary appears to have solved the problem
113a. It is likely (that) Mary will solve the problem
113b. Mary is likely to solve the problem

The main characteristic of raising verbs is that they can take the expletive element *it* as a subject. Thus, while *be certain*, for example, is a raising predicate, *be confident* is not, as shown by the fact that *be confident* cannot take the expletive *it* as a subject:

114a. It is certain (that) Mary will win
114b. Mary is certain to win

115a. *It is confident (that) Mary will win
115b. *Mary is confident to win
115c. Mary is confident (that) she will win

At the moment, the correlation between the ability to take an expletive subject and the ability to host the subject of another clause seems to be arbitrary. However, in Chapter 5 we will see that it is related to a peculiar lexical property of raising verbs/predicates, as opposed to other verbs/predicates.

3.4.3 Conditions on NP-movement

3.4.3.1 The Tensed S Condition   It was pointed out above that one of the differences between the raising construction (110) and its non-raising counterpart (109) is that the verb of the embedded clause in the raising construction is not conjugated. In fact, this verb cannot be conjugated, as witnessed by the ungrammatical status of the following example:

116a. *Mary seems has solved the problem
116b. *[S [NP *Mary*]ᵢ *seems* [tᵢ *has solved the problem*]]

At the moment, we will understand by 'conjugated verb' a verb which bears a Tense marker. A verb which bears a Tense marker is **Tensed**, and a verb which does not bear a Tense marker is **non-Tensed**. Notice, however, that the terms 'Tensed' and 'non-Tensed', strictly speaking, apply to S rather than to verbs. This is because Tense is a constituent of AUX, not V, as we have seen. Non-Tensed clauses differ from the Tensed ones in that they instantiate the element *to* under the AUX node, instead of a Tense marker. Accordingly, the structure of the non-Tensed embedded clause in (110), for example, is as in (117). A more detailed discussion of the differences between the two types of clause is included in Chapter 5. The relevance of Tense to the present discussion lies in its crucial role in determining NP-movement.

117.

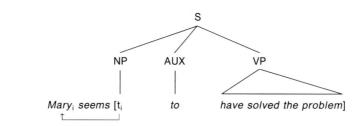

Going back to (116), this example illustrates a condition on the application of NP-movement, known as the **Tensed S Condition (TSC)**. The latter has the effect of preventing NP-movement from moving an NP out of a tensed clause. Following the strategy adopted in this chapter, this condition can be built into the definition of NP-movement, as in (118):

118. **NP-movement**
     Move NP to an empty subject position, unless NP is contained in a Tensed S (clause) which excludes the targeted subject position.

This version of NP-movement excludes (116) on the grounds that the embedded subject is NP-moved out of a Tensed clause. In the grammatical raising construction (110) the embedded clause is non-Tensed, hence the fact that NP-movement of its subject is legitimate.

3.4.3.2 The Specified Subject Condition   The following examples illustrate another condition on NP-movement:

119a. Mary appears to be likely to win

119b. [NP *Mary*]ᵢ *appears* [tᵢ *to be likely* [tᵢ *to win*]]

120a. *John appears it is likely to win
120b. *[NP *John*]ᵢ *appears* [*it is likely* [tᵢ *to win*]]

In (119) the NP *Mary* moves from the subject position of the most embedded clause to the subject position of the next clause (up), and finally to the subject position of the root clause. In (120), however, *Mary* moves directly to the subject position of the root clause, since the subject position of the intervening clause is filled. This type of movement is called **super-raising**, and usually results in ungrammaticality.

The ungrammatical status of (120) results from the fact that the NP *Mary* has been moved across another subject. The fact that NP-movement across a subject results in ungrammaticality can be seen in situations which do not necessarily involve super-raising. Compare the following examples:

121a. John is believed to have beaten Bill
121b. [NP *John*]ᵢ *is believed* [tᵢ *to have beaten Bill*]

122a. *Bill is believed John to have beaten
122b. *[NP *Bill*]ᵢ *is believed* [*John to have beaten* tᵢ]

In (121) the NP subject of the embedded clause *John* is moved to the subject position of the root passive clause. This instance of NP-movement does not cross over a subject. In contrast, the instance of NP-movement in (122), where *Bill* is moved from the object position of the verb in the embedded clause to the subject position of the root passive clause, crosses over a subject, namely *John*. The ungrammatical status of (122) confirms that NP-movement cannot move an NP (whether it is a subject or an object) across a subject.

This condition on NP-movement is known as the **Specified Subject Condition (SSC)**. A possible way of incorporating it into the definition of NP-movement is as in (123):

123. **NP-movement**
     Move NP to an empty subject position, unless
     (i) NP is contained in a tensed clause which excludes the targeted subject position (TSC) or
     (ii) NP is separated from the targeted subject position by a specified subject (SSC).

This version of NP-movement rules out (120) and (122), on the grounds that they involve NP-movement across a (specified) subject.

3.4.4 Summary

NP-movement is involved in the derivation of passives and raising constructions, and has the distinctive property of moving an NP to an empty subject position. Like *Wh*-movement, NP-movement is also subject to some conditions, which have been incorporated into its definition. One condition, called the Tensed S Condition (TSC), prevents NP-movement from moving an NP out of a Tensed clause. Another condition, called the Specified Subject Condition (SSC), prevents NP-movement from moving an NP across a subject.

3.5   *Extraposition and Heavy NP Shift*

Compare the following examples (the style in (125) is typical of news bulletins):

124a. Details of a secret plan to finance the rebels have emerged
124b. *Details* [PP *of a secret plan to finance the rebels*] *have emerged*
125a. Details have emerged of a secret plan to finance the rebels
125b. *Details have emerged* [PP *of a secret plan to finance the rebels*]

The PP between brackets is the complement of the noun *details* in both examples. In (124) it appears where it is 'understood', i.e. in the complement position of the noun. However, in (125) it appears in the sentence-final position, following the verb. Presumably, the PP complement of the noun in (125) has moved from its D-structure position inside the NP containing *details* to the sentence-final position. The transformational rule responsible for this movement is called **Extraposition**.

126.

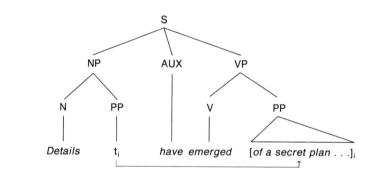

We will assume, for the moment, that extraposed PPs are structurally represented as the rightmost daughters of VP, so that (125) has the S-structure shown in (126). Except for Affix-hopping, Extraposition differs from the movement transformations discussed so far in that it operates rightward (it is an instance of **rightward movement**).

Extraposition can be defined as follows:

127. **Extraposition**
     Move XP and attach it to the right side of VP.

As with the other transformations, the use of the variable XP is intended to capture the fact that categories other than PP can be extraposed. In the following example, the extraposed category is a relative S':

128a. A man has come forward who claims to be the killer
128b. D-str: [S [NP *A man* [S' *who claims to be the killer*]] *has* [VP *come forward*]]
128c. S-str: [S [NP *A man* t_i] *has* [VP *come forward* [S' *who claims to be the killer*$_i$]]]

Recall (from above) that relative clauses are constituents of complex NPs whose head noun they modify.

Now, compare the following examples:

129a. Mary returned all the books she had borrowed to the library
129b. *Mary* [VP *returned* [NP *all the books she had borrowed*] [PP *to the library*]]

130a. Mary returned to the library all the books she had borrowed
130b. *Mary* [VP *returned* [PP *to the library*] [NP *all the books she had borrowed*]]

The NP *all the books she had borrowed* is a complement of the verb *return*. The latter takes an NP and an (optional) PP as complements, so that its subcategorization frame is roughly of the form: [— NP (PP)]. In (129) the two complements of the verb appear in the order specified in the subcategorization frame, with NP preceding PP. In (130), however, the order of the two complements is reversed, with NP following PP.

131.

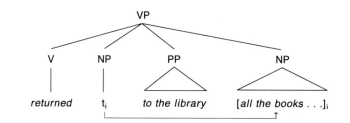

The order shown in (130) is the result of a transformational rule which moves the NP complement from its base-generated position immediately following the verb (and preceding the PP complement) and attaches it to the right side of VP. This is shown in (131). The transformational rule responsible for this operation is called **Heavy NP Shift**. The name of the transformation is intended to reflect the fact that the rule applies only to NPs which are 'heavy', where 'heavy' is vaguely understood to mean several constituents. The NP *the book*, for example, is not 'heavy' in the intended sense, and therefore cannot be subject to Heavy NP Shift:

132a. *Mary returned to the library the book
132b. *Mary* [VP *returned* t$_i$ [PP *to the library*] [NP *the book*]$_i$]

133a. Mary returned the book to the library
133b. *Mary* [VP *returned* [NP *the book*] [PP *to the library*]]

Thus, although Heavy NP shift resembles Extraposition in that it moves a category and attaches it to the right side of VP, it differs in that it applies to 'heavy' NPs only.

There are various ways of defining the rule of Heavy NP Shift, although the notion 'heavy' remains difficult to define precisely. A possible way of defining Heavy NP Shift is as follows:

134. **Heavy NP Shift**
   Move a 'heavy' NP and attach it to the right side of VP.

The inclusion of the expression 'heavy NPs' in the definition ensures that ungrammatical sentences such as (133) are excluded, on the grounds that the NP moved is not 'heavy' in the intended sense.

To summarize, two additional transformations have been briefly discussed in this section: Extraposition and Heavy NP Shift. The two transformations are similar in that they both move a category and attach it to the right side of VP. However, they differ crucially in that Heavy NP Shift applies only to 'heavy NPs'.

3.6 *Conclusions and Revisions*

The attempt to extend the model constructed in the previous chapter to sentences which involve displaced categories has resulted in the introduction of a new set of rules called transformations. The latter apply to representations, called Deep Structures (D-structures), generated by PS rules in combination with LIR, and derive modified representations, called Surface Structures (S-structures). The modifications introduced by transformations range between displacing (moving) a category from one position to another designated position in the sentence, to inserting new material.

To ensure that transformations do not over-generate (i.e. derive ungrammatical sentences), certain specific conditions were built into their definitions. Basically, these in-built conditions help define the domains over which transformations (can) apply. On two occasions it was felt necessary to introduce conditions which differ in that they serve as 'filters' on representations derived by transformational rules, rather than as conditions on the application of the transformations themselves. The underlying idea is that transformations can be allowed to over-generate in a limited way, with the undesirable sentences excluded by conditions applying to representations derived by transformations.

As a result of introducing transformations, the syntactic component of the model now consists of two sub-components. One sub-component, sometimes called the Base, consists of PS rules. The other sub-component, called the Transformational sub-component, consists of transformations. The Base generates D-structure representations where categories are generally located where they are expected to be, that is, where they are 'understood'. These structures then serve as input to the rules of the transformational sub-component which introduce certain modifications into them, and derive S-structure representations as output.

The revised model can be graphically represented as in (135).

135.

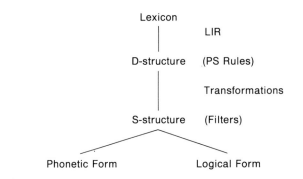

Recall from the previous chapter that Phrase Markers derived by the syntactic component are submitted, separately, to the Semantic and Phonological components. The Semantic Component assigns the Phrase Marker a semantic representation, often called **Logical Form**. On the other hand, the Phonological Component assigns the Phrase Marker a phonetic representation, often called the **Phonetic Form**.

Exercises

Exercise 1

Outline a derivation for each of the following examples. You are expected to provide a D-structure and an S-structure for each sentence, and to justify the involvement of a transformation, if any:

1. John kicked the ball
2. John did not kick the ball
3. Did John kick the ball?
4. What did John kick?
5. The ball was kicked by John
6. John seems to have kicked the ball

Exercise 2

Explain how the following ungrammatical sentences are excluded in the context of the model developed:

1. *John kicked rarely the ball
2. *John not kicked the ball
3. *What do you know somebody who bought?
4. *What do you know where John kicked?
5. *John seems has kicked the ball
6. *The ball seems John to have kicked

Exercise 3

It has been claimed that for certain sentences to be properly derived, the transformational rules involved have to be ordered with respect to each other, such that one rule has to apply first before the other can apply. Explain whether the transformational rules involved in the derivation of each of the following sentences need to be ordered with respect to each other:

1. Did Mary solve the problem?
2. George does not like broccoli
3. Has John fixed the car?
4. What did Mary buy?
5. Is Bill in the garden?

Exercise 4

It has been claimed that the constructions in (1b) and (2b) are derived from the same underlying representations as (1a) and (2a), respectively:

1a. I gave a book to John
1b. I gave John a book

2a. I sent a letter to Mary
2b. I sent Mary a letter

Try to work out the derivation involved, and discuss the status of the transformational rule it entails in the context of the model developed so far.

Exercise 5

It has been claimed that the *Wh*-island Condition and the Cyclicity Condition express one and the same condition on *Wh*-movement, instead of two separate conditions. Evaluate this claim in relation to the following examples:

1a. How do you know that John fixed the car?
1b. *How do you know whether John fixed the car? (*answer*: with a crowbar)

Further Reading

The role of transformations in the derivation of sentences and their implications for the thoery of Grammar are discussed in Chomsky (1957, 1965), Lees (1963), and Mathews (1964), although the idea had already been entertained in earlier work. At this stage, and in the subsequent years, transformations were said to have the format briefly discussed at the beginning of this chapter, which consists of a Structural Description (SD) and a Structural Change (SC). Moreover, different constructions were thought to involve different transformations, so that transformations were construction specific: a transformation for passives, a transformation for raising constructions, a transformation for *wh*-questions, a transformation for *yes/no* questions, and so on. A good overview of these transformations can be found in Akmajian and Heny (1975). See also Baker (1978).

Although the attempt to restrict the proliferation of transformations and to reduce some of them to single and more general transformations were already evident in Chomsky (1973), where the general rule NP-Movement is discussed, it did not materialize in a forceful way until Chomsky (1977b). The latter collapsed a number of individual transformations into the more general rule *Wh*-Movement, which applies across a broad range of constructions. That these constructions have similar underlying properties had already been clear from such major works as Ross (1967), Emonds (1970/1976), and Chomsky (1973).

Most of the transformations discussed in this chapter will be further discussed in the subsequent chapters. On the properties of Topicalization see Chomsky (1977b), and on Extraposition see Baltin (1983; 1984), Guéron (1980), and Guéron and May (1984). On the phenomenon of preposition-stranding and the structure of PPs in general see van Riemsdijk (1978) and references therein.

Early discussions of trace (or Trace Theory) can be found in Chomsky (1977a, b), Fiengo (1977), Lightfoot (1977), and Wasow (1979). A survey of the literature which linked the phenomenon of *wanna*-contraction to trace theory can be found in Postal and Pullum (1982).

The programme aimed at restricting the number of transformations, inevitably, was accompanied by a parallel attempt to collapse conditions on individual transformations into a smaller number of more general conditions applying to general transformations such as *Wh*-Movement and NP-Movement. The notion 'transformational cycle' as a condition on derivations is discussed in Chomsky (1965) and subsequent work. Other conditions not discussed in this chapter, such as the A-over-A condition, are discussed in Chomsky (1968; 1973). One of the most influential works as far as generalized conditions on *Wh*-Movement are concerned is Ross (1967). The latter identifies and discusses the island conditions, two of which were mentioned in this chapter. Some of Ross's island conditions were further reduced to more general conditions in Chomsky (1973) and later work to be discussed in Chapter 8 of this book.

Chomsky (1973) also introduces the Specified-Subject Condition and the Tensed-S Condition. The conditions on the transformations which affect non-phrasal categories, e.g. SAI, are discussed in Emonds (1970/1976), where the distinction between root and non-root transformations is introduced. The latter work was also influential in restricting movement of phrasal categories to specific positions already available in the structure (see next Chapter). Emonds (1978) deals with the difference in behaviour between auxiliary verbs and main verbs.

Another landmark in the programme to restrict the power of transformations is Chomsky (1970) 'Remarks on Nominalizations'. Most of the arguments in this paper were directed towards a growing trend, known as Generative Semantics, which attributed what was seen by some linguists as 'excessive power' to transformations, as a consequence of the idea that meaning is exclusively determined at D-structure. This led to the postulation of detailed D-structure representations which included decomposed representations of complex predicates, with transformations having the role of assembling them into single syntactic units in the course of the derivation. The thrust of Chomsky's arguments is that (certain) morphological rules which derive complex categories must be confined to the Lexicon, and that these categories are represented as single complex units in the Syntax. This view came to be known as the Lexicalist Hypothesis, and has engendered an intense debate about the scope of the rules of Morphology and their place in the Grammar (see Further Reading, Chapter 2).

The idea of surface filters as a means of restricting the power of transformations is discussed in Perlmutter (1971), and later (re)appeared in a more developed way in Chomsky and Lasnik (1977), where the Doubly Filled Comp Filter is introduced, together with a number of others. The filters-based model outlined in this paper was the precursor of the principle-based model discussed in the remaining chapters of this book.

4

X-Bar Theory

Contents

4.1 *The Status of PS Rules and the Lexical Insertion Rule*

In Chapter 2 we saw that the constituent structures of phrasal categories are largely determined by the subcategorization properties of lexical items. For example, the structure of VP in a sentence which includes a transitive verb, e.g. *hit*, will consist of V and NP, and the structure of VP in a sentence which includes an intransitive verb, e.g. *smile*, may consist of V only, and so on. There is thus a clear implicational relationship between subcategorization frames and the PS rules which generate phrasal categories, illustrated in (1a–e) (read ⇒ as 'implies'):

1a.	*hit*:	[— NP]	⇒	1a.′	VP	→ V NP
1b.	*smile*:	[—]	⇒	1b.′	VP	→ V
1c.	*think*:	[— S′]	⇒	1c.′	VP	→ V S′
1d.	*give*:	[— NP PP]	⇒	1d.′	VP	→ V NP PP
1e.	*rely*:	[— PP]	⇒	1e.′	VP	→ V PP

Each of the subcategorization frames in the left column implies the PS rule in the right column. The subcategorization frame of *think* in (1c), for example, implies the PS rule in (1c′); and the subcategorization frame of *give* in (1d) implies the PS rule in (1d′); and so on. The observed implicational relationship between subcategorization frames and PS rules extends to other lexical categories, nouns, adjectives, etc.

In view of this, there is a sense in which PS rules simply duplicate information explicitly specified in subcategorization frames. Most of the information about the constituent structures of phrasal categories ('made explicit' by PS rules) can be derived from ('read off') the subcategorization frames of the corresponding lexical categories. Obviously, this duplication of information is undesirable, on the grounds that it makes the Grammar unnecessarily complicated. We should therefore seek ways of eliminating it, presumably, by eliminating PS rules. If successful, this move will in actual fact result in the elimination of the whole of the Categorial Sub-component (Base), a major simplification indeed.

Obviously, the move to eliminate PS rules entails the availability of an alternative mechanism which would determine the structural representation of lexical categories on the basis of their lexical properties. Among other things, the mechanism will have to determine how complements are structurally represented in relation to the categories which subcategorize for them, as well as how non-complements such as adjectives and adverbs are structurally represented in relation to the categories they modify. The mechanism in question would also have to cater for the non-lexical categories S and S′, ideally on a par with lexical categories, rather than separately. Recall that the PS rule which expands S (S → NP AUX VP) encodes crucial information which determines the grammatical function 'subject' (NP-daughter-of-S or [NP S]).

In fact, the implications of the move to eliminate the Categorial Sub-component go beyond the functions of PS rules, to include those of LIR. Recall that the latter makes reference to terminal nodes in Phrase Markers generated by PS rules. The reference includes both the categorial features of the terminal node and the context in which it is situated, in relation to the categorial features and the subcategorization properties of lexical items. The function of matching lexical items with appropriate nodes situated in appropriate contexts is crucial in excluding a certain class of ungrammatical sentences. In view of this, any revision which will result in the elimination of LIR will have to include a mechanism which performs the functions previously performed by LIR.

The alternative mechanism which determines the structural representation of categories to be discussed in this chapter is called **X-bar Theory**, and the principle which ensures that the lexical properties of lexical items are accurately reflected in structural representations is called the **Projection Principle**. The revisions undertaken in this chapter have radical implications for the nature of the Grammar and its organization, discussed at the end of this chapter. We will start first by discussing the Projection Principle.

4.2   *The Projection Principle*

Part of the function of LIR was to ensure that sentences such as (2) are included and sentences such as (3) are excluded:

2a. Mary solved the problem
2b. *Mary* [VP *solved* [NP *the problem*]]
3a. *Mary solved
3b. *Mary* [VP *solved*]
4.   *solve* [— NP]

Another part of the function of LIR is to introduce lexical items into Phrase Markers. In a sense, LIR has the nature of a transformational rule with conditions incorporated into it. It performs the operation of introducing lexical items, but this operation is subject to the conditions that, first, the terminal node must have the same categorial properties as the lexical items, and, secondly, the terminal node must be situated in a context which matches the subcategorization properties of the lexical item. Note, however, that the desired result can be achieved simply by requiring that the lexical properties of lexical items, as represented in (4) with respect to the verb *solve*, for example, be 'projected onto', i.e. accurately reflected in, structural representations. (4) includes information relating to both the categorial features of the lexical item and its subcategorization properties.

The requirement in question can take the form of a simple and general principle which will act as a condition on the structural representation of lexical categories, and can be defined as follows (Chomsky, 1981):

5. **Projection Principle (PP)**
   Representations at each syntactic level (i.e. LF, D- and S-structure) are projected from the lexicon, in that they observe the subcategorization properties of lexical items.

PP incorporates the condition that representations 'observe the subcategorization properties of lexical items', where the term 'subcategorization' is understood to include categorial features and subcategorization requirements. Representations which do not observe this condition, such as (3), are therefore excluded. Another essential part of the condition is that the subcategorization properties of lexical items be observed at 'each syntactic level (i.e. LF, D- and S-structure)'. D-structure and S-structure are syntactic levels in that they are characterized by syntactic rules, as opposed to (for example) lexical or phonological rules (Chapter 2). So far, we have not discussed evidence showing that LF, the level where meaning relations are determined, is also syntactic in nature. Such evidence will be discussed in the next chapter. For the moment, it is perhaps sufficient to remember that subcategorization properties play a crucial role in determining meaning relations, particularly in sentences which involve a displaced complement. The fact that the topicalized object in *This problem, I can solve* is interpreted as the logical object of the verb relates to the fact that the verb is transitive, among other things.

The property of PP as a condition which holds for all syntactic levels of representation has an important consequence on the presence of traces in subcategorized positions. In Chapter 2 we discussed evidence showing that movement transformations leave a trace behind. The evidence consisted of examples where traces are visible to certain rules of the Grammar, in particular the rule which contracts *want* and *to* to *wanna* in Colloquial English. Because traces arise at a post-D-structure level, we faced the problem of providing a formal motivation for their presence as legitimate categories in structural representations. At that stage, the formal motivation could only be provided in terms of a stipulation, which we called the Trace Convention:

6. **Trace Convention**

Movement transformations leave a trace.

Now we are in a position to derive at least some of the effects of the Trace Convention from a general and independently needed principle of the Grammar, namely PP.

Consider (7b, c) below as candidates for the S-structure representation of (7a):

7a. This problem, I can solve
7b. *This problem, I can* [VP [V *solve*]]
7c. *This problem*ᵢ*, I can* [VP [V *solve*] [NP tᵢ]]

(7b) is excluded by PP, on the grounds that it does not observe the subcategorization properties of the transitive verb *solve*. (7c), however, is not excluded by PP, as the transitive verb *solve* has an NP object, the trace. Thus the presence of a trace in the object position of the verb in the S-structure (and LF) representation of (7a) follows from PP. In other words, in a model which incorporates PP, the presence of the trace in the S-structure (and LF) representation of (8a), and similar examples, does not need to be stipulated in terms of the Trace Convention.

It looks, therefore, as though, as far as subcategorized positions are concerned, the presence of traces follows from a general principle of the Grammar. Obviously, the presence of traces in non-subcategorized positions, e.g. the subject position, cannot be motivated on the same grounds, as subjects do not figure in the subcategorization frames of lexical items. However, although we cannot yet eliminate the Trace Convention completely, we have taken the first step towards achieving this goal. Further steps will follow later in this chapter.

4.3   *X-Bar Theory*

While PP ensures that the subcategorization properties of lexical items are (accurately) reflected in structural representations, it does not specify how complements, for example, are structurally represented with respect to the lexical categories which subcategorize for them. This role is performed by different conditions, called the principles of X-bar Theory, or the **X-bar Schemata**. In this section, we will discuss the nature and role of these schemata. As it will transpire, some of these schemata are in fact no more than formal statements of generalizations abstracted from PS rules.

4.3.1   Heads and Maximal Projections

The PS rules which generate lexical categories recognize one level of categorial representation above X, the phrasal level XP. This can be clearly seen in (8a–d) below, which are abstracted from the corresponding PS rules discussed in Chapter 2:

8a. VP → . . . V . . .
8b. NP → . . . N . . .
8c. AP → . . . A . . .
8d. PP → . . . P . . .

Read from right to left, these rules encode the generalization that the structural representation of every category includes a phrase level, i.e. XP. For example, the structural representation of V includes VP, the structural representation of N includes NP, and so on. Let us call the phrasal level of (XP) the **maximal projection** (of X). Read from left to right, the rules in (8a–d) convey a different, but related, generalization: every XP has X as an obligatory constituent. For example, VP has V as an obligatory constituent, NP has N as an obligatory constituent, and so on. Let us call the obligatory constituent of a maximal projection the **head** (of that maximal projection). This generalization is related to the previous one in the sense that it actually follows from it. If the structural representation of every category includes a maximal projection, then every maximal projection will include the category of which it is the maximal projection (i.e. the head).

This core property of PS rules can be captured in terms of the following schema:

9. XP → . . . X . . .

(9) is a schema in the sense that it represents a property which all members of the class of PS rules discussed have in common. It is to be seen as essentially a condition on the structural representation of categories. Its content can be understood to mean that the structural representation of every category must have the form shown in (9), where X has the same categorial value on both sides of the arrow: if $X = V$, $XP = VP$, and if $X = N$, $XP = NP$, and so on.

Although schema (9) basically captures a common property of PS rules, there is a sense in which it is more restrictive than PS rules. Because the latter are rewrite rules, and because systems of rewrite rules generally make it possible in principle to rewrite a given symbol as one or a combination of any (number of) symbols, nothing seems to exclude unattested representations of the type illustrated in (10a, b):

10a. *VP → N
10b. *NP → PP VP

However, these rules are excluded by schema (9), on the grounds that they do not observe the condition that every maximal projection must have a head, and that a maximal projection exists in so far as it is a projection of a lexical head category, and therefore has the same categorial value as the head.

4.3.2   Specifiers and Complements

One of the serious shortcomings of PS rules is the fact that they do not reflect structurally the distinction between subcategorized and non-subcategorized categories in relation to the head. For example, the rule which generates the NP in (11a) below has the form shown in (11b), and gives rise to the structure in (11c).

11a. Mary's solution to the problem
11b. NP → NP N PP

11c.

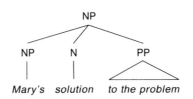

The PP *to the problem* is the complement of the noun *solution*, and the NP *Mary* is its (logical) subject. However, both the PP complement and the NP subject are structurally represented as sisters to the head N, and therefore to each other. This is an undesirable situation, if only because it seems to undermine the claim that grammatical functions are structurally based, so that subjects and complements are expected to have different structural relations with respect to the lexical head. Therefore, what is needed is a structure of NP where the subject and the complement have different structural relations with respect to the head N. Recall (from Chapter 2) that the notions 'complement' and 'sister' are closely related, so that the complement of a head is invariably structurally represented as its sister. In view of this, it seems that it is the structural relation that the subject has with the head N in (11b, c) which needs to be modified.

The modification required can be achieved by recognizing an additional level of categorial representation intervening between the head and its maximal projection. This intervening level will include the head and its complement, but exclude the subject. With respect to (11a) above, this modification will yield the structure in (12) below, where the intervening level is called N' (read 'N-bar'). Unlike the PS rule-based structure (11b, c), (12) clearly makes a structural distinction between the subject of NP and the complement of N. The former is the daughter of NP and sister of N', and the latter is the daughter of N' and sister of N. We will see below, and in the subsequent chapters, that the presence of the X' level of representation has a number of other major advantages. For the moment, let us outline the schemata which underlie structure (12).

12.

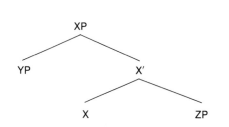

The schemata in question are as in (13a, b). (14) is the structure they imply:

13a. XP → YP X'
13b. X' → X ZP

14.

Y and Z, like X, are variables. With respect to structure (12) YP is the NP subject, and ZP the PP complement of N. X' is called the **single-bar** projection, the underlying idea being that there is a hierarchical relation between the different projections which is reflected in terms of the number of bars associated with each projection. This is shown more clearly in (15a, b) below, which are notational variants of (13a, b):

15a. X″ → Y″* X′
15b. X′ → X⁰ Z″*

The hierarchy is from 'double-bar' to 'single-bar' to 'zero-bar', or vice versa. The double-bar projection (X″) is what we referred to above as the maximal (or phrasal) projection (XP), and X⁰ is the head. Either of the two notations in (13a, b) and (15a, b) can be used, although the one in (13a, b) is used more often. Note that schemata (13a, b) and (15a, b) subsume schema (9) above, in that they also encode the head requirement.

The asterisk associated with Y″ (YP) and Z″ (ZP) in (15a, b) means 'zero or more occurrences of some maximal projection'. Z″ (ZP) in (15b) stands for the complement of the head. Obviously, the number and nature of complements is usually determined by the subcategorization properties of the head. The noun *solution* in (11a) above has a PP complement, whereas the noun *Mary* in (16), for example, does not:

16a. Mary solved the problem

16b.

NP
|
N′
|
N
|
Mary

The X-bar schemata apply to the other lexical categories in a similar way, so that the structural representation of each includes a maximal projection (XP) and a single-bar projection (X′), in addition to the head (X). As with NPs, the single-bar projection, i.e. V′, A′ and P′, is the domain of the head (V, A, or P) and its complement (ZP):

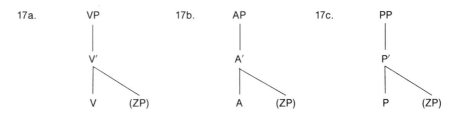

17a. VP 17b. AP 17c. PP

Y″ in (15a) stands for **Specifier (Spec)**. The latter is a functional term which refers to the maximal projection which is a daughter of XP and a sister to X′. The Spec of the NP in (14) above is the NP subject *Mary*, and the Spec of the NP in (18a) below is the Det element *the*. Note that, according to (15a), Spec must be a maximal projection, i.e. an XP category. However, it is not clear whether Det has a maximal projection (DetP?) of its own, on a par with other lexical categories. The representation of Det is a problem at the moment, and will remain so until Chapter 6, where a more detailed discussion of its exact status is included.

Presumably, other lexical categories take specifiers as well, depending on their properties. Having said that, specifiers are generally optional, in the sense that one can have an NP, for example, without a specifier, as shown in (16) above. In this respect, specifiers are different from complements: the presence or absence of complements is regulated by PP in combination with the subcategorization properties of lexical items. There is no equivalent condition which requires categories to have a specifier.

18a. The solution to the problem

18b.

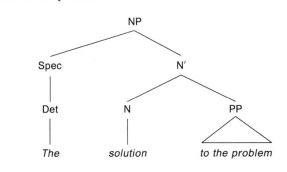

4.3.3   Adjuncts

4.3.3.1   Adjectives and Adverbs   Adjectives and VP-adverbs are among the non-sub-categorized categories generated by PS rules. The two rules are reproduced here for reference :

19a. NP → $\left\{ \begin{array}{c} NP \\ Det \end{array} \right\}$ (Adj) N . . .

19b. VP → (ADV) V . . . (ADV)

Given that adjectives and VP-adverbs are not complements of the categories they modify, they are excluded from the X′ (single-bar) domain, i.e. the domain which includes the head and its complements. However, it is not equally obvious that adjectives and adverbs are excluded from the Spec position, meaning that it is not clear they are not specifiers. The decision whether adjectives and adverbs are specifiers of the lexical categories they modify needs to be based on some evidence.

   Starting with adjectives, they differ from specifiers of NP in a number of respects, two of which will be discussed here. Both respects relate to the fact, encoded in rule (19a) above and illustrated in (20a), that Det and an NP subject cannot co-occur in the pre-N domain.

20a. *Mary's the solution to the problem

20b.

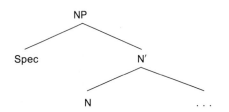

Given structure (20b), the inability of Det and an NP subject to co-occur in the pre-N domain follows from the assumption that they are both specifiers, i.e. categories which occupy the Spec position of NP. (20a) is ungrammatical because there are two categories which compete for a single position. If adjectives were specifiers of NP, we would expect them to be unable to co-occur with either Det or an NP subject in the pre-N domain. However, we know (from Chapter 2) that this is not the case. In fact, adjectives usually co-occur with either of these categories:

21a. Mary's final solution to the problem
21b. [NP [NP *Mary's*] [AP *final*] [N *solution*] . . .]
22a. The final solution to the problem
22b. [NP [Det *The*] [AP *final*] [N *solution*] . . .]

Another respect in which adjectives differ from specifiers is that specifiers tend to be unique. Each category can only have one specifier, as shown by the ungrammatical example (20a) above. In the X-bar system, this restriction on the number of specifiers follows from the existence of a single Spec position in every phrasal structure. Adjectives differ in that they can be 'stacked', so that more than one adjective can be found in a single NP. (23a, b) below are classic examples of 'stacking':

23a. A tall dark handsome stranger
23b. The big red car

The differences between adjectives and specifiers discussed are sufficiently compelling to warrant the conclusion that adjectives are not specifiers and, therefore, do not occupy the Spec position of NP.

The order of adjectives with respect to the specifier and the head suggests that they occupy a position intervening between Spec and N. Looking at structure (12/20b) above, it is not clear what this position is. The fact that adjectives can be 'stacked', as shown in (23a, b), indicates that we should not be looking for a unique position as such. Rather, adjectives should somehow be 'added' to the structure in (12/20b). More formally, adjectives are said to be **adjoined** to a given projection, and their representation is in terms of an **adjunction** structure. The term 'adjunction' can be loosely understood to mean the 'extension' of a given category, in the manner illustrated in (24):

24.

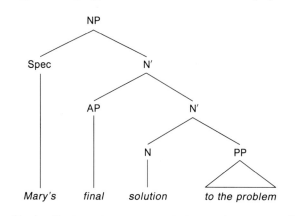

The operation of 'extending' a category amounts to creating a copy of it, hence the fact that there are two occurrences of N' in (24). The newly created copy of N' serves as the mother node for the adjoined AP. Note, however, that because the newly created N' node is only an 'extension' or a copy of N', the adjunction structure in (24) means that AP in fact has an ambiguous relationship with N': AP is both the sister and the daughter of N'. Strange though this may sound from a real-life perspective, it is precisely this property of adjuncts which distinguishes them (in structural terms) from complements and specifiers. Complements and specifiers do not have ambiguous relationships: the former are daughters of X' but sisters of X, and the latter are sisters of X' but daughters of XP. The important aspect of the adjunction structure illustrated in (24) is that it enables us to reflect in structural terms the fact that adjectives are neither complements nor specifiers of the noun they modify.

Turning now to VP-adverbs, we need to decide whether they are adjoined to a projection of V or occupy the Spec position of VP. Since we have not discussed specifiers of verbs yet, an examination of the data of the type carried out above with respect to adjectives and specifiers of nouns is not possible. To anticipate the discussion of specifiers of verbs below and in Chapter 6, it is unlikely that VP-adverbs occupy this position. They are more likely to be adjoined to a projection of the verb, on a par with adjectives in relation to nouns. Note that there is a sense in which VP-adverbs parallel adjectives in function, as witnessed by the following examples:

25a. The army's total destruction of the city
25b. [NP [NP *The army's*] [AP *total*] *destruction of the city*]
26a. The army totally destroyed the city
26b. *The army* [VP [ADV *totally*] *destroyed the city*]

The VP-adverb in (25) modifies the verb in the same way its adjectival counterpart in (26) modifies the noun. If the modification relation in (25) is expressed in terms of an adjunction structure, as we have concluded, the parallel modification relation in (26) is likely to be expressed in terms of an adjunction structure too.

Another respect in which adverbs also parallel adjectives which we can mention here relates to the fact that adverbs can also be 'stacked', although to a lesser degree than adjectives:

27a. John repeatedly viciously attacked Bill
27b. *John* [VP [ADV *repeatedly*] [ADV *viciously*] *attacked Bill*]
28a. Mary cleverly (only) partially solved the problem
28b. *Mary* [VP [ADV *cleverly*] [ADV *partially*] *solved the problem*]

It seems that, as with adjectives, adverbs do not occupy a unique (Spec) position, but are adjoined (added) to an existing projection of V.

The conclusion that adjectives are adjoined to N′ was determined on the basis of the order of the adjective in relation to the specifier and the head noun. The order of VP-adverbs in relation to AUX elements and the verb suggests that it can be adjoined either to V′, as shown in (29a), or to VP, as shown in (29b):

29a.

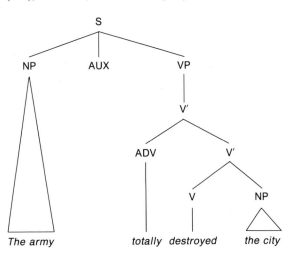

29b.

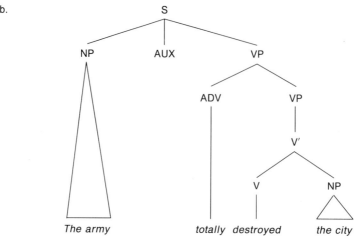

Both structures lead to the derivation of the order where the VP-adverb precedes the verb and follows the AUX elements which do not Affix-hop onto the verb. For reasons of uniformity and consistency, given the observed parallelism with adjectives, we will assume for the moment that VP-adverbs are adjoined to V′, rather than to VP.

Reasons of uniformity and consistency also dictate that the VP-adverb in example (30) below is adjoined to V′, even though it occupies a different linear position:

30a. John fixed the car quickly
30b. *John* [VP *fixed the car* [ADV *quickly*]]

Recall (from Chapter 2) that some VP-adverbs can occur in the final position of VP, as shown in the PS rule (19b) above. This fact does not necessarily mean that VP-final adverbs have a different structural representation from that of VP-initial adverbs. The adjunction structures discussed so far are all instances of left-adjunction, in the sense that the 'extension' is located to the left of the category adjoined to. In principle, however, the 'extension' can also be located to the right of the category adjoined to, as shown in (31). In this structure the VP-adverb is right-adjoined to V′, whereas in (29a) above the VP-adverb is left-adjoined to V′. The difference between the two adjunction structures is only

31.

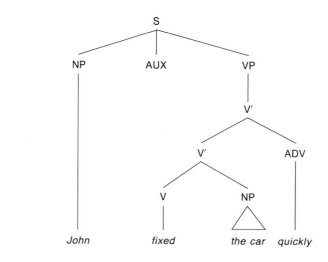

in the directionality of adjunction. Structurally, the VP-adverb has exactly the same status and the same ambiguous relationship with V′ in both structures.

***4.3.3.2** Relative Clauses*   Recall (from the previous chapters) that the bracketed clauses in examples (32) and (33) below have different relations with respect to the noun:

32a. The suggestion that John should resign is absurd
32b. [NP *The suggestion* [S′ *that* [S *John should resign*]]] . . .

33a. The suggestion that John made is absurd
33b. [NP *The suggestion*ᵢ [S′ Oᵢ *that* [S *John made* tᵢ]]] . . .

In (32) the bracketed S′ is the complement of the noun *suggestion*, the latter being a member of the class of nouns which subcategorize for a clausal complement. In (33), however, S′ is a restrictive relative clause, which has an adjective-like function with respect to the noun.

34.

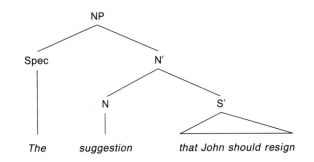

The   suggestion   that John should resign

As the complement of the noun, the bracketed S′ in (32) is presumably situated inside N′, the domain of the head and its complements. The structure involved is shown in (34).

As an adjective-like modifier of the noun, the relative S′ in (33) is expected to have the same structural status as adjectives. This means that it is adjoined to N′, although in this situation right-adjunction, rather than left-adjunction, is involved.

35.

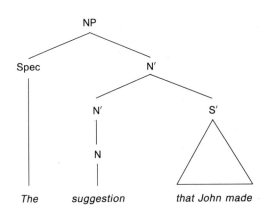

The   suggestion   that John made

Right-adjunction to N' accounts for the fact that relatives usually follow the noun they modify, contrary to adjectives which usually precede the noun they modify. Apart from this difference, relatives and adjectives have exactly the same structural status, given the observed similarity in function between them.

4.3.3.3   Adjunction Structures and X-Bar Theory   The adjunction structures discussed so far can be captured in terms of the following schemata:

36a. X' → YP X' (or X' YP)
36b. XP → YP XP (or XP YP)

(36a) refers to adjunction to the single-bar projection, and (36b) to adjunction to the double-bar (phrasal) projection. The information included in brackets reflects the availability of right-adjunction, in addition to left-adjunction. Note that, strictly speaking, adjunction structures are inconsistent with the principle underlying X-bar Theory that each projection differs in terms of the number of bars associated with it (X'' → X' → X^0). This is because adjunction does not result in the creation of a projection with one less (or more) bars, but in the creation of a projection with the same number of bars as the category adjoined to.

It could be argued on this basis that the adjunction schemata in (36a, b) do not belong to the domain of X-bar Theory. According to this view, adjunction structures, to the extent that they exist, will remain a mystery, in so far as they do not seem to form part of the set of permissible structures. Another view would be to add the adjunction schemata to the set of the X-bar schemata discussed above, so that adjunction structures become part of the set of permissible structures. This will be the case despite the fact that the adjunction schemata are somehow different in nature from the other X-bar schemata. A third view would be to argue that since adjunction structures are simply 'extensions' of the projections permitted by X-bar schemata, there is a sense in which they are not necessarily inconsistent with the principles of X-bar Theory. The logical outcome of this view is that the adjunction schemata do not need to be added to the X-bar schemata. We are not going to resolve the issue here. We shall continue to assume that adjunction structures do exist, and leave open the question of how they fit in with the principles of X-bar theory.

4.3.4   Summary

The structural representation of lexical categories is determined by the principles of X-bar Theory. The latter take the form of schemata, inasmuch as they capture the common properties of individual PS rules. The core structural relations defined by X-bar schemata are 'specifier of X' and 'complement of X'. The specifier of a lexical category is represented as the daughter of the maximal projection and the sister of the single-bar projection. On the other hand, the complement of a lexical category is represented as the sister of the lexical head and the daughter of the single-bar projection. A third structural relation arguably defined by the principles of X-bar Theory is that of 'adjunct'. Adjuncts, such as adjectives and adverbs, are structurally represented as 'extensions' of one of the X-bar projections of the lexical category they modify, and therefore tend to have an ambiguous relationship with the projection they are adjoined to.

4.4   *X-Bar Theory and Non-lexical Categories*

So far, the discussion has been restricted to lexical categories. It is important to see whether the non-lexical categories, S and S', can be brought into line with the lexical ones, so that the structural representation of the non-lexical categories is also governed by the principles of X-bar Theory. A priori there are no particular reasons to assume that the non-lexical categories must have the same structural properties as the lexical ones. However, the principles of X-bar Theory arguably will gain more credibility if it turns out that the structural representation of the non-lexical categories is fundamentally similar to that of the lexical ones.

4.4.1   The X-Bar Structure of S: IP

4.4.1.1   INFL as the Head of S   To determine the X-bar structure of S, we need first to decide which of its three major constituents is likely to be the head. Looking at (37a, b), the most likely candidate seems to be AUX:

37a. S → NP AUX VP

37b.

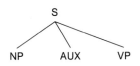

NP and VP are phrasal categories, and therefore neither of them is likely to be the head of S. Given their status as phrasal categories (i.e. maximal projections), and their order in relation to AUX, NP and VP are more likely to be, respectively, the specifier and the complement of the head of S. On the other hand, the fact that AUX is not a phrasal category suggests it is probably the head of S. Let us then assume that AUX is indeed the head of S. The next step is to assign S a structure which is consistent with the principles of X-bar theory, that is, a structure where AUX has a single-bar projection which dominates it and its complement, and a maximal projection which dominates its specifier.

Before we take this step, let us first resolve a confusion surrounding the use of the term 'AUX'. The latter has been used so far to refer to a node in the structure of S, and in its full form (auxiliary) to the verbs *be* and *have*. Recall (from Chapter 3) that these auxiliary verbs are not members of the AUX node, in the sense that they do not originate under AUX. Rather, they originate inside VP and are moved to AUX via V-movement in tensed clauses. To avoid the confusion created by the term 'AUX' we shall refer to the node which intervenes between NP and VP in (37a, b) by the term **INFLECTION**, usually shortened to **INFL** or just **I**. The term 'Inflection' can be justified on the grounds that the node in question hosts Tense, which is a typical member of the set of inflectional categories (see Chapter 2).

In fact, Tense is not the only inflectional member of AUX. Another inflectional member of this node is the 'subject marker' *-s*, found with regular verbs in third person singular present tense conjugations. The distribution of this inflectional category is identical to that of Tense in most respects:

38a. Mary does not like John, but Jane does
38b. Does Mary like John?

In (38a) and (38b) the inflectional category -*s* appears on *do*, presumably as a result of being left stranded. In the first clause of (38a), -*s* is stranded as a result of Neg blocking Affix-hopping (from moving the inflectional categories of AUX) onto V, and in (38b) it is stranded as a result of AUX-movement to COMP (Chapter 3). In the second clause of (38a), -*s* is stranded as a result of the deletion of VP. All these facts show that the inflectional category -*s* is a member of AUX, on a par with Tense, thereby providing further justification for renaming AUX **INFLECTION**.

Note that -*s* is not a Tense morpheme, even though its appearance is restricted to the present tense paradigm in Standard English:

39a. I smile	39c. You smile	39e. She/he smiles
39b. *I smiles	39d. *You smiles	39f. *She/he smile
39g. We smile	39i. You smile	39k. They smile
39h. *We smiles	39j. *You smiles	39l. *They smiles

These examples show that -*s* cannot appear with any member of the present tense-paradigm, but is restricted to the third person singular member. In other words, -*s* appears when the subject is third-person singular. The subject and -*s* are said to agree in the features of person, gender and number, known as the **agreement features**. The inflectional morpheme -*s* is said to belong to the category **Agr(eement)**, just as the past tense morpheme -*ed* is said to belong to the category Tense. In languages which have richer inflectional systems, a different Agr morpheme appears with each member of the conjugation paradigm. Now, rather than assuming that English is different in that it instantiates an Agr morpheme only in the third-person singular conjugation, it is more plausible to assume that it instantiates a different Agr morpheme in each member of the conjugation paradigm. Unlike the third person singular morpheme, the others are simply abstract in nature. This view attributes the situation in English to the more general fact that its inflectional system is generally poor compared to that of other languages, and not to some peculiar grammatical property.

In the previous chapter we used the expression 'Tensed clause' to refer to clauses which instantiate Tense under AUX (now I(NFL(ECTION))). A general property of English is that clauses which instantiate Tense also invariably instantiate Agr, and clauses which do not instantiate Tense also invariably do not instantiate Agr. Clauses which instantiate Tense and Agr are often called **finite**, and the ones which do not instantiate Tense and Agr are called **non-finite**. Restricting our attention to finite clauses for the moment, they have the structure shown in (40), where I(NFLECTION) is the head, and IP the equivalent of S in the previous structure. VP is the complement of I, situated under the I′ projection of I. The NP subject, on the other hand, is in the Spec position, immediately dominated by IP.

40.

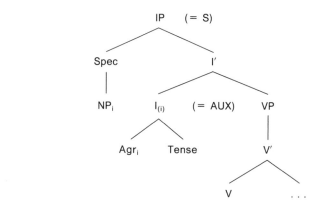

Thus, just as the subject of NP is located in the Spec position of NP (Spec-NP), as we saw above, so the subject of the sentence (i.e. IP) is located in the Spec position of IP (Spec-IP).

The co-indexation of the Agr category under I and the NP subject in Spec-IP encodes the agreement relation between them in person, gender and number. In this situation the subject is said to be in **Spec-Head Agreement** with (the Agr category of) I. Note that Spec-Head Agreement is mandatory, in the sense that, if the subject bears agreement features which are different from those of Agr, ungrammaticality results. This is illustrated by the ungrammatical examples in (39) above, where the features of the subject are inconsistent with those of Agr. To exclude these examples, Spec-Head Agreement can be considered as a condition which regulates the relationship between heads and their specifiers. A possible way of defining it is as in (41):

41. **Spec-Head Agreement**
   A head (X) and its specifier (Spec-XP) must agree in relevant features.

The relevant features for (the Agr category of) I and a specifier occupying Spec-IP are person, gender and number, among others to be discussed in the subsequent chapters. For Ns and their Det-specifiers the relevant features are number (*These/*this children*), possibly among others. Later on in this chapter we will see that other types of feature can enter Spec-Head Agreement relations.

It seems that the non-lexical category IP (alias S) can successfully be assigned a structure consistent with the principles of X-bar Theory. The theoretical advantage of the revision introduced relates to the desirability of the generalization that the structural representation of all categories (both lexical and non-lexical) is governed by the same principles. The empirical advantages, on the other hand, will become clear as we move along. For the moment note that all the grammatical relations and processes expressed in terms of the previous structure can also be expressed in terms of structure (40).

4.4.1.2 *Spec-IP and the Extended Projection Principle* It was pointed out earlier that specifiers are generally optional, in the sense that it is possible to have a category which does not have a specifier. However, IP seems to be an exception to this otherwise general property. Consider the following examples, discussed in Chapter 3 in the context of NP-movement:

42a. Mary seems to have solved the problem
42b. *Mary*$_i$ *seems* [t$_i$ *to have solved the problem*]

43a. *(It) seems that Mary has solved the problem
43b. *It seems that [Mary has solved the problem*]

Recall that the derivation of the raising construction (42a) involves movement of the subject NP *Mary* from the subject position of the non-finite embedded clause to the subject position of the root clause. This movement cannot apply in (43) because the embedded clause is tensed/finite (the Tensed S Condition). In this example, *Mary* remains in the subject position of the embedded clause, and the subject position of the root clause is obligatorily filled with the 'semantically empty' NP *it*.

One could ask with respect to (43a) why the presence of *it* should be obligatory despite the fact that this element is 'semantically empty'. A plausible answer to this question is that the presence of *it* is forced by some condition of the grammar which requires the Spec position of IP (i.e. the subject position of the sentence) to be filled. The obligatory presence of a 'semantically empty' element in the Spec position of IP in the absence of a 'meaningful' subject can also be seen in other constructions:

44a. A unicorn is in the garden
44b. *(There) is a unicorn in the garden

Like the expletive *it*, the element *there* is also 'semantically empty', as shown by the fact that its absence in (44a) (or its presence in (44b)) has no effect on the meaning of the sentence. In (44a) the NP *a unicorn* occupies the subject position (i.e. Spec-IP), whereas in (44b) it does not. In the latter example, the subject position is obligatorily filled with *there*. Here again, one could ask why the presence of this element is obligatory despite the fact that it is 'semantically empty'. The answer is likely to be the same as above: its presence seems to be required by some formal requirement of the grammar on Spec-IP.

The formal requirement in question is called the **Extended Projection Principle (EPP)**, and is sometimes defined as in (45):

45. **Extended Projection Principle**
    Clauses must have a subject.

Recall that PP requires subcategorized categories to be present in structural representations, but says nothing about non-subcategorized categories such as subjects. (45) extends this requirement to subjects, hence the term 'extended'. However, we will assume here that the two principles are independent of each other, in the sense that EPP does not subsume PP. Given its definition in (45), EPP is a condition on subjects, whereas PP is a condition on subcategorized categories. Note that what is meant by 'subject' in (45) is a 'formal subject', i.e. a category which occupies the subject position of the clause, irrespective of whether the category in question is a 'meaningful' NP, as in (42) and (44a), or an expletive, as in (43) and (44b).

One reason for keeping the two principles separate from each other relates to a difference in the level of representation at which they apply. We have seen that PP applies at all levels of syntactic representation, a requirement which is incorporated into its definition. EPP, however, does not have the same scope in that it does not hold for D-structure representations. The reason has to do with the derivation of raising constructions such as (42a) above, outlined in (46a, b) below, and the derivation of passives outlined in (47b, c):

46a. D-structure
     [IP [NP e] *seems* [*Mary to have solved the problem*]
46b. S-structure
     [IP [NP *Mary*]i *seems* [ti *to have solved the problem*]

47a. The problem was solved (by Mary)
47b. D-structure
     [IP [NP e] *was solved the problem (by Mary)*]]
47c. S-structure
     [IP [NP *The problem*]i *was solved* ti *(by Mary)*

Recall (from Chapter 3) that in the derivation of raising constructions and passives the subject position which serves as a landing site for the moved NP is empty at D-structure, as shown in (46a) and (47b). In other words, the D-structure representation for raising constructions and passives lacks a subject. It follows that EPP does not hold for D-structure representations, unlike PP, which holds for all syntactic levels of representation including, crucially, D-structure. EPP holds for S-structure and LF representations only. The root clause in the S-structure representation (46b) satisfies EPP as a result of the movement of the NP *Mary* (from the embedded clause) to its subject position. The same is true for the S-structure representation of the passive in (47c), where the sentence also acquires a subject via movement. The embedded clause in (46c) satisfies EPP via the trace in the subject position, left behind by movement of the NP subject to the root clause.

Note that, like PP, EPP has a crucial implication for traces and the Trace Convention. We concluded above that the presence of traces in subcategorized positions follows from PP, paving the way towards deriving the effects of the Trace Convention. However, because PP says nothing about non-subcategorized categories such as subjects, the presence of traces in subject positions of clauses does not follow from it. Now the presence of a trace in a subject position evacuated by movement does follow from a general principle, namely EPP, and therefore does not need to be stipulated. The presence of the trace in the subject position of the embedded clause in the S-structure representation (66c) is crucial for the clause to satisfy EPP. Thus, it seems that the effects of the Trace Convention are indeed derivable from general and independently needed principles of the Grammar.

Given the manner in which raising constructions and passives satisfy EPP, it is tempting to conclude at this stage that it is perhaps EPP which motivates (forces) NP-movement in raising constructions and passives. NP-movement enables the clauses with empty subject positions to acquire a subject, thereby avoiding a violation of EPP. When NP-movement cannot apply, as in (43a, b), where the embedded clause is tensed/finite, a 'semantically empty' element is inserted in the subject position as a last-resort measure to save the sentence from being excluded by EPP. The question of what motivates movement transformations will be one of the most frequently recurring themes in the forthcoming chapters, where more light will be shed on the various factors which motivate movement processes.

4.4.1.3 *Non-finite Clauses and PRO Subjects*   Consider the following examples in the light of EPP:

48a. John wanted for Bill to leave
48b. *John wanted for* [$_{IP}$ *Bill to leave*]

49a. John wanted Bill to leave
49b. *John wanted* [$_{IP}$ *Bill to leave*]

50a. John wanted to leave
50b. *John wanted* [$_{IP}$ e *to leave*]

In all three examples, the verb *wants* has a non-finite clause as complement. In (48) and (49) the complement clause has a subject, *Bill*. However, in (50) the complement clause apparently does not have a subject, a situation which, if true, should give rise to a violation of the EPP. Note that (50) is not a raising construction, and therefore cannot be said to have the derivation shown in (51a):

51a. *[$_{IP}$ [$_{NP}$ *John*]$_i$ *wanted* [$_{IP}$ t$_i$ *to leave*]]

51b. *It wants that John will leave

Recall (from Chapter 3) that the distinctive property of raising verbs such as *seem* is the fact that they can take the expletive *it* as a subject. (51b) shows that *want* does not belong to this class of verbs. Therefore, derivation (51a), which otherwise results in avoiding a violation of EPP, is excluded.

As shown in its definition, EPP does not make a distinction between finite and non-finite clauses, and therefore is expected to hold of both types of clause. It follows that the embedded non-finite clause in (50) must have a subject which is, presumably, a null category. Obviously, the null category in question cannot be a trace, given that the derivation outlined in (51a) is excluded. The null category in question, like null *wh*-phrases found in relatives without an overt *wh*-phrase (see Chapter 3), must be base-generated, meaning that it is present in D-structure representations. This null category is **PRO** (read 'big PRO'), a label which reflects the fact that it has certain properties in common with (overt) pronouns, shown in (53) below. (52) is the structural representation of (50) with PRO in the subject position of the embedded clause:

52. *John*ᵢ *wanted* [IP PROᵢ *to leave*]

53a. John said (that) he would leave
53b. *John*ᵢ *said (that)* [IP *he*ᵢ *would leave*]

The co-indexation of PRO with the NP subject of the root clause *John* in (52) conveys the information that the two categories have the same reference, just as *John* and the pronoun *he* in (53) also have the same reference. (52) is said to be a **control** construction, where *John* controls PRO. Control is to be understood as a relationship of 'reference-assignment', so that the control relationship between *John* and PRO in (52) amounts to the former assigning a reference to the latter. Control is also a relationship of identification whereby the controller identifies the content of the null category PRO (see Chapter 3).

54.

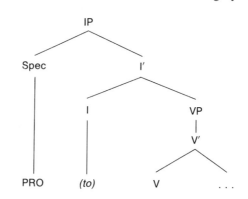

For reasons which will be discussed in detail in Chapter 7, PRO is restricted to the subject position of non-finite clauses. As pointed out above, non-finite clauses differ from their finite counterparts in that they lack the Tense and Agr categories under I. Instead, they instantiate the element *to*, which is generally a marker of non-finiteness. Accordingly, non-finite clauses have the representation shown in (54).

The reason why *to* is included between parentheses has to do with the fact that there are other types of non-finite clauses which do not instantiate this element. An example of such clauses is the **gerund**. The distinctive property of gerunds is that they instantiate the bound morpheme *-ing*, which differs from its counterpart in sentences such as *John is reading a book* in that it does not necessarily denote an ongoing event. The gerund in (55) below, for example, does not denote an event in the process of taking place:

55a. John dislikes eating in public
55b. *John dislikes* [PRO *eating in public*]

Like the other non-finite clauses, gerunds also instantiate PRO in the subject position. The question which arises with respect to gerundive clauses is what exactly occupies their head position I. Note that, according to the principles of X-bar Theory, the head position has to be filled for X-bar structures to be **licensed**. In other words, the various levels of categorial representation, including the X⁰ level, exist in so far as they are projections of a given category (inflectional or otherwise). In finite clauses I^0, I', and IP are projections of the inflectional categories Agr and Tense, and in non-finite clauses with *to* they are projections of *to*. With respect to gerundive clauses, it is possible that I^0, I', and IP are the projections of the bound morpheme *-ing*. The latter originates under I and subsequently Affix-hops onto the verb. If this is the correct analysis for gerunds, they do not give rise to a problem as far as the licensing of the X-bar projections of I is concerned.

However, even if the analysis briefly outlined turns out to be inappropriate, the X-bar projections of I in gerundive clauses can still be justified independently. Suppose that finiteness is a feature [+/– FINITE], on a par with the categorial features [+/– V] and [+/– N] (Chapter 2), and the feature [+/– Q] associated with the COMP of declarative and interrogative clauses (Chapter 3). The typology of I as determined by the feature [+/- FINITE] can be captured as follows:

56a. I   →   [+/– FINITE]
56b. [+ FINITE]   →   Agr, Tense
56c. [– FINITE]   →   to, $\emptyset$

(56a–c) can be understood to mean that the feature specification [+ FINITE] is realised in terms of the Agr and Tense categories, and the feature specification [– FINITE] is realised either as *to* or as nothing. The idea is that the presence of a feature is sufficient to license X-bar projections, so that in gerundive clauses the X-bar projections of I are licensed by the feature [– FINITE]. Recall (from Chapter 2) that even categories such as verbs and nouns are essentially bundles of categorial features (with positive and negative values), so that their X-bar projections are in actual fact licensed by (categorial) features. The same is true of COMP in relation to the features [– Q] (declarative clauses) and [+ Q] (interrogative clauses).

4.4.2 Small Clauses

Now, compare the following examples:

57a. John considers Bill to be incompetent
57b. *John considers* [IP [NP Bill] [I' *to* [VP *be* [AP *incompetent*]]]]
58a. John considers Bill incompetent
58b. *John considers* [*Bill incompetent*]

In both examples the verb *consider* has a non-finite clause as complement. However, the two clauses differ in that the one in (57) instantiates *to* and the verb *be*, whereas the one in (58) instantiates neither of these two categories. The embedded clause in (58) is called a **small clause**, mainly because it lacks the I-element *to*. In fact, this element is excluded from small clauses altogether:

59. John considers Bill (*to) incompetent

The fact that small clauses also cannot be introduced by a complementizer is a property which they share with non-small clauses in the same environment:

60a. *John considers that/for Bill to be incompetent
60b. *John considers that/for Bill incompetent

The reason why neither type of clause in these examples can be introduced by a complementizer will be discussed in Chapter 6. To the extent that (60a, b) imply the absence of COMP and (therefore) S', the latter property is not exclusive to small clauses.

The status of the small clause in (58), among other environments, as a clause has mainly been related to the fact that its subject displays certain properties usually associated with subjects. We will not review the evidence here, although we will take this point into consideration in the analysis to be outlined. The question we will try to deal with first is whether the (obligatory) absence of *to* in small clauses affects the licensing of the X-bar projections of I. Given the discussion of gerundive clauses above, the absence of *to* does not necessarily imply the absence of I. However, the issue with respect to small clauses such as the one in (58) also involves the verb *be*. Like *to*, this verb is also excluded:

61. *John considers Bill be incompetent

In the structure of IP outlined above, VP has the status of the complement of I, so that I can be said to take VP as complement. Thus, if I were present we would expect VP to be present too. In view of this, it remains mysterious why *be* cannot appear as shown in (61). Reversing the argument, the fact that *be* cannot appear implies that VP is absent, and if VP is absent then I is likely to be absent too, on the assumption that the absence of a complement implies the absence of the head which subcategorizes for it.

The plausible hypothesis seems to be that the small clause in (58) lacks I and (therefore) its X-bar projections, and V and (therefore) its X-bar projections. Looking at the structure of the non-small clause in (57) the categories we are left with are the NP subject and the predicative AP. Bearing in mind that the NP subject must occupy a subject position, the small clause can be assigned the structure shown in (62):

62.

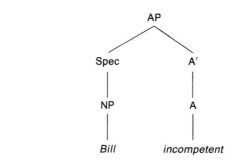

The status of the small clause as an AP is determined by the categorial nature of the predicate, which in (58) is an adjective. The NP *Bill* has the status of a subject by virtue of occupying the Spec position of AP, just as it has the status of a subject in the NP *Bill's incompetence* by virtue of occupying the Spec position of NP. The notion 'subject' is generally understood to mean the category which occupies the Spec position of a given XP.

Categories other than AP can also function as a small-clause complement. In (63) the small clause is a PP and in (64) it is a VP.

63a. The captain expects the drunken sailors (*to) off the ship immediately

63b.

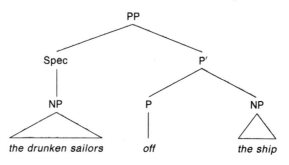

64a. John made Bill (*to) read the whole book

64b.

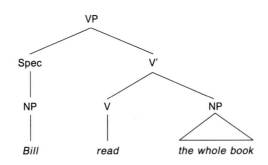

(64) is a called a **causative** construction, with an interpretation paraphrasable as 'John caused Bill to read the whole book.' A more detailed discussion of causative constructions in English and other languages is included in Chapter 9.

Now, consider example (65) below, where the small-clause complement is an NP, in comparison to the examples in (66):

65a. John considers Bill a genius
65b. *John considers* [? *Bill* [NP *a* [N' *genius*]]]
66a. Mary's solution to the problem
66b. The solution to the problem
66c. *Mary's the solution to the problem

The analysis outlined above assigns the subject of the small clause to the Spec position of the small clause. However, in (65) the Spec position of the NP small clause is occupied by the Determiner *a*. This raises the question as to which position *Bill* (the subject of the NP small clause) occupies. Recall that Det and an NP subject are usually in complementary distribution, as shown in examples (66a–c). Recall also that it was this fact which led to the conclusion that both categories occupy the Spec position of NP. In view of this, the co-occurrence of the NP subject with Det in the pre-N' domain in (65) is unexpected. A solution to this problem will be outlined in Chapter 6, in the context of a more detailed discussion of the structure of noun phrases.

4.4.3 The X-Bar Structure of S′: CP

4.4.3.1 COMP as the Head of S′ As with S, we need to determine which category is the head of S′. The decision with respect to S′ is relatively straightforward. Looking at (67), the head is likely to be COMP, IP (alias S) being a maximal projection.

67a. S′ → COMP IP

67b.

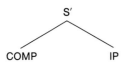

Assigning S′ a structure consistent with the principles of X-bar theory gives the result shown in (68), where **C** stands for Comp(lementizer), and **CP** for **Comp(lementizer) Phrase** (alias S′).

68.

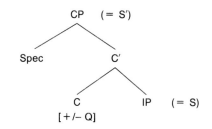

As pointed out in chapter 3, declarative clauses are marked with the feature [− Q], and interrogative clauses with the feature [+ Q], so that in (68) the X-bar projections of C are the projections of these features. As far as embedded clauses are concerned, the feature [− Q] is optionally realised as *that* when IP is finite, and as *for* when IP is non-finite.

69a. I think (that) John should leave
69b. *I think* [CP [C' (*that*) [IP *John should leave*]]]
70a. I want (for) John to leave

70b.

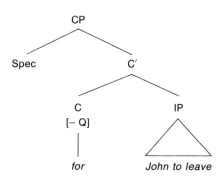

The fact that the type of complementizer which appears under C depends on whether I is finite or non-finite implies a link between C and I, which we will not pursue here.

As for embedded yes/no clauses, the feature [+ Q] can be realized as *if* or have its presence indicated by *whether*. We will assume here that *whether* is a *wh*-phrase associated with yes/no questions, and is base-generated under Spec-CP.

71a. I wonder if John has left
71b. *I wonder* [CP [C' *if* [IP *John has left*]]]
72a. I wonder whether John has left

72b.

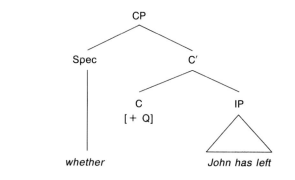

The important point to remember about (72) is that *wh*-phrases are located under Spec-CP, while complementizers are located under C. This arrangement has important implications for the representation of moved *wh*-phrases and auxiliaries in *wh*-questions to which we turn now.

A major problem with the structure based on the PS rule S′ → COMP S is that it makes available only one position in the pre-S domain, so that in a *wh*-question such as (73) below the moved *wh*-phrase and the auxiliary are both represented under the COMP node:

73a. Who did Mary see?

73b.

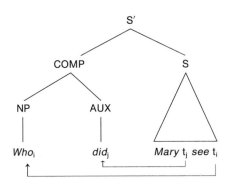

Moreover, the two categories located under COMP belong to different levels of categorial representation. While *did* (i.e. AUX or I) is a head, the *wh*-phrase is a phrasal category (maximal projection). Presumably, a given category cannot be both a head and a phrasal projection, as representation (73b) seems to imply with respect to COMP. Contrary to (73b), the structure based on the principles of X-bar Theory does not have these problems. (74) makes available two positions in the pre-IP domain, one of which is a head position (C) and the other a phrasal position (Spec-CP). The *wh*-phrase is located under the phrasal position (Spec-CP), and I (alias AUX) is located under the head position (C):

74.

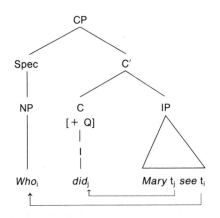

4.4.3.2 *Spec-CP and Wh-questions*   We have seen that IP differs from other categories in that its Spec position is required (by EPP) to be filled at S-structure. Judging from some of the examples above, where Spec-CP is empty, it seems that CP is not subject to a similar requirement. However, this does not seem to be true for all types of CP.

Apparently, CPs whose head (C) is marked with the feature [+ WH] (i.e. *wh*-clauses) seem to be required to have their Spec position filled by a *wh*-phrase. Consider the following examples:

75a. I wonder who Mary saw
75b. *I wonder* [$_{CP}$ *who*$_i$ [$_{C'}$ [+ WH] [$_{IP}$ *Mary saw* t$_i$]]]

76a. *I wonder Mary saw who
76b. **I wonder* [$_{CP}$ e [$_{C'}$ [+ WH] [$_{IP}$ *Mary saw who*]]]

The verb *wonder* subcategorizes for a [+Q] clause obligatorily, which can either be [− WH] (i.e. an (indirect) yes/no question), as in (71) and (72) above, or [+ WH] (i.e. an (indirect) *wh*-question), as in (75) and (76). Example (76), compared to (75), shows that Spec-CP cannot remain empty when C is [+ WH].

The requirement that the Spec position of a *wh*-clause be filled holds for root *wh*-questions as well. Example (78) is ungrammatical if it is intended as a *wh*-question:

77a. Who did Mary see?
77b. [$_{CP}$ *Who*$_i$ [$_{C'}$ *did*$_j$ [+ WH] [$_{IP}$ *Mary* t$_j$ *see* t$_i$]]]?

78a. *Mary saw who?
78b. *[$_{CP}$ e [$_{C'}$ [+ WH] [$_{IP}$ *Mary saw who*]]]?

The intended interpretation for (78) as a *wh*-question is conveyed by the presence of the feature [+ WH] in C (as well as by the question mark or rising intonation). Obviously, (78) is grammatical if interpreted as an echo-question, but this is beside the point. As pointed out in Chapter 3, echo-questions are not (wh-) questions: they are not marked for the feature [+ WH]. Thus echo-questions are irrelevant to the requirement that clauses which are [+ WH] must have their Spec position filled with a *wh*-phrase.

Thus, it seems that [+ WH]-CPs are subject to a requirement which in essence is similar to EPP in relation to IPs. The difference, given the discussion above, is that, while EPP holds of all types of IPs, including the non-finite ones, the CP-related requirement holds only of [+ WH]-CPs. We will call the CP-related requirement the **[+ WH]-CP Principle** (instead of the more logical but cumbersome name Extended Extended Projection Principle), and define it as in (79):

79. [+ WH]-CP Principle
A [+ WH]-CP must have a specifier.

Like EPP, the [+ WH]-CP Principle holds of S-structure and LF representations, but not of D-structure representations. Pursuing the parallelism with EPP, just as it is possible that NP-movement in raising constructions and passives is motivated by EPP, as shown above, it is also possible that *Wh*-movement in *wh*-questions is motivated by the [+ WH]-CP Principle – the *wh*-phrase has to move to Spec-CP to provide the [+ WH]-CP with a specifier necessary for it to satisfy the [+ WH]-CP Principle. Note that it is not necessary to specify that the specifier intended in (79) must be a *wh*-phrase. This will follow from the Spec-Head Agreement requirement discussed earlier. The relevant feature for C and a specifier occupying Spec-CP is [+/− WH]. Because C in *wh*-questions bears the feature [+ WH], only a phrase bearing the same feature, i.e. a *wh*-phrase, can occupy Spec-CP.

As a final remark, it is possible that the [+ WH]-CP Principle also holds for yes/no questions as well. Recall from above that embedded yes/no questions can either instantiate *if* under I or *whether* under Spec-CP. To the extent that the latter is a *wh*-phrase, it seems that yes/no questions are possibly also specified for the feature [+ WH], so that, technically, yes/no questions and *wh*-questions are identical. Assuming this to be the case, it follows from (79) that all yes/no questions include a *wh*-phrase in Spec-CP. In embedded clauses the *wh*-phrase can either be realised as *whether* or, presumably, as a null *wh*-phrase, whereas in root sentences it is invariably realized as a null category. Evidence that embedded [+ WH] yes/no interrogatives probably include a null *wh*-phrase can be gleaned from examples such as the following:

80a. *How do you wonder whether/why John fixed the car?
80b. *How do you wonder if John fixed the car?
80c. *How_i do you wonder [CP (wh-XP) [C' if [IP John fixed the car t_i]]]?

(80a) involves a violation of the *Wh*-island Condition, triggered by movement of the *wh*-phrase out of the embedded *wh*-island (Chapter 3). Example (80b) shows that the *wh*-island violation arises even when an overt *wh*-phrase is missing. Assuming that the defining characteristic of *wh*-islands is that they include a *wh*-phrase in Spec-CP, it follows that the embedded yes/no interrogative in (80b) includes a null *wh*-phrase in Spec-CP, as shown in (80c). The fact that an overt *wh*-phrase and *if* cannot co-occur, as shown in **I wonder whether/if John fixed the car*, can be attributed to an appropriately modified version of the Doubly Filled COMP Filter (Chapter 3).

4.4.4 Summary

The non-lexical categories S and S' can be assigned a structure determined by the principles of X-bar Theory. The head of S is I (alias AUX) and its maximal projection is IP (alias S). The single-bar projection of I (I') dominates the head I and VP which functions as the complement of I. The maximal projection IP dominates the subject of the sentence. I can either be [+ FINITE] (finite clauses) or [− FINITE] (non-finite clauses). Spec-IP (the subject position) is subject to a special condition (EPP) which requires it to be filled by S-structure (clauses must have a subject). Non-finite clauses without an overt subject have the null category PRO as a subject. Small clauses are categorially realized as the maximal projection of the predicate, which is usually a lexical category. Subjects of small clauses occupy the Spec position in the X-bar structure of the predicate. The head of the non-lexical category S' is C(OMP) and its maximal projection is CP. The single-bar projection (C') dominates the head C and IP which functions as the complement of C. C can be either [+ WH] (interrogative) or [− WH] (declarative). When it is [+ WH] it is subject to a special condition (The [+WH]-CP Principle) which requires its specifier position to be filled by S-structure ([+WH]-CPs must have a specifier).

4.5 *The Structure Preserving Hypothesis and Movement Types*

4.5.1 Substitution Movements

So far, we have not discussed the question of whether the principles of X-bar theory hold at all syntactic levels of representation or just at D-structure. If they hold at all syntactic levels of representation, the implication is that transformations do not have the power to modify D-structure representations in such a way as to derive S-structure and LF representations which are inconsistent with the principles of X-bar theory. If, on the other hand, the scope of the principles of X-bar Theory is restricted to D-structure, the implication is that transformations can introduce modifications which result in violations of the principles of X-bar theory at the post-D-structure levels. The former scenario is arguably more desirable, on the grounds that it places further constraints on the power of transformations, and maintains a certain degree of uniformity of structure at all syntactic levels of representation.

The idea that the principles of X-bar theory apply at all levels of syntactic analysis implies that transformations 'preserve' D-structure representations. At this stage, this implication is basically a hypothesis, in the sense that its validity needs to be verified against the various types of transformation discussed in Chapter 3, among others. The hypothesis can be formulated as in (81) (adapted from Emonds (1976)):

81. Structure-Preserving Hypothesis
   Transformations are structure-preserving.

Here we will understand by a 'structure-preserving transformation' any transformation which leads to the derivation of a structure which is consistent with the principles of X-bar theory. Thus, all transformations which, for example, move a category to an (empty) position licensed by the principles of X-bar theory are 'structure-preserving'. On the other hand, all transformations which require the creation of a new node not licensed by the principles of X-bar theory are not 'structure preserving'. Such transformations are said to be 'structure-building'.

Transformations which move a category to an empty position are called **substitution transformations**. A prominent example of substitution transformations is NP-movement, involved in the derivation of passives (82) and raising constructions (83):

82a. The problem was solved (by Mary)
82b. D-structure:

   $[_{IP}$ e $[_{I'}$ *was* $[_{VP}$ *solved* $[_{NP}$ *the problem*$]]]]$
82c. S-structure:

   $[_{IP}$ $[_{NP}$ *The problem*$]_i$ $[_{I'}$ *was* $[_{VP}$ *solved* $t_i]]]$

83a. Mary seems to have solved the problem
83b. D-structure:

   $[_{IP}$ e I $[_{VP}$ *seems* $[[_{NP}$ *Mary*$]$ *to have solved the problem*$]]]$
83c. S-structure:

   $[_{IP}$ $[_{NP}$ *Mary*$]_i$ I $[_{VP}$ *seems* $[t_i$ *to have solved the problem*$]]]$

In both constructions NP-movement moves an NP to an empty subject position (i.e. Spec-IP). Thus, NP-movement is trivially 'structure-preserving'.

Other prominent examples of substitution movements are *Wh*-movement and, to some extent, also I-to-C movement (alias SAI):

84a. Which problem did Mary solve?
84b. D-structure:

   $[_{CP}$ e $[_{C'}$ e $[_{IP}$ *Mary* $[_{I'}$ *did* $[_{VP}$ *solve* $[_{NP}$ *which problem*$]]]]]]$
84c. S-structure:

   $[_{CP}$ $[$*Which problem*$]_i$ $[_{C'}$ $[_{I'}$ *did*$]_j$ $[_{IP}$ *Mary* $[_{I'}$ t_j $[_{VP}$ *solve* $t_i]]]]]$?

Wh-movement moves the *wh*-phrase to an empty Spec position of CP, whereas I-to-C movement moves I to the empty C position. In the latter case, the term 'empty' is interpreted to mean 'devoid of lexical material', though not of features. Recall that the C of interrogative clauses is specified with the feature [+ WH]. *Do*-support, involved in the derivation of (84), has been ignored because it is not crucially relevant to the discussion.

Thus, NP-movement, *Wh*-movement and I-to-C movement are all 'structure-preserving', essentially because they are substitution movements. However, the other transformations, i.e. Topicalization, I-to-V movement (alias Affix-hopping), V-to-I movement (alias V-raising to AUX), Extraposition, and Heavy NP Shift, are not substitution movements, as they do not move a category to a base-generated empty position. The question of whether these transformations are also 'structure-preserving' needs discussion.

4.5.2   Adjunction Movements

A typical example of a 'structure-building' transformation is Topicalization, as formulated in Chapter 3. Recall that Topicalization moves a category and attaches it to the (left side of) S (now IP), thereby creating a new node.

85a. This problem, I can solve
85b. I believe that this problem, I can solve

85c.

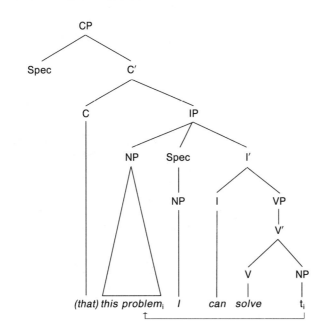

Structure (85c) is obviously inconsistent with the principles of X-bar theory, as the NP node created by Topicalization is not licensed by any of the X-bar schemata discussed above. We therefore need to assign (85a, b) an alternative structure which is consistent with the principles of X-bar theory, if we are to maintain the position that all transformations are 'structure-preserving' in the sense explained above.

To the extent that the schemata which license adjunction structures, discussed above, can be considered to be among the principles of X-bar theory, (85a, b) can be assigned the structure shown in (86), where the topicalized category is left-adjoined to IP.

86a. XP → YP XP (or XP YP)

86b.

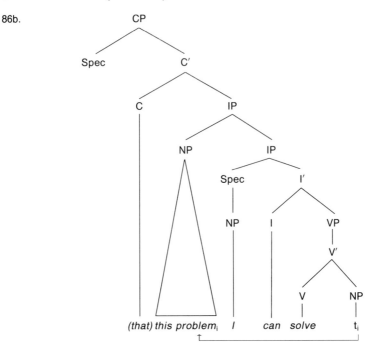

According to this analysis, Topicalization can be said to be non-'structure-building', as, strictly speaking, it does not create a new node but simply 'extends' an existing one (IP). More generally, Topicalization, as analysed in (86), does not give rise to a structure which is inconsistent with the principles of X-bar theory, assuming that the latter include the adjunction schema in (86a), where XP = IP.

   The re-analysed version of Topicalization, outlined in (86), means that Topicalization is now an **adjunction** movement. Other 'structure-building' transformations can also be re-analysed as adjunction movements. These include Extraposition and Heavy NP Shift, which were said (in Chapter 3) to attach the category they move as the rightmost constituent of VP. These transformations can be said to right-adjoin the category they move to VP, thereby deriving an adjunction structure.

   Turning now to I-to-V movement and V-to-I movement, they were said (in Chapter 3) to attach the category they move to V, and to I, respectively:

87a. Mary solved the problem
87b. [$_{IP}$ *Mary* [$_{I'}$ t$_i$ [$_{VP}$ *solve* + [I]$_i$ *the problem*]]]

88a. Mary has solved the problem
88b. [$_{IP}$ Mary [$_{I'}$ [$_V$ *have*]$_i$ + I [$_{VP}$ t$_i$ *solved the problem*]]]

We have so far been vague about how exactly I in (87) and V in (88) are 'attached' to V and I, respectively. We are now in a position to be more explicit about this notion. The moved head category (I or V) can be said to adjoin to the host head category (V or I), deriving the complex head structures shown in (88a) and (89b).

89a. I-to-V movement   89b. V-to-I movement

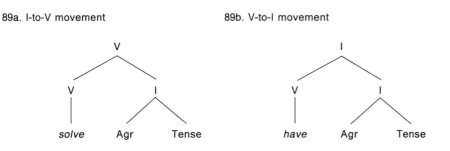

Because V is the host in I-to-V movement, the head category derived by adjunction to V is a complex V (89a), and because I is the host in V-to-I movement, the complex head category derived by adjunction to V is I (89b).

Note that the adjunction schemata discussed above deal only with adjunction to maximal projections and to single-bar projections. To accommodate the structures in (89a, b) we need to introduce a new adjunction schema for head-adjunction:

90. X → X Y (or Y X)

As with the other adjunction structures, the head-adjunction structures derived by I-to-V and V-to-I movements will be incompatible with the principles of X-bar theory if the latter are assumed to include schema (90).

4.5.3 Summary

In this section we addressed the question of whether the principles of X-bar Theory hold at all levels of syntactic representation (D-structure, S-structure, and LF) or are restricted to D-structure. The issue boils down to whether transformations should be allowed to derive structures which are incompatible with the principles of X-bar theory. Considerations relating to the need to restrict the power of transformations and to maintain a certain degree of uniformity of structure at all syntactic levels seem to favour the view that transformations should not be expected to derive structures which are incompatible with the principles of X-bar Theory. Instead, transformations should be expected to be 'structure-preserving'. Substitution transformations, such as NP-movement, *Wh*-movement, and I-to-C movement, are trivially 'structure-preserving' since they involve movement to an empty position. Adjunction transformations, such as Topicalization, I-to-V movement, and V-to-I movement, are arguably also 'structure-preserving' on the assumption that X-bar theory includes adjunction schemata among its principles.

4.6 *Conclusions and Revisions*

We started this chapter by considering the role of PS rules in the grammar. It transpired that their role was largely superfluous, as most simply duplicate information included in the lexical entries of categories. This fact raised the possibility that PS rules could be eliminated completely, and with them the Categorial Component of the Base, leading to a major simplification of the overall structure of the Grammar.

The role of ensuring that the subcategorization properties of lexical items are properly reflected in structural representations has been attributed to a simple principle called the Projection Principle (PP), which applies at all syntactic levels of representation. PP subsumes the role of LIR, as well as deriving the effects of the Trace Convention with respect to subcategorized positions.

The role of defining the major aspects of the structural representation of categories fell to a limited set of principles called the principles of X-bar Theory. The latter mostly take the form of schemata, in the sense that they capture certain common properties of phrase structures, and function as constraints on the structural representation of categories, both lexical and non-lexical. The assumption that these principles hold at all syntactic levels of representation leads to a situation where they also serve as conditions on the types of transformation allowed, such that only those which are 'structure-preserving' are possible.

In addition to these principles, there is the Extended Projection Principle (EPP) which requires (both finite and non-finite) clauses to have a subject. Non-finite clauses which do not have an overt subject have the null category PRO as the subject. Unlike PP, EPP does not hold at D-structure. Like PP, however, it derives some of the effects of the Trace Convention, this time with respect to the (non-subcategorized) subject position. *Wh*-questions (and possibly also yes/no questions) are subject to a condition, called the [+WH]-CP Principle, which requires *Wh*-clauses to have a (*wh*-)specifier at S-structure. This condition is in essence similar to the condition imposed by EPP on IPs, suggesting that perhaps they both derive from some more general requirement of the Grammar (Chapter 7).

The consequence of these radical revisions is that the Grammar is increasingly becoming principle-based instead of rule-based. In the previous, rule-based model the Categorial Component, for example, consisted of category-specific rules which by virtue of being category-specific contained redundant information. In contrast, the revised model consists of general, non-category-specific principles which serve as conditions on representations. The principles of X-bar theory, for example, do not make reference to specific categories, but express generalizations which hold across categories, including the non-lexical ones. The replacement of specific rules by general principles represents a major step towards a concept of Grammar as a system of general principles which defines . possible representations.

The resulting model is better described in terms of levels of representation and conditions on these levels, rather than in terms of components. (91) provides a graphic representation of the model as conceived so far. Some principles apply to all syntactic levels of representation, whereas others are limited to some. For example, while PP holds at all syntactic levels, EPP does not hold at D-structure.

An important aspect of the model outlined in (91) is that the levels of representation are characterized by the kinds of condition which apply or do not apply to them. For example, D-structure is characterized by (among other things) the fact that EPP does not apply to it, whereas other principles do. We expect our investigations in the forthcoming

91.

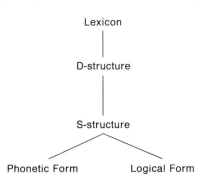

Lexicon

D-structure

S-structure

Phonetic Form   Logical Form

chapters to reveal further distinctive characteristics of the various levels of representation. If, on the other hand, our investigations reveal a strong (i.e. (near-)complete) parallelism between two given levels of representation, the *raison d'être* for one of them as a distinct level will cease to exist, and a revision will become inevitable. Just as a given component can become superfluous in the process of searching for an adequate theory of language, a given level of representation can also become superfluous.

Exercises

Exercise 1

The PP constituents *of soccer* and *with talent* in (1) below are said to have different structural relations with respect to the noun. Determine the structural status of each constituent on the basis of (2–5), among other examples you may think of:

1. The player of soccer with talent
2. *The player with talent of soccer
3. The player of soccer and basketball
4. The player with talent and (with) a future
5. *The player of soccer and with talent

Exercise 2

Determine the structure of VP in (1) on the basis of (2–5), among other examples you may think of:

1. Mary will organize a meeting at home in the afternoon
2. Mary will organize a meeting at home in the afternoon, and John will probably do so too
3. Mary will organize a meeting at home in the afternoon, and John will probably do so in the evening
4. Mary will organize a meeting at home in the afternoon, and John will probably do so in the café in the evening

Exercise 3

Discuss the structural status of the bracketed constituents in the following examples in the context of X-bar theory:

1. [Presumably], John is the instigator of all the troubles
2. John arrived [after Mary had left]
3. Bill went to London [to see his parents]
4. [Reading a detective story] is fun
5. [That John should leave suddenly] is puzzling

Exercise 4

The bracketed constituents in (1) and (2) below have been claimed to occupy the Spec position of the adjective they modify (Spec-AP):

1. Mary is [very] intelligent
2. Bill is [rather] suspicious of John

Evaluate this claim in relation to (3) and (4) below, where AP is a small clause complement of the root verb:

3. I consider Mary [very] intelligent
4. I find Bill [rather] suspicious of John

Exercise 5

Example (1) is ambiguous between two interpretations, shown in A and B:

1. The French student
   A. The student who studies French
   B. The student who is French

In (A) *French* is the complement of *student*, whereas in (B) it is an adjective modifier of *student*. Determine the structural status of *French* in (1) with the interpretation in (A). In doing so, you may want to take into consideration the following examples:

2. The dismissal of John has been condemned
3. John's dismissal has been condemned
4. *The John's dismissal has been condemned

What do these examples reveal about the position of *French* in (1) with the interpretation in (A)?

Further Reading

The fundamentals of X-bar theory are outlined in Chomsky (1973) and later refined in Emonds (1976), Jackendoff (1977), Chomsky (1981) and Stowell (1981). The latter and later Chomsky (1986b) were influential in extending the principles of X-bar Theory to non-lexical categories, complementing earlier work by Bresnan (1970) and Fassi Fehri (1980) in relation to COMP/S'.

Discussions of the structure of small clauses can be found in Chomsky (1981), Stowell (1981), and Kayne (1984). A different view is expressed in Williams (1980; 1983). Chomsky (1986b) presents the analysis outlined in this chapter, which is an attempt to assign small clauses a structure consistent with the principles of X-bar Theory.

The Projection Principle and the Extended Projection Principle are discussed at length in Chomsky (1981). This is a substantial and highly technical piece of work which set research on the way to developing a principle-based theory of Grammar. Most of the ideas discussed in this chapter and subsequent ones can be traced to this book. For example, the book includes a discussion of the relationship between PRO and the Extended Projection Principle, as well as a discussion of its referential properties to be outlined in detail in Chapter 7 of this book.

The typology of movements discussed in this chapter is outlined in Chomsky (1986b), although it was evident from earlier work, in particular Chomsky (1981). The book also mentions the relevance of this typology to the Structure-Preserving Hypothesis, introduced in Emonds (1976).

5

Theta Theory

Contents

5.1 C-Selection and S-Selection

In the previous chapters we used the expressions 'logical subject' and 'logical object' to refer to the semantic functions of NPs. In some sentences the semantic functions of NPs correspond to their grammatical functions, whereas in others they do not:

1a. John hit Bill
1b. [$_{IP}$ *John* I [$_{VP}$ *hit* [$_{NP}$ *Bill*]]]
2a. Bill was hit (by John)
2b. [$_{IP}$ *Bill*$_i$ *was* [$_{VP}$ *hit* [$_{NP}$ t$_i$] (*by John*)]]

In the active sentence (1), the semantic functions of the two NP's *John* and *Bill* correspond with their grammatical functions, such that the former is both the semantic (logical) and the grammatical subject of the sentence and the latter the semantic (logical) and grammatical object of the verb. In the passive sentence (2), however, the semantic functions of the two NPs do not correspond with their grammatical functions. The NP *Bill* has the semantic function of object, since it undergoes the act described by the verb, whereas grammatically it is the subject of the sentence, since it occupies the Spec position of IP and is in a Spec-Head Agreement relation with (the Agr category of) I at S-structure. On the other hand, the NP *John* inside the *by*-phrase apparently has the semantic function of subject, although grammatically it is not the subject of the sentence, since it does not occupy the subject position and is not in Spec-Head Agreement with (the Agr category of) I.

Recall (from Chapter 3) that the property of passives just mentioned was partly the reason for analysing the NP *Bill* in (2a), for example, as being base-generated in the object position of the verb and subsequently moved to the subject position of the sentence, as shown in (2b). The reasoning goes as follows: the (transitive) verb *hit* subcategorizes for an NP, and by virtue of PP (the Projection Principle) it must have an NP object at all syntactic levels of representation. Since the NP *Bill* is semantically the object of the verb, it is this NP which is assumed to be base-generated in the object position, to satisfy the subcategorization properties of the verb. There is a sense in which this reasoning entails that subcategorization in terms of syntactic categories such as NP is based on some kind of 'semantic subcategorization', such that the NP which functions as the grammatical object is also the semantic (logical) object of the verb.

Subcategorization in terms of syntactic categories such as NP is called **categorial selection (c-selection)**, and selection in terms of semantic categories, loosely referred to above as 'semantic subcategorization', is called **semantic selection (s-selection)**. S-selection is largely determined by the inherent meaning (the conceptual structure) of lexical items. The verb (or concept) *hit*, for example, entails two participants, a subject participant who performs the act of 'hitting' and an object participant who suffers the act of 'hitting'. On the other hand, the verb (or concept) *run*, as in *Mary ran fast (towards the shed)*, entails only one subject participant, i.e. the individual who does the 'running'. Just as c-selection operates in terms of syntactic categories, s-selection operates in terms of semantic categories, called **thematic roles** (or **theta-roles**). The verb *hit*, for example, is said to s-select two thematic roles, an **agent** (the subject participant), and a **patient** (the object participant). The verb *decide*, as in *Mary decided that John should leave*, also s-selects two participants, the second of which, i.e. the clause *(that) John should leave*, is a **proposition**. Other verbs may select a different number of participants with different thematic roles, as we will see below.

The observation made above that c-selection seems to be based on s-selection is interesting in so far as it suggests that perhaps one is reducible to the other. The fact that the verb *hit* c-selects an NP arguably follows from the fact that it s-selects a participant with the thematic role patient in the first place. Similarly, the fact that the verb *run*, as in *Mary ran fast*, does not c-select an NP arguably follows from the fact that it does not s-select an object participant in the first place. Suppose that a correspondence relation can be established between thematic roles and syntactic categories, such that individual categories serve as the 'canonical structural realisation' (CSR) of specific thematic roles. The CSR of agent, for example, will typically be NP, and the CSR of proposition will typically be a clause. It follows from this situation that c-selection does not need to be mentioned in lexical entries: the c-selectional properties of lexical items are derivable from their s-selectional properties in terms of the relation 'CSR'.

This conclusion, if correct, has important implications for the relevance of semantic categories to syntax. We have seen that subcategorization properties play a crucial role in the syntactic representations of sentences. The relationship between the subcategorization properties of lexical items and their syntactic representations is mediated by PP, which is a syntactic principle. We will see below that the relationship between the thematic properties of lexical items and their syntactic representations is also mediated by a syntactic principle, called the **Theta Criterion**, which applies at LF but the effects of which extend to other levels of syntactic representation by virtue of PP. Recall that LF is the level where sentences are assigned a semantic representation, and therefore the level where thematic relations are determined. In this chapter we will learn more about the properties of LF, and what we will learn will confirm the idea that LF is essentially a syntactic level of representation.

The Theta Criterion belongs to a sub-theory of Grammar called **Theta Theory**, on a par with X-bar Theory. The implication of the existence of these sub-theories for the overall organization of the Grammar will be discussed at the end of this chapter. To anticipate, as a result of adding Theta Theory, the Grammar is gradually acquiring a **modular** structure, where each of the sub-theories represents a **module** (Chapter 1). Each module is self-contained and consists of a set of principles which constrain relevant aspects of representations. The (principles of the) modules interact with each other in a well-defined manner, to either include or to exclude certain representations.

Before we embark on a discussion of Theta Theory, note that it is still less well-understood in some respects than other modules of the Grammar. As it will transpire on occasion in this chapter, it is sometimes hard to draw clear conclusions relating to the thematic properties of certain sentences, and therefore hard to evaluate their theoretical implications.

5.2   *Arguments, Quasi-arguments, and Operators*

5.2.1   Arguments and Thematic Roles

The s-selectional properties of lexical items are often described in terms of terminology borrowed from Logic. Verbs are referred to as **predicates**, so that this concept of 'predicate' is slightly different from the concept we have been using so far to refer to the material included under the VP node in the sentence (Chapter 2). The participants involved in the event depicted by a predicate are called **arguments**. The verb *hit*, for example, is a predicate which takes two arguments, and the verb *run* (in the intransitive sense) is a predicate which takes only one argument. Verbs which take two arguments, e.g.

kick, are called **two-place** predicates, and verbs which take one argument, e.g. *run* (as in *Mary ran towards the shed*), are called **one-place** predicates, where 'place' corresponds, roughly, to 'argument'. Information relating to arguments of predicates is called the **argument structure** (of predicates).

The number of arguments associated with a given lexical item determines the number of thematic roles the lexical item can assign, such that to every argument there corresponds a thematic role in the **thematic structure** of the lexical item. Lexical items are said to **assign** thematic roles to the arguments they select, subject to certain structurally based conditions to be discussed below. Here, we will adopt the notation in (3) below to represent argument and thematic structures:

3a. *hit*: < 1, 2 >
       < Agent, Patient >
3b. *run*: < 1 >
       < Agent >

Arguments are represented by arabic numbers included between angled brackets, and thematic roles are represented by their individual names included between angled brackets. The argument and thematic structures represent the selectional properties of lexical items, included in their lexical entries along with various other types of information. Later in this chapter we will introduce a modification in representations (3a, b) which will distinguish between subject arguments and object arguments.

An argument is usually defined as a referring expression, i.e. an expression which corresponds to (or picks out) an individual or an entity in a given world (or discourse domain). Thus, *the teacher*, *the book*, and *John* in (4a) below are all referring expressions in the sense defined, and therefore arguments. However, the expletive ('semantically empty') elements *it* in (4b) and *there* in (4c) and (4d) are not referring expressions, and therefore non-arguments:

4a. The teacher gave the book to John
4b. It seems that Mary has solved the problem
4c. There is a unicorn in the garden
4d. There seems to be a unicorn in the garden

Arguments can also be propositions, i.e. clauses (both 'normal' and 'small'):

5a. John considers Bill to be incompetent
5b. John considers Bill incompetent
5c. Mary decided that John should leave

The verbs *consider* and *decide* in these examples each take two arguments, one of which is a proposition. Propositions are arguments in the sense that they refer to a state of affairs in a given world.

Thematic roles can be collectively defined as the roles assigned to the arguments which participate in a given event. The definition of individual thematic roles, however, is much less clear in some cases. While some of the terms adopted are almost self-explanatory, e.g. agent/actor, others are much less so. Here we will content ourselves with illustrating the major thematic roles recognized in the literature, while pointing out some of the difficulties which arise from an attempt to determine the thematic role of a given expression in certain contexts:

6a. The boy likes the girl
6b. *The boy* (**experiencer**), *the girl* (**theme**)

7a. Bill prepared the dinner for Mary
7b. *Bill* (**agent**), *the dinner* (**patient**), *Mary* (**benefactive**)

8a. Mary put the book on the shelf
8b. *Mary* (**agent**), *the book* (**theme**), *the shelf* (**location**)

9a. Bill gave the book to John
9b. *Bill* (**agent**), *the book* (**theme**), *John* (**goal**)

10a. Mary stole the money from the thief
10b. *Mary* (**agent**), *the money* (**theme**), *the thief* (**source**)

11a. John opened the door with the key
11b. *John* (**agent**), *the door* (**patient/theme**), *the key* (**instrumental**)

The patient role is generally understood to imply a change in state, and the theme role to imply a change in location or position. However, it is not clear sometimes whether the thematic role involved should be characterized as patient or theme. For example, it is not clear whether *the door* in (11) should be characterized as patient, on the grounds that it has changed in state, from being closed to being open, or as theme, on the grounds that it has undergone a change in position, or both. Here, we will drop the term 'patient' and subsume the situation of change in state under the definition of 'theme', so that the latter implies a change in position or state or both.

5.2.2 Quasi-arguments

Some expressions seem to share properties with both arguments and non-arguments. This is the case of the so-called 'weather-*it*':

12a. It sometimes rains after snowing
12b. *It sometimes rains after* [PRO *snowing*]

13a. It is difficult to predict their next move
13b. *It is difficult* [PRO *to predict their next move*]

'Weather-*it*' is similar to the expletive *it* in that it is apparently a non-referring expression. At the same time, it differs from the expletive *it* in that it can control PRO, as shown in (12). That the expletive *it* cannot function as a controller of PRO is shown in (13), where PRO has an arbitrary interpretation for lack of a controller, or an antecedent to assign it a reference. The ability to function as a controller of PRO is a property of referring expressions (i.e. arguments), given that control is essentially a relation of reference-assignment. The fact that 'weather-*it*' can control PRO implies that it has argumental properties, although it is apparently a non-referring expression.

Expressions with this type of ambivalent nature are sometimes called **quasi-arguments**. This term can be understood more generally to refer to expressions which function as arguments of a special class of predicates and have an interpretation peculiar to the situations described by those predicates. Like straightforward arguments, quasi-arguments are also assigned a thematic role, although the thematic role they are assigned is a special one in that it is peculiar to the situations they are associated with. 'Weather-*it*', for example, can be said to be assigned a 'weather' thematic role by the verb of which it is a special argument.

The term 'quasi-argument' is sometimes also used to refer to noun phrases in idiomatic phrases such as the ones in the following examples:

14a. John took advantage of Bill
14b. John kicked the bucket

An idiomatic phrase is generally a phrase the meaning of which does not derive directly from a combination of the literal meaning of its individual constituents. The idiomatic meaning 'exploit', for example, cannot be derived compositionally from the meanings of the individual words in (14a), and the same is true for the idiomatic meaning 'die' in relation to (14b). In the latter case, the expression *the bucket* does not refer to an entity in the real world (a 'vessel for holding or carrying water or milk'). The fact that *the bucket* is not a referring expression in the idiomatic meaning implies that it is not an argument. At the same time, the presence of *the bucket* is necessary for the idiomatic meaning to be conveyed, as shown by the fact that its absence or replacement by another expression results in ungrammaticality or the loss of the idiomatic meaning:

15a. *John kicked
15b. John kicked the jug

While (15a) is ungrammatical, (15b) can only have the literal meaning, derived compositionally from the meanings of the individual words. This implies that, although *the bucket* is a non-referring expression, it functions as a special argument of the verb *kick* in its idiomatic use. The relationship between *the bucket* and the verb *kick* in the idiomatic meaning of (15b) is somewhat similar to the relationship between 'weather-verbs' and 'weather-*it*', in that it is special and restricted to a peculiar interpretation. Thus, as with 'weather-verbs' and 'weather-*it*', the verb *kick* can be said to assign a special thematic role to *the bucket*, partly responsible for the idiomatic meaning.

Assuming this to be the case, the question arises as to whether the idiomatic *kick* is the same verb as the non-idiomatic *kick* which assigns a theme role to its object argument in examples such as (15b). To the extent that the two *kicks* differ in meaning, it could be argued that they have separate entries in the Lexicon, just like homophonous words such as *bank* as in *Bank of Scotland* and *bank* as in *bank of the River Thames*. On the other hand, given that the idiomatic meaning is the result of combining *kick* and the expression *the bucket*, it could be argued further that the two items are entered together in the Lexicon as a single complex item, with the meaning 'die'. The status of *kick the bucket* as a lexical complex seems initially to be supported by the fact that, unlike ordinary objects, *the bucket* cannot undergo passivization (NP-movement to the subject position). Thus, the passive (16b) below cannot have the idiomatic meaning that its active counterpart in (14b) has:

16a. Advantage was taken of John
16b. The bucket was kicked by John

However, this is not true of all idioms, as the passive (16a) does have the idiomatic meaning that its active counterpart (14a) has. The properties of idioms, in particular variations in the properties of individual idioms, are still not well understood; we shall therefore have no more to say about them here.

5.2.3   Operators and Variables: Quantifier Raising

5.2.3.1   Wh-Phrases   *Wh*-phrases are non-referring expressions, since, unlike names such as *Mary*, they do not pick out specific individuals or entities in a given world. For reasons which will become clear below, they are sometimes called **quasi-quantifiers**. The status of *wh*-phrases as non-arguments initially raises a problem with respect to *wh*-questions such as (17):

17a. Which problem did Mary solve?

17b. D-structure:

[$_{CP}$ e [$_{IP}$ *Mary* [$_{I'}$ *did* [$_{VP}$ *solve* [$_{NP}$ *which problem*]]]]*?*

17c. S-structure:

[$_{CP}$ *Which problem*$_i$ *did*$_j$ [$_{IP}$ *Mary* [$_{I'}$ t$_j$ [$_{VP}$ *solve* t$_i$]]]]*?*

The verb *solve* is a two-place predicate, and therefore expected to have two arguments. Yet in (17) it apparently has only one argument, *Mary*, the object *wh*-phrase being a non-argument.

Note, however, that in the S-structure representation (17c) the *wh*-phrase does not occupy the object position of the verb. The latter is occupied by the trace of the moved *wh*-phrase. Traces of *wh*-phrases are said to have the status of (logical) **variables** in the LF representation of *wh*-questions, and *wh*-phrases have the status of (logical) **operators**. The LF representation of (17), for example, is as in (18a), and has the logical interpretation shown in (18b), where the trace of the *wh*-phrase is replaced with a variable:

18a. [$_{CP}$ *Which problem*$_i$ *did*$_j$ [$_{IP}$ *Mary* [$_{I'}$ t$_j$ [$_{VP}$ *solve* t$_i$]]]]*?*

18b. *for which problem* x, [Mary solved x]

The *wh*-operator (wh-phrase), located outside IP, is said to **bind** the variable in the object position. From a formal point of view, variables can in principle be assigned a **value** (a reference) among the set of values defined by the operator: *what*, for example, narrows the reference to non-humans (or non-animates), and *who* narrows the reference to humans (or animates). It follows that there is a sense in which variables are arguments, on a par with names and other referring expressions. In view of this, the two-place predicate *solve* in the *wh*-question (17a) does indeed have two arguments in the LF representation (18), the name *Mary* and the variable trace of the *wh*-phrase. In the next section we shall discuss a more precise definition of the notion 'variable'.

The LF representation (18a) of example (17a) looks identical to its S-structure representation (17c). However, there are sentences whose LF representations are significantly different from their S-structure representations. Consider the following example, which is an instance of so-called **multiple *wh*-questions**:

19a. Who solved which problem?

19b. S-structure:

[$_{CP}$ *Who*$_i$ [$_{IP}$ t$_i$ I [$_{VP}$ *solved* [$_{NP}$ *which problem*]]]]*?*

(19a) is an (information-seeking) *wh*-question, even though one of the two *wh*-phrases it includes is **in situ**, meaning located in the (object) position where it is base-generated. Multiple *wh*-questions raise an interesting problem which can be stated with respect to (19) as follows: if the LF representation of (19a) is identical to the S-structure (19b), i.e. if the object *wh*-phrase remains in the object position in the LF representation, we will have a situation where the two-place predicate *solve* has only one argument, the variable trace in the subject position. The object, being a *wh*-phrase, is a non-argument.

This reasoning leads to the plausible conclusion that something happens in the derivation of multiple *wh*-questions such as (19a), in the mapping from S-structure onto LF, which results in an LF representation consistent with the argument structure of the verb. Somewhat predictably, what happens is that the *wh*-phrase in the object position of the verb in (19) also moves to Spec-CP, leaving a variable trace behind which functions as the object argument of the verb. This transformational operation derives the LF representation in (20a) below, with the logical interpretation in (21b), from the S-structure representation in (19b) above:

20a. [CP [*Who*]ᵢ [*which problem*]ⱼ *did* [IP tᵢ I [VP *solve* tⱼ]]]?

20b. *for which person* x *and which problem* y, [x *solved* y]

Thus, by assuming that the *wh*-phrase in situ in the S-structure representation (19b) moves to Spec-CP in the mapping from S-structure onto LF, we derive an LF representation where the two-place predicate *solve* does indeed have two arguments – the two variable traces.

The movement transformation which applies in the mapping (from S-structure) onto LF does not have a 'visible' effect on word order, contrary to the movement transformations which apply in the mapping (from D-structure) onto S-structure. Recall (from the previous chapter) that the model of Grammar branches off at the level of S-structure into the separate levels of PF and LF, with PF the 'visible' and LF the 'invisible' level. Thus, any reordering operation which takes place prior to or at the level of S-structure will be ('visibly') reflected in PF, but any reordering operation which takes place after S-structure, i.e. in the mapping from S-structure onto LF, as in (20), will not be ('visibly') reflected in PF. The word order in the PF representation of the multiple *wh*-question (19a) is as it is in the S-structure representation (19b). Movement operations which take place prior to or at the level of S-structure are sometimes called **overt** movements, and the ones which take place in the mapping from S-structure onto LF are called **covert** movements.

In view of the fact that the transformation which derives the LF representation (20a) involves movement of a *wh*-phrase to Spec-CP, it is tempting to call it *Wh*-movement. However, recall (from the previous chapter) that *Wh*-movement is a substitution movement, in the sense that it moves a *wh*-phrase to an empty Spec-CP position. The transformation involved in (20a) cannot be a substitution movement, as Spec-CP is already filled with the subject *wh*-phrase moved there by *Wh*-movement in the mapping from D-structure onto S-structure. Given that the only other type of movement allowed is adjunction (see previous chapter), it follows that the transformation in question is an adjunction movement. Here, we will assume that this movement transformation adjoins the moved *wh*-phrase to the *wh*-phrase already in Spec-CP, deriving the adjunction structure shown in (21). The transformation which moves categories in the mapping

21.

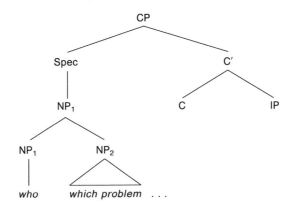

from D-structure onto LF is called **Quantifier Raising (QR)**. Recall from above that *wh*-phrases are called quasi-quantifiers. The true (or genuine) quantifiers are the subject of our next discussion.

5.2.3.2   Quantified Phrases   Consider the following examples:

22a. John suspects everyone
22b. S-str: [$_{IP}$ *John* I [$_{VP}$ *suspects* [$_{NP}$ *everyone*]]]

23a. Mary suspects someone
23b. S-str: [$_{IP}$ *Mary* I [$_{VP}$ *suspects* [$_{NP}$ *someone*]]]

Expressions such as *every*(*one*), *some*(*one*), *each* (*one*), *all*, among others, are called **quantifiers**. Unlike names such as *John*, quantifiers are non-referring expressions: they do not refer to a specific individual in a given world. Formally speaking, one cannot substitute a constant for a quantifier in the logical representation of quantified expressions. (22) basically means that if you find an individual you can expect *John* to suspect him/her, and (23) means that of all the individuals in a given world there is/exists at least one whom *Mary* suspects. Together with *all*, *every*(*one*) is called a **universal** quantifier, while *some*(*one*) is called an **existential** quantifier.

As non-referring expressions, and therefore non-arguments, quantified phrases present us with the same problem as *wh*-phrases in situ (in multiple *wh*-questions). If the LF representations of (22a) and (23a) remain as they are in (22b) and (23b), we will have a situation where the two-place predicate *suspect* has only one argument, instead of the two arguments specified in its argument structure. The analysis outlined above for *wh*-phrases in situ carries over to quantified phrases, so that quantified phrases also undergo QR in the mapping from S-structure onto LF. The movement transformation leaves a variable trace behind which functions as the object argument of the verb. Accordingly, the LF representations of (22) and (23), derived by QR, are as shown in (24) and (25) below, respectively:

24a. [$_{IP}$ *everyone*$_i$ [$_{IP}$ *John* I [$_{VP}$ *suspects* t$_i$]]]

24b. *for every person* x, [John suspects x]

25a. [$_{IP}$ *someone*$_i$ [$_{IP}$ *Mary* I [$_{VP}$ *suspects* t$_i$]]]
25b. *for some person* x, [*Mary suspects* x]

Unlike *wh*-phrases raised by QR, quantified phrases raised by QR are adjoined to IP. A discussion of this discrepancy between quantified phrases and *wh*-phrases affected by QR will take us too far afield, and therefore will be avoided here. Evidence for the idea that *wh*-phrases in situ and quantified phrases are moved in the mapping from S-structure onto LF will be discussed in the subsequent chapters. Here we will briefly discuss the usefulness of this transformation in accounting for the ambiguity of sentences with multiple quantified expressions.

Multiple quantification usually gives rise to ambiguity of meaning, so that (26) below (pronounced with neutral intonation) has at least two different interpretations (or readings):

26a. Everyone suspects someone
26b. S-str: [$_{IP}$ [$_{NP}$ *Everyone*] I [$_{VP}$ *suspects* [$_{NP}$ *someone*]]]

(26) can have a 'distributed' reading whereby each individual suspects a different individual, so that *Mary* suspects *John*, *Bill* suspects *Donald*, *Jane* suspects *Fred*, and

so on. (26) can also have the (different) reading whereby the same individual is suspected by everyone, so that *John, Mary, Fred* and so on all suspect *Donald*. The first interpretation can be paraphrased as 'Everyone has someone whom he/she suspects', and the second as 'There is someone whom everyone suspects'.

More formally, in the first (distributed) reading *everyone* is said to have **scope** over *someone*. In the second reading, however, the scope relation between the two quantified expressions is the reverse, so that *someone* has scope over *everyone*. Using different terminology, in the first interpretation *everyone* is said to have the **wider/broader** scope, whereas in the second interpretation it is *someone* which has the **wider/broader** scope. The notion 'wider/broader' is, in a sense, visibly illustrated in the paraphrases given above. In the first paraphrase, 'Everyone has someone whom (s)he suspects', *everyone* is outside (wider than) *someone*, so that *someone* is within (inside) the scope of *everyone*. However, in the second paraphrase, 'There is someone whom everyone suspects', it is *someone* which is outside (wider than) *everyone*, so that *everyone* is within (or inside) the scope of *someone*.

As with grammatical relations in general, we expect relations of scope to have a structural basis. Scope can be structurally defined as in (27) (the two definitions are adapted from May (1985) and Reinhart (1976), respectively):

27. **Scope**
    The scope of A is the set of nodes that A c-commands in the LF representation.

28. **C-command**
    A c-commands B iff the first branching node dominating A also dominates B (and A does not dominate B).

The definition of scope makes use of the notion 'c-command', defined in (28). To illustrate the effects of these definitions consider the abstract structures in (29). In (29a) A c-commands B because the first branching node which dominates A, i.e. C, also dominates B (and A does not dominate B). In (29b), however, A does not c-command B, because the first branching node which dominates A, i.e. D, does not dominate B. Now, because A c-commands B in (29a), A has scope over B, and because A does not c-command B in (29b), A does not have scope over B.

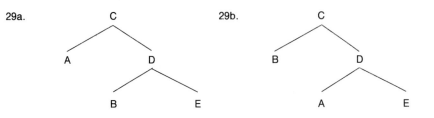

29a.   29b.

Going back to (26), the different scope relations between the two quantified expressions which underlie the two different interpretations can be represented in terms of the two different LF representations (30) and (31) below. (30) represents the first reading, and (31) the second reading:

30a. [IP *Everyone*ᵢ [IP *someone*ⱼ [IP tᵢ I [VP *suspects* tⱼ]]]]

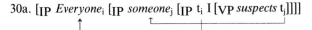

30b.

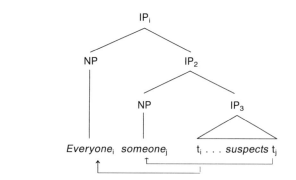

31a. [$_{IP}$ *someone*$_i$ [$_{IP}$ *Everyone*$_j$ [$_{IP}$ t$_j$ I [$_{VP}$ *suspect* t$_i$]]]]

31b.

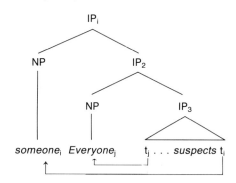

Both structures involve multiple adjunction to IP of the quantified expression (NP) moved by QR. In (30), *everyone* has scope over *someone*, because the first branching node which dominates *everyone*, i.e. IP$_1$, also dominates *someone*. Note that the reverse relation does not hold in this structure, i.e. *someone* does not have scope over *everyone* because *someone* does not c-command *everyone*. In (31), *someone* c-commands *everyone*, and therefore has scope over it, but *everyone* does not c-command *someone*, and therefore does not have scope over it.

The idea underlying this analysis is that the ambiguity of sentences with multiple quantified phrases such as (26) is a function of their LF representations. In other words, the fact that such sentences have two possible interpretations follows from the possibility that they can have two different LF representations which give rise to two different scope relations between the quantified expressions. On the other hand, the possibility that ambiguous sentences such as (26) can have two LF representations is allowed by the assumption that quantified expressions undergo a movement transformation (QR) in the mapping from S-structure onto LF. Note that in the S-structure representation, (26b), of (26a), the quantified expression in the subject position (Spec-IP) asymmetrically c-commands the quantified expression in the object position. If the two quantified expressions are not assumed to undergo movement in the mapping onto LF, the scope ambiguity of (26a) will be hard to explain in structural terms. On the assumption that the scope relations between quantified expressions are indeed a function of their structural relations, the asymmetrical c-command relation between the two quantified expressions in the S-structure representations of sentences with multiple quantification will result in the availability of only one reading, contrary to fact.

5.2.4 Summary

The lexical entries of lexical items include an argument structure and a thematic structure which encode their selectional properties. Referential expressions are arguments, whereas non-referential expressions are non-arguments. The latter group includes expletives, *wh*-phrases, and quantified expressions. *Wh*-phrases in situ and quantified expressions undergo a movement transformation, called Quantifier Raising (QR), in the mapping from S-structure onto LF. QR leaves a variable trace which acts as the argument of the verb at the LF level. The movement undergone by quantified expressions in the mapping onto LF makes it possible to account for the scope ambiguities characteristic of sentences with multiple quantification. The scope ambiguities of these sentences are a function of their LF representations.

5.3 *The Structural Representation of Argument Structures*

5.3.1 Internal and External Arguments

So far, we have not discussed how the argument/thematic structures of lexical items are mapped onto structural representations, such that an object argument/thematic role is assigned to an object position and a subject argument/thematic role to a subject position. In view of the fact that 'object' and 'subject' are structure-based (functional) terms (see Chapter 2), it is somewhat inaccurate to use them to refer to arguments/thematic roles in argument/thematic structures. The terms usually used in relation to argument/thematic structures are **internal** and **external**. In a sentence like *The boy hit the ball*, *the ball* is the internal argument of the verb *hit*, and *the boy* its external argument.

Structurally, the terms 'internal' and 'external' correspond to the object position and the subject position, respectively:

32a. The boy hit the ball

32b.

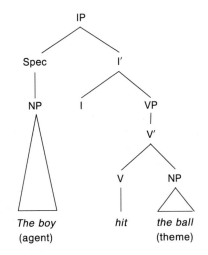

33a. Mary's translation of the book

33b.

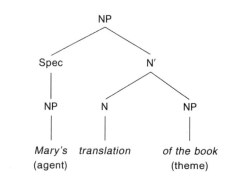

In both (32) and (33) the internal/theme argument is located inside (internal to) the single-bar projection of the lexical head. However, the two examples differ in that in the sentence (32) the external/agent argument of the verb is located outside (external to) the maximal projection of the verb (VP), whereas in the NP (33) the agent/external argument of the noun is located outside the single-bar projection of the noun (N′). We will take this discrepancy between sentences and NPs to suggest that, structurally, the notions 'external' and 'internal' are to be understood in relation to the single-bar projection of the lexical head rather than the maximal projection. This means that an external argument/thematic role is assigned to a position outside (external to) the single-bar projection of the lexical head, and an internal argument/thematic role is assigned to a position inside (internal to) the single-bar projection of the lexical head.

Having said that, there is a need for a mechanism to ensure that arguments/theta-roles are assigned to appropriate positions. A general fact about certain arguments/thematic roles is that they have an invariable status with respect to the external/internal dichotomy. For example, an agent argument/thematic role is invariably assigned to an external position. One way of ensuring that arguments/thematic roles are assigned to appropriate positions is to assume that arguments/thematic roles are specified in lexical entries as to whether they are internal or external. Here, we will adopt the notation in (34) below to distinguish between external and internal arguments/thematic roles (the symbol Ø indicates the absence of an argument/thematic role):

34a. *put*: agent < theme, location >
34b. *hit*: agent < theme >
34c. *run*: agent < Ø >

The internal arguments/thematic roles are included inside (internal to) the angled brackets, and the external argument/thematic role is located outside (external to) the brackets. Given the argument/thematic structures in (34a–c), the external argument/thematic role will be mapped onto an appropriate external position and the internal arguments/thematic roles onto internal positions. For the moment we shall assume, as we did in relation to subcategorization frames, that the order of internal arguments/thematic roles is specified in lexical entries, although in the next chapter we shall discuss reasons to believe that this does not need to be the case.

Lexical heads are said to **directly theta-mark** their internal arguments, and **indirectly theta-mark** their external argument. As with certain other terms, there is both a structural basis and a meaning (semantic?) basis for this terminological distinction. Structurally, internal arguments are sisters to the lexical head which selects them, whereas external arguments are not. Recall (from Chapters 2 and 4) that there is a close connection between the notion 'semantic/logical object' (internal argument) and the structural notion of sisterhood. Thus the internal argument (object) has a closer structural relation to the lexical head than does the external argument (subject). In Chapter 8 we shall see that this structural distinction between internal arguments and external arguments is reflected in a distinction in the range of certain grammatical processes affecting them.

As far as meaning is concerned, there is evidence which suggests that the thematic role of the external argument is determined by a combination of the meanings of the lexical head and its internal argument(s). Consider the following examples:

35a. John threw a ball
35b. John threw a fit (John is epileptic)
36a. John cut the bread
36b. John cut his finger

In (35a) *John* has an agent role, in both the idiomatic and non-idiomatic meanings of the sentence. In (35b), however, *John* can hardly be said to have an agent role. Likewise, in (36a) *John* has the agent role, whereas in (36b), with the reading where it is John's finger which is cut, *John* does not necessarily have the agent role. Thus the internal argument seems to play a role in determining the nature of the thematic role assigned to the external argument. In contrast, the external argument does not play a role in determining the nature of the thematic role assigned to the internal argument: replacing the external argument in (35) and (36) by a different one does not affect the nature of the thematic role assigned to the internal argument.

The external thematic role is sometimes said to be assigned via **predication**, where the term 'predicate', in this situation, refers to the lexical head and its internal arguments (the original notion of predication (Chapter 2)). In structural terms, the domain which includes the lexical head and its internal argument is VP in sentences. The theta-marking of the external argument is indirect in the sense that it is mediated by V' (or VP) in sentences. In contrast, the theta-marking of the internal argument is not mediated by any (intermediate) category, as the internal argument is a sister to the lexical head. We shall now discuss another situation where the lexical head is sometimes also said to indirectly theta-mark one of its arguments.

5.3.2   Objects of Prepositions

Consider the following examples:

37a. Mary put the book *(on the shelf)
37b. *Mary* I [$_{VP}$ *put* [$_{NP}$ *the book*] [$_{PP}$ *on* [$_{NP}$ *the shelf*]]]
37c. *put*: agent <theme, location>

38a. Mary gave the book *(to John)
38b. *Mary* I [$_{VP}$ *gave* [$_{NP}$ *the book*] [$_{PP}$ *to* [$_{NP}$ *John*]]]
38c. *give*: agent <theme, goal>

In both sentences the PP (indirect object) is an obligatory complement of the verb. The thematic role assigned to the NP object of the preposition is part of the thematic structure of the verb, as shown in (37c) and (38c). This means that the object of the preposition is in fact an internal argument of the verb. However, unlike the theme argument, the location argument and the goal argument are not structurally represented as sisters to the verb, but as sisters to the preposition.

In this situation, the verb is sometimes said to indirectly theta-mark the argument structurally represented as the object of the preposition. This relationship is indirect in the sense that it is mediated by the preposition, in the way shown in (39):

39. . . . [$_{VP}$ V NP [$_{PP}$ P NP]]

The verb theta-marks PP, under sisterhood, and the head of PP (i.e. P) **transmits** this theta-role to its NP object, also under sisterhood. The role of the preposition in this respect is restricted to transmitting to its object a thematic role originally assigned by the verb. The implication is that the preposition involved does not have a thematic structure of its own.

Now, compare (37) and (38) with the examples in (40) and (41).

40a. John baked fresh bread (for his guests)
40b. *John* I [$_{VP}$ *baked* [$_{NP}$ *fresh bread*] [$_{PP}$ *for* [$_{NP}$ his *guests*]]]
40c. *bake*: agent < theme, (benefactive) >
40c′. *bake*: agent < theme >

41a. John opened the door (with a key)
41b. *John* I [$_{VP}$ *opened* [$_{NP}$ *the door*] [$_{PP}$ *with* [$_{NP}$ *a key*]]]
41c. *open*: agent < theme, (instrumental) >
41c′. *open*: agent < theme >

Contrary to what is found in (37) and (38), the occurrence of the PP in these examples is not obligatory. In this situation, it is not clear whether the object of the preposition is an argument of the verb, so that the argument/thematic structure of the verb is as in (40c) and (41c), or is not an argument of the verb, so that the argument/thematic structure of the verb is as in (40c′) and (41c′). In the former scenario, the object of the preposition will have a status similar to that of the object of the preposition in (37) and (38) above, except that its occurrence is optional. Its theta-marking by the verb will operate as shown in (39). On the latter scenario, however, the object of the preposition will not have a similar status. Rather, its status will be similar to that of adjuncts, i.e. modifying constituents which are not part of the argument structure of the lexical head, and whose occurrence is usually optional. Its theta-marking will operate as shown in (42):

42. . . . [$_{VP}$ [$_{V'}$ V] [$_{PP}$ P NP]]]

The implication of this analysis is that the benefactive and instrumental prepositions in (40) and (41), unlike the dative and locative prepositions in (37) and (38), have a thematic structure of their own, on a par with verbs and other lexical categories. While the prepositions in (37) and (38) simply transmit to their object a thematic role originally assigned by the verb (to PP), the prepositions in (40) and (41) assign a thematic role of their own to their object. We will not try to settle the issue here.

Remaining with the topic of prepositions, a distinction is sometimes drawn between 'semantically empty' prepositions and other prepositions. For example, the preposition *on* in (37) is not 'semantically empty', since it contributes to the overall meaning of the sentence. Thus, its replacement with another (locative) preposition, e.g. *under*, results in a change of meaning (location). On the other hand, the preposition *of* found in NPs such as (33a) above, reproduced below as (43a), is said to be 'semantically empty', on the grounds that it does not contribute to the overall meaning of the NP:

43a. Mary's translation of the book
43b. Mary translated the book

As shown in sentence (43b), the presence of the preposition *of* is not necessary to convey the meaning underlying the thematic relation between the lexical head and its theme argument. Its obligatory presence in NPs such as (43) is motivated by some purely formal consideration, rather than by considerations of meaning involving thematic relations. The function of the preposition *of* in NPs will be discussed in the next chapter.

5.3.3 Argument Positions and Theta-Positions

The structural representation of argument/thematic structures gives rise to a typology of positions in the clause structure, which will be shown below and in the subsequent chapters to play a crucial role in determining certain grammatical relations. Positions can now be classified as to whether they are **A-positions** (argument positions) or **A′-positions** (A-bar or non-argument positions), and whether they are **θ-positions** (theta-(marked) positions) or **θ′-positions** (theta-bar or non-theta-(marked) positions).

An A-position is a position where an argument can be base-generated. Thus, all complement positions of lexical heads are A-positions, since these positions are usually occupied by the internal arguments of lexical heads. The subject position of IP (Spec-IP) and the subject position of NP (Spec-NP) are also A-positions, given that they are the positions where the external arguments of the verb and the noun are usually base-generated. The positions where arguments are not base-generated are A′-positions. These include the Spec position of CP (Spec-CP) and adjoined positions. Recall that Spec-CP is usually filled with *wh*-phrases moved from inside IP or (in the case of *whether*) base-generated there. Likewise, adjoined positions are occupied either by a moved category, as in Topicalization, or (in the case of adjectives and adverbs) by modifying categories which are not arguments of the lexical head.

A θ-position is a position which is assigned a thematic role by the lexical head. Thus, all complement positions of lexical heads are θ-positions, given that these positions are occupied by the internal arguments of the lexical head. However, not all subject positions are θ-positions. Whether the subject position is a θ-position in a given sentence depends on whether the lexical head assigns an external thematic role. In sentences which include a verb which assigns an external thematic role, the subject position is a θ-position. However, in sentences which include a verb which does not assign an external thematic role, the subject position is a θ′-position. Typical examples of the latter type are raising verbs. Recall that the subject position of clauses which include a raising verb can be occupied either by a subject moved from the embedded clause (44) or by the expletive *it* (45):

44a. Mary seems to have solved the problem
44b. *Mary*$_i$ *seems* [t$_i$ *to have solved the problem*]

45a. It seems that Mary has solved the problem
45b. *It seems* [*that Mary has solved the problem*]

46. *seem*: Ø < proposition >

The subject *Mary* in (44) is the external argument of the embedded verb *solve* which assigns it its external thematic role. The raising verb *seem* does not have an external thematic role of its own to assign, as shown in (46). For this reason the subject position of its clause can be occupied by an argument moved from another subject position, as in (44), or by a non-argument (an expletive), as in (45). Because raising verbs do not assign an external thematic role, the subject position of their clause is usually a θ′-position. We now have an explanation for the fact, pointed out in Chapter 2, that raising verbs are characterized by their ability to take the expletive (non-argument) *it* as a subject.

The other θ'-positions are Spec-CP and adjoined positions, which are usually occupied by non-arguments. Because these positions are usually occupied by non-arguments they are not assigned a thematic role, and because they are not assigned a thematic role they are θ'-positions. At this stage, it should be clear that while all A'-positions are also θ'-positions, not all A-positions are also θ-positions. While complement positions are usually both A-positions and θ-positions, there is no similar complete overlap with respect to the subject position of the sentence. We saw above that the subject position of the sentence (Spec-IP) is an A-position. However, whether it is a θ-position or a θ'-position depends on whether the verb of the sentence assigns an external thematic role. If the verb of the sentence assigns an external thematic role, the subject position is a θ-position, and if it does not assign an external thematic role (e.g. a raising verb), the subject position is a θ'-position. Thus there is no complete overlap between the class of A/A'-positions and the class of θ/θ'-positions.

5.3.4   Summary

Arguments/thematic roles of lexical items come specified as to whether they are internal or external. Internal arguments/thematic roles are assigned to internal positions, and external arguments/thematic roles to external positions, where the terms 'internal' and 'external' are understood in relation to the single projection of the lexical head. Lexical heads directly theta-mark their direct objects, and indirectly theta-mark their indirect objects and their subjects. Positions in structures can be classified according to the A/A' and θ/θ' dichotomies. Generally, A-positions are the positions where an argument can be base-generated, and A'-positions are the positions where an argument is not base-generated. θ-positions are the positions assigned a thematic role, and θ'-positions are the positions not assigned a thematic role.

5.4   *The Theta Criterion*

5.4.1   The Theta Criterion and the Projection Principle

Consider the following example:

47a. *John seems (that) Mary has solved the problem
47b. *John seems [CP (that) [IP Mary has solved the problem]]

In this sentence there is only one external thematic role available, assigned by the verb *solve* of the embedded clause to the argument *Mary*. Being a raising verb *seem* does not assign an external thematic role. However, the subject position of its clause is occupied by an argument, namely *John*. Recall that when this position is occupied by a non-argument the sentence is grammatical (*It seems that Mary has solved the problem*). Thus, the ungrammaticality of (47) seems to be due to the fact that it includes an argument which is not assigned a thematic role. This conclusion implies the condition that each argument must be assigned a thematic role. When this condition is violated, as in (47), ungrammaticality results.

With this in mind, consider now the following examples:

48a. *There solved a problem
48b. *There I [VP solved a problem]

49a. *Mary solved there

49b. *Mary I [VP solved [there]]

These examples represent the opposite situation, where the number of thematic roles available exceeds the number of arguments present. The verb *solve* has both an internal and an external thematic role to assign, but (48) and (49) include only one argument each, *there* being a non-argument. Thus the ungrammaticality of (48) and (49) seems due to the fact that one of the thematic roles of the verb is not assigned to an argument. This conclusion implies the condition that each thematic role must be assigned to an argument. When this condition is violated, as in (48) and (49), ungrammaticality results.

The two conditions we have identified represent two clauses of a more general condition on the representation of thematic structures called the **Theta Criterion**:

50. **Theta Criterion**
    a. Each argument must be assigned a thematic role.
    b. Each thematic role must be assigned to an argument.

The Theta Criterion is a condition on representations, and has the effect of excluding those where an argument is not assigned a thematic role or a thematic role is not assigned to an argument. Which of the three levels of representation (D-, S-structure, or LF) the Theta Criterion applies at is an important question to which we turn now.

Consider the following examples:

51a. Who solved which problem?

51b. D-str: [CP e [IP *Who* I [VP *solved* [*which problem*]]]]?

51c. S-str: [CP *Who*$_i$ [IP t$_i$ I [VP *solved* [*which problem*]]]]?

51d. LF: [CP *Who*$_i$ *which problem*$_j$ [IP t$_i$ I [VP *solved* t$_j$]]]]?

52a. John suspects everyone

52b. D-str: [CP e [IP *John* I [VP *suspects* [*everyone*]]]]

52c. S-str: [CP e [IP *John* I [VP *suspects* [*everyone*]]]]

52d. LF: [CP e [IP *everyone*$_i$ [IP *John* I [VP *suspects* t$_i$]]]]]

The D-structure and S-structure representations of (51a) and (52a) suggest that the Theta Criterion cannot be said to apply at D-structure and S-structure. In the D-structure of (51b), both the subject and the object positions are filled with non-arguments, and in the S-structure (51c) at least the object position is filled with a non-argument. Not until the LF level (51c) are both argument positions filled with arguments, namely the variable traces of the *wh*-phrases raised by QR. A similar situation is found in (52). Not until the LF level (52d) is the internal argument position of the verb filled with an argument, namely the variable trace of the quantified phrase raised by QR in the mapping from S-structure onto LF.

The conclusion which emerges is that the Theta Criterion applies at LF – which is not surprising, given that LF is the level where meaning relations, which crucially include thematic relations, are determined. However, the situation is more complicated than it seems. The Theta Criterion is a condition on the structural representation of the thematic structures of lexical categories. The thematic structures of lexical categories encode their selectional and therefore lexical properties. The lexical properties of categories are required by PP (the Projection Principle) to be observed at all syntactic levels of representation (D-, S-structure, and LF) (see Chapter 4). It follows from this situation that the Theta Criterion must hold at all levels of representation (by virtue of PP). At the same time, we have seen in (51) and (52) that their D-structure and S-structure representations involve a violation of the Theta Criterion. As a matter of fact, this is one of the major problems with the theory developed here, which we shall not try to solve here.

5.4.2   The Theta Criterion and Chains

5.4.2.1   A-Chains and A'-Chains   Consider the following examples:

53a. Mary seems to have solved the problem
53b. [$_{IP}$ *Mary*$_i$ I [$_{VP}$ *seems* [t$_i$ *to have solved the problem*]]]

54a. *Mary believes to have solved the problem
54b. *[$_{IP}$ *Mary*$_i$ I[$_{VP}$ *believes* [t$_i$ *to have solved the problem*]]]

Recall that raising verbs such as *seem* do not assign an external thematic role. The verb *believe* differs from raising verbs in that it assigns an external thematic role, as shown in *John believes Mary to have solved the problem*. Comparing the two examples (53) and (54), the crucial difference seems to be that, whereas the raised argument in (53) is assigned only one (external) thematic role, by the verb of the embedded clause, its counterpart in (54) is assigned two (external) thematic roles, one by the verb of the embedded clause and the other by the verb of the root clause. It seems, therefore, that the ungrammaticality of (54) is due to the fact that the raised argument is assigned two thematic roles, although there may be other considerations involved. This conclusion implies another condition on the assignment of thematic roles: that each argument be assigned one and only one thematic role.

One way of incorporating this condition into the Theta Criterion is to include a uniqueness condition in its definition, as in (55):

55. **Theta Criterion**
    a. Each argument must be assigned one and only one thematic role.
    b. Each thematic role must be assigned to one and only one argument.

Note that example (54) does not necessarily force a **uniqueness condition** on clause (b), although it does force a uniqueness condition on clause (a). However, it is not difficult to see why a uniqueness condition should also be incorporated into clause (b). The number of arguments associated with a given lexical head usually corresponds to the number of thematic roles the lexical head assigns. The possibility of allowing one thematic role to be assigned to more than one argument will mean that, in principle, a head can take any number of arguments, an undesirable consequence. It will also lead to ambiguity of thematic functions in relation to individual arguments, also an undesirable consequence for obvious reasons.

Let us now go back to example (53). Given that the assignment of thematic roles is determined at LF, the external thematic role of the verb of the embedded clause, strictly speaking, is assigned to the trace of the raised NP. Recall that the subject position of clauses containing a raising predicate is a θ'-position. The trace, located in a θ-position, is said to **transmit** the thematic role it receives to its antecedent located in a θ'-position. The trace and its antecedent are said to form a (movement) **chain**, where the antecedent, i.e. the raised NP in (53), is the **head** (of the chain) and the trace is the **root/tail** (of the chain).

The crucial implication of (53) is that the Theta Criterion should be viewed as a condition on the assignment of thematic roles to individual arguments as well as argument chains. As a matter of fact, the Theta Criterion can be exclusively viewed as a condition on chains, if we extend the notion 'chain' to include non-moved categories, such as *Mary* and *the problem* in *Mary solved the problem*. Chains will then differ as to whether they consist of one member, e.g. {*Mary*} and {*the problem*} in the previous sentence, or more than one member, e.g. {*Mary, t*} in example (53). Although this discussion requires that we substitute the expression 'argument chain' for the term 'argument' in the definition of the Theta Criterion, we will leave the definition as it is in (55).

The idea that the Theta Criterion holds for chains implies a severe restriction on movement transformations, so that only those which move an argument (from a θ-position) to a θ′-position are allowed. Movement of an argument (from a θ-position) to another θ-position will result in the derivation of a chain with two thematic roles, in violation of the Theta Criterion. It is precisely for this reason that raising of the NP *Mary* to the subject position of the root clause in (54) is excluded: the derived chain {*Mary, t*} has two thematic roles, the external thematic role of the embedded verb, assigned to *t*, and the external thematic role of the root verb, assigned to *Mary*. Our next step is to check whether the other movement transformations discussed in chapter 3 are consistent with this requirement. The discussion of NP-movement in passives is postponed to a later section in this chapter. The transformations which affect head categories such as I and V are ignored here, as they are not directly relevant to the discussion.

The following examples illustrate Topicalization, *Wh*-movement, and QR:

56a. This problem, I can solve
56b. [$_{CP}$ e [$_{IP}$ *This problem*$_i$ [$_{IP}$ *I can* [$_{VP}$ *solve* t$_i$]]]]

57a. Which problem did Mary solve?
57b. [$_{CP}$ *Which problem*$_i$ *did* [$_{IP}$ *Mary* I [$_{VP}$ *solve* t$_i$]]]?

58a. John suspects everyone
58b. [$_{CP}$ e [$_{IP}$ *everyone*$_i$ [$_{IP}$ *John* I [$_{VP}$ *suspects* t$_i$]]]]

Although (at least) some of these transformations do not affect arguments as such, they all have in common with NP-movement the fact that their target is a θ′-position. Recall that Spec-CP and adjoined positions are θ′-positions, so that the movement chains derived by Topicalization, *Wh*-movement, and QR all have a single thematic role each, assigned to the trace. The chains derived by Topicalization, *Wh*-movement, and QR differ from the chains derived by NP-movement in one important respect. The target of NP-movement (Spec-IP) is an A-position, so that the chain derived by this movement is an **A-chain** (i.e. a chain whose head is located in an A-position). On the other hand, the target of Topicalization, *Wh*-movement and QR is an A′-position, and therefore the chain derived by them is an **A′-chain** (i.e. a chain whose head is located in an A′-position). As far as the Theta Criterion is concerned, the relevant member of (at least some) A′-chains is the variable trace, as the head is usually a non-argument.

5.4.2.2 Raising to Object   Consider the following examples:

59a. John believes Mary to be a genius
59b. John considers Bill to be a fool

The NPs *Mary* and *Bill* are the external arguments of the embedded predicates (*be*) *a genius* and (*be*) *a fool*, respectively. Therefore, they are expected to occupy the external argument position of the embedded clause, i.e. the Spec position of IP. However, these NPs exhibit certain properties which seem to suggest that they function grammatically as the direct objects of the root verbs *believe* and *consider*, even though thematically they are related to the predicate of the embedded clause.

Some of these properties are illustrated in the following examples, using (59) for illustration:

60a. John believes her/*she to be a genius
60b. Mary is believed to be a genius
60c. John (sincerely) believes (*sincerely) Mary to be a genius

(60a) shows that when the NP in question is a pronoun, it is realized as the objective form of the pronoun *her/him/them*, rather than the subjective form *she/he/they*. This fact suggests that the NP is the direct object of the root verb. (60b) shows that the NP in question can move to the subject position of the root clause when the verb of this clause is in the passive form. This fact also suggests that the NP is the direct object of the root verb, given that the property of moving to the subject position in passives is exclusively associated with the direct object of the passive verb in Standard English. Finally, (60c) shows that a VP-adverb cannot intervene between the root verb and the NP in question, just as a VP-adverb generally cannot intervene between the verb and its direct object (see Chapter 3).

An obvious way of reconciling the fact that the NP in question is the external argument (subject) of the embedded predicate with the fact that it has object-like properties is to assume that it is base-generated in the external argument position (subject position) of the embedded clause and subsequently moved to the object position of the root verb. This instance of NP-movement can be called Subject-to-Object raising (or Raising-to-Object):

61a. D-str: [$_{IP}$ *John* I [$_{VP}$ *believes* [$_{NP}$ e] [$_{IP}$ *Mary to be a genius*]]]
61b. S-str: [$_{IP}$ *John* I [$_{VP}$ *believes* [$_{NP}$ *Mary$_i$*] [$_{IP}$ t$_i$ *to be a genius*]]]

62a. The problem was solved
62b. [$_{IP}$ *The problem$_i$* was [$_{VP}$ *solved* t$_i$]]

The reasoning underlying the derivation in (61) is in essence similar to the reasoning underlying the derivation of passives in (62). Recall that the derivation of passives is intended to reconcile the status of the moved NP as the internal argument of the verb with the fact that it has subject-like properties: it occupies Spec-IP and is in Spec-Head Agreement with (the Agr category of) I.

However, while the derivation of passives is consistent with the Theta Criterion, as we will see below, the derivation outlined in (61) is not. Notice that the analysis outlined in (61) assumes the presence of an empty object position in the root clause at D-structure which is subsequently filled by the moved NP. In the current system, object positions exist in so far as they are the structural realization of the internal argument of the lexical head. It follows that every existing object (internal argument) position is assigned a thematic role by the lexical head which selects it (otherwise it would not exist). In view of this, movement of the external argument of the embedded predicate to the object position in the root clause shown in (61), and, in fact, movement to a selected (object) position in general, inevitably leads to the derivation of a chain with two thematic roles, and therefore to a violation of the Theta Criterion.

The analysis of the constructions in (59) which is consistent with the Theta Criterion is the non-movement analysis shown in (63) below, where the embedded subject remains in the embedded subject position at S-structure:

63a. D/S-str: *John believes [Mary to be a genius]*
63b. D/S-str: *John considers [Bill to be a fool]*

Notice, however, that although this analysis succeeds in avoiding a violation of the Theta Criterion it still has the major task of explaining the object-like properties of the embedded subject noted above. Unfortunately, for this we will have to wait until the next chapter, where some notions crucial to the analysis are introduced and explained. At the moment, note that the root verbs which occur in constructions such as (63a,b) belong to a limited class of verbs, sometimes called **believe-type** verbs.

5.4.2.3 *Dative Shift*   Compare the following examples:

64a. Mary gave the book to John
64b. Mary I [$_{VP}$ gave [$_{NP}$ the book] [$_{PP}$ to John]]
65a. Mary gave John the book
65b. Mary I [$_{VP}$ gave [$_{NP}$ John] [$_{NP}$ the book]]

The two sentences are synonymous, although they differ in the order of complements and in the presence versus absence of the preposition *to*. In (64) the goal argument *John* appears as the indirect object, but in (65) it occupies the position of the direct object and, moreover, displays direct object-like properties:

66a. John was given the book (by Mary)
66b. Mary (reluctantly) gave (*reluctantly) John the book

The possibility that (65) is also derived from the (common) underlying structure (64b), by a transformation which changes the order of the two arguments (and deletes the preposition *to*), is excluded by the Theta Criterion. Whether the two arguments are assumed to switch places or the goal argument alone is assumed to move to an empty complement position located to the left of the theme argument, a chain with two thematic roles will inevitably be derived.

We are therefore forced to assume, at least for the time being, that (64a) and (65a) derive from different D-structures, shown in (64b) and (65b), where the two arguments have different positions, and therefore different functions. There is evidence which suggests that the pattern [V NP NP] shown in (64), called **Dative Shift**, is unlikely to be derived by a transformational rule from an underlying structure with the order [V NP PP]. Although a substantial number of verbs which select two internal arguments, e.g. *give, send, buy*, allow the Dative Shift pattern, there are verbs which do not. For example, although the verb *donate* is close in meaning to the verb *give*, it does not tolerate the Dative Shift pattern. Likewise, although the verb *transmit* is close in meaning to the verb *send*, it does not tolerate the Dative Shift pattern:

67a. Mary donated (the) money to the charity
67b. *Mary donated the charity (the) money

68a. Mary sent the letter to John
68b. Mary sent John the letter

69a. Mary transmitted the message to John
69b. *Mary transmitted John the message

Transformational rules are usually not sensitive to individual lexical items, given that they operate on (classes of) categories. In view of this, it is unlikely that the Dative Shift pattern is derived by a transformational rule, as the rule in question would have to be made sensitive to individual lexical items to exclude ungrammatical sentences such as (67b) and (69b). If the Dative Shift pattern is derived at all, it must be in terms of a rule which applies in the Lexicon and affects the argument structure of certain verbs but not of others. The nature of some of these rules is the subject of our discussion in the next section.

5.4.3   Summary

The assignment of thematic roles is subject to a condition called the Theta Criterion. The latter establishes a one-to-one correspondence between thematic roles and arguments, such that each argument is assigned one and only one thematic role and each thematic role is assigned to one and only one argument. In essence, the Theta Criterion is a well-formedness condition on chains, which has the consequence of restricting movement of arguments to θ'-positions (non-theta-marked positions). Movement to θ-positions (theta-marked positions), e.g. selected complement positions, is excluded on the grounds that it leads to the derivation of chains with two thematic roles. Chains fall into two classes, A-chains, derived by movement to A-positions, and A'-chains, derived by movement to A'-positions.

5.5   *Argument Structures and Lexical Rules of Derivation*

5.5.1   Verbal Passives

Compare the passive sentence in (70) to its active counterpart in (71):

70a. The problem was solved (by Mary)
70b. [$_{IP}$ *The problem*$_i$ *was* [$_{VP}$ *solved* t$_i$ (*by Mary*)]]

71a. Mary solved the problem
71b. [$_{IP}$ *Mary* I [$_{VP}$ *solved the problem*]]

The ability of the internal argument to move to the subject position in the passive sentence (70) implies, given the Theta Criterion, that the subject position of passives (like that of raising predicates) must be a θ'-position. However, looking at the active sentence (71), we see that the verb *solve* does indeed assign an external thematic role to the subject position of its clause. Comparing the two sentences, it seems that the verb assigns the external thematic role when it is in the active form, but not when it is the passive form. Why?

Before we move on to a possible explanation for the noted difference between active and passive verbs, a word about the *by*-phrase. The optional presence of the *by*-phrase in passives, among other properties, suggests that it has the structural status of an adjunct. On the other hand, its linear position suggests that it is right-adjoined to VP (or V'), as shown in structure (72). Although the *by*-phrase is somehow associated with the external argument of the passive verb, it is unlikely that it receives the external thematic role of the passive verb in the way external arguments receive theirs from active verbs. We are in fact forced to assume, as pointed out above, that passive verbs do not assign an external

72.

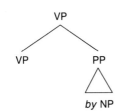

by NP

thematic role. If they did, there would be no reason why it should not be assigned to the canonical external argument position (Spec-IP) instead of to an adjunct.

Passive verbs are derived by attachment of the **passive morpheme** -*ed*/-*en* to the active form of (regular) verbs. This process of affixation does not result in the derivation of a new category; what is derived from attaching the passive morpheme to the (active form of the) verb is still a verb. Recall (from Chapter 2) that there are (derivational) affixes which do not change the categorial nature of the base forms they attach to in the Lexicon. In view of this, it is not implausible to assume that the process which derives passive verbs from active verbs takes place in the Lexicon. Let us assume further that the lexical rule in question does more than simply attach the passive morpheme to the base (active) form of the verb. More precisely, the rule in question affects the argument structure of the base verb in such a way as to 'suppress' its external argument. The complex rule involved can be represented as in (73):

73a. *solve*: $[+ V; - N] (= V)$
  agent $<$ theme $> \rightarrow$
73b. *solved*: $[+ V; - N] (= V)$
  Ø $<$ theme $>$

The derived passive form in (73b) differs from the base active form in (73a) in that its argument/thematic structure lacks an external argument/thematic role. However, the two forms are identical categorially, even though the passive form (73b) has the additional passive morpheme. Now, since the argument/thematic structure of the passive verb does not include an external argument/thematic role, the subject position of passive sentences is a θ'-position, and therefore a legitimate target for a moved argument. The chain derived by movement of the internal argument to the subject position in passives has only one thematic role, and is therefore consistent with the Theta Criterion. The situation is, however, more complicated than it seems, as we will discover shortly.

5.5.2. Adjectival Passives

Compare the passive sentence above with the examples in (74a, b):

74a. The island was uninhabited
74b. The performance was uninterrupted

The participles *uninhabited* and *uninterrupted* in these examples are said to be instances of **adjectival passives**, as opposed to their counterpart in (70) above which is an instance of **verbal passives**. The participles in (74a, b) are passive in the sense that their internal argument surfaces as the subject of the sentence, on a par with the verbal passive in (70). On the other hand, they are adjectival because they display properties usually associated with adjectives.

One of the adjectival properties of the participles in (74a, b) relates to their ability to take the negative prefix *un*-. This prefix usually attaches to adjectives, as shown in (75a), but never to verbs, as shown in (75b) below (recall that the negative prefix *un*- should be distinguished from the homophonous 'reversative' prefix found in verbs such as *to unbutton, to unpack, to uncover* (Chapter 1)):

75a. unhappy, unkind, unsympathetic
75b. *to uninhabit (an island), *to uninterrupt (a performance)

Secondly, these participles can modify nouns, as shown in (76a,b), a function which is usually associated with adjectives, and which excludes verbs altogether:

76a. The uninhabited island
76b. The uninterrupted performance

Thirdly, they can function as complements of verbs such as *remain* and *seem*, which usually select adjectives but not verbs:

77a. The island seemed uninhabited
77b. The performance remained uninterrupted

All three properties, among others, indicate that the participles in (74a, b) above are adjectival in nature, and therefore categorially distinct from verbal passives.

The relevant part of the rule involved in the derivation of adjectival passives from a base verb can be stated as in (78):

78a. *inhabit*: $[+ \text{ V} - \text{N}]$ $(= \text{V})$ $\Rightarrow$
78b. *inhabited*: $[+ \text{ V} + \text{N}]$ $(= \text{A})$

Recall (from Chapter 2) that adjectives have the feature complex shown in (78b). Recall also that the categorial features of a derived complex are determined by the features of the affix, which acts as the head of the derived complex. It follows that the adjectival features of the participle in (78b) are the features of the affix *-ed*, the base being a verb. Comparing the rule in (78a, b) to the rule in (73) above, involved in the lexical derivation of verbal passives, it seems that we are dealing with two different, though homophonous, affixes. The affix which appears on verbal passives has verbal features, so that when it is affixed to a verb the derived complex is still a verbal category. On the other hand, the affix which appears on adjectival passives has adjectival features, so that when it is affixed to a verb the derived complex is an adjectival category.

Turning now to the argument/thematic structure of adjectival passives, we saw above that they resemble verbal passives in that their internal argument surfaces in the subject position of the sentence. Initially, this suggests that adjectival passives have a derivation similar to that of verbal passives, i.e. that they undergo a lexical process which 'suppresses' the external argument/thematic role of the base verb, and a syntactic process (NP-movement) which moves their internal argument to the subject position of the sentence. However, for reasons which we will not explore here, adjectival passives are often assumed to have a different derivation, whose main characteristic is that it is exclusively lexical. The steps of the derivation relevant to our discussion so far are listed in (79) (adapted from Borer (1984b) and Levin and Rappaport (1986)):

79. **Properties of Adjectival Passive Formation (APF)**

    a. Affixation of the passive morpheme *-ed/-en*
      e.g. interrupt → interrupted
    b. Change of category
      e.g. interrupt: $[+\text{V} -\text{N}]$ → interrupted: $[+\text{V} +\text{N}]$
    c. Suppression of the external role of the base verb
      e.g. interrupt: agent $<$theme$>$ → interrupted: $\emptyset$ $<$theme$>$
    d. Externalization of an internal role of the base verb
      e.g. interrupted: $\emptyset$ $<$theme$>$ → theme $<\emptyset>$

Given this derivation, sentences which include adjectival passives, such as (74b) above, have the structural representation shown in (80):

80a. The performance was uninterrupted
80b. D-str. [IP *The performance* I [VP [V *was*] [AP *uninterrupted*]]]
80c. S-str. [IP *The performance* I [VP [V *was*] [AP *uninterrupted*]]]

The crucial difference between adjectival passives and verbal passives, so far, is that adjectival passives do not involve movement of the internal argument to the subject position in the Syntax. The externalization of the internal argument takes place in the Lexicon, and the internal argument is mapped directly onto the subject position of the sentence, as shown in (80b, c). In verbal passives, however, the externalization of the internal argument takes place in the Syntax, as the internal argument is mapped directly onto the internal argument position at D-structure.

5.5.3   Implicit Arguments

According to the analysis so far, the lexical derivation of both verbal passives and adjectival passives involves the 'suppression' of the external argument/thematic role of the base verb. However, there is evidence which suggests that, while the lexical derivation of adjectival passives does indeed involve the 'suppression' of the external argument/thematic role, this is unlikely to be the case in the lexical derivation of verbal passives. Verbal passives will be shown to include an **implicit** external argument which does not have a counterpart in adjectival passives.

One piece of evidence relates to the *by*-phrase. Unlike verbal passives, adjectival passives do not seem to tolerate a *by*-phrase:

81a. The ball was kicked (by Mary)
81b. The room was unoccupied (*by Mary)

The role of the *by*-phrase in verbal passives such as (81a) is to specify the identity of the individual who performs the act described by the verb, i.e. the external argument. When the *by*-phrase is missing, the external argument is said to have an arbitrary interpretation, roughly paraphrasable as '(some)one' (Chapter 3). The fact that the interpretation of verbal passives involves an external argument (even when the *by*-phrase is missing) implies that, contrary to what we assumed earlier, their external argument is not 'suppressed'. In contrast, the interpretation of adjectival passives does not involve an external argument, hence the fact that they do not tolerate a *by*-phrase. Adjectival passives are sometimes said to have a **state** reading, as opposed to verbal passives, which tend to have an **event** reading. (81b), for example, describes the state of the room at a given point in time rather than the event which led to the room being unoccupied.

Another piece of evidence relates to subject-oriented (or agent-oriented) adverbs such as *deliberately* and *intentionally*, so called because they tend to modify the external argument, typically agent. These adverbs can occur freely with verbal passives, but not so with adjectival passives:

82a. The ball was (intentionally) kicked (by Mary)
82b. The room was (*intentionally) unoccupied

In the verbal passive (82a) the adverb modifies the external argument of the verb, even when the *by*-phrase is missing. Once again, this suggests that the external argument/thematic role of verbal passives is somehow 'implicit'. On the other hand, the fact that adjectival passives do not tolerate subject-oriented adverbs implies that they lack a corresponding 'implicit' external argument/thematic role.

The third piece of evidence relates to the phenomenon of control, briefly discussed in the previous chapter. Verbal passives allow control of the PRO subject of a non-finite purpose clause, whereas adjectival passives do not:

83a. The ball was kicked (to make a point)
83b. *The ball was kicked* [PRO *to make a point*]

84a. The room was unoccupied (*to make a point)
84b. **The room was unoccupied* [PRO *to make a point*]

The controller of PRO in the verbal passive (83) is the 'implicit' external argument of the passive verb. (84) indicates that, contrary to verbal passives, adjectival passives lack this argument/thematic role.

The evidence reviewed so far shows clearly that it is inaccurate to assume, as we did above, that the external argument of the base verb is 'suppressed', i.e. eliminated, in the lexical derivation of verbal passives. To the extent that the term 'suppressed' can be used in relation to the derivation of verbal passives, it should be understood to mean 'suspended', i.e. not eliminated but at the same time not assigned to the external argument position. Recall that it is necessary to assume that the external thematic role is not assigned to Spec-IP, as movement of the internal argument to this position in the Syntax, typical of verbal passives, would be incompatible with the requirement of the Theta Criterion. Obviously, it is desirable to clarify the status of 'suspended' or 'implicit' arguments in relation to the structural representation of passives. However, this task will not be carried out here. The reader is referred to the Further Reading section for some related references.

5.5.4   Ergatives and Middles

Compare the following examples:

85a. John broke the vase
85b. The vase broke

English, like many other languages, has a class of verbs which enter into a **transitivity/ ergativity alternation** of the type illustrated in (85). In (85a) the verb *break* has two arguments, an agent, realized as the subject, and a theme, realized as the object. In (85b), however, the verb *break* has only the theme argument, this time realized as the subject. In the latter example, the verb resembles verbal and adjectival passives, although, unlike verbal and adjectival passives, it does not seem to display a morpheme which could be related to this property. The verb is said to be **transitive** in (85a) and **ergative** in (85b). Among the other verbs which enter into the transitivity/ergativity alternation are *open*, *crack*, *bend*, *shorten*, *drop* and *spin*.

Two major questions arise in relation to the transitive/ ergative pairs. First, what is the status of the external argument/thematic role in the ergative member of the pair (85b)? Is it 'eliminated', as in adjectival passives, or simply 'suspended', as in verbal passives? Secondly, which of the two members of the pair is derived and which is basic? Is the ergative member derived from the transitive member or the other way round? Obviously, it is desirable not to have a separate entry for each member. Semantically related categories should be derivable one from the other, unless there are reasons to believe otherwise. Since the answer to the second question somewhat depends on the answer to the first, we shall deal with the first question first.

An obvious way of checking whether the external argument/thematic role in the ergative member is 'eliminated' or simply 'suspended' is to apply the tests discussed above in relation to verbal and adjectival passives:

86a. The vase broke (*by John)
86b. The vase broke (*intentionally)
86c. The vase broke (*to prove a point)

As shown by these examples, ergatives are incompatible with a *by*-phrase (86a), an agent-oriented adverb (86b), and with control of a PRO subject of a purpose clause (86c). Thus ergatives pattern with adjectival passives, rather than verbal passives, leading to the conclusion that their external theta-role is 'eliminated', rather than simply 'suspended'.

Having concluded that, there are in principle two possible ways of deriving (85b), where the internal argument occupies the (external) subject position. One is that the theme argument is externalized by a lexical rule of the type involved in the derivation of adjectival passives. This means that the theme argument is mapped directly onto the subject position at D-structure, as shown in (87) below. The other possibility is that, while the external argument is 'eliminated', the theme argument remains unaffected, as in the derivation of verbal passives. This means that the theme argument is mapped onto an internal argument position at D-structure, and subsequently moved to the subject position by NP-movement, as shown in (88):

87a. *break* $_{(trans)}$: agent < theme > → *break* $_{(erg)}$: theme < Ø >
87b. D-str. [$_{IP}$ the vase [$_{VP}$ broke]]

88a. *break* $_{(trans)}$: agent < theme > → *break* $_{(erg)}$: Ø < theme >
88b. D-str. [$_{IP}$ e [$_{VP}$ *broke the vase*]]
88c. S-str. [$_{IP}$ *The vase*$_i$ [$_{VP}$ *broke* t$_i$]]

(87) represents an exclusively lexical derivation of ergatives, whereas (88) represents a partly lexical and partly syntactic derivation of ergatives. The lexical part of the derivation 'eliminates' the external argument of the base, and the syntactic part moves the internal argument to the subject position. As far as English is concerned, it is not clear which of the two analyses is the more plausible. However, there is fairly strong evidence from other languages in favour of the analysis outlined in (88), i.e. the partly lexical, partly syntactic derivation of ergatives. The reader is referred to the Further Reading section on this point.

Let us now turn to the second question: which of the two members of the pair (ergative or transitive) is derived and which is basic? The idea that the external thematic role is 'eliminated', shared by the two analyses outlined in (87) and (88), presupposes that it is the ergative member which is derived from the transitive member, by the 'elimination' of the external argument/thematic role of the transitive member. However, this is by no means the only possibility. It is conceivable that the transitive member is derived from the ergative member by a lexical operation which adds an external argument to the argument structure of the ergative member:

89. *break* $_{(erg)}$: Ø < theme > → *break* $_{(trans)}$: agent < theme >

This analysis implies that the semantic structure of the transitive *break* is more complex than it appears, so that example (85a) above means something like 'John caused the vase to be broken'. This reading is sometimes referred to as the **causative** reading, and the lexical process shown in (89) as **causativization**. We will not try to decide between the two analyses here. A detailed analysis of causative constructions in English and other languages is included in Chapter 9.

Ergatives are traditionally distinguished from another class of verbs, called **middles**, although the latter resemble ergatives in that their internal argument appears in the subject position, and in that, in English, they do not display a morpheme which could be related to this property. The verbs *translate* and *bribe* in (90a, b) are said to have a middle use (or reading):

90a. Greek translates easily
90b. Bureaucrats bribe easily

A distinctive property of middles is that they are usually 'adorned'. This is most frequently done with adverbs, as in (90a, b), but other elements can also serve this function, such as negation (92a), a quantified subject (92b), among other elements. Examples (91a, b) show that 'adornment' is obligatory with middles:

91a. *Greek translates
91b. *Bureaucrats bribe

92a. This bread doesn't/won't cut
92b. Not many/few bureaucrats bribe

Obviously, an adequate analysis of middles should be able to explain, among other things, why they have to be 'adorned'. However, this task is beyond the limits of this book. Here, we shall simply outline some basic properties of middles bearing on their argument/thematic structure.

Although middles resemble ergatives in that their subject is thematically an internal argument, the interpretation of middles is said to differ fundamentally, in that it involves an agent, on a par with that of verbal passives. The sentence in (90a), for example, means, roughly, 'It is easy for one to translate Greek'. No such reading is possible with ergatives, so that 'The vase broke' does not mean 'Someone broke the vase'. Having said that, the agent reading of middles is incompatible with the fact that, unlike verbal passives, they fail the usual tests for the presence of an 'implicit' external argument/thematic role:

93a. *The book sold (quickly) by Mary
93b. *The book sold voluntarily
93c. *The book sold (widely) [PRO to make money]

In this respect, middles pattern with ergatives and adjectival passives, rather than with verbal passives, although, as noted above, they resemble verbal passives in that an agent argument/role figures in their interpretation. A proper analysis for middles will, therefore, have to reconcile these apparently contradictory properties. As this task is beyond the limits of this book, we will leave the issue open, and turn to a discussion of how middles can be derived.

As with ergatives, middles can a priori be derived in one of two possible ways. One possibility is that the internal argument/thematic role of the base verb is externalized in the Lexicon, in which case the theme role will be mapped directly onto the subject position at D-structure, as shown in (94) below. The other possibility is that the internal argument/ thematic role of the base is not affected by the lexical rule, in which case it will be mapped onto the internal argument position at D-structure, and subsequently moved to the subject position by NP-movement, as shown in (95):

94a. *bribe* (trans) : agent < theme > → *bribe* (middle) : theme < Ø >
94b. D-str. [$_{IP}$ *Bureaucrats* [$_{VP}$ *bribe easily*]

95a. *bribe* (trans) : agent < theme > → *bribe* (middle) : Ø < theme >
95b. D-str. [$_{IP}$ e I [$_{VP}$ *bribe bureaucrats easily*]]
95c. S-str. [$_{IP}$ *Bureaucrats*$_i$ I [$_{VP}$ *bribe* t$_i$ *easily*]]

The analysis outlined in (94) represents an exclusively lexical derivation of middles, whereas the one in (95) represents a partly lexical and partly syntactic derivation of middles. Note with respect to the latter that, because of the Theta Criterion, the subject position has to be a θ'-position, even though the external argument figures in the interpretation of middles.

5.5.5   Derived nominals

Compare the sentences in (96) with the noun phrases in (97):

96a. The barbarians destroyed the city
96b. *The barbarians destroyed
96c. *There destroyed the city

97a. The barbarians' destruction of the city was awful
97b. The destruction of the city was awful
97c. The destruction was awful

Examples (96a–c) illustrate the familiar fact that arguments of verbs must be syntactically realized, a consequence of the Theta Criterion and PP. Examples (97a–c), on the other hand, show that the corresponding arguments of the related noun do not have to be syntactically realized. This implies that the derivation of nouns from verbs affects the argument structure of the base verb, such that the syntactic realization of the arguments becomes non-obligatory.

   As far as the external argument/thematic role is concerned, it can be affected in one of the two possible ways discussed above. It can either be 'eliminated', as in the derivation of adjectival passives, or simply 'suspended', as in the derivation of verbal passives. The usual tests for detecting the presence of an 'implicit' external argument give a positive result:

98a. The destruction of the city (by the barbarians)
98b. The deliberate destruction of the city
98c. The destruction of the city [PRO to prove a point]

It seems, therefore, that derived nominals resemble verbal passives in that their external argument/thematic role is 'implicit', though apparently not syntactically realized. Presumably, whatever the nature of the analysis for verbal passives it should be possible to extend it to derived nominals.

   Another respect in which derived nominals seem to resemble verbal passives, as well as other complex predicates, relates to the ability of the internal argument to appear in the subject position of NP, giving rise to a construction sometimes referred to as 'nominal passive' or 'passive in NP':

99a. The city's destruction (by the barbarians)
99b. D-str. [$_{NP}$ e [$_{N'}$ *destruction the city*]
99c. S-str. [$_{NP}$ *The city$_i$'s* [$_{N'}$ *destruction* t$_i$]

If (99a) is an instance of passivization in the sense associated with verbal passives, then it has the derivation outlined in (99b,c), where the internal argument is base-generated in the complement position and subsequently moved to the subject position via NP-movement.

   However, there are reasons to doubt the apparent parallelism with verbal passives, chief among them the fact that complements of certain nouns cannot appear in the subject position of the NP. Compare the 'nominal passives' in (100a,b) with their verbal counterparts in (100a,b):

100a. *The book's discussion (by Mary)
100b. *The issue's avoidance (by John)

101a. The book was discussed (by Mary)
101b. The issue was avoided (by John)

The contrast illustrated by these examples implies a restriction on the ability of internal arguments of nouns to appear in the subject position of the noun phrase, known as the **Affectedness Constraint**. For an internal argument of a noun to be able to appear in the subject position of the NP, it has to be affected by the event depicted by the head noun, where an affected NP is, roughly, one which undergoes a change in state or location. The internal argument of *destruction*, for example, is affected in the intended sense, whereas the internal argument of *discussion* and *avoidance* are not, hence the fact that they cannot appear in the subject position of NP.

The Affectedness Constraint is not likely to be a condition on NP-movement, since the latter would have to be made sensitive to the categorial nature of the predicate (whether it is a verb or a noun). Rather, the Affectedness Constraint suggests an exclusively lexical derivation, so that the internal argument in so-called 'nominal passives' is directly mapped onto the subject position. Notice that the definition of 'affected' is similar to the definition of 'theme', implying a lexical rule which makes specific reference to 'theme'. The status of the external argument in 'nominal passives' remains somewhat obscure, as in verbal passives. It is neither 'eliminated' nor, apparently, syntactically realized, but, somehow, 'suspended'. A possible analysis for the status of 'implicit' agentive arguments in NPs will be discussed in Chapter 7.

5.5.6 Summary

Lexical rules of derivation can affect the argument/thematic structure of lexical items. The lexical derivation of verbal passives involves the 'suspension' of the external argument/ thematic role of the base, such that it is neither assigned to the external argument position (Spec-IP) nor 'eliminated' altogether. This implies that the subject position of passives, like that of raising predicates, is a θ'-position, and therefore a legitimate target for a moved argument. The lexical derivation of adjectival passives, on the other hand, involves the total 'elimination' of the external argument/thematic role, and, moreover, the externalization of the internal argument. The lexical derivation of ergatives and middles also seems to affect the argument structure of the base. Ergatives and middles super- ficially resemble verbal and adjectival passives, in that they apparently lack a syntactically realized external argument/theta-role, and that their internal argument surfaces in the subject position of the sentence. The question of whether the internal argument is externalized in the Lexicon or moved to the subject position in the Syntax was left open. Finally, the lexical rules which derive nouns from verbs also seem to affect the argument structure of the base verb. The evidence discussed seems to suggest that the external argument/thematic role is simply 'suspended', as in verbal passives, and that, in examples where the internal argument appears in the subject position of NP ('nominal passives'), the process of externalization apparently takes place in the Lexicon, rather than in the Syntax.

5.6 Conclusions and Revisions

In this chapter we discussed the selectional properties of lexical items relating to their argument and thematic structures. Lexical categories are said to s-select a certain number of arguments to which they assign a corresponding number of thematic roles. To the extent that a correspondence relation can be established between semantic categories and syntactic categories, the selectional properties of lexical items can be reduced to their s-selectional properties.

The structural representation of argument and thematic structures of lexical items is subject to a syntactic condition called the Theta Criterion. The latter establishes a one-to-one correspondence relation between thematic roles and arguments, such that every argument is assigned a single thematic role and every thematic role is assigned to a single argument. Essentially, the Theta Criterion is a well-formedness condition on argument chains, where the notion 'chain' may include a moved argument and its trace, or a non-moved argument alone. The Theta Criterion essentially holds at LF, where thematic relations are determined, but by virtue of PP it is expected to hold also at the levels of S-structure and D-structure.

A consequence of the Theta Criterion is that it forces movement of non-argument categories such as *wh*-phrases and quantified phrases from argument positions (to non-argument positions) in the mapping from S-structure onto LF. Movement of these categories leaves a trace which has the status of a variable, and therefore an argument capable of being assigned a thematic role. The transformation which displaces non-argument categories in the mapping from S-structure onto LF is called Quantifier Raising (QR). Its introduction into the model confirms the idea that LF is a syntactic level in much the same way as S-structure and D-structure.

Another consequence of the Theta Criterion is that movement of arguments is possible only to positions which are not assigned a thematic role (θ'-positions), as movement to positions which are assigned a thematic role (θ-positions) would lead to the derivation of argument chains with more than one thematic role. All the movement transformations which affect arguments discussed so far are arguably consistent with this requirement. For example, the instance of NP-movement involved in the derivation of raising constructions is consistent with the Theta Criterion, given that raising predicates do not assign an external thematic role, as a lexical property.

A third consequence of the Theta Criterion, in combination with PP, is that the processes which affect the argument/thematic structures of lexical items are confined to the Lexicon. For example, the process which results in the inability of verbal passives to assign an external thematic role to the subject position of the sentence, has to take place in the Lexicon. This ensures that the subject position of verbal passives is a θ'-position, and therefore a legitimate target for movement of the internal argument in the Syntax.

The Theta Criterion belongs to a sub-theory of the Grammar called Theta Theory. Theta Theory has a status parallel to that of X-bar Theory, so that the overall structure of Grammar consists of sub-theories, sometimes called modules. The Grammar can then be said to have a modular structure, where each module deals with a different aspect of the representation and derivation of sentences, although the output as a whole is the result of an interaction between the principles of the various modules.

Exercises

Exercise 1

The examples below have been argued to require a relaxation of the uniqueness condition incorporated in the definition of the Theta Criterion, in particular the condition that an argument can only be assigned a single thematic role:

1. John left the room angry
2. Bill reached the finish line exhausted
3. Mary hammered the nail flat
4. Jane ate the fish raw
5. Bill painted the wall black

Explain why these examples apparently require a relaxation of the uniqueness condition, and try to see whether it is possible to analyse them in such a way that a revision of the Theta Criterion is not required.

Exercise 2

Consider the following example, which illustrates an interesting way in which *wh*-phrases interact in scope with the universal quantifier *everyone*:

1. What did everyone buy for John?
   A. Mary bought John a suit, Jane a sweater, and Bill a tie
   B. Everyone bought John a tie

(1) is ambiguous between two interpretations, so that either (A) or (B) would be an appropriate answer for it. In the interpretation shown in (A) the *wh*-phrase has scope over the universal quantifier *everyone*, whereas in interpretation (B) it is the universal quantifier which has scope over the *wh*-phrase.

Explain whether interpretation (B) of (1) is problematic for the argument that the scope properties of quantified expressions, including *wh*-phrases, are a function of their structural positions.

Exercise 3

Discuss the argument structure of the verb in each of the following pairs of examples:

1a. The horse jumped (over) the fence
1b. The rider jumped the horse over the fence

2a. The dog walked to the park
2b. Mary walked the dog to the park

3a. The horse raced across the barn
3b. Bill raced the horse across the barn

Exercise 4

It has been argued that the following examples are problematic for Theta Theory:

1. They mentioned it to him that he was not shortlisted
2. John resents it very much that Bill is always late
3. Bill would hate it for John to resign
4. They demand it of all students that they attend regularly

Explain why these examples appear to be problematic, and try to outline an analysis for them consistent with the Theta Criterion.

Exercise 5

Discuss the argument/thematic structure of the verbs *spray* and *load* in the following examples:

1a. John sprayed paint on the wall
1b. John sprayed the wall with paint

2a. John loaded hay on the truck
2b. John loaded the truck with hay

You are expected to discuss (among other things) the question of whether the different orders of the internal arguments can be derived in the syntax or must be base-generated.

Further Reading

Allwood *et al.* (1977) discusses the link between Logic and Linguistics (Logic for Linguistics). The terminology relating to thematic roles has been inherited from traditional grammar, and its relevance to linguistic theory within the generative tradition is established in Gruber (1965; 1976), Jackendoff (1972) and, more formally, in Freidin (1978) and Chomsky (1981). For a more comprehensive study of argument structures see Higginbotham (1985) and Grimshaw (1990). Chomsky (1981) also includes an extended discussion of the typology of positions in relation to the dichotomies theta-/non-theta-position and argument/non-argument position.

   The properties of LF as presented in this chapter, in particular the idea that quantified phrases undergo a movement (QR) in the mapping from S-structure onto LF, are discussed in Chomsky (1977a) and May (1977; 1985). The notion of 'c-command', which plays a crucial role in the LF representation of sentences as well as in other aspects of the theory to be discussed in the next chapters, appears in Reinhart (1976). The latter and Reinhart (1979; 1983) represent a coherent alternative view of the interpretation of quantified expressions and the properties of logical representations in general. The issues relating to LF have given rise to a large body of literature, some of which will be mentioned in the relevant remaining chapters. Baker (1970), Bresnan (1970), Kuno and Robinson (1972), and Chomsky (1973) include some of the early discussions of the distribution of *wh*-phrases and the properties of multiple *wh*-questions. On the mechanisms underlying the movement of *wh*-phrases at LF, see Higginbotham and May (1981) and Aoun *et al.* (1981).

Raising to Object appeared in the typology of transformations outlined in Rosenbaum (1967), and has given rise to one of the most exciting controversies. Postal (1974) is a substantial and formidable defence of Raising to Object. Evaluations of arguments for and against raising can be found in Bresnan (1976) and Lightfoot (1976). Some of the arguments against Raising to Object are outlined in Chomsky (1973; 1981). Dative Shift has also given rise to an exciting debate, with arguments for and against. Among the early analyses are Chomsky (1965), Green (1974), Emonds (1976), and Oehrle (1976). Some of the more recent references on Dative Shift are Hornstein and Weinberg (1981), Stowell (1981), Chomsky (1981), Czepluch (1982), Kayne (1984), Larson (1988), and Baker (1988). For a recent debate see Jackendoff (1990) and Larson (1991).

The question of whether rules which affect the argument structure of lexical items should all be confined to the Lexicon or distributed between the Lexicon and Syntax has given rise to a large body of data. Among the relevant references are Williams (1981; 1982), Chomsky (1981), Marantz (1984), Borer (1984b), Keyser and Roeper (1984), Burzio (1986), Jaeggli (1986), Levin and Rappaport (1986), Roberts (1987), Zubizarreta (1987) and Baker (1988). The view that all these rules, including the rule which results in the change of the grammatical function of the internal argument in passives, should be confined to the Lexicon, is one of the major tenets of Lexical Functional Grammar. Among the major references on this particular version of Generative Grammar are Bresnan (1982b).

6

Case Theory

Contents

6.1   *The Case Filter and the Visibility Hypothesis*

6.1.1   The Problem

Compare the following examples:

1a. *John to leave suddenly is foolish
1b. *[CP [C′ e [IP *John* [I′ *to* [VP *leave suddenly*]]]]] *is foolish*
2a. For John to leave suddenly is foolish
2b. [CP [C′ (*For*) [IP *John* [I′ *to* [VP *leave suddenly*]]]]] *is foolish*
3a. That John should leave suddenly is surprising
3b. [CP [C′ *That* [IP *John* [I′ *should* [VP *leave suddenly*]]]]] *is surprising*

All three examples have a clause (CP) as the subject. Each clausal subject has an overt NP subject of its own, *John.* In (1) and (2) the clausal subject is non-finite, whereas in (3) it is finite. Comparing the three examples, the following descriptive generalization emerges: an overt NP cannot occur in the subject position of a non-finite (subject) clause (1), unless the overt NP is preceded by the **prepositional complementizer** *for* (2).

An early attempt to deal with (1) consisted of postulating the filter in (4) below, which has the effect of excluding representations which include the sequence it specifies (adapted from Chomsky and Lasnik (1977)):

4. **NP-to-VP Filter**
   *[NP-to-VP], except in the context [*for* —].

Although (4) correctly rules out (1) and correctly rules in (2), it is somewhat *ad hoc*, in that it fails to explain, among other things, why the presence of the prepositional complementizer *for* in (2) succeeds in rescuing the sequence.

Notice also that PRO, unlike overt NPs, can occur in the subject position of a non-finite clause. Moreover, PRO is incompatible with the presence of *for* in Standard English:

5a. To leave suddenly is foolish
5b. [CP e [IP PRO [I′ *To* [VP *leave suddenly*]]]] *is foolish*
6a. *For to leave suddenly is foolish
6b. *[CP *For* [IP PRO [I′ *to* [VP *leave suddenly*]]]] *is foolish*

Presumably, a more desirable analysis would be one which explains why overt NPs cannot appear in the subject position of (subject) non-finite clauses unless they are preceded by a prepositional complementizer, and why PRO behaves differently.

6.1.2   The Case Filter

As a first step towards developing such an analysis, consider the following examples, together with table (10):

7a. For $\left\{\begin{array}{l} \text{*he} \\ \text{him} \\ \text{*his} \end{array}\right\}$ to leave suddenly is foolish

7b. [CP *For* [IP *him to* [VP *leave suddenly*]]] . . .

$$
\text{8a.} \left\{ \begin{array}{l} \text{He} \\ \text{*Him} \\ \text{*His} \end{array} \right\} \text{showed} \left\{ \begin{array}{l} \text{*he} \\ \text{him} \\ \text{*his} \end{array} \right\} \text{to} \left\{ \begin{array}{l} \text{*they} \\ \text{them} \\ \text{*their} \end{array} \right\}
$$

8b. [CP [IP *He I* [VP *showed him* [PP *to them*]]]]

$$
\text{9a.} \left\{ \begin{array}{l} \text{*He} \\ \text{*Him} \\ \text{His} \end{array} \right\} \text{attempt to leave suddenly surprised everybody}
$$

9b. [IP [NP *His* [N′ *attempt* [CP e [IP PRO *to leave suddenly*]]]]] . . .

10. | *Subjective forms* | *Objective forms* | *Possessive forms* |
|---|---|---|
| a. I | a′. me | a″. my |
| b. you | b′. you | b″. your |
| c. he | c′. him | c″. his |
| d. she | d′. her | d″. her |
| | | |
| e. we | e′. us | e″. our |
| f. you | f′. you | f″. your |
| g. they | g′. them | g″. their |

Apart from certain exceptions (gaps in the paradigm), pronouns in Standard English generally have three different forms: a **subjective** form (10a–g), an **objective** form (10a′-g′), and a **possessive** (or **genitive**) form (10a″-g″). The subjective form occurs in the subject position of finite clauses (8a,b), the objective form following verbs and prepositions (8a,b), and the genitive form in the subject position of NPs (9a,b). Thus each form of the pronoun is associated with a specific syntactic environment.

The different forms of pronouns are said to reflect the **Case** properties of NPs. The idea is that NPs are **assigned** Case by neighbouring head categories which bear a specific structural relation of **locality** to them. Leaving aside genitive Case for the moment, an NP in the subject position (Spec-IP) of a finite clause is assigned subjective Case by finite I. In contrast, an NP in the subject position of a non-finite clause is not assigned subjective Case. The reason is that non-finite I, unlike finite I, does not have the ability to assign (subjective) Case, for reasons which will be discussed below. On the other hand, an NP in the object position of a preposition or a transitive verb is assigned objective Case by the preposition or transitive verb. In contrast to transitive verbs, intransitive verbs cannot assign objective Case. The relationship between transitivity and the ability to assign objective Case is discussed in detail later in this chapter.

In a number of languages with rich inflectional morphology, the Case properties of NPs are overtly reflected in terms of distinct morphological markers, called **Case-markers**. In English, where inflectional morphology is comparatively poorer, the Case properties of NP's are overtly shown only in the different forms of pronouns listed in table (10) above. On the assumption that Case is a property of NPs in general, it would be rather implausible to take the view that in English only pronominal NPs have Case properties. It is more plausible to adopt the view that all types of NP in English have Case properties, and that English differs in that these Case properties are overtly shown in pronominal NPs only. With non-pronominal NPs the Case properties are represented in terms of abstract Case-markers, much like the subject Agr markers (chapter 4).

Bearing this in mind, let us assume that NPs have Case because they are required by a general principle of Grammar to have Case. In other words, let us assume that the distribution of NPs is subject to a condition which requires that they have Case. The condition in question is called the **Case Filter**, and can be formulated as in (11) below (adapted from Chomsky 1981):

11. **Case Filter**
    *NP if NP has phonetic content and has no Case.

It is clear from its definition that the Case Filter is restricted to NPs which have phonetic content, i.e. overt NPs. This means that null NPs such as PRO, and possibly others, are not subject to the condition expressed by the Case Filter. Let us see how (11) helps explain the contrast between (1) and (3) above, and why the presence of the prepositional complementizer *for* in (2) makes it possible for an overt NP to occur in the subject position of the non-finite clause.

The relevant parts of these examples are reproduced here for reference:

12a. *John to leave suddenly . . .
12b. *[CP [C′ e [IP *John* [I′ *to* [VP *leave suddenly*]]]]]

13a. For John to leave suddenly . . .
13b. [CP [C′ *(For)* [IP *John* [I′ *to* [VP *leave suddenly*]]]]]

14a. That John should leave suddenly . . .
14b. [CP [C′ *That* [IP *John* [I′ *should* [VP *leave suddenly*]]]]]

Recall that Case is assigned to an NP by a head category which bears a close structural relationship to it, to be defined below. Thus, an NP has Case if it is in the 'vicinity' of a Case-assigning category. Recall also that not all categories assign Case. For example, non-finite I does not assign subjective Case, and intransitive verbs do not assign objective Case. In (14) the NP subject *John* is assigned subjective Case by finite I, and therefore satisfies the Case Filter. In (12), however, I is non-finite, and therefore does not assign subjective Case to the NP subject. This means that the NP subject *John* in this example fails to be assigned Case, and is therefore in violation of the Case Filter. Finally, in (13), where I is also non-finite, the NP subject is assigned Case by the prepositional complementizer *for*, and therefore satisfies the Case Filter. This is precisely the sense in which the presence of *for* helps rescue a representation where an overt NP is in the subject position of a non-finite clause. Notice that in this situation the NP subject is assigned objective Case, indicated in example (8) above by the fact that only the objective form of the pronoun is allowed in this context.

As pointed out, the Case Filter does not apply to non-overt NPs such as PRO, by definition. Consequently, PRO is expected to be able to occur in non-**Case-marked** environments. These include the subject position of a non-finite clause not preceded by the prepositional complementizer *for*, shown in (5) above. The reason why PRO, unlike overt NPs, cannot be preceded by *for*, as shown in (6) above, will be discussed in Chapter 7 in the context of a broader account of the distribution of PRO and its referential properties.

The idea that the Case Filter applies to overt NPs only can be understood to mean that it is a condition on the phonetic representation of (overt) NPs, and therefore applies at the PF (Phonetic Form) level. The implication would be that the Case Filter is not relevant to LF (Logical Form) representations. Initially, this view may look incompatible with the fact that Case properties encode information relating to the grammatical functions of NPs, which obviously play a crucial role in determining meaning relations. Recall that the terms 'subject(ive)' and 'object(ive)' refer to the grammatical functions of NPs. However, it is important to remember that the grammatical functions of NPs are determined by their structural positions (Chapter 2), so that although Case properties encode information about (reflect) the grammatical functions of NPs they do not determine them. Moreover, there seems to be no one-to-one correspondence between Subjective Case and Objective Case, on the one hand, and the grammatical functions subject and object, on the other. For example, objective Case does not necessarily invariably imply the grammatical function 'object'. In (7/13), for example, the NP *John/him* has the grammatical function 'subject', by virtue of occupying Spec-IP (i.e. the subject position), but is assigned objective Case, rather than subjective Case. Having said that, there have been attempts in the literature to make Case relevant to LF representations, and therefore to meaning relations. One such attempt is known as the **Visibility Hypothesis**.

6.1.3 The Visibility Hypothesis

The Visibility Hypothesis incorporates the claim that the function of Case is to make NPs 'visible' for theta-marking, a process which takes place at LF (Chapter 5). The implication of this hypothesis is that Case is a property of arguments in general (i.e. expressions which receive a thematic role) and not just overt NPs.

The Visibility Hypothesis has two major advantages. First, it makes it possible to dispense with the Case Filter altogether, since its effects, at least with respect to argument NPs, will derive from Visibility: an NP argument which does not have Case will not receive a thematic role, and therefore is excluded by the Theta Criterion. The second major advantage of the Visibility Hypothesis is that it accounts for the fact that variables (traces of *wh*-phrases and quantified phrases) occur in Case-marked positions, although they are null categories:

15a. Who bought what?
15b. [$_{CP}$ *Who*$_i$ *what*$_j$ [$_{IP}$ t$_i$ I [$_{VP}$ *bought* t$_j$]]]

15c. *for which person* x, *for which thing* y, [x *bought* y]
16a. John suspects everybody
16b. [$_{CP}$ e [$_{IP}$ *everybody*$_i$ [$_{IP}$ *John* I [$_{VP}$ *suspects* t$_i$]]]]

16c. *for every person* x, [*John suspects* x]

Recall that variables have the status of arguments and therefore receive a thematic role at LF. In the context of the Visibility Hypothesis, the reason why variables occur in Case-marked positions follows from their status as arguments, and therefore need to be 'visible' for theta-marking.

Although the Visibility Hypothesis has the two advantages mentioned, it leaves certain related facts unexplained. One such fact has to do with PRO and its distribution:

17a. To leave suddenly is foolish
17b. [$_{CP}$ e [$_{IP}$ PRO [$_{I'}$ *To* [$_{VP}$ *leave suddenly*]]]] . . .
18a. John planned to leave suddenly
18b. *John planned* [$_{CP}$ e [$_{IP}$ PRO [$_{I'}$ *to* [$_{VP}$ *leave suddenly*]]]]

In both examples PRO is an argument which receives a thematic role from the verb *leave*. Yet PRO is in a non-Case-marked position, contrary to what is expected in the context of the Visibility Hypothesis. This problem is discussed in more detail in Chapter 7, where a possible solution to it is outlined and evaluated.

Another fact relates to the expletive NPs *it* and *there*. The problem raised by these elements is the converse of the one raised by PRO. Expletive NPs usually occur in Case-marked positions even though as non-arguments they are not assigned a thematic role:

19a. It seems that John is leaving soon
19b. There is a unicorn in the garden

However, it could be argued that this property of expletives is not necessarily incompatible with the Visibility Hypothesis. The latter implies the requirement that only NPs which have Case can receive a thematic role. It does not necessarily follow from this requirement that all NPs which have Case will receive a thematic role. Recall that the Theta Criterion independently excludes assignment of thematic roles to non-arguments. Having said that, the fact that expletives invariably occur in Case-marked positions is significant, and should be accounted for by an adequate theory of Case. A possible solution to the problem raised by expletive NPs will be discussed below. For the moment, note that a logical consequence of the Visibility Hypothesis is that propositional arguments, such as the embedded CP in (19a), are also expected to have Case.

We will not decide between the two approaches to Case here. We will use the expression 'Case Requirement' in a neutral way, leaving open the question of whether it takes the form of a Case Filter or follows from the Theta Criterion as implied by the Visibility Hypothesis. In the rest of this chapter, we will discuss the role that Case plays in the representation and derivation of sentences.

6.1.4   Summary

Each NP is assigned Case by a neighbouring head category which bears a specific structural relationship of locality to it. An NP in the subject position of a finite clause is assigned subjective Case by finite I, and an NP following a transitive verb or a preposition is assigned objective Case by the transitive verb or preposition. Non-finite I and intransitive verbs do not assign Case. The Case assigned to NPs is shown overtly in pronominal NPs, but has an abstract realization in non-pronominal NPs. NPs are required to have Case either by a condition which takes the form of a Case Filter applying at PF or, as implied by the Visibility Hypothesis, the need to be visible for theta-marking at LF.

6.2   *Government, Adjacency and Spec-Head Agreement*

So far, we have been using the term 'objective' to refer to the Case assigned by transitive verbs and prepositions, and the term 'subjective' to refer to the Case assigned by finite I. These terms are in fact cover terms for distinct individual Cases associated with each class of the categories mentioned. The (objective) Case assigned by transitive verbs is called **accusative**, and the (objective) Case assigned by prepositions is frequently called **oblique**. On the other hand, the (subjective) Case assigned by finite I is called **nominative**. In this section we will discuss the structural conditions under which each of these Cases is assigned.

6.2.1   Government

Accusative Case and oblique Case are generally assigned by transitive verbs and prepositions to their NP object. It could be concluded on this basis that, like internal

20.

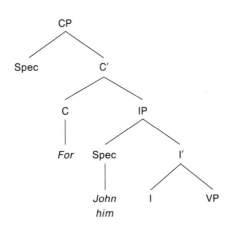

thematic roles, these Cases are also assigned under the structural relationship of sisterhood. However, this conclusion would be inaccurate, as in (8) and (13) above the prepositional complementizer *for* is not a sister of the subject of the non-finite clause to which it assigns (oblique) Case. The relevant part of the structure is reproduced in (20). In view of this, what is needed is a structural relationship which includes sisterhood as well as locality relationships of the type illustrated in (20). The structural relationship in question will serve as a condition under which Case is assigned.

The structural relationship in question is known as **Government**, and can, for the moment, be defined as in (21):

21. **Government**
 A governs B iff
 (i) A is an X^0 category.
 (ii) A c-commands B.

The notion 'c-command' (Chapter 5) plays a crucial role in the definition of government. C-command defines the government domain of a head, just as it defines the scope domain of quantified expressions in LF representations (Chapter 5). The definition of c-command is reproduced here for reference:

22. **C-command**
 A c-commands B iff
 (i) A does not dominate B and B does not dominate A.
 (ii) The first branching node dominating A also dominates B.

Let us see, first, how government subsumes the relationship of sisterhood, using (23a,b) for illustration. According to clause (i) of the definition of government (21), the class of **governors** is restricted to X^0 (head) categories. This means that in (23a,b) only V and P qualify as governors, ignoring the internal structure of NP. In (23a) V governs NP because (i) V is a head category, and (ii) V c-commands NP. The same relationship exists

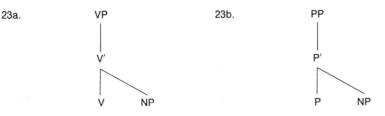

between P and its NP complement in (23b), confirming that government subsumes the sisterhood relationship between heads and their complements. Thus, heads assign Case to their NP complements under government.

Turning now to the configuration in (20) above, *for* (under C) governs the NP in Spec-IP because (i) *for* is a head category, and (ii) *for* c-commands NP. The underlying generalization here is that if a head governs a maximal projection, the head also governs the Spec position of that maximal projection. Because *for* governs IP in (20), it also governs the Spec position of IP, occupied by the subject. Thus, although *for* and the NP subject of the non-finite clause are not sisters, a government relationship exists between them, so that *for* assigns Case to the NP subject of the finite clause under government. Below, we will see other situations where a head category governs and assigns Case to an NP which is not its complement/sister. These considerations further highlight the need for the structural condition of government, which subsumes sisterhood but extends beyond it to include other locality relationships.

24.

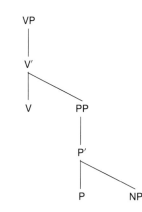

There is, however, a sense in which government, as defined in (21), is not sufficiently restrictive. For example, in a configuration such as (24), it allows the verb to govern, and potentially assign Case to, the NP complement of the preposition. Since NP complements of prepositions receive their (oblique) Case from the preposition itself, the verb in (24) should be prevented from governing the NP complement of the preposition and potentially assigning it (accusative) Case. Thus, the definition of government should be made more restrictive, basically by incorporating into it a condition which would prevent a 'distant' governor from governing a category which has a 'closer' governor. With respect to (24), V should be prevented from governing the NP complement of P on the grounds that NP has a closer governor, namely P.

This condition is known as **Minimality**, and can be defined as in (25):

25. Minimality Condition
In the configuration $[_{XP} \ldots X \ldots [_{YP} \ldots Y \ldots ZP] \ldots]$ X does not govern ZP.

The configuration in (25) corresponds to the one in (24), where X = V, YP = PP, Y = P and ZP = NP. The Minimality Condition prevents the verb from governing the NP complement of P in this configuration. Put more simply, the Minimality Condition prevents a head from governing into the domain of another head category. There are various ways of incorporating the Minimality Condition into the definition of Government the following being one such way:

26. **Government**
    A governs B iff
    (i) A is an X^0 category.
    (ii) A c-commands B.
    (iii) Minimality is respected.

It will become clear in the subsequent chapters that government plays a crucial role in determining most grammatical relations.

6.2.2 Adjacency

Government is the core condition of UG which regulates Case-assignment in all languages. It has been suggested that individual languages may choose to add another condition to the core condition of government on Case-assignment. For example, it has been suggested that English makes use of the condition of **adjacency**, in addition to government, in regulating Case-assignment. This means that in English a head category has both to govern and to be adjacent to an NP to be able to assign it Case. Consider the following examples, discussed in Chapters 3 and 4 in relation to Affix-hopping (I-lowering):

27a. *John makes frequently mistakes
27b. *[$_{IP}$ *John* [$_{I'}$ + [$_V$ *make*]$_i$ [$_{VP}$ *frequently* [$_{VP}$ t$_i$ *mistakes*]]]]

28a. John frequently makes mistakes
28b. [$_{IP}$ *John* [$_{I'}$ t$_i$ [$_{VP}$ *frequently* [$_{VP}$ *make* + [I]$_i$ *mistakes*]]]]

These examples were cited as evidence that, in English, main verbs do not raise to I (across the left-adjoined VP-adverb). Rather, I lowers to the main verb inside VP. The question why (27) is ungrammatical, i.e. the reason why an adverb cannot intervene between the verb and its NP object, was left open. In the context of an earlier framework which did not assume the possibility of V-raising to I, the ungrammaticality of (27) was attributed to a violation of the adjacency condition on Case-assignment. This explanation can be incorporated into the current framework in the following way. Movement of the verb to I is prevented from taking place on the grounds that it yields a representation where the verb is not adjacent to its NP object, and therefore cannot assign it Case.

This explanation gains credibility when (27) and (28) are compared to the following examples:

29a. John knocked repeatedly on it
29b. John repeatedly knocked on it

The complement of the verb in these examples is a PP, i.e. a category which is not subject to the Case Requirement. In this situation, the adverb can appear intervening between the verb and its PP complement (29a), as well as preceding the verb (29b). The fact that a VP-adverb can intervene between the verb and a PP complement but not between a verb and an NP complement lends support to the Adjacency Condition on Case-assignment in English. The verb is required to be adjacent to its complement only in situations where the verb assigns it Case. In situations where the verb does not assign Case to its complement, the verb can move to I. Note that (29a) seems to suggest that main verbs can move out of VP in English in the situation it illustrates. We will not pursue this possibility here.

The Adjacency Condition on Case-assignment has also been credited with the advantage of determining the order of complements inside VP in situations where a verb selects more than one complement:

30a. Mary put the book on the table
30b. *Mary* I [$_{VP}$ *put* [$_{NP}$ *the book*] [$_{PP}$ *on the table*]]

31a. *Mary put on the table the book
31b. **Mary* I [$_{VP}$ *put* [$_{PP}$ *on the table*] [$_{NP}$ *the book*]]]

32a. Mary persuaded Bill to leave
32b. *Mary* I [$_{VP}$ *persuaded* [$_{NP}$ *Bill*] [$_{CP}$ PRO *to leave*]]

33a. *Mary persuaded to leave Bill
33b. **Mary* I [$_{VP}$ *persuaded* [$_{CP}$ PRO *to leave*] [$_{NP}$ *Bill*]]]

So far, the correct ordering of complements inside VP has been achieved in terms of a stipulation: internal arguments are ordered with respect to each other in lexical entries. However, the order [V NP PP], illustrated in (30), and the order [V NP CP], illustrated in (32), can arguably be considered as following from the Adjacency Condition. Because the NP complement needs to be assigned Case, and because Case is assigned under adjacency, the NP complement has to be adjacent to the verb. The ungrammatical order [V PP NP], illustrated in (31), and the ungrammatical order [V CP NP], illustrated in (33), are excluded on the grounds that they involve a violation of the Adjacency Condition, and ultimately a violation of the Case Requirement.

6.2.3   Spec-Head Agreement

We have seen that nominative (subjective) Case is assigned by finite I. A close look at the configuration involving an NP subject in Spec-IP and a finite I reveals that the definition of government needs to be revised to accommodate nominative Case-assignment. In this configuration I does not c-command Spec-IP, owing to the intervening I' projection (a branching node). Therefore, I does not govern the NP in Spec-IP, and consequently should not be able to assign it (nominative) Case. If we wish to maintain that all Cases are assigned under government, our task will be to revise the definition of government – more precisely, the definition of c-command – to accommodate the configuration in (34). If, on the other hand, we find reasons to believe that the assignment of nominative Case takes place under a different condition, we can maintain the definition of government as is. The position we will take here is a mixture of both views. We will assume that the assignment of nominative Case takes place under a condition which includes government as well as another relation.

34.

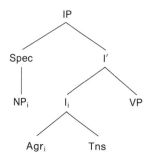

The assignment of nominative Case can be accommodated under government simply by substituting the term 'maximal projection' for the term 'branching node' in the definition of c-command, as shown in (35a) below (the version in (35a) is sometimes referred to as **m-command**):

35a. **C-command**

A c-commands B iff

(i) A does not dominate B and B does not dominate A.

(ii) The first *maximal projection* which dominates A also dominates B.

35b. **Government**

A governs B iff

(i)   A is an X^o category.

(ii) A c-commands B.

(iii) Minimality is respected.

According to the previous definition of c-command, a branching node (I′, V′, P′, etc.) is sufficient to block a c-command relation. The consequence is that head categories do not c-command, and therefore do not govern, their specifiers. The revised version in (36a) differs in that only a maximal projection (IP, VP, PP, etc.) can block a c-command relation. Consequently, head categories c-command, and therefore govern, their specifiers. It is not difficult to see that by adopting the revised definition of c-command, it becomes possible for I in (34) to govern Spec-IP and assign nominative Case to the NP occupying it. The c-command domain of I is IP, and, obviously, IP also includes Spec-IP. The reason why we need to assume that the subject is governed by finite I will become clearer in Chapter 8, which deals with movement processes.

There is a sense in which the subject in the Spec position of a finite IP has a special relationship with I. Recall that I assigns nominative Case to an NP in Spec-IP only if I is finite, that is, only if I has Agr and Tense. When I is non-finite an NP in Spec-IP is assigned objective Case by an external governor, such as the prepositional complementizer *for*. Recall also (from Chapter 4) that in finite clauses the subject is in Spec-Head Agreement with (the Agr category of) I. Some of the relevant examples from Standard English are reproduced here, together with the definition of Spec-Head Agreement:

36a. He/she smiles

36b. *He/she smile

37. **Spec-Head Agreement**

A head (X) and its specifier (Spec-XP) must agree in relevant features.

Examples such as (36b) are excluded on the grounds that they involve a violation of Spec-Head Agreement. Note that, because heads govern their specifiers under the revised definition of (c-command and) government, there is a clear sense in which Spec-Head Agreement involves government. In view of this, Spec-Head Agreement can be understood to mean that for a head and an NP to be in Spec-Head Agreement, the head must both govern NP and share with it relevant (agreement) features.

Given the special relationship between finite I and the subject in Spec-IP, it is plausible to assume that the assignment of nominative Case by finite I to the subject operates under Spec-Head Agreement. This amounts to saying that government alone, though necessary, is not sufficient for the assignment of nominative Case. In non-finite clauses, I does not assign nominative Case to the subject in Spec-IP because I is not in Spec-Head Agreement with the subject. We will assume that this is so not only because I does not agree with the subject, but also because non-finite I does not govern the subject, non-finite I being inherently a non-governor. Later on in this chapter the relationship between nominative

Case and agreement between finite I and the subject in finite clauses and lack of agreement in non-finite clauses will be made much more precise.

6.2.4   Summary

Objective Case (accusative and oblique) and subjective Case (nominative) are both assigned under government. The latter is a locality condition which includes the relationship of sisterhood, the relationship between a head and the specifier of its complement, and the relationship between a head and its own specifier. The assignment of nominative Case differs in that, in addition to government, it also requires an agreement relation with I. For an NP to receive nominative Case from I, it has to be governed by I and share the same agreement features with the (Agr category of) I. The relation which incorporates these two conditions is Spec-Head Agreement.

6.3   *Objective Case*

6.3.1   Objective Case and Transitivity

Traditionally, an intimate link is assumed to exist between the ability to assign objective Case and transitivity, such that transitive categories are the categories which assign objective Case. Prepositions usually take an NP complement to which they assign (oblique) Case, so that prepositions are generally transitive in nature. As for verbs, there does not seem to be a strict correlation between the property of selecting an obligatory NP argument and the ability to assign (accusative) Case. A given verb may select an obligatory NP argument and not assign it Case. Examples of such verbs are *rely* and *approve* in its use illustrated in (39):

38a. The boy relies on the girl
38b. *The boy relies

39a. Mary does not approve of John's behaviour
39b. *Mary does not approve

40a. John kicked the ball
40b. *John kicked

The function of the prepositions *on* and *of* in (38a) and (39a) is to assign Case to the NP argument selected by the verb. Unlike *rely* and *approve*, the verb *kick* in (40a) is transitive, and therefore does not need to rely on a preposition to assign Case to its internal NP argument.

There is a parallelism between verbs such as *rely* and *approve*, on the one hand, and (derived) nouns and adjectives, on the other. Generally, nouns and adjectives cannot c-select NP complements, meaning that their internal argument can never be realized as a (bare) NP. When the internal argument of a noun or an adjective is realized as an NP, the latter is invariably preceded by a preposition:

41a. The destruction *(of) the city
41b. The translation *(of) the book

42a. Mary is proud *(of) her achievements
42b. Bill is keen *(on) soccer

To the extent that transitivity and the ability to assign objective Case are one and the same thing, it appears that nouns and adjectives are never transitive.

With respect to derived nouns, such as *destruction* and *translation*, this is presumably the result of the lexical process which derives them from related transitive verbs. We saw in Chapter 5 that the lexical process which derives nouns from verbs affects the argument/ thematic structures of the base verbs. For example, the structural realization of the otherwise obligatory (internal) arguments of the base verb is optional with derived nouns (*The destruction (of the city) was a mistake*). It seems that the lexical process which derives nouns from verbs also affects the Case properties of transitive base verbs, so that an intransitive noun is derived from a transitive verb. It is possible that there is a link between the loss of the ability to assign objective Case and the optionality of internal arguments, such that one follows from the other. However, we will not try to establish such a link here.

The correlation between transitivity and the ability to assign objective Case goes some way towards solving certain problems raised by the attempt to reduce c-selection to s-selection, thereby dispensing with c-selection in lexical entries (Chapter 6). The idea is that to each semantic category there corresponds a syntactic category which represents its Canonical Structural Realization (CSR). A potential problem with this attempt is that two lexical items which s-select the same semantic category may c-select different syntactic categories. For example, the verbs *hear* and *listen* both s-select a theme argument, but while *hear* can c-select an NP (*I heard him*), *listen* cannot (*I listened *(to) him*). Likewise, while the verbs *ask*, *wonder*, and *care* all s-select a proposition, only *ask* c-selects NP:

43a. I asked what time it was
43b. I asked (about) the time

44a. I wondered what time it was
44b. I wondered *(about) the time

45a. I didn't care what time it was
45b. I didn't care *(about) the time

Whether a given verb c-selects an NP or another category arguably follows from whether the verb is transitive, and therefore a Case-assigner, or intransitive, and therefore a non-Case assigner. This means that the selectional properties of 'similar' verbs are basically the same, but that differences in their Case properties may result in their internal argument being realized as an NP or an NP preceded by a preposition which acts as a Case-assigner. Because *hear* and *ask* assign objective Case, meaning that they are transitive, their internal argument can be realized as a bare NP. On the other hand, because *listen*, *wonder*, and *care* do not assign objective Case, meaning that they are intransitive, their internal argument cannot be realized as a bare NP.

6.3.2   Exceptional Case-Marking (Objective Subjects)

Two instances of objective Case-assignment have been discussed so far. One instance relates to situations where a transitive category assigns Case to an NP which is its (internal) argument. The other instance relates to situations where a transitive category assigns Case to an NP which is not its argument. The latter is found in examples where the subject of a non-finite clause is assigned objective Case by an external governor. In (46), below, reproduced from above, the subject of the non-finite clause is assigned (objective) Case by the prepositional complementizer *for*:

46a. For him to leave suddenly . . .
46b. [$_{CP}$ *For* [$_{IP}$ *him* [$_{I'}$ *to* [$_{VP}$ *leave suddenly*]]]]

Note that the NP subject in this example is thematically related to the predicate of the clause, and does not bear any thematic relation to the category which assigns it Case. Case-assignment in situations which do not involve a thematic relationship between the assigner and the assignee is known as **Exceptional Case-Marking (ECM)**.

Although (46) is technically an instance of ECM, the term is more often associated with sentences such as the following:

47a. I believe John to be intelligent
47b. I believe [John to be intelligent]

48a. I believe him/(*he) to be intelligent
48b. I (sincerely) believe (*sincerely) him to be intelligent
48c. He is believed to be intelligent

We concluded in Chapter 5 that the analysis of (47a) which is consistent with the Theta-Criterion is the one outlined in (47b), where the NP subject of the embedded non-finite clause remains in its D-structure position (does not move to a selected object position in the matrix clause). At the same time, it was pointed out that this analysis is apparently inconsistent with the fact that the NP in question displays properties usually associated with objects rather than with subjects. (48a) shows that, when pronominal, the NP subject appears in the objective form rather than the subjective form. (48b) shows that a VP-adverb cannot intervene between the NP subject and the root verb, as is usually the case between verbs and their NP objects. Finally, (48c) shows that the NP subject can move to the subject position of the root clause when the verb of the root clause is in the passive form, a typical property of direct objects. All three properties indicate that the NP subject, sometimes called the **ECM subject**, is somehow also the object of the root verb.

The inconsistency disappears once we assume that the ECM subject, although thematically related to the predicate of the embedded clause, is assigned (objective) Case by the verb *believe* of the root clause – an instance of ECM. Because the ECM subject bears a Case relationship to the root verb which is identical to the Case relationship between verbs and their direct objects, it is not surprising that the ECM subject behaves as if it were the direct object of the root verb. In other words, ECM subjects are hybrid grammatical constructs, in so far as they are subjects with respect to X-bar Theory (and Theta-Theory) and objects with respect to Government Theory and Case Theory. In a modular system of the type discussed here, this situation should not come as a surprise.

The same situation is found in examples where the embedded clause is a small clause (Chapter 5):

49a. I consider John intelligent
49b. *I consider* [$_{AP}$ *John* [$_{A'}$ *intelligent*]]

50a. I consider him/*he intelligent
50b. I (sincerely) consider (*sincerely) him/John intelligent

The relationship between the subject of the small clause and the root verb also exhibits the properties of verb–direct object relationships. As in the previous situation, this is due to the fact that the subject of the small clause is assigned objective Case by the root verb, even though the subject of the small clause is thematically related to the predicate of the small clause.

The verbs which assign accusative Case to an NP which is not their internal argument are called **ECM verbs**. The transitive nature of these verbs is shown independently by the fact that they can take a bare NP object, in addition to their ability to take a (small) clausal complement:

51a. I believed it/him
51b. I considered the offer seriously
51c. I was expecting it/him

52a. *My belief John to be intelligent
52b. My belief that John is intelligent

Example (52a) shows that the (derived) nominal counterparts of ECM verbs cannot occur in an ECM context. This is to be expected on the conclusion that nouns do not assign (objective) Case.

Recall (from earlier) that objective Case is assigned under the structural condition of government. Thus, in all situations of Exceptional Case-Marking discussed we expect the Case-assigner to govern the NP it Case-marks. With respect to the situation illustrated in (46) above, we have seen that the prepositional complementizer does indeed govern the NP subject of the non-finite IP. The generalization that government of a maximal projection implies government of the specifier of that maximal projection extends to examples where the embedded clause is a small clause. The configuration involved is shown in (53). Because the root verb governs its small clause complement, it also governs the Spec position of the small clause (Spec-XP), occupied by the ECM subject.

53.
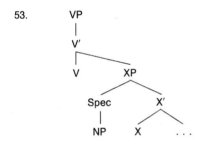

The situation with respect to non-small ('normal') clausal complements is not equally straightforward. Non-small clauses are canonically realized as CP, implying the structure in (54b), where the ECM subject is separated from the ECM verb by both CP and IP:

54a. I believe John to be intelligent
54b. *I believe* [CP [C' e [IP *John to be intelligent*]]]

The issue we need to address here is whether a head category should be allowed to govern across two maximal projections. Note that if C qualifies as a governor for the subject in (54), it will prevent the ECM verb from governing Spec-IP, and therefore from assigning it Case, by virtue of Minimality. On a more general note, it is undesirable to allow a head category to govern across two maximal projections simply because this step would undermine the idea that government is essentially a locality relation. The root verb in (54) is simply 'too far away' from the NP in the embedded Spec-IP to govern it. Assuming this to be the case, (54b) is unlikely to be the structure underlying the ECM construction in (54a).

As a first step towards determining the structure of ECM constructions such as (54a), consider the following example:

55a. *I believe that John/him/he to be intelligent
55b. *I believe* [CP [C' *that* [IP *John/him/he to be intelligent*]]]

This example illustrates the fact that the presence of the complementizer *that* in ECM constructions gives rise to ungrammaticality. Assuming that (55) is excluded on the grounds that the NP subject of the embedded clause fails to be assigned Case, the following conclusion can be drawn. The presence of CP, implied by the complementizer *that* in (55), prevents the root verb from governing, and therefore assigning Case to, the subject of the embedded clause. It follows from this that the ECM construction in (54a), where the verb assigns accusative Case to the subject of the embedded clause, lacks the category CP. Accordingly, (54a) has the structure shown in (56b):

56a. *I believe* [IP *John to be intelligent*]

56b.

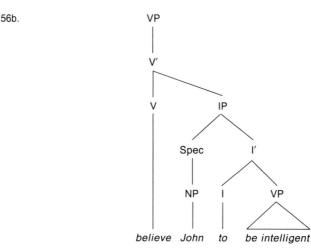

In this configuration the root verb governs the subject in the embedded Spec-IP for the same reason that the root verb in structure (53) above governs the subject of the small clause. As a matter of fact, the structure in (56) is identical to the one in (52), where the complement XP = IP.

ECM verbs such as *believe* are sometimes said to trigger **CP-deletion/reduction**, as a lexical property. Alternatively, ECM verbs can be said to c-select either IP or CP (*I believe that John is intelligent*), depending on whether the selected clause includes a subject which is dependent on an external governor for Case. In the context of a framework where c-selection reduces to s-selection, this will amount to saying that propositional arguments can be canonically realized either as CP or as IP, again with the choice dependent on whether the selected proposition includes a subject in need of an external source for Case.

6.3.3   Dative Shift

In Chapter 5 we discussed a class of verbs which enter into the Dative Shift alternation, whereby the indirect object and the direct object appear to shift places:

57a. Mary gave a book to John
57b. *Mary* I [VP *gave* [*a book*] [*to John*]]

58a. Mary gave John a book
58b. *Mary* I [VP *gave* [*John*] [*a book*]]

We concluded that it was unlikely that (58) derives from a D-structure with the order shown in (57) by a transformational process which reorders the theme and goal arguments of the verb and deletes the preposition *to*. Rather, (58) is base-generated as it is, with the goal argument adjacent to the verb and the theme argument to its right. Here we will discuss the implications that the Dative Shift pattern (58) has for Case Theory.

(57) apparently does not raise any problems for Case Theory. The NP argument adjacent to the verb (theme) receives accusative Case from the verb, and the NP argument inside PP (goal) receives oblique Case from the preposition. It is the Dative Shift construction in (58) which raises some fairly intractable problems, as it includes two NPs but, apparently, only one source for (objective) Case. One of the questions which needs to be resolved is whether verbs which select two arguments assign two accusative Cases. If we maintain that the Case properties of lexical categories somehow reflect their argument structures, so that a given verb which selects two internal arguments can assign two Cases, it is possible, in principle, that the two NPs in (58) are assigned one Case each by the verb. If, on the other hand, we maintain that lexical categories can only assign one Case, we need to work out the source of the Case assigned to the second NP in (58), its nature, and the condition under which it is assigned.

Starting with the former hypothesis, if the two NPs in (58) both receive their Case from the verb, we should expect both of them to behave like direct objects of the verb. For example, we should expect both NPs to be able to 'passivize', i.e. to move to the subject position of the sentence when the verb is in the passive form. Underlying this argument is the idea that the ability to 'passivize' is a unique property of direct objects, i.e. NPs which receive accusative Case from the verb. Consider the following examples from Standard English:

59a. John was given a book
59b. *John*ᵢ was [VP *given* [tᵢ] [*a book*]]

60a. *A book was given John
60b. **A book*ᵢ was [VP *given* [*John*] [tᵢ]]

(59) was cited in Chapter 6 as evidence that it is the goal (first) argument which has the properties of a direct object in Dative Shift constructions. (60) illustrates the fact that in Standard English the theme (second) argument does not have the properties of a direct object. In view of this, it is unlikely that the theme (second) argument in Dative Shift constructions such as (58) receives Case from the verb.

There have been attempts in the literature to attribute verbs such as *give* in Standard English the ability to assign two Cases, although a distinction is drawn between the two. For example, Chomsky (1981) has suggested that these verbs have, as a lexical property, the ability to assign a 'secondary' Case to the second NP, in addition to the 'primary' Case assigned to the first (adjacent) NP. The structure postulated in the context of this analysis is the one in (61), where the second argument is a daughter of VP, while the first argument is a daughter of V'. Presumably, the difference in syntactic behaviour between the two NPs, illustrated in (59) and (60) above, follows from the distinction made between

61.

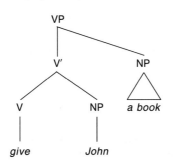

'primary' and 'secondary' Case. Only NPs which receive 'primary' Case qualify as true direct objects of the verb, and therefore only these NPs are able to 'passivize'.

According to the analysis outlined in (61) the ability to assign 'secondary' Case is lexically determined, so that verbs which select two internal arguments can be expected to differ as to whether they assign a 'secondary' Case. The advantage of this analysis is that it can account for the fact, discussed in Chapter 5, that the verb *donate* does not tolerate the Dative Shift pattern (**Mary donated the charity money*) simply by assuming that this verb lacks the ability to assign a 'secondary' Case. On the other hand, to the extent that Case-assignment in English operates under Adjacency, the analysis outlined in (61) would either have to assume that Adjacency is somehow waved in Dative Shift constructions or interpret the structure in such a way that an adjacency relation of some sort holds between the second NP and the verb.

The second hypothesis, that the verb assigns only one Case in Standard English Dative Shift constructions, has also been suggested in the literature. A number of analyses based on this hypothesis have in common the assumption that Dative Shift constructions involve a 'hidden' PP which contains the goal argument. According to this analysis, Dative Shift constructions differ from their paraphrases with the order [V NP PP] only in that, first, the PP containing the goal argument is ordered before the theme argument and, secondly, the head of PP is null. Ignoring certain differences in implementation, the structure implied is roughly as in (62a), where the symbol Ø under P means 'null'. (62b) is the structure of the related constructions with the order [V NP PP], presented below for comparison. Given structure (62a), the sources of Case for the two NP complements, their nature, and the conditions under which they are assigned are the same as in (62b). This is to say that the theme NP is assigned accusative Case by the verb, and the goal NP is assigned oblique Case by the null preposition.

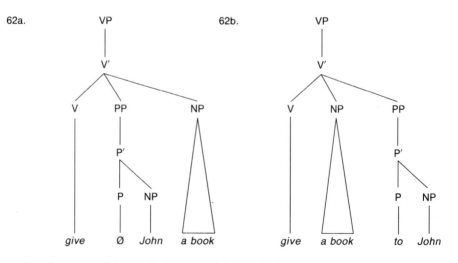

The advantage of the analysis outlined in (62) is that it minimizes differences between the Dative Shift construction and the related construction illustrated in (62b). Given that in both constructions the arguments bear the same thematic relationships to the verb, it is natural to assume that they also bear the same structural relationships to the verb in both constructions. We will come back to this issue in more detail in Chapter 9. For the moment, notice that this analysis shares with the previous one the Adjacency problem, given that the second NP in (62a) is not adjacent to the verb. The analysis outlined in (62a) apparently also has the problem of explaining why *donate* does not tolerate Dative Shift.

6.3.4 Summary

There is a close connection between transitivity and the ability to assign objective Case, such that the former reduces to the latter. A given category can be intransitive even though it may select an internal argument, suggesting that selection of an internal argument and the ability to assign objective Case do not go hand in hand. Intransitive categories which select an internal (non-propositional) argument are characterized by the fact that their (non-propositional) argument cannot be realized as a bare NP. Transitive categories are the ones which assign objective Case to the NP argument they select. Some of these categories can also assign objective Case to an argument they do not select, a situation known as Exceptional Case-Marking. As far as categories which select two NP arguments are concerned, it is not clear whether they assign objective Case to both NP arguments or whether one of the two arguments selected is assigned Case by an independent source.

6.4 *Genitive Case and the DP Hypothesis*

6.4.1 Subjects of Noun Phrases and Genitive Case

Genitive Case was said earlier to be assigned to subjects of noun phrases:

63a. His/John's house
63b. Her/Mary's translation of the book
63c. Its/the city's destruction by the barbarians

Note that a genitive subject can have one of a number of possible thematic roles. In (63a) it is a possessor, in (63b) an agent, and in (63c) a theme. The genitive form of pronouns represents overt marking of the genitive Case assigned to subjects of noun phrases. As for non-pronominal subjects, genitive Case can be said to be overtly marked by the morpheme *'s*. To the extent that this is the function of *'s*, non-pronominal genitive noun phrases also show overt Case marking in English.

The questions we will concern ourselves with in this section are, first, what the source of genitive Case is in noun phrases, and, secondly, under which condition genitive Case is assigned. The structure of noun phrases we have been assuming so far is the one in (64), where the subject occupies Spec-NP.

We concluded above that nouns do not assign Case (nouns are intransitive), on the grounds that their internal NP argument is invariably preceded by a preposition. In view of this, the NP subject in (64) cannot be said to receive (genitive) Case from N. Note that, even if nouns did have the ability to assign Case, it would be rather bizarre for the Case of

64.

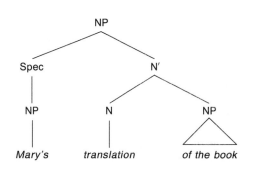

the noun in (64), for example, to be assigned to the subject rather than to the complement. Recall that it is generally the case that lexical categories have a closer relationship with their complements than with subjects, an asymmetry which is structurally reflected in (64) by the fact that the complement is a sister to N whereas the subject is not.

It seems that there is no apparent source for the genitive Case assigned to subjects of noun phrases, and yet there must be one. As a first step towards resolving this paradox, we will discuss certain properties of noun phrases which indicate that they have a structure which is more complex than the one shown in (64). The revised structure suggested by these properties will reveal a clear source for the genitive Case assigned to subjects of noun phrases.

6.4.2 Noun Phrases and Clauses

There are a number of respects in which noun phrases seem to resemble full clauses, suggesting that they have a structure which parallels that of full clauses. Initially, this can be seen simply by comparing the noun phrase in (65a) with its clausal counterpart in (65b):

65a. Mary's translation of the book
65b. Mary translated the book

Like sentence (65b), the noun phrase (65a) has a propositional content, in the sense that it includes a lexical category, a complement, and a subject. It differs only in that its lexical category is a noun, rather than a verb, and that the complement is preceded by a preposition. The second property follows from the first, on the assumption that nouns, unlike verbs, do not assign Case. (65a) also differs from (65b), this time crucially, in that it lacks a Tense category. It is the ability of clauses to instantiate Tense which enables them to function as complete sentences, assuming that a 'complete sentence' is a proposition which is anchored in time in terms of Tense. The fact that noun phrases do not instantiate Tense can be considered the reason why they cannot function as 'complete sentences', even though they may have a propositional content. Having said that, crucial though this difference is between noun phrases and clauses, it does not necessarily bear on the structural parallelism between them.

The similarities between noun phrases and clauses go much further. In Chapter 5 we discussed a construction, called the 'passive in NP' or 'nominal passive', where the internal argument of the noun appears in the subject position of the noun phrase and the external argument inside a *by*-phrase located to the right of the noun. This construction is illustrated in (63c) above, and is reproduced in (66a) below, together with a corresponding verbal passive:

66a. The city's destruction (by the barbarians)
66b. The city was destroyed (by the barbarians)

Although it was concluded in Chapter 5 that 'nominal passives' are probably derived differently from verbal passives, the superficial similarities between the two constructions is arguably suggestive of fundamental structural similarities between noun phrases and clauses.

A further similarity between noun phrases and clauses concerns the distribution of **anaphoric** expressions such as the reciprocal *each other*. The distribution of anaphoric expressions is discussed in detail in the next chapter, so our discussion of it here will be brief. Generally, first, an anaphor must have an antecedent in the sentence and, secondly, the antecedent must be located inside the 'local domain' of the anaphor:

67a. *The players*ᵢ *blame each other*ᵢ
67b. **The manager*ⱼ *blames each other*ᵢ

68a. *The players think (that) the manager blames each other
68b. **The players*ᵢ *think (that)* [*the manager*ⱼ *blames each other*ᵢ]

69a. The manager thinks (that) the players blame each other
69b. *The manager*ⱼ *thinks (that)* [*the players*ᵢ *blame each other*ᵢ]

Examples (67a,b) illustrate the fact that an anaphor must have an antecedent in the sentence. In (67b) *The manager* does not qualify as an antecedent for *each other* because it is not plural–*each other* requires a plural antecedent as in (67a). Example (68) shows that an antecedent for the anaphor, when present in the sentence, cannot be 'too far away' from the anaphor. Although *the players* is plural and therefore can be an antecedent for the anaphor, it is not sufficiently 'close' to the anaphor. Example (69) shows that the antecedent is appropriately 'close' to the anaphor when the antecedent is included in the same clause as the anaphor. The clause which immediately contains the anaphor is the 'local domain' of the anaphor. In (67b) the anaphor does not have an antecedent at all, and in (68) the antecedent is not included in the 'local domain' of the anaphor.

With this in mind, consider now the following examples:

70a. The manager heard their criticism of each other
70b. The manager heard [their₁ criticism of each other₁]

71a. *The players heard his criticism of each other
71b. *The players₁ heard [his₂ criticism of each other₁]

These examples show that the noun phrase, included between brackets, can function as the 'local domain' of an anaphor. The ungrammaticality of (71), when compared to example (70), is due to the fact that the antecedent of the anaphor (*the players*) is not located inside the noun phrase which includes the anaphor. Thus, noun phrases are clause-like in that, like clauses, they can also serve as a 'local domain' for an anaphor.

6.4.3 The DP Hypothesis

A plausible way of capturing the observed similarities between noun phrases and clauses is by assigning noun phrases a structure which parallels that of clauses. The intended structure is shown in (72a), where D is short for Det(erminer). (72b) is the structure of the clause, provided below for comparison. (72a) incorporates the claim that D is the head of the 'noun phrase', rather than its specifier. Moreover, D is a non-lexical (or **functional**) category which parallels I in IP, so that 'noun phrase' (DP), like IP, is the maximal projection of a functional category. Like IP too, the functional head of 'noun phrase' has a lexical category as a complement, except that this lexical category is NP rather than VP. Taking the parallelism with IP further, the subject position of 'noun phrase' is Spec-DP, just as Spec-IP is the subject position of IP:

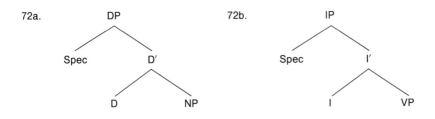

Let us now see how the hypothesis that 'noun phrases' have the structure in (72a), called the **DP Hypothesis**, solves our original problem, which is to find a source for the genitive Case assigned to subjects of 'noun phrases'. Although 'noun phrases' are now technically DP's we shall continue to use the expression 'noun phrase' (included between quotation marks) as a transitional term of reference.

It was observed above that 'noun phrases' differ from clauses in that they do not instantiate a Tense category. However, there are no reasons which suggest that 'noun phrases' do not instantiate an Agr category; there is in fact substantial evidence for the presence of an Agr category in 'noun phrases', some of which is discussed later on in this chapter. The parallelism with IPs suggests that the Agr category, presumably, is instantiated under D, so that D can be said to have the content shown in (73):

73. D → (Agr) Def

Def refers to the in(definiteness) property of 'noun phrases', which we will assume here to be marked in terms of the feature complex [+/− Def]. This means that Def in (73) is a 'bundle' of features in much the same way that Agr is a bundle of the features number, gender, and person. Having said that, (73) does not incorporate a specific claim about the fairly complex issue of definiteness and the related issue of specificity in 'noun phrases'.

Assuming (73), we are now in a position to answer the question concerning the source of genitive Case assigned to subjects of 'noun phrases', and the condition under which it is assigned. Genitive Case is assigned to subjects of 'noun phrases' under Spec-Head Agreement with (the Agr category of) D, just as nominative Case is assigned to subjects of finite clauses under Spec-Head Agreement with (the Agr category of) I. Accordingly, the structure of a 'noun phrase' such as the one in (74a) below is as in (74b):

74a. Mary's translation of the book

74b.

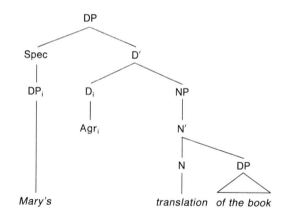

Notice that the subject and the complement are also DPs, with an internal structure similar to that of the overall DP which includes them. With the revision introduced, every (instance of a) 'noun phrase' is a DP, so that the Case Requirement now holds for DPs (not NPs): every (overt) DP must have Case.

In (73) the Agr category is included between parentheses to convey the information that its occurrence is optional. This implies that there are DP's which do not instantiate Agr, just as there are IPs (non-finite clauses) which do not instantiate Agr. The DPs which do not instantiate Agr arguably are the ones which include determiners such as (in)definite articles and others. (75a), for example, has the representation shown in (75b):

75a. The translation of the book

75b.

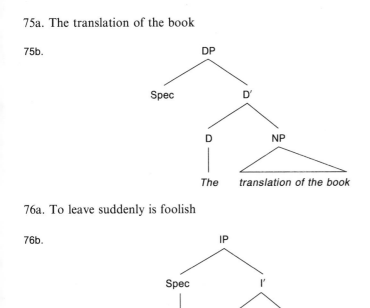

76a. To leave suddenly is foolish

76b.

Accordingly, the presence of a determiner arguably can be taken as an indication of the absence of Agr under D, just as *to* is an indication of the absence of Agr under I in (non-finite) clauses such as (76). This generalization serves as the basis on which Abney (1987) has suggested an analysis for the co-occurrence restriction on determiners and subjects in 'noun phrases' to which we turn now.

The co-ccurrence restriction on determiners and subjects in 'noun phrases' is illustrated in (77a) below, and encoded in rule (77b):

77a. *Mary's the translation of the book

77b. NP → $\left\{ \begin{matrix} \text{Det} \\ \text{NP} \end{matrix} \right\}$N′

Underlying (77b) is the assumption that subjects of 'noun phrases' and determiners occupy the same position, and hence cannot co-occur. Initially, this property of 'noun phrases' may appear problematic for the DP analysis, where determiners and DP subjects occupy different positions, D and Spec-DP, respectively. However, in the context of the DP analysis the co-occurrence restriction shown in (77a) is a consequence of the more fundamental fact that Agr and determiners are mutually exclusive. The reasoning underlying this analysis is as follows: the appearance of a determiner implies the absence of Agr, and the absence of the latter implies that a subject in Spec-DP does not have a source for (genitive) Case, and therefore is excluded. The situation in (77a) is similar to the situation found in non-finite clauses such as (78), where an overt subject co-occurs with *to*.

78a. *John to leave suddenly is foolish
78b. *[CP e [IP *John* [I' *to* [VP *leave suddenly*]]]] . . .

The restriction shown in (78) is a consequence of the fact that *to* implies the absence of Agr, and the absence of the latter implies that an overt DP subject is excluded from the subject position on the grounds that it fails to be assigned Case.

Recall that an overt subject is allowed in the subject position of a non-finite clause in situations where there is an external governor, e.g. an ECM verb, which assigns it Case. Here again we find a parallelism between clauses and 'noun phrases':

79a. I believe John/him to have left suddenly
79b. *I believe* [IP *John/him* [I' *to* [VP *have left suddenly*]]]

80a. I consider John/him a great athlete
80b. *I consider* [DP *John/him a great athlete*]

(80) involves a small clause complement whose subject is exceptionally Case-marked by the root verb. This example was identified in Chapter 4 as a problem for the small-clause analysis outlined there, which assigns the subject of the small clause to the Spec position of the maximal projection which realizes the small clause. The problem arose as a result of assigning the small clause in (80) an NP structure, with the consequence that both the subject of the small clause and the determiner are competing for the (same) Spec-NP position. In the context of this (NP-based) analysis, (80) is surprising in that it represents an exception to the otherwise rigid restriction on the co-occurrence of NP subjects and determiners in 'noun phrases'.

81.

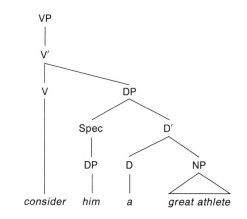

In the context of the DP analysis, however, (80) is not expected to be problematic, given that the subject and the determiner are assumed to occupy different positions, so that (80) has the structure shown in (81). (80) shows that the co-occurrence restriction on DP subjects and determiners holds only in the absence of an external Case-assigner for the subject, just as (79) shows that an overt DP subject is excluded from the subject position of a non-finite clause only in the absence of an external Case-assigner for the subject. This conclusion confirms that examples where a DP subject and a determiner cannot co-occur involve a violation of the Case Requirement on DPs.

6.4.4 Pronouns and Agr

So far, we have been treating pronouns as (pro-forms for) nouns. However, there is evidence which suggests that pronouns are (pro-forms for) DPs, in the sense that they occupy the D position of DP, rather than the N position. Part of the evidence has to do with examples such as the following, read/pronounced without an intonation break after the pronoun:

82a. You politicians/warmongers
82b. We humans/victims

83a. *You the politicians
83b. *We the humans

(82a,b) show that pronouns, in particular *you* and *we*, can function as (play the role of) determiners, on a par with articles and other determiners. Examples such as (83a,b) have been cited as evidence that the pronoun is a determiner, on the grounds that it cannot co-occur with another determiner. However, given the discussion above, this restriction does not necessarily mean that the pronoun occupies the D position. Even if the pronoun were in Spec-DP it would still be excluded, for the same reason that DP subjects are generally excluded in the presence of a determiner and the absence of an external Case-governor. There are, however, other facts which indicate that pronouns occupy the D position not only in examples (82a,b) but in general.

Consider the following examples:

84a. You politicians must be ashamed of $\begin{Bmatrix} \text{*yourself} \\ \text{yourselves} \\ \text{*themselves} \end{Bmatrix}$

84b. We sheep always blame $\begin{Bmatrix} \text{*myself} \\ \text{ourselves} \\ \text{*yourselves} \end{Bmatrix}$

These examples show that the number and person features of the subject, indicated by the reflexive element in the object position, are encoded in the pronoun. In (84a) the person feature of the subject is exclusively marked on the pronoun, whereas the number feature is marked on both the pronoun and the noun. In (84b), which includes an irregular noun which does not show number, both the number and person features are overtly marked on the pronoun.

The following examples show that the Case of the noun phrase is also marked on the pronoun:

85a. We/*us politicians know how to make empty promises
85b. The public despises us/*we politicians
85c. The public is against us/*we politicians

On the assumption that the agreement features and the Case of a 'noun phrase' are encoded in its head, the pronoun in the type of 'noun phrases' discussed must be in the head position, i.e. D.

The evidence discussed is part of the more general and independent fact that pronouns are essentially bundles of agreement features. The pronoun *she*, for example, is a bundle of the features third person (person), feminine (gender), singular (number), and the pronoun *we* is a bundle of the features first (person), plural (number). The person, gender, and number features are basically the features which make up the category Agr, so that pronouns are in fact no more than the morphological realization of the Agr category. In view of this it is not surprising that pronouns occupy the D position. Examples (85a–c), and more generally the fact that pronouns show Case distinctions, indicate that Case is also one of the features of the Agr category. This means that the process we have been calling Case-assignment to the subject in examples such as (86a) and (86b) below is essentially a process of 'matching' the Case feature of the Agr category I/D with the Case feature of the Agr category of the subject:

86a. He translated the book
86b. His translation of the book

86c.

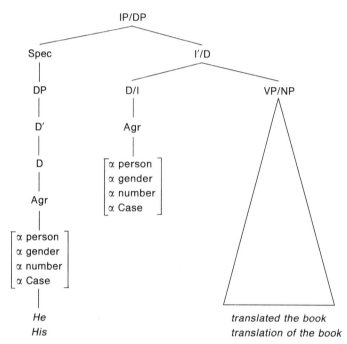

The Greek letter alpha is a variable which encodes the value of each feature. By virtue of Spec-Head Agreement the values of the features of the Agr categories in (86c) must be identical: if the value of the Case feature, for example, is nominative in one it must be nominative in the other, and if it is genitive in one it must be genitive in the other, and so on. In this context, ungrammatical examples from Standard English such as **His/him left early* and **He/him translation of the book*, which show a lack of agreement in the Case feature, are on a par with ungrammatical examples such as **You/we smiles*, which show a lack of agreement in the person and number features. Both types of example are excluded on the grounds that they involve a violation of Spec-Head Agreement. Although the term 'Case-assignment' becomes inaccurate in this context, we will continue to use it as a metaphor for what is essentially an agreement relation involving the Case feature.

Going back to examples (82a,b), they have the structure shown in (87a), where the pronoun is situated under D, and the noun under N. (87b) is the structure of the DP subject in (86a,b) isolated below for emphasis. The point is that DPs which consist of a pronoun only have a DP structure which consists of the X-bar projections of D only:

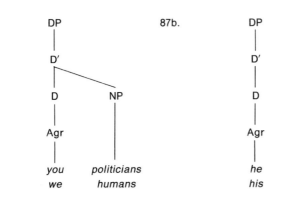

87a.   87b.

6.4.5   Gerundive Noun Phrases

Consider the following examples, which include a gerundive phrase (Chapter 4):

88a. John's keeping a rottweiler frightens his neighbours
88b. Bill resents John's keeping a rottweiler
88c. Mary is against John's keeping a rottweiler

Externally, the gerundive phrase illustrated in these examples displays properties usually associated with 'noun phrases'. For example, it occurs in positions typically reserved for 'noun phrases', such as the object position of transitive verbs like *resent* (88b), and the object position of prepositions like *against* (88c), in addition to their ability to occur in the subject position of a finite clause (88a). Moreover, the subject of the gerundive phrase bears genitive Case, as shown in (88a–c), which is a typical property of subjects of 'noun phrases'.

Internally, however, the gerundive phrase illustrated in (88a–c) displays properties which indicate the presence of a VP. First of all, the object of *keep(ing)* is assigned accusative Case, implying that its Case-governor is a verb. If the Case-governor of the object were a noun we would expect the presence of a preposition, for reasons which should be familiar by now. Another property which indicates the presence of VP relates to the fact that in certain contexts the gerundive phrase in question can include a VP-adverb modifying the gerund:

89a. John's continually picking arguments with Mary irritates Bill
89b. Bill's habitually lying about his whereabouts is intriguing

On the assumption that VP-adverbs, as their name suggests, adjoin to VP, (89a,b) imply the presence of a VP inside the gerundive phrase.

In the context of the (previously adopted) NP-analysis of 'noun phrases', the mixed properties of the gerundive phrases discussed raise a serious problem. The (NP) structure they imply is shown in (90). The top NP accounts for the fact that externally these phrases are 'noun phrases', and VP accounts for their internal verbal properties. The NP-daughter-of-NP is the subject of the 'noun phrase'. However, (90) is clearly inconsistent with the principles of X-bar Theory, and is therefore excluded. Moreover, it is not clear

90.

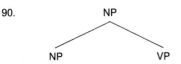

91.

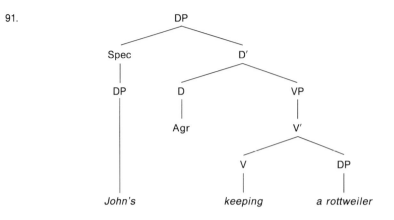

from which source the subject receives its genitive Case. However, in the context of the DP analysis these phrases can be assigned a structure which is consistent with both their mixed properties and the principles of X-bar theory, shown in (91). (91) differs from the types of DP discussed (above) in that the complement of D is VP. VP accounts for the internal verbal properties of the phrase, and DP accounts for its external nominal properties. Genitive Case is assigned to the subject via Spec-Head Agreement with (the Agr element of) D, in line with overt subjects of DPs in general.

6.4.6   Summary

The NP analysis of 'noun phrases' proved inadequate in accounting for the genitive Case assigned to the subject, and in capturing some significant parallelisms between 'noun phrases' and clauses. The latter suggest that 'noun phrases' should be assigned a structure which parallels that of clauses. The revised structure of the 'noun phrase' is one where D is the head of the 'noun phrase', with NP as its complement in certain 'noun phrases', and Spec-DP as the subject position. In this structure genitive Case is assigned – more precisely, determined – via Spec-Head Agreement with D, in situations where D instantiates an Agr category. Pronouns have been argued to be the morphological realization of the Agr element of D, and therefore occupy the D position. The DP-analysis for 'noun phrases' has also been shown to account for the mixed and otherwise problematic properties of gerundive 'noun phrases'. The structure of gerundive 'noun phrases' is one where the complement of D is VP.

6.5   *Case and Movement*

In this section we will discuss the ways in which Case Theory interacts with movement transformations. We will start first with DP-movement (alias NP-movement), and then move on to *Wh*-movement and Quantifier Raising, included under the general heading 'Operator-movement'.

6.5.1 DP-movement

6.5.1.1 Raising Constructions Raising constructions involve movement of a DP subject from an embedded non-finite clause to the subject position of the root (finite) clause. When the embedded clause is finite, DP-movement is prevented from taking place by the Tensed S Condition (TSC) (Chapter 3). Consequently, an expletive DP appears in the subject position of the root clause:

92a. John seems to be happy
92b. [IP [DP *John*i] *seems* [[DP ti] *to be happy*]]

93a. It seems (that) John is happy
93b. [IP [DP *It*] *seems (that)* [[DP *John*] *is happy*]]

In Chapter 4 it was tentatively suggested that DP-movement in (92) is motivated by EPP, (the principle which requires every clause to have a (formal) subject). Movement of the embedded subject to the subject position of the root clause enables the root clause to acquire a subject and thereby satisfy EPP. When DP-movement is prevented from taking place, as in (93), the expletive DP *it* is inserted in the subject position of the root clause for the purpose of ensuring that the root clause satisfies EPP.

However, there are reasons which apparently cast doubt on the possibility that DP-movement in (92) is motivated by EPP. Part of the reasoning underlying the EPP-based analysis is that EPP can be satisfied simply by inserting a formal, expletive DP in the subject position of the root clause, as shown in (93). It remains mysterious, though, why this process cannot apply to (92), thereby rendering movement of the embedded subject unnecessary:

94a. *It seems John to be happy
94b. *[IP [DP *It*] *seems* [[DP *John*] *to be happy*]]

This example is consistent with EPP, and yet it is ungrammatical. Somehow, it seems that DP-movement is obligatory in raising constructions whenever it is possible, that is, whenever the embedded clause is non-tensed. A possible way of maintaining the EPP-based analysis is to argue that expletive-insertion (like *Do*-support (Chapter 3)) is a 'last resort' option, in the sense that it is triggered only when a movement process is prevented from taking place by some principle of the Grammar. When movement is possible, as would be the case in (94), expletive-insertion is excluded altogether, by virtue of being a 'last resort' mechanism. In (93), however, expletive-insertion applies legitimately because DP-movement is prevented from taking place by TSC. Although this is not an implausible analysis, the standard view concerning the motivation behind DP-movement relies on the Case Requirement rather than on EPP.

The reasoning underlying the Case-based analysis is as follows. When the embedded clause is non-finite, as in (92), its overt DP subject cannot receive Case via Spec-Head Agreement with (non-finite) I, and is therefore in danger of being excluded by the Case Requirement. To avoid this prospect, the DP subject moves to the subject position of the root finite clause, where it receives nominative Case via Spec-Head Agreement with (finite) I. The ungrammatical example (94) represents a situation where the embedded DP subject remains in its non-Case-marked D-structure position, and is therefore excluded by the Case Requirement. In the context of this (Case-based) analysis, the fact that movement of the embedded DP subject results in the root clause acquiring a subject, thereby satisfying EPP, is simply a by-product of the need to circumvent the Case Requirement, rather than the prime reason for movement.

6.5.1.2 *Passives and Ergatives (Burzio's Generalization)*   Passives such as (95) below involve movement of a DP object to the subject position. As in raising constructions, the DP in question cannot remain in its D-structure position even when the subject position is filled with a formal expletive subject (96):

95a. The ball was kicked (by John)
95b. [$_{IP}$ [$_{DP}$ *The ball*$_i$] *was* [$_{VP}$ *kicked* [$_{DP}$ t$_i$]]]

96a. *It was kicked the ball (by John)
96b. *[$_{IP}$ [$_{DP}$ *It*] *was* [$_{VP}$ *kicked* [$_{DP}$ *the ball*]]]

The parallelism with raising constructions suggests that DP-movement in passives is also motivated by Case considerations, rather than by EPP. Presumably, (96) excludes the possibility that DP-movement in passives is motivated by EPP, unless, of course, one adopts the argument that expletive-insertion is a 'last resort' strategy in the sense explained above.

Additional evidence for the hypothesis that DP-movement in passives is motivated by Case can be gleaned from examples such as (97a,b) below, where the complement of the passive verb is a clause, rather than a DP:

97a. It was decided that John should resign
97b. It was believed that John would resign

Because the complement is not a DP, and therefore not subject to the Case Requirement, it does not have to be in Spec-IP. Consequently, the subject position is filled with an expletive DP for the purpose of satisfying EPP. This example suggests that movement of the complement of the passive verb to Spec-IP in passives is obligatory only when the complement is a DP, confirming the Case-based analysis for DP-movement: the DP object in passives moves to Spec-IP to receive Case.

Now, if movement of the DP object in passives is motivated by Case, the implication is that verbal passives cannot assign Case. Since the active counterpart of *kick*, for example, is clearly transitive (*The boy kicked the ball*), it seems that the inability of passive verbs to assign accusative Case is the result of the affixation of the passive morpheme to the active base form. In Chapter 5 we discussed evidence showing that the affixation of the passive morpheme to an active base verb results in the derived (passive) verb being unable to assign its external thematic role to the subject position, although there are indications that the external thematic role is not eliminated altogether. Now we are led to conclude that the affixation of the passive morpheme to a transitive base verb also results in the derived verbal passive being unable to assign accusative Case to its object. The passive morpheme is often said to 'absorb' the (accusative) Case of the passive verb, thereby forcing the DP object to move to the subject position where it receives (nominative) Case via Spec-Head Agreement with (the Agr element of finite) I.

In Chapter 5 we also discussed a class of verbs, called ergatives, which resemble passives in that their internal argument appears in the subject position, and is placed there via DP-movement. As with passives too, the internal argument of ergative verbs cannot remain in the object position:

98a. The vase broke
98b. [$_{IP}$ [$_{DP}$ *The vase*$_i$] I [$_{VP}$ *broke* [$_{DP}$ t$_i$]]]

99a. *It broke the vase
99b. *[IP [DP *It*] I [VP *broke* [DP *the vase*]]

If it is the case that DP-movement is generally motivated by Case considerations, it follows that ergative verbs do not assign (accusative) Case to their object. This is despite the fact that, unlike passives, ergative verbs do not exhibit a morpheme which can be said to 'absorb' the (accusative) Case of the transitive (or causative) base from which they derive (*John broke the vase*). It is for this reason that ergatives, and also passives, are called **unaccusatives**, a term which is intended to capture the property whereby these verbs select an internal argument but do not assign accusative Case to it.

The similarity between passives and ergatives suggests the generalization that verbs which do not assign an external thematic role to the subject position seem also to be unable to assign accusative Case to their internal argument (and vice versa). Recall (from Chapter 5) that ergatives, like passives, do not assign an external thematic role to the subject position. This generalization was made in Burzio (1986) and came to be known as **Burzio's Generalization**. The version in (100) is from Chomsky (1986a):

100. **Burzio's Generalization**
    A verb (with an object) Case-marks its object iff it theta-marks its subject.

As a generalization, (100) should, obviously, be derivable from some general principle of the Grammar, a task which will not be undertaken here.

6.5.1.3   *The Subject-inside-VP Hypothesis*   So far, the Spec position of VP has not been attributed a role in the representation and derivation of sentences. This is a rather surprising gap, which suggests that something has probably been overlooked. In this section, we will see that Spec-VP, far from remaining idle, plays a crucial role in the representation of subjects of sentences. The link between this issue and Case theory will become clear as we proceed.

Consider the following examples, intended as approximations (in word order) of French examples discussed in Sportiche (1988):

101a. *All* the travellers have drunk from the well
101b. The travellers have *all* drunk from the well

In both examples the **floating quantifier** *all* modifies the subject *the travellers*. However, only in (101a) is the quantifier adjacent to the DP it modifies. Assuming that modification relations are structurally based and imply adjacency (Chapter 5), it follows that the quantifier in (101b) is somehow structurally related to the DP it modifies, even though the two categories are separated by the auxiliary verb *have*. The situation we have here is no different from a number of other situations we have encountered so far, where two related categories, e.g. a verb and its object, appear separated from each other rather than adjacent. We have dealt with these situations by assuming that the two related categories are base-generated adjacent to each other, and that one of them is affected by a movement transformation. The same reasoning can be applied to the quantifier in relation to the DP subject it modifies in (101b).

The question we need to answer is which of the two related categories is affected by movement, the quantifier or the DP it modifies. One possibility could be that the complex is base-generated in the position it occupies in (101a), which is, presumably, Spec-IP. The derivation of (101b) will then involve lowering of the quantifier to a position intervening between the finite auxiliary verb, located under I, and the main verb. Although this derivation both establishes a structural relationship between the quantifier and the DP it modifies, and accounts for their order in (101b), there is an alternative analysis which implements one of the more familiar movement transformations, namely DP-movement. The alternative analysis is that the complex is base-generated in the position occupied by the quantifier in (101b), and that the order in (101b) is derived by a DP-movement process to Spec-IP which affects *the travellers* only, stranding the quantifier behind in the original position of the complex. According to this analysis, (101a) differs only in that the movement affects the whole of the complex, instead of just *the travellers*.

The two derivations implied by this analysis are as outlined in (102a,b), where movement of the auxiliary from inside VP to I is ignored:

102a. [IP [*All* [*the travellers*]ᵢ *have* [VP [t]ᵢ [V′ *drunk from the well*]]]]
102b. [IP [*The travellers*]ᵢ *have* [VP [*all* tᵢ] [V′ *drunk from the well*]]]]

The position intervening between the auxiliary (under I) and the main verb (inside VP) is assumed to be Spec-VP, the only position in this environment made freely available by X-bar Theory, short of adopting an adjunction structure. If this is the right analysis for (101a/102a) and (101b/102b), these examples can be said to show that subjects are base-generated in Spec-VP and subsequently moved to Spec-IP. The usefulness of example (101b/102b), in particular, lies in the fact that the position of the quantifier gives an indication of the D-structure position of the subject: to the extent that this position is Spec-VP, the latter is the position occupied by subjects of sentences at D-structure.

The reason why DP subjects have to move to Spec-IP (from Spec-VP) can be related to Case Theory if Spec-VP is assumed to be a non-Case-marked position, on a par with the object position of passives and ergatives. Like its counterparts in passives and ergatives, the DP-subject in simple sentences such as (103) moves to Spec-IP to receive nominative Case under Spec-Head Agreement with I:

103a. The boy kicked the ball

103b.

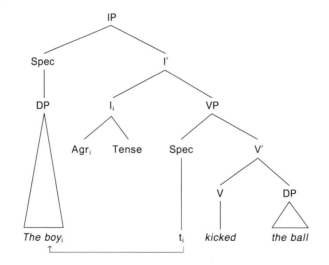

Ungrammatical examples such as *It/there (has) the boy kicked the ball*, where the subject remains in Spec-VP and Spec-IP is filled with a formal expletive subject, can be invoked as evidence that Spec-VP is a non-Case-marked position, although this example, like the others above, can be explained away in terms of the idea that expletive-insertion is a last resort option. In the rest of this book we will refer to Spec-VP as the thematic subject position and to Spec-IP as the grammatical subject position.

Besides the fact that the **Subject-inside-VP Hypothesis** fills an otherwise surprising gap in the representation and derivation of sentences, it arguably also has other theoretical advantages. One could suggest, for example, that the hypothesis makes possible a closer connection between the structural representation of lexical categories and their argument/thematic structures. By including all the arguments of lexical categories inside their X-bar projections (at D-structure), we are effectively implying that X-bar projections are basically the structural representations (domains) of lexical categories together with their argument/thematic structures. Prior to the Subject-inside-VP Hypothesis, it was not possible to make this close connection between X-bar structures and argument/thematic structures, as the subject was assumed to be base-generated outside VP. Note that the implication of this reasoning is that expletive subjects do not originate in Spec-VP, as they are not part of the argument/thematic structures of the verbs they occur with. Expletives are therefore inserted directly under the grammatical subject position of the sentence, possibly by a transformation similar to Do-support (Chapter 3).

As a final remark, the analysis outlined for subjects of sentences extends to subjects of DPs in a natural way, so that a DP such as (104a) can be said to have the derivation shown in (104b):

104a. Mary's translation of the book

104b.

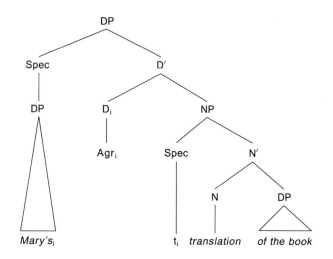

The DP subject is base-generated in Spec-NP, and subsequently moves to Spec-DP, presumably for the same reason that DP subjects of sentences move to Spec-IP. Spec-NP (the D-structure (thematic) position of the subject) is non-Case-marked, presumably for the same reason its counterpart in sentences (Spec-VP) is also non-Case-marked.

6.5.1.4   Case and A-Chains (TSC)   The idea that DP-movement is motivated by Case considerations implies that DP-movement takes place from a non-Case-marked position to a Case-marked position. Consequently, the A-chain derived by DP-movement has only one Case, assigned to the head of the chain. This general property of A-chains suggests that there is probably a one-to-one correspondence between A-chains and Case, which parallels the one-to-one correspondence between (A-)chains and thematic roles (chapter 5). Recall that the latter property of (A-)chains was encoded in the (definition of the) Theta Criterion by incorporating into it a uniqueness condition, such that a chain can have one and only one thematic role (or theta-position). To take a similar step with respect to the Case Requirement, we need first check whether A-chains with two Case positions are indeed excluded.

Consider the following, not unfamiliar, example:

105a. *John seems is happy
105b. *$[_{IP}$ $[_{DP}$ *John*$]_i$ *seems* $[[_{DP}$ t$]_i$ *is happy*$]]$

Up to this stage, we have been excluding this example in terms of TSC, that is, the condition which prevents DP-movement from moving a DP out of a finite clause. Notice, however, that (105) also involves a situation where the DP *John* moves from one Case-marked position (the subject position of the embedded finite clause) to another Case-marked position (the subject position of the root finite clause), leading to the derivation of an A-chain with two Cases. In view of this, (105), and similar examples, actually show that A-chains are indeed subject to a uniqueness condition with respect to their Case properties. Once the Case Requirement is revised to this effect, TSC can then be dispensed with altogether. The condition it encodes is an epiphenomenon, in so far as it is part of a more fundamental restriction on the Case properties of A-chains.

There are various possible ways of incorporating the uniqueness condition in question into the definition of the Case Requirement. The following version is suggested in Chomsky (1986a):

106. **Case Requirement**
A chain is Case-marked if it contains exactly one Case-marked position.

Recall that the notion 'chain' is understood in the broader sense which includes DPs not involved in movement. (106), like the Theta Criterion, is best understood as a well-formedness condition on chains: for a chain to be well-formed with respect to its Case properties, it has to satisfy the requirement specified in (106). Note that the definition in (106) is not specific to A-chains, implying that it applies to A'-chains as well. We turn to a discussion of A'-chains.

6.5.2 Operator-movement: Variables and Case

We have seen that DP-movement results in the derivation of A-chains where the head (the moved DP) is in a Case-marked position and the tail/root (the trace) is in a non-Case-marked position. This is to be expected on the assumption that DP-movement is motivated by Case considerations. A'-chains, derived by *Wh*-movement and QR, differ in that it is their root/tail position which is Case-marked:

107a. What did John kick?
107b. $[_{CP}$ *What*$_i$ $[_{C'}$ *did* $[_{IP}$ *John* I $[_{VP}$ *kick* t$_i]]]]$?

107c. For which thing x, John kicked x

108a. John suspects everyone
108b. $[_{IP}$ *everyone*$_i$ $[_{IP}$ *John* I $[_{VP}$ *suspects* t$_i]]]$

108c. For every x, John suspects x

In both examples the trace of the A'-chain, derived by *Wh*-movement in (107) and QR in (108), is situated in a Case-marked position. However, despite this fundamental difference between A-chains and A'-chains, the latter are also consistent with the Case Requirement, in that, at least in examples of the type illustrated in (107) and (108), they include a unique Case-marked position.

Presumably, the reason why A'-chains differ from A-chains with respect to their Case position is that movement of operators (*wh*-phrases and quantified phrases) is not motivated by Case considerations. We saw in Chapter 4 that movement of *wh*-phrases in the syntax (overt *Wh*-movement) is motivated by the [+ WH]-CP Principle, i.e. the principle which requires [+ WH]-CPs to have a specifier by S-structure. On the other hand, movement of quantified phrases and *wh*-phrases in situ in the mapping from S-structure onto LF (covert movement) is sometimes said to be motivated by scope considerations. Given that quantified and *wh*-phrases logically tend to have scope over the whole sentence (107c/108c), and given the structural basis of scope (c-command), the quantified/*wh*-phrase has to be in a c-commanding position with respect to the whole sentence at LF.

There is, however, a more fundamental reason why traces of operators are in Case-marked positions whereas DP traces are not. Recall that traces of operators have the status of variables at LF (107c/108c), contrary to DP-traces, which have the status of anaphors, as we shall see in Chapter 7. Assuming an approach to Case in terms of the Visibility Hypothesis, variables have Case because as arguments they are required (by the Theta Criterion) to be assigned a thematic role. Recall that in the context of the Visibility Hypothesis the assignment of thematic roles to arguments is dependent on arguments having Case. The fact that traces of operators have Case, as a defining property, then follows.

6.5.3 Structural versus Inherent Case: Expletive-argument Chains and Partitive Case

A common property of nominative and accusative Cases is that, first, they do not necessarily involve a thematic relation between the assigner and the assignee and, secondly, they are determined at S-structure. Nominative Case is assigned to the DP subject via Spec-Head Agreement with finite I, and does not involve a thematic relation between I and the DP subject. Nominative Case is determined at S-structure in the sense that it takes place subsequent to movement of the DP subject to Spec-IP, either from Spec-VP (Subject-inside-VP Hypothesis), the Spec-IP position of a non-finite embedded clause (raising constructions) or from the object position of an unaccusative verb (passives and ergatives). As for accusative Case, although in most situations it involves categories which are thematically related, i.e. the verb and its internal argument, it can also involve categories which are not thematically related, i.e. an ECM verb and an ECM subject. The fact that accusative Case can be determined subsequent to movement can be seen in examples such as the following:

109a. I believe him to have been sacked
109b. *I believe* [$_{IP}$ *him$_i$ to have been sacked* t$_i$]

110a. I expect him to abandon the race
110b. *I expect* [$_{IP}$ *him$_i$ to* [$_{VP}$ t$_i$ [$_{V'}$ *abandon the race*]]]

In (109) the assignment of accusative Case to *him* by the ECM verb *believe* takes place subsequent to the movement of *him* from the object position of the embedded passive verb to the subject position of the embedded clause. A similar situation exists in (110), except that in this case movement takes place from the Spec-VP position to the Spec-IP position of the embedded clause.

A Case which is determined at S-structure and does not necessarily involve a thematic relation between the assigner and the assignee is called **structural** Case. Nominative and accusative are therefore both structural Cases. Note that in the context of the DP Hypothesis, genitive Case also qualifies as a structural Case, as it is assigned via Spec-Head Agreement with D, which does not bear a thematic relation to it. Genitive Case is also arguably determined at S-structure, in so far as subjects of DPs, like subjects of sentences, are base-generated in the Spec position of the maximal projection which assigns them a thematic role (the Subject-inside-NP Hypothesis), and subsequently moved to Spec-DP. A Case which is determined at D-structure and involves a thematic relation between the assigner and the assignee is called **inherent** Case. Of the Cases discussed in this chapter, oblique Case, assigned by prepositions to their complement, qualifies as inherent Case. As far as the data discussed in this book are concerned, there are apparently no reasons to believe that oblique Case can be assigned subsequent to movement. Moreover, prepositions generally assign oblique Case to a DP which they also theta-mark, either in terms of a thematic role of their own or a thematic role they receive from the verb (Chapter 5).

With this in mind, consider now the following examples:

111a. Three girls arrived
111b. There arrived three girls

112a. A car approached
112b. There approached a car

The verbs *arrive* and *approach* belong to a subclass of the class of verbs we referred to above (and in chapter 5) as ergative/unaccusative. Their distinctive property is that their unique argument can either appear in the subject position (Spec-IP), as in (111a) and (112a), or in the postverbal position, as in (111b) and (112b). In the latter case, the expletive *there* appears in the subject position. The question which examples (111b) and (112b) raise is how the DPs in the postverbal position satisfy the Case Requirement, given that the verb is unaccusative (does not assign accusative Case).

Various answers to this question have been suggested, one of which relies on the notion of 'Case-transfer'. The idea is that the expletive in the Case-marked subject position is co-indexed with the DP in the postverbal position and forms with it an 'expletive-argument chain'. Within this chain a process of 'Case transfer' takes place, whereby the expletive in the Case-marked subject position transfers the nominative Case it receives from I to the argument in the non-Case-marked postverbal position. This way, the postverbal DP, or, rather, the 'expletive-argument chain', can be said to satisfy the Case Requirement. An interesting consequence of the notion of the 'expletive-argument' chain is that it offers a possible solution to a problem, pointed out earlier in this chapter, that expletives give rise to in relation to the Visibility Hypothesis. The problem is that expletives invariably occur in Case-marked positions even though, as non-arguments, they are not dependent on Case. If expletives can be shown to be invariably linked to an argument in a non-Case-marked position, as in (111b) and (112b) above, the fact that they occur in Case-marked positions can be said to follow from their role as the Case-marked member of the 'expletive-argument chain'.

The analysis arguably extends to examples such as (113) and (114) below, on the assumption that in both examples the clausal argument is linked to the expletive DP:

113a. It seems that John left suddenly
113b. *It$_i$ seems* [$_{CP}$ *that John left suddenly*]$_i$

114a. They consider it inappropriate that John left suddenly
114b. *They consider* [$_{AP}$ *it$_i$* [$_{A'}$ *inappropriate*]] [$_{CP}$ *that John left suddenly*]$_i$

(113) includes a raising verb which does not assign an external thematic role and, by virtue of Burzio's Generalization, does not assign Case to its internal argument either. Although the complement of the raising verb in (113) is a CP, it is expected to be assigned Case under the Visibility Hypothesis by virtue of being an argument. If the CP complement is assumed to be linked to the expletive in the Case-marked subject position, CP satisfies the Case Requirement by virtue of being in an 'expletive-argument chain'. Example (114) includes an expletive in the subject position of the small-clause complement, and is linked to the extraposed CP. Note that in this example the position occupied by the expletive is not only Case-marked, it is also theta-marked, which is unexpected. However, these facts arguably follow from the role of the expletive in the 'expletive-argument chain'.

Going back to examples (111b) and (112b), Belletti (1988) has offered an alternative analysis which exploits the fact that the postverbal subject must be indefinite. The ungrammaticality of examples (115b) and (116b) is due to the fact that the postverbal subject is definite. Examples (115a) and (116a) show that no such restriction applies to preverbal subjects:

115a. Mary arrived
115b. *There arrived Mary

116a. The car approached
116b. *There approached the car

Belletti relates this property of these constructions to the fact that in Icelandic, among other languages, indefinite arguments generally have distinct Case properties from definite arguments. More precisely, they receive a special Case known as **partitive**, which Belletti argues is an inherent Case in the sense explained above. Belletti generalizes this property of indefinite arguments in Icelandic to all languages, arguing that in English it is simply masked by the fact that the language has poor Case morphology. Belletti argues further that all verbs have, as a lexical property, the ability to assign partitive Case to an argument they theta-mark. However, only indefinite arguments are compatible with partitive Case, so that when the internal argument of a given verb is not indefinite, assignment of partitive Case does not take place. According to this analysis, the postverbal argument in (111b) and (112b) above receives partitive Case from the unaccusative verb by virtue of being theta-marked by the verb as well as by virtue of being indefinite. In (115b) and (116b), however, the postverbal argument does not receive partitive Case from the unaccusative verb, on the grounds that partitive Case is incompatible with indefinite arguments.

6.5.4   Summary

We have discussed reasons to believe that DP-movement is generally motivated by Case consideration. DPs move to a Spec-IP position because they cannot receive Case in their D-structure position. In raising constructions this is due to the fact that the embedded I is non-finite, and in passives and ergatives to the fact that passive and ergative verbs lack the ability to assign (accusative) Case to their internal argument. The Case-based analysis for DP-movement makes it possible to revise the representation of subjects in sentences along the lines of the Subject-inside-VP Hypothesis. The latter postulates that thematic subjects of sentences are base-generated in Spec-VP and subsequently moved to Spec-IP, for Case reasons. Among the advantages of the Subject-inside-VP Hypothesis is that it makes it possible to have a close connection between X-bar structures and thematic/argument structures of lexical categories. X-bar structures are basically the structural projections of the thematic/argument structures of lexical categories.

The A-chains derived by DP-movement have a single Case position, a fact which reflects a uniqueness condition on the Case properties of chains, incorporated into the Case Requirement. A'-chains also have this property, but differ in that their Case-marked position is usually the root of the chain, rather than the head. This fact arguably follows from the status of traces of operators as variables, and therefore as arguments in need of Case.

Finally, a distinction is drawn between structural Case and inherent Case. The former is determined at S-structure, and does not necessarily involve a thematic relation between the assigner and assignee. Examples of structural Case are nominative, accusative, and, according to the DP Hypothesis, also genitive. Inherent Case is determined at D-structure, and involves a thematic relation between the assigner and the assignee. Examples of inherent Case are oblique, assigned to objects of prepositions, and arguably also partitive, assigned to indefinite arguments of unaccusative verbs.

6.6   *Conclusions and Revisions*

In this chapter we discussed the Case properties of 'noun phrases', and the mechanisms of the Grammar regulating them. 'Noun phrases' are subject to a condition, called here the Case Requirement, which requires them to have Case. The Case Requirement can either take the form of a Case Filter, which applies at PF and excludes overt 'noun phrases' which lack Case, or can be made to follow from the Theta Criterion in terms of the Visibility Hypothesis – 'noun phrases', especially arguments, need to have Case to be visible for theta-marking at LF.

The empirical basis for the Case Requirement relates to the fact that the appearance of a 'noun phrase' in certain non-Case-marked environments gives rise to ungrammaticality. A 'noun phrase' is in a Case-marked environment if it is in a specific structural relation of locality, called government, to a transitive category, or if it is in a Spec-Head Agreement relation with a functional category which instantiates the Agr category. Spec-Head Agreement involves government as well as agreement in the grammatical features of person, gender, number, and Case. The Cases assigned under government alone are accusative (assigned by transitive verbs), oblique (assigned by prepositions), and possibly also partitive (assigned to indefinite 'noun phrases' by (un)accusative verbs). The Cases assigned under Spec-Head agreement are nominative (assigned via Spec-Head Agreement with finite I) and genitive (assigned via Spec-Head Agreement with D).

The necessity to account for genitive Case-assignment, as well as certain significant structural similarities between 'noun phrases' and clauses, has led to the conclusion that 'noun phrases' have a structure which parallels that of clauses. 'Noun phrases' are DPs, headed by the functional category D which may have either NP or VP (gerundive DPs) as its complement. In certain 'noun phrases' D instantiates the Agr category, but in others (arguably the ones which include determiners) it does not. Pronouns occupy the D position, on the grounds that they are the morphological realization of the (agreement features, including Case, of the) Agr category under D.

Cases fall into two major classes, structural and inherent. Structural Cases are determined at S-structure, and do not necessarily involve a thematic relation between the assigner and the assignee. Examples of structural Case are nominative, accusative and genitive. Inherent Cases are determined at D-structure and involve a thematic relation between the assigner and the assignee. Examples of inherent Case are oblique, and arguably also partitive.

The Case Requirement is also responsible for DP-movement (alias NP-movement) processes. DP-movement seems invariably to take place from a non-Case-marked position to a Case-marked position. This suggests that DPs move to Case-marked positions because they cannot receive Case in their D-structure positions. The fact that DP-movement from a Case-marked position (to another Case-marked position) leads to ungrammaticality, in turn, suggests that there is a uniqueness condition on A-chains, such that they can only have one Case-marked position. This requirement holds for A'-chains as well, although the latter differ in that their Case position is usually the root rather than the head position.

The modular aspect of the theory of Grammar emerged clearly in this chapter in relation to the interaction between the principles of the various modules. For example, Case Theory interacts with X-bar Theory and Government Theory insofar as the latter define the locality relations under which Case is assigned. The interaction between these theories is best illustrated in ECM constructions, where the ECM DP is a subject with respect to X-bar Theory (it occupies Spec-IP) but patterns with objects with respect to Government and Case Theory (it is governed and assigned Case by the verb). On the other hand, the Visibility Hypothesis, to the extent that it is viable, establishes a clear dependency relation between Case Theory and Theta Theory: assignment of a thematic role to a DP is made dependent on the DP having Case.

A third issue which illustrates clearly the interaction between the principles of separate modules of the Grammar relates to DP-movement. The latter is motivated by Case considerations, in the sense that DPs move to Case-marked positions because they cannot receive Case in their D-structure positions. The consequence is that the positions to which DPs move need not be specified in the definition of the transformation itself. Moreover, the fact that this position must be the subject position of a finite clause which includes a verb which does not assign an external thematic role, follows from the principles of Case Theory in combination with the principles of Theta Theory. The condition that DP-movement can affect a DP included in a tensed clause (TSC) also does not need to be specified in the definition of DP-movement. This condition now follows from the principles of Case Theory, in particular the requirement that chains have a unique Case position.

Exercises

Exercise 1

Outline a derivation for each of the following examples:

1. The temperature is believed to have dropped
2. Which athlete is likely to be banned?
3. It is hard to be seen to be losing

You are expected to (i) determine what motivates each movement step in the derivation, (ii) identify the nature of each chain, and (iii) explain the Case properties of each chain.

Exercise 2

Examples (1) and (2) below seem to suggest that *be easy* is a raising predicate, so that (2) involves raising of *John* from the embedded clause to the subject position of the root clause:

1. It is easy to please John
2. John is easy to please

Discuss the problems that this derivation gives rise to, and try to outline an alternative analysis which is less problematic.

Exercise 3

The following examples include so-called **Bare-NP Adverbs**, which are DPs functioning as adverbial modifiers:

1. Bill arrived this morning
2. The children went that way

Discuss the status of Bare-NP Adverbs in these examples with respect to the Case Requirement on DPs. Make sure you consider both the Case Filter and the Visibility Hypothesis.

Exercise 4

The bracketed constituents in the examples below are sometimes called **cognate objects**, which are special DPs etymologically related to the verbs they occur with:

1. He smiled [a strange smile]
2. He ran [a good run]

Given the intransitive nature of the verbs in these examples, discuss the status of the bracketed DPs with respect to the Case Requirement.

Exercise 5

We have concluded in this chapter that nouns (and adjectives) do not assign Case, so that in example (1) below the semantically empty preposition *of* is inserted for the purpose of assigning Case to the DP complement of the noun. Bearing this in mind, consider a derivation for raising constructions and passives which involves insertion of the preposition *of* to assign Case to the DP in the non-Case-marked position, thereby rendering its movement unnecessary. However, this derivation is excluded, as shown by examples (2) and (3):

1. The translation of the book
2. *It/there was kicked of the ball
3. *It/there seems of John to be happy

What do examples (2) and (3) suggest in relation to the rule of insertion?

Further Reading

The theory of Case discussed in this chapter is mainly due to Rouveret and Vergnaud (1980) and Vergnaud (1982), further refined in Chomsky (1981; 1986a), Grimshaw (1981), and Pesetsky (1982). One of the original motivations for Case theory was to handle the cases which in Chomsky and Lasnik (1977) were handled in terms of the NP-to-VP Filter, in addition to other related cases. The Visibility Hypothesis appears in Chomsky (1981; 1986a) and is attributed to Joseph Aoun.

The theory of government is developed in Chomsky (1981), and its precise definition has been the subject of an intense debate. For a discussion of some definitions and their empirical implications, see Aoun and Sportiche (1983). The issue of adjacency in relation to Case-assignment is discussed in Stowell (1981) and Chomsky (1981). The relevance of Spec-Head agreement to Case is discussed in Chomsky (1986b), Borer (1986), Koopman (1987), Koopman and Sportiche (1991), and Chomsky (1991c).

The idea that the head of the noun phrase is D (the DP Hypothesis), and the idea that pronouns are D elements, are discussed in Postal (1966), Brame (1981; 1982), Hudson (1987), and Abney (1987). The parallelism in structure and other properties between noun phrases and clauses, is also discussed in Horrocks and Stavrou (1987) and Szabolcsi (1987). Abney (1987) also includes an extended discussion of the structure of gerunds with external nominal properties. For a detailed study of the syntax of noun phrases in general see Giorgi and Longobardi (1991).

The interaction between DP-movement and Case is discussed in Burzio (1986) and Chomsky (1981; 1986a). The idea that certain verbs which select an internal argument do not assign it Case (unaccusative verbs) appears in Perlmutter (1978). An alternative analysis for passives is presented in Baker *et al.* (1989). The Subject-inside-VP Hypothesis is discussed in Kitagawa (1986), Kuroda (1988), Sportiche (1988), and Koopman and Sportiche (1991).

The relevance of Case to variables is discussed in Chomsky (1981; 1986a). The latter also includes a discussion of the distinction between structural and inherent Case. The idea of partitive Case as an inherent Case is suggested in Belletti (1988) in the context of an alternative analysis to the expletive-argument chain analysis for *there*-constructions discussed in Chomsky (1981; 1986a).

7

Binding Theory and Control

Contents

7.1   *DP-Types*

In the previous chapter we discussed the distribution of DPs as determined by their Case properties in combination with the principles of Case Theory. In this chapter we shall discuss the distribution of DPs as determined by their referential properties in combination with the principles of a module of Grammar called **Binding Theory**. A section of the chapter is devoted to a discussion of the referential properties and distribution of PRO, which are believed to be regulated by a different module of Grammar called **Control Theory**. The properties of PRO and the factors which determine its interpretation are still poorly understood, and therefore our discussion of them will be descriptive in most parts, and somewhat speculative in others. Another (vaguely related) section is devoted to a discussion of the mechanism of **Licensing** and the principle of **Full Interpretation**, which play a crucial role in the derivation and representation of sentences.

7.1.1   Overt DPs

As far as their referential properties are concerned, overt DPs fall into three different classes: **anaphors**, **pronouns**, and **Referential Expressions (R-expressions)**. The class of anaphors includes **reflexives**, such as *himself* and *themselves*, and **reciprocals**, such as *each other*. These elements (anaphors) have in common the fact that they are dependent for their reference on an antecedent included in the sentence:

1a. The players blamed themselves/each other
1b. *The players$_i$ blamed themselves$_i$/each other$_i$*
2a. *The manager blamed themselves/each other
2b. **The manager$_i$ blamed themselves$_j$/each other$_j$*

The anaphor has an antecedent in (1), *the players*, but does not have an antecedent in (2). The DP *the manager* does not qualify as antecedent for the anaphor in (2) because it does not share the same features with the anaphor. Differences in features imply differences in referential values, indicated in terms of indices. The DP subject and the anaphor in (2) have different indices, and therefore different referential values.

Pronouns differ from anaphors in that they do not have to have an antecedent in the sentence. (3a) below, for example, can either have the interpretation shown in (3b), where the pronoun refers back to the subject of the root clause, or the interpretation shown in (3c), where the pronoun refers to an individual included in the discourse context (i.e. an individual known to the speaker and the listener):

3a. The manager suspects that the players blame him
3b. *The manager$_i$ suspects that the players blame him$_i$*
3c. *The manager$_i$ suspects that the players blame him$_j$*

The class of R-expressions includes names, such as *John, Mary, Bill*, and referring DPs, such as *the manager, the players, the table*. Unlike anaphors and pronouns, R-expressions cannot have an antecedent in the sentence. (4a) below, for example, cannot have the interpretation shown in (4b), where the R-expression *the manager* is co-indexed with the pronoun in the subject position of the root clause:

4a. He suspects that the players blame John
4b. **He$_i$ suspects that the players blame John$_i$*

4c. *He$_i$ suspects that the players blame John$_j$*

In (4c) the pronoun and the R-expression are not co-indexed, meaning that the pronoun is not the antecedent of the R-expression. The term 'antecedent' is understood for the moment to mean a DP which precedes and bears the same index as an anaphor, a pronoun, or an R-expression. Later on we shall discuss a more precise definition of the term 'antecedent'.

The referential properties of DPs can be assumed to be encoded in them in terms of referential features, together with the agreement features. In the previous chapter we saw that pronouns are basically the morphological realization of the Agr element of D, more precisely, of the (agreement) features person, number, gender and Case. There is a sense in which reflexives are also the morphological realization of the same features, and therefore probably also occupy the D position in DP. The difference between pronouns and reflexives lies in an additional feature complex relating to anaphoricity and pronominality, formally represented as [+/− a(naphoric)] and [+/− p(ronominal)]. Anaphors (reflexives and reciprocals) have the feature-specifications [+a, −p], whereas pronouns have the feature-specifications [−a, +p]. The anaphoric feature of reflexives is arguably spelled out by the *self*-morpheme of the complex *pro + self*. R-expressions differ from anaphors and pronouns in that they are neither anaphoric nor pronominal, and therefore have the feature-specifications [−a, −p]. The fourth logical possibility, [+a, +p], does not seem to have a corresponding member among overt DPs. It does, however, have one among null DPs, to which we turn now.

7.1.2 Null DPs

On the assumption that the anaphoric and pronominal features are properties of all DPs, null DPs are expected to be specified for these features as well. So far, we have encountered three different types of null DP: DP-traces, variables, and PRO. DP-traces are found in raising constructions such as (5) below, and passives such as (6), among others:

5a. The manager seems to have resigned
5b. *The manager$_i$ seems* [t$_i$ *to have resigned*]

6a. The manager is believed to have resigned
6b. *The manager$_i$ is believed* [t$_i$ *to have resigned*]

Because DP-traces arise as a result of DP-movement, they invariably have an antecedent in the sentence, namely the moved DP itself. Recall that movement involves automatic co-indexation between the moved category and the trace. Thus DP-traces pattern with lexical anaphors in that they invariably have an antecedent in the sentence. We therefore conclude that DP-traces are anaphoric expressions, with the feature-specifications [+a, −p].

Variables (i.e. traces of *wh*-phrases and quantified phrases) also arise as a result of movement:

7a. Who does the manager blame?
7b. *Who$_i$ does* [$_{IP}$ *the manager* I [$_{VP}$ *blame* t$_i$]]

7c. *for which person* x, *the manager blames* x

8a. The manager blames everyone

8b. *everyone*$_i$ [$_{IP}$ *The manager* I [$_{VP}$ *blames* t$_i$]]

8c. *for every person* x, *the manager blames* x

Unlike DP-traces, however, variables do not depend on their antecedent for reference. This is because the antecedents of variables, in particular *wh*-phrases and quantified phrases, are not referential expressions (Chapter 5). Recall that, in A'-bar chains involving an operator and a variable, it is the variable which functions as an argument, occupying the Case-marked and theta-marked position of the chain. Recall also that variables have the status of referential expressions, on a par with names and other referring expressions. This means that variables have the feature specifications [– a, – p].

The third null DP is PRO, found in the subject position of non-finite clauses situated in certain contexts:

9a. The manager tried to resign

9b. *The manager*$_i$ *tried* [PRO$_i$ *to resign*]

9c. **The manager*$_i$ *tried* [PRO$_j$ *to resign*]

10a. The manager doesn't know how to organize the team

10b. *The manager*$_i$ *doesn't know how* [PRO$_i$ *to organize the team*]

10c. *The manager*$_i$ *doesn't know how* [PRO$_j$ *to organize the team*]

PRO seems to share properties with both anaphors and pronouns, depending on the context in which it occurs. In (9), for example, PRO must have an antecedent in the sentence, as shown by the fact that the interpretation in (9c) is excluded. In (10), however, PRO can either have an antecedent in the sentence or outside the sentence. In (10b) PRO has an antecedent in the sentence, i.e. *the manager*, whereas in (10c) it does not have an antecedent in the sentence. In the latter case PRO is said to have an **arbitrary** interpretation, roughly paraphrasable as 'one'. The fact that in (10) PRO does not have an antecedent in the sentence shows that in this particular context it displays properties usually associated with pronouns. Together, these properties of PRO suggest that it has the feature specifications [+ a, + p].

The fourth logical combination, [– a, + p], does not seem to have a corresponding member among the types of null DPs discussed so far. However, in Chapter 9 we shall discuss an additional null category which has exactly these features (i.e. the features of a pure pronoun). Note that, between them, overt and null DPs discussed so far instantiate all the logical combinations of the anaphoric and pronominal features. The combination [+ a, – p] is instantiated by reflexives, reciprocals, and DP-traces. The combination [– a, + p] is instantiated by overt pronouns. The combination [– a, – p] is instantiated by overt R-expressions and variables. Finally, the combination [+ a, + p] is instantiated by PRO.

The first three classes correspond to the three-way distinction pointed out above with respect to overt DPs, which includes anaphors, pronouns, and R-expressions. As we shall see below, the distribution and interpretation of these three classes of DPs (both overt and null) are regulated by the principles of Binding Theory. PRO, however, forms a different class all by itself, whose distribution and interpretation are regulated by the principles of Control Theory.

7.1.3   Summary

The referential properties of DPs (both overt and null) are encoded in terms of feature complexes combining anaphoric and pronominal features. Reflexives, reciprocals, and

DP-traces are pure anaphors. Pronouns (and a null category to be discussed in Chapter 9) are pronominal. Names, referring expressions, and variables are neither anaphoric nor pronominal, and are called R-expressions. Finally, PRO is both anaphoric and pronominal.

7.2   *Binding and Co-referentiality*

Consider the following example:

11a. *The manager's assistants blame himself
11b. *[DP [*The manager's*]i *assistants*] *blame himself*i

12.

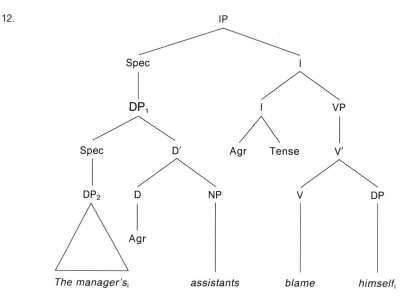

The notion 'antecedent' was temporarily defined above as the category which precedes and bears the same index as an anaphor or a pronoun. Both conditions are met by *the manager* in (11), and yet the relationship between this category and the anaphor seems to be illegitimate. The structure of this example is more clearly shown in (12). DP_2 (*the manager*) does not c-command the anaphor, owing to the intervening DP_1 – the first maximal projection which dominates DP_2 is DP_1, and the latter does not dominate the anaphor. In general terms, categories included inside a DP subject of a sentence cannot c-command out of the DP subject. What example (11/12) shows is that anaphors impose a certain structural condition on their antecedent, such that the antecedent must c-command the anaphor. Our descriptive statement concerning anaphors should then be revised to read that anaphors must have a c-commanding antecedent in the sentence. This is confirmed by the following example, where (the whole of) DP_1 (*the manager's assistants*) is the antecedent of the anaphor:

13a. The manager's assistants blame themselves
13b. [*The manager's assistants*]i *blame themselves*i

Because DP_1 c-commands the anaphor, the relationship between the two expressions is legitimate.

With this in mind, consider now example (14) below, in comparison to example (15) reproduced from above:

14a. His assistants blame John
14b. *His$_i$ assistants blame John$_i$*
14c. *His$_i$ assistants blame John$_j$*

14d. He suspects that the players blame John
14e. **He$_i$ suspects that the players blame John$_i$*
14f. *He$_i$ suspects that the players blame John$_j$*

(14a) can either have the interpretation shown in (14b) or the one in (14c). The interpretation which concerns us here is the one in (14b), where the R-expression *John* has the same reference as the pronoun *his*. Initially, this interpretation looks inconsistent with the conclusion reached earlier, on the basis of (14e), that R-expressions cannot have an antecedent in the sentence. When (14b) is compared to (14e), however, a more precise descriptive generalization emerges. An R-expression cannot have a c-commanding antecedent in the sentence. In (14b) the pronoun does not c-command the R-expression, and hence the relationship between them is legitimate. In (14e), however, the pronoun c-commands the R-expression, hence the fact that the pronoun cannot serve as antecedent for the R-expression.

The examples discussed show that a distinction needs to be drawn between two types of co-referentiality relation. One holds under the structural condition of c-command, while the other does not. The former is called **binding**, and can be defined as follows:

15. **Binding**
    A binds B iff:
    (i) A is co-indexed with B.
    (ii) A c-commands B.

According to this definition, binding relations form a subset of the set of co-referentiality relations. Co-referentiality needs only satisfy the condition of co-indexation, whereas binding needs to satisfy both the condition of co-indexation and the condition of c-command. In other words, for two co-referential categories (i.e. two co-indexed categories) to be in a binding relation, the **binder** has to c-command the **bindee**.

Let us now go back to examples (11) and (14). To rule out (11) we now have to revise our conclusion with respect to anaphors, to the effect that anaphors must be bound in the sentence. Although *the manager* is co-referential with the anaphor *himself*, it does not bind the anaphor for lack of c-command. Consequently, the anaphor is not bound in this sentence, and hence the fact that the sentence is excluded. To rule in (14b) we also have to revise our generalization with respect to R-expressions, to the effect that R-expressions cannot be bound in the sentence. Because the pronoun *his* in (14b) does not c-command the R-expression *the manager*, the pronoun does not bind the R-expression. Consequently, the R-expression is not bound in (14b), its relationship with the pronoun being one of mere co-referentiality. In contrast, the relationship between the pronoun and the R-expression in (14e) is a relationship of binding, as the pronoun c-commands the R-expression. Consequently, the R-expression is bound in this example.

The structural domain we have been mentioning so far is 'sentence': anaphors must be bound in the sentence, pronouns do not have to be bound in the sentence, and R-expressions cannot be bound in the sentence. However, investigation of more data reveals that the structural domain in question needs to be made much more precise. In the next section we shall try to identify the binding domain of anaphors and pronouns, and to formulate a formal condition on their distribution in relation to this domain. R-expressions are discussed separately in the subsequent section, for reasons which will become clear there.

7.3 *Anaphors and Pronouns*

7.3.1 Distribution

In the previous chapter we discussed examples which showed that the 'local domain' in which an anaphor must be bound can be just a clause, rather than the whole sentence:

16a. The manager suspects (that) the players blame themselves
16b. *The manager$_j$ suspects* [$_{IP}$ *the players$_i$ blame themselves$_i$*]

17a. *The players suspect (that) the manager blames themselves
17b. **The players$_i$ suspect* [$_{IP}$ *the manager$_j$ blames themselves$_i$*]

(16) shows that the anaphor can be bound inside the (embedded) clause containing it. (17) shows that in this context the anaphor must be bound inside the embedded clause. The DP *the players* in the subject position of the root clause, though co-referential with the anaphor, apparently cannot serve as a binder for the anaphor. Presumably this is because the co-referential DP is located outside the (embedded) clause containing the anaphor. Examples (16) and (17) together show that the 'local domain' of an anaphor can be smaller than a (whole) sentence.

We also discussed examples which showed that the 'local domain' of an anaphor can be even narrower than a (whole) clause:

18a. The manager heard the players' stories about each other
18b. *The manager$_j$ heard* [$_{DP}$ *the players'$_i$ stories about each other$_i$*]

19a. *The players heard the manager's stories about each other
19b. **The players$_i$ heard* [$_{DP}$ *the manager's$_j$ stories about each other$_i$*]

(18) shows that an anaphor can be bound inside the DP immediately containing it. (19) shows that in this context the anaphor must be bound inside the DP containing it. *The players* in the subject position of the sentence cannot serve as a binder for the anaphor, as it is located outside the 'local domain' of the anaphor.

The precise definition of the 'local domain' within which an anaphor must be bound will, obviously, have to take into account the common properties of clauses and DPs. This domain will then have to be specified in the definition of the principle of Binding Theory which regulates the distribution of anaphors. Pending the definition of 'local domain', the principle which regulates the distribution of anaphors, called **Binding Condition A (BC A)**, can be formulated as in (20):

20. **Binding Condition A**
    Anaphors must be bound inside a 'local domain'.

Assuming (20), all ungrammatical examples involving a situation where the anaphor is not bound in an appropriate 'local domain' are ruled out by BC A. Note that BC A is also expected to regulate the distribution of DP-traces, given that they are also anaphoric in nature, as concluded earlier. The 'local domain' within which an anaphor must be bound is then expected to correspond to the domain within which DP-movement takes places. We shall return to this issue below.

Let us now see whether there is a parallel condition on the distribution of pronouns in relation to a potential antecedent. It was pointed out above that pronouns may, but need not, have an antecedent in the sentence. This conclusion was reached on the basis of the following example, reproduced from above:

21a. The manager suspects (that) the players blame him
21b. *The manager$_i$ suspects* [$_{IP}$ *the players blame him$_i$*]
21c. *The manager$_i$ suspects* [$_{IP}$ *the players blame him$_j$*]

The interpretation represented in (21b) involves a binding relation between the pronoun in the embedded clause, and the subject of the root clause. The interpretation represented in (21c) does not involve a similar relation, as the two categories are not co-indexed. (21) may initially give the impression that pronouns are not subject to a binding condition which refers to a given 'local domain'. However, when other examples are examined it turns out that pronouns are indeed subject to a binding condition which makes reference to the same 'local domain' as the one referred to by the condition which regulates the distribution of anaphors (i.e. BC A).

Consider the following examples, which include the same context as (16) and (17) above:

22a. The manager suspects (that) the players blame them
22b. *The manager suspects* [$_{IP}$ *the players$_i$ blame them$_j$*]
22c. **The manager suspects* [$_{IP}$ *the players$_i$ blame them$_i$*]

23a. The players suspect (that) the manager blames them
23b. *The players$_i$ suspect* [$_{IP}$ *the manager$_j$ blames them$_k$*]
23c. *The players$_i$ suspect* [$_{IP}$ *the manager$_j$ blames them$_i$*]

(22a) can have the interpretation shown in (22b), where the pronoun refers to individuals understood in the discourse context. However, (22a) cannot have the interpretation shown in (22c), where the pronoun is bound by the subject of the embedded clause. (23a) can have the interpretation in (23b), where the pronoun refers to individuals understood in the discourse context, and can also have the interpretation in (23c), where the pronoun is bound by the subject of the root clause. The crucial interpretations are the ones in (22c) and (23c). Together, they show that the pronoun cannot be bound by an antecedent included in the same clause as the pronoun, although it can be bound by an antecedent located outside the clause containing the pronoun.

Note that the domain in which the pronoun cannot be bound in (22c), i.e. the embedded clause, is exactly the same domain where an anaphor must be bound, as we have seen. At this stage it starts to look as though pronouns are required to be **free** (not bound) in precisely the same domains where anaphors are required to be bound. This suspicion is confirmed when the following examples, which include the same DP context as (18) and (19) above, are examined:

24a. The manager heard the players' stories about them
24b. *The manager heard* [$_{DP}$ *the players'$_i$ stories about them$_j$*]
24c. **The manager heard* [$_{DP}$ *the players'$_i$ stories about them$_i$*]

25a. The players heard the manager's stories about them
25b. *The players$_i$ heard* [$_{DP}$ *the manager's$_j$ stories about them$_k$*]
25c. *The players$_i$ heard* [$_{DP}$ *the manager's$_j$ stories of them$_i$*]

The crucial interpretations are the ones in (24c) and (25c). Together, they show that a pronoun cannot be bound inside the DP containing it, although it can be bound by an antecedent located outside the DP containing the pronoun. This situation is the reverse of that found with anaphors. Recall that an anaphor must be bound inside the DP domain in (24) and (25).

The conclusion that pronouns are required to be free in precisely those domains where anaphors are required to be bound implies the following binding condition on the distribution of pronouns, called **Binding Condition B (BC B)**:

26. **Binding Condition B**
    Pronouns must be free in a 'local domain'.

Assuming (26), all examples involving a situation where a pronoun is not free in its 'local domain' are excluded. Our next task is to try to find the appropriate definition for 'local domain'. A possible way of arriving at a viable definition is by attempting to answer the question: What are the requirements that a given domain must satisfy, besides including the anaphor/pronoun, for it to qualify as a 'local domain'? Recall from above that the domain in question will have to make reference to common properties of clauses and DPs.

7.3.2   Governing Category (NIC and SSC)

7.3.2.1   The Governor (NIC)   As a first step towards answering the question above, consider the following examples:

27a. The managers expected each other to resign
27b. *The managers$_i$ expected* [$_{IP}$ *each other$_i$ to resign*]

28a. The managers expected them to resign
28b. **The managers$_i$ expected* [$_{IP}$ *them$_i$ to resign*]

Both examples include a non-finite clause embedded under an ECM verb. (27) shows that an anaphor can occur in the ECM subject position and be bound by the subject of the root clause. Predictably, a pronoun is excluded from this context, as shown by (28). The reading of (28a), whereby the pronoun is not bound by the subject of the root, has been ignored, as it is irrelevant to the discussion. Now compare (27) and (28) with (29) and (30) below, where the embedded clause is finite:

29a. *The managers expected (that) each other would resign
29b. **The managers$_i$ expected* [$_{IP}$ *each other$_i$ would resign*]

30a. The managers expected that they would resign
30b. *The managers$_i$ expected* [$_{IP}$ *they$_i$ would resign*]

The striking fact about these examples is that they present a situation which is the reverse of the one found in (27) and (28). An anaphor is excluded from the subject position of an embedded finite clause, whereas a pronoun is allowed. This contrast suggests that finiteness plays a role in determining 'local domain'.

An early attempt to deal with this issue was based on a condition called the **Nominative Island Condition (NIC)**, where the notion 'island' is as explained in Chapter 3 in relation to movement transformations. The idea is that a subject position which is assigned nominative Case is an island with respect to binding, so that an anaphor, for example, cannot refer out of it. Accordingly, (29) is excluded on the grounds that it involves a violation of NIC. In contrast, a subject position which is not assigned nominative Case is not an island, so that an anaphor, for example, can refer out of it, to an antecedent in the root clause. This is the situation found in (27), where the embedded subject position occupied by the anaphor is assigned accusative Case by the root ECM verb.

There is a clear sense in which NIC is to overt anaphors what TSC (the Tensed S Condition) is to DP-traces. Recall that TSC excludes DP-movement out of tensed (finite) clauses:

31a. John seems to be happy
31b. *John$_i$ seems* [t$_i$ *to be happy*]

32a. *John seems is happy
32b. *John$_i$ seems* [t$_i$ *is happy*]

Notice, however, that (32) is also excluded by NIC, on the assumption that DP-traces are anaphors. The subject position of the embedded clause in this example is assigned nominative case, and is therefore an island for the anaphoric DP-trace occupying it. In view of this, TSC can be dispensed with altogether, on the grounds that its effects are derivable from NIC. Thus, what looked initially like a condition on the DP-movement transformation turns out to be part of a more general condition on the representation of anaphoric categories, including DP-traces.

Let us now tease out the content of NIC and its implications, with the purpose of incorporating its effects into the definition of 'local domain'. Nominative Case implies finite I, and finite I implies that the subject position of the clause is governed (see Chapter 6). In view of this, it could be concluded that the presence or absence of a governor plays a role in determining the 'local domain' in which an anaphor must be bound and a pronoun must be free. Let us assume, then, that 'local domain' is the domain which includes the anaphor/pronoun as well as the governor of the anaphor/pronoun. A domain which does not include the governor of the anaphor/pronoun does not qualify as 'local domain' even though it may include the anaphor/pronoun. In (27) and (28) above, where the anaphor/ pronoun is governed (and assigned Case) by the root verb, the 'local domain', of the anaphor/pronoun is the root clause. The embedded clause in these (ECM) examples does not qualify as the 'local domain' for the anaphor/pronoun, simply because it does not include the governor of the anaphor/pronoun, even though it includes the anaphor/ pronoun.

The embedded finite clause in (29) and (30) differs in that it includes the governor of the anaphor/pronoun, namely finite I, and therefore qualifies as the 'local domain' for the anaphor/pronoun. Accordingly, we expect an anaphor to be bound in this domain and a pronoun to be free. However, the anaphor is not bound in this domain (embedded clause) in (29), implying a violation of BC A. On the other hand, the pronoun is free in the embedded clause in (30), and therefore no violation of BC B is involved. Notice with respect to this example that, although the subject of the root clause binds the pronoun, the subject is located outside the 'local domain' of the pronoun – the pronoun is still free in its 'local domain'.

7.3.2.2   The Subject (SSC)   Now consider the following examples:

33a. The managers expected the players to blame each other
33b. *The managers$_i$ expected* [*the players$_j$ to blame each other$_j$*]
33c. *The managers$_i$ expected* [*the players$_j$ to blame each other$_i$*]

34a. The managers expected the players to blame them
34b. *The managers$_i$ expected* [*the players$_j$ to blame them$_j$*]
34c. *The managers$_i$ expected* [*the players$_j$ to blame them$_i$*]

At an earlier stage, these examples were dealt with separately from the ones discussed above, in terms of another condition on binding relations. The condition in question is the Specified Subject Condition (SSC) discussed in chapter 3 in relation to DP-movement. With respect to (33) and (34), SSC encodes the condition that anaphors be bound in the domain of the nearest subject, and pronouns be free in the domain of the nearest subject. The nearest subject to the anaphor/pronoun in (33) and (34) is the embedded subject, and the domain of the embedded subject is the embedded clause. Therefore, in these examples we expect an anaphor to be bound inside the embedded clause and a pronoun to be free. In (33c) the anaphor is not bound in the embedded clause, and in (34b) the pronoun is not free in the embedded clause, and hence both interpretations are excluded. The interpretations in (33b) and (34c), however, are consistent with the requirement that anaphors be bound and pronouns be free in the domain of the nearest subject.

In Chapter 3 SSC was invoked to exclude DP-movement across a subject, thereby ruling out ungrammatical examples such as the following:

35a. *The managers are expected the players to blame
35b. *The managers$_i$ are expected [the players$_j$ to blame t$_i$]

It is possible now to reason that DP-movement across a subject is ruled out because it gives rise to representations where the DP-trace, which is an anaphor, is not bound in the domain of its nearest subject. The nearest subject to the DP-trace in (35) is the subject of the embedded clause, and the domain of this subject is the embedded clause. In (35) the anaphoric DP-trace is not bound in the embedded clause, giving rise to a violation of the requirement that anaphors be bound in the domain of the nearest subject (SSC). Thus, just as the effects of TSC with respect to DP-movement were shown above to be part of a more general pattern which includes overt anaphors, the effects of SSC with respect to DP-movement are also part of a more general pattern which includes overt anaphors. Thus, TSC and SSC are not really conditions on DP-movement, but are part of a more general condition on representations, only some of which are derived by DP-movement.

The content of SSC implies that the subject plays a crucial role in determining 'local domain'. The presence of a subject in a given domain results in a situation where an anaphor must be bound in this domain (the domain of the subject) and a pronoun must be free. Presumably, the absence of a subject in a given domain is expected to yield the opposite results. Consider the following examples:

36a. The players heard stories about each other
36b. The players$_i$ heard [$_{DP}$ stories about each other$_i$]
37a. *The players heard his stories about each other
37b. *The players$_i$ heard [$_{DP}$ his$_j$ stories about each other$_i$]

The DP containing the anaphor in (36) apparently does not have a subject. Consequently, DP does not qualify as the 'local domain' for the anaphor, even though it includes the governor of the anaphor. The 'local domain' of the anaphor in this example is the whole sentence, which also includes a binder for the anaphor. The DP in (37) differs in that it has a subject, the pronoun *his*. Consequently, this DP qualifies as the 'local domain' for the anaphor, in which the anaphor is expected to be bound. However, in (37) the anaphor is not bound inside DP, and hence the interpretation is ruled out. Thus, it seems that the striking contrast between (36) and (37) is due to the absence of a subject for the DP in (36) and its presence in (37). This conclusion confirms that the subject indeed plays a crucial role in determining the 'local domain' of anaphors, and presumably, also pronouns.

7.3.2.3 Definition   We are now in a position to answer the question raised above: what requirements must a given domain satisfy to qualify as 'local domain' for an anaphor/ pronoun? The discussion above suggests the following answer: for a given domain to qualify as 'local domain' for an anaphor or a pronoun, it must include, in addition to the anaphor/pronoun, the governor of the anaphor/pronoun (the NIC cases) and a subject (the SSC cases). A domain of this type is sometimes called a **Complete Functional Complex (CFC)**, i.e. a domain where 'all grammatical functions compatible with its head are realised in it – the complements necessarily, by the projection principle, and the subject, which is optional unless required [by a principle of grammar]' (Chomsky, 1986a: 169). Recall that subjects are obligatory with clauses, by virtue of EPP. However, there is no equivalent principle which requires DPs to have a subject, despite their clause-like character, so that subjects are optional with DPs. It is for this reason that a finite clause is invariably a CFC, and therefore a 'local domain', whereas a DP is a 'local domain' apparently only when the subject is realized in it.

The term often used to refer to 'local domain' is **Governing Category (GC)**, defined as in (38):

38. **Governing Category**
    The GC of A is the minimal domain which contains A, the governor of A, and a subject.

With the definition of GC stated separately, Binding Conditions A and B can now be defined as follows:

39a. **Binding Condition A**
    An anaphor must be bound in its GC.

39b. **Binding Condition B**
    A pronoun must be free in its GC.

These definitions account for the distribution of anaphors and pronouns in all the contexts discussed so far, which represent the core contexts. There are other arguably marginal contexts which seem to require some qualifications (see Exercises at the end of the chapter).

Note that the element which crucially determines the 'local domain' (or GC) of anaphors and pronouns is the subject. Some of the NIC cases which have motivated the inclusion of 'governor' in the definition of 'local domain' are amenable to an alternative analysis in terms of Case Theory, rather than Binding Theory. The core cases are reproduced here with reflexives:

40a. The player expected himself to win
40b. *The player expected himself would win

It was pointed out above that reflexives are the morphological realization of the Agr features together with the [+a] feature, and hence their internal structure *pro + self*. Recall (from the previous chapter) that the Agr features include the Case feature, in addition to person, gender, and number features. Now, the fact that the pro-part of reflexives corresponds to the objective series of pronouns implies that reflexives are inherently invariably specified for an objective Case feature. In view of this, the reason why reflexives cannot occur in a nominative subject position can be attributed to a violation of Spec-Head Agreement, rather than a condition of Binding Theory: the (objective) Case feature of the reflexive is incompatible with the (nominative) Case feature of the Agr category of finite I. In other words, (40b) is excluded for the same reason that examples such as *Him/his will win* or, more significantly, *The player expected him would win* are also excluded.

In contrast to (40b), example (40a) does not involve a situation of Case conflict, as the embedded non-finite I lacks Agr and therefore does not enter into a Spec-Head Agreement relation with the ECM subject. To the extent that this analysis is viable, the notion 'governor' can be dropped from the definition of 'local domain' (GC).

7.3.3 Summary

Anaphors are required to be bound and pronouns to be free in a 'local domain', called Governing Category (GC). The GC of anaphors and pronouns is the minimal domain which contains the anaphor/pronoun, the governor of the anaphor/pronoun, and a subject. The requirement that the GC of the anaphor/pronoun include the governor subsumes the cases which previously fell under NIC. On the other hand, the requirement that the GC include a subject subsumes the cases which previously fell under SSC.

7.4 R-Expressions

7.4.1 A-binding versus A'-binding

We have seen that R-expressions differ from pronouns and anaphors in that they can never be bound, although they can be co-referential with another expression in the sentence. This seems to be the case irrespective of the distance between the R-expression and a potential binder. In (41) below, for example, the R-expression *the players* is separated from the pronoun *they* by three clausal boundaries, and yet the R-expression cannot be bound by the pronoun, as shown in (41b):

41a. They say (that) the journalists claim (that) the public thinks (that) the manager blames the players
41b. *They$_i$ say [(that) *the journalists claim* [(that) *the public thinks* [(that) *the manager blames the players$_i$*]]

Recall that in example (42) below, reproduced from above, the pronoun does not bind the R-expression, although the two categories are co-referential:

42a. His assistants blame John
42b. His$_i$ assistants blame John$_i$

In this example the pronoun does not bind the R-expression co-indexed with it because the pronoun does not c-command the R-expression.

Example (41) shows clearly that GC ('local domain') discussed above in relation to anaphors and pronouns does not play a role in the distribution of R-expressions. Therefore, the definition of the binding condition which regulates the distribution of R-expressions is not expected to make reference to GC. The condition in question is called **Binding Condition C (BC C)**, and can be defined as in (43):

43. **Binding Condition C**
    An R-expression must be free (everywhere).

Essentially, BC C amounts to the statement that R-expressions are incompatible with binding. This is not surprising if binding is understood to be a relationship of reference-assignment. Recall that reflexives and pronouns are no more than bundles of features which have the function of restricting the set of possible antecedents, e.g. *herself* implies a feminine, singular antecedent and *he* a masculine, singular antecedent. Anaphors and pronouns are dependent on an antecedent for reference, either directly, as in *The manager blames himself*, or indirectly, as in *He blames himself*, where the reflexive depends on the pronoun which in turn depends on a discourse antecedent. In view of this, it is not surprising that R-expressions are incompatible with binding (cannot be bound). This conclusion can be understood to mean that, perhaps, BC C does not need to be stated as a binding condition. However, certain properties of R-expressions to be discussed below will show that BC C needs to be stated, albeit in a slightly different form than shown in (43).

The conclusion that R-expressions cannot be bound extends to variables as well, although initially this may not seem to be the case. The following examples are reproduced from above:

44a. Who does the manager blame?
44b. *Who$_i$ does* [$_{IP}$ *the manager* I [$_{VP}$ *blame* t$_i$]]?

44c. *For which person* x, *the manager blames* x

45a. The manager blames everyone
45b. *everyone$_i$* [$_{IP}$ *The manager* I [$_{VP}$ *blames* t$_i$]]

45c. *for every person* x, *the manager blames* x

In each of these examples the variable is co-indexed with a c-commanding operator – the *wh*-phrase in (44) and the quantified phrase in (45). The relationship between an operator and a variable, such as in (44) and (45), is traditionally called binding. In view of this, one might conclude that variables are inconsistent with BC C, with the implication that they are somehow different from overt R-expressions. However, there is a clear difference between the binding relation referred to by BC C and the binding relation in (44) and (45). The former, as pointed out above, is a relation of reference-assignment, whereby the antecedent assigns a reference to the bindee. The binding relation in (46) and (47), however, cannot be said to be one of reference-assignment, for the simple reason that operators are not referential expressions and therefore do not have a reference to assign.

We therefore need to make a formal distinction between two types of binding relation. The type of binding which involves reference-assignment is called **A-binding** and the type of binding which involves an operator and a variable is called **A'-binding** (read 'A-bar binding'). In the former (A-binding), the binder is usually an argument located in an A-position, whereas in the latter (A'-binding), the binder is usually an operator (a non-argument) located in an A'-position. Given this distinction, the binding conditions listed above are conditions on A-binding relations and do not hold for A'-binding relations. In other words, the theory of binding which incorporates Binding Conditions A, B, and C is a theory of A-binding, and as such irrelevant to A'-binding relations of the type in (44) and (45). This does not necessarily mean that BC C does not apply to variables at all. As R-expressions, variables are expected to be subject to BC C, as with overt R-expressions. That this is the case is shown in the following example:

46a. Who does John claim the players blame?
46b. **Who$_i$ does* [*John$_i$ claim* [*the players blame* t$_i$]]?

(46a) cannot have the interpretation shown in (46b), where the individual *wh*-enquired about is the same as the individual who makes the claim. This is because this interpretation involves the pattern of indexation shown in (46b), where the variable is co-indexed with the subject of the sentence which is in a c-commanding position with respect to the variable. This co-indexation results in the variable being A-bound by the subject, and is excluded by BC C. Thus, like overt R-expressions, variables cannot be bound (anywhere).

Having said that, there are certain grammatical contexts where a variable is actually A-bound. The following example, which includes a relative clause, illustrates one such context:

47a. The manager (whom/that) the players like most is Bill
47b. *The manager*ᵢ [Oᵢ [*the players like* tᵢ *most*]] *is Bill*

The variable in the object position of the relative clause is A-bound (and assigned a referential value) by the head noun of the relative clause. This relationship is clearly inconsistent with BC C as formulated above. The latter should exclude (47) for the same reason it excludes (46), among others. Thus, BC C should be revised so as to include (47) while still excluding (46) and similar examples.

There is a significant difference between (46) and (47) which gives an indication as to the revision required. In (46) the A-binder intervenes between the variable and its operator, whereas in (47) the A-binder does not intervene between the variable and its operator. This difference implies that a variable cannot be A-bound only if the A-binder intervenes between the variable and its operator. When the A-binder does not intervene in the intended sense, the variable can be A-bound by it. This amounts to saying that operators determine the 'local domain' in which variables must be free (cannot be bound), so that the definition of GC C must make reference to this particular notion of 'local domain'. Chomsky (1986a) has suggested the following version of BC C:

48. **Binding Condition C**
    An R-expression must be A-free in the (c-command) domain of its operator.

This definition allows (47), where the A-binder is not located in the (c-command) domain of the operator of the variable, but excludes cases such as (46), where the A-binder is located in the (c-command) domain of the operator of the variable. The c-command domain of the operator is the 'local domain' of R-expressions, i.e. the domain in which R-expressions cannot be bound.

Note that although the 'local domain' of R-expressions appears to be different from that of anaphors and pronouns, the fact that operators, which determine the 'local domain' of R-expressions, are specifiers (of CP), and the fact that subjects, which determine the 'local domain' of anaphors and pronouns, are also specifiers (of IP) suggest that perhaps the same notion of 'local domain' applies to all three types of expression. The possibility that the definition of the 'local domain' of anaphors and pronouns does not need to make reference to the governor, discussed above, makes this prospect more realistic. We will come back to this issue in Chapter 8.

7.4.2   Crossover and A'-bound Pronouns

The following examples illustrate a phenomenon known as **Crossover**:

49a. Who did he see?
49b. **Whoᵢ did* [IP *heᵢ* I [VP *see* tᵢ]]?

49c. *for which person* x, x *saw* x

50a. Who did his boss see?

50b. **Who_i did [IP [DP his_i boss] I [VP see t_i]]?*

50c. *for which person* x, x's *boss saw* x

(49a) cannot have the interpretation shown in (49b,c), where the pronoun in the subject position is co-referential with the variable and, by transitivity, with the *wh*-phrase. (50a) cannot have the interpretation shown in (50b,c), with a similar pattern of indexation. In both examples the *wh*-phrase has **crossed over** a co-indexed pronoun in the subject position. (49) is an instance of **Strong Crossover (SCO)** and (50) an instance of **Weak Crossover (WCO)**, the reason being that the ungrammaticality of the latter is felt to be weaker than that of the former.

(49) is ruled out by BC C, as it involves a situation where the variable is A-bound by the pronoun located in the subject position of the sentence. (50), however, is not ruled out by BC C, nor by any other binding condition for that matter. The pronoun in the subject position of DP does not c-command the variable, and therefore does not bind it. The fact that the *wh*-phrase binds the pronoun should not be of significance, as the binding relationship involved is an instance of A'-binding. Various analyses have been suggested in the literature to account for the Crossover phenomena, which we will not discuss here for lack of space. Descriptively, the condition involved can be stated as follows:

51. **Crossover**
    A variable cannot be co-indexed with a pronoun to its left.

Obviously, as a descriptive statement (51) should be derivable from general and independent principles.

The Crossover effects also arise with quantified phrases raised at LF. (52a) below, for example, cannot have the interpretation shown in (52b,c), and (53a) cannot have the interpretation shown in (53b,c):

52a. He saw everyone

52b. **everyone_i [IP He_i I [VP saw t_i]]*

52c. for every x, x saw x

53a. His boss saw everyone

53b. **everyone_i [IP [DP [His_i] boss] I [VP saw t_i]]*

53c. *for every* x, x's *boss saw* x

(52) is an instance of SCO and (53) an instance of WCO. The fact that variable traces of quantified expressions pattern with the variable traces of *wh*-phrases should not come as a surprise at this stage. However, (52) and (53) do represent strong evidence for movement of quantified expressions at LF (Chapter 5). Only if the quantified expressions are assumed to move and leave a variable behind can examples (52) and (53) be accommodated under the descriptive generalization in (51). Moreover, although co-indexation with a quantified expression is excluded in (53), co-indexation with an R-expression occupying the same position is not. Recall from above that the interpretation shown in (54b) of (54a) below is possible, as the subject pronoun does not bind the R-expression in the object position:

54a. His boss saw John

54b. *His_i boss saw John_i*

Because R-expressions do not undergo QR at LF, the crossover effect does not arise. Thus, the contrast between (53b) and (54b) strongly supports the hypothesis that quantified phrases undergo movement at LF.

The expression 'to its left' in (51) is significant, as a variable *can* be co-indexed with a pronoun to its right. For example, (55a) below can have the interpretation shown in (55b, c), and (56a) can have the interpretation shown in (56b,c):

55a. Who claims (that) he is innocent?
55b. *Who$_i$* [$_{IP}$ t$_i$ *claims* [*he$_i$ is innocent*]]*?*

55c. *for which person* x, x *claims* x *is innocent*

56a. Everyone claims (that) he is innocent
56b. *Everyone$_i$* [$_{IP}$ t$_i$ *claims* [$_{IP}$ *he$_i$ is innocent*]]

56c. *for every person* x, x *claims* x *is innocent*

Note that in these examples, as well as in the Crossover examples above, the pronoun is A'-bound. A'-bound pronouns are sometimes said to have a **bound variable** interpretation, meaning that they logically translate as variables as shown in (55c) and (56c), for example. Note, however, that if A'-bound pronouns are assumed to be represented as variables at LF, (55) and (56) will involve a violation of BC C. The pronoun-cum-variable will be A-bound by the variable trace of the operator in the domain of the operator. We shall say no more about this issue, except for a brief comment later concerning the level at which binding conditions apply.

7.4.3   Parasitic Gaps (Adjunct Islands)

The following example illustrates a somewhat unusual construction called **parasitic gap construction**:

57a. Which article did John file without reading?
57b. *Which article$_i$ did John file* [e$_i$] *without reading* [e$_i$]*?*
57c. *for which article* x, *John filed* x *without reading* x

This construction contains two variables (gaps), represented by the symbol 'e'. One variable is in the object position of *file*, the other in the object position of *reading*. The presence of two variables (in Case-marked argument positions) should in principle imply two distinct operators. However, in (57) there is apparently only one operator, the *wh*-phrase *which article*.

An analysis of (57) along the lines outlined in (58) below, whereby the *wh*-phrase is base-generated in the position of the rightmost gap, then moved to the next gap, and finally to its surface position, is excluded, for a number of reasons:

58. *Which article$_i$ did John file* [e$_i$] *without reading* [e$_i$]*?*

First, movement into the second gap (the object position of *file*) is movement from a theta-marked position (the object position of *reading*) to another theta-marked position, and therefore is excluded by the Theta-Criterion (Chapter 5). Secondly, movement into the second gap is also movement from a Case-marked position to another Case-marked position, which is excluded by the condition that chains have one Case (position) (Chapter 6). Thirdly, this same movement would be movement out of an adjunct phrase, which is generally excluded. Adjuncts are said to be islands, on a par with *wh*-

clauses (the *Wh*-Island Condition) and complex noun phrases (the Complex NP Condition), discussed in Chapter 3. The fact that adjuncts are islands for movement is shown in (59):

59a. *Which article did John disappear without reading?
59b. *_Which article_$_i$ _did John disappear_ [_without reading_ t$_i$]?

59c. *for which article* x, *John disappeared without reading* x

The phrase *without reading x* is an adjunct, the verb *disappear* being intransitive. Because the phrase is an adjunct it is an island to movement, so that (59) is excluded by a condition on movement which for the moment we will call the **Adjunct Island Condition**. If the parasitic gap construction in (57) above did involve *wh*-movement out of the (same) adjunct phrase (as (59), it should be ungrammatical for the same reason that (59) is ungrammatical.

This conclusion implies that *Wh*-movement of the *wh*-phrase in (57) takes place directly from the object position of the verb *file*, as shown in (60):

60. *Which article*$_i$ *did John file* t$_i$ [*without reading* [e]]?

Given (60), the question we need to answer is how the gap inside the adjunct phrase arises. The answer outlined in (61) below is suggested in (Chomsky 1986b):

61. . . . *without* [CP O$_i$ [IP *reading* t$_i$]]

According to this analysis, the gap inside the adjunct phrase arises as a result of the movement of a null operator to the Spec-CP position inside the adjunct phrase. Note that because this movement operates inside the adjunct phrase it does not give rise to a violation of the Adjunct Island Condition.

An important aspect of the analysis outlined in (61) is that it assimilates (the adjunct phrase of) parasitic gap constructions to relative clauses with a null *wh*-phrase, illustrated in (62) below. (63) is a parasitic gap construction which involves a relative clause with a null *wh*-phrase, provided here for comparison:

62a. This is the article I filed
62b. *This is the article*$_i$ [CP O$_i$ [IP *I filed* t$_i$]]

63a. This is the kind of article you must read before you file
63b. *This is the kind of article*$_i$ [CP O$_i$ [IP *you must read* t$_i$]]

63c. *before* [CP O$_j$ [IP *you file* t$_j$]]

Recall (from Chapter 3) that relative clauses such as the one in (62) involve movement of a null operator to the Spec-CP position of the relative clause. The adjunct phrase in (61) and its counterpart in (63) are claimed to involve a similar movement of a null *wh*-phrase.

In Chapter 3 we used island effects as diagnostic tests for the presence of movement in relatives without an overt *wh*-phrase. Now, if parasitic gap constructions do indeed involve movement of a (null) *wh*-phrase inside the adjunct phrase, we expect the island effects to show up if the gap is included within an island embedded inside the adjunct phrase. What we need to do is make the adjunct phrase of the parasitic gap construction more complex by embedding inside it a complex 'noun phrase' or a *wh*-island, as in (64) and (65):

64a. *This is the report which John published before announcing the plan to discuss

64b. *before* [CP O$_i$ [IP PRO *announcing* [DP *the plan* [PRO *to discuss* t$_i$]]]]

65a. *This is the report which John filed before disclosing when to discuss

65b. *before* [CP O$_i$ [IP PRO *disclosing* [CP *when* [IP PRO *to discuss* t$_i$]]]]

The adjunct phrase, which is the focus of our attention here, is represented separately in (64b) and (65b). (64b) includes a complex 'noun phrase' out of which movement of the null *wh*-phrase has taken place. (65b) includes a *wh*-island out of which movement of the null *wh*-phrase has taken place. The fact that the adjunct phrase exhibits the island effects, as shown by the status of (64) and (65), implies that it does indeed involve movement of a null *wh*-phrase, on a par with relatives with a null *wh*-phrase.

An important property of parasitic gap constructions is the fact that the two gaps (variables) have the same referential value (index), and logically translate as one and the same variable (57c). To account for this fact, Chomsky (1986b) suggests a mechanism of **chain composition**, whereby the two independently derived A'-chains are fused together into a single, complex chain, the members of which bear the same index. Technically, this merger results in a situation where the *wh*-phrase in (57), for example, is related to both gaps (via co-indexation), and therefore A'-binds both variables occupying them.

A number of other properties of parasitic gap constructions, however, are not easy to account for. First, the gap (variable) inside the adjunct phrase is **parasitical** upon the presence of a variable inside the main clause. This is shown in the following examples, neither of which includes a variable inside the main clause. (66) has an overt DP in the object position in the main clause, and (67) has a DP-trace in this position:

66a. *John filed the report without reading

66b. *John filed the report* [*without reading* [e]]

67a. *The report was filed without reading

67b. *The report$_i$ was filed* t$_i$ [*without reading* [e]]

The variable in the main clause is said to license the **parasitic gap** in the adjunct phrase. Because (66) and (67) do not include a variable in the main clause, the parasitic gap in the adjunct phrase is not licensed.

Secondly, the licensing variable must not c-command the parasitic gap. In all examples of parasitic gap constructions above, the licensing variable is in the object position of the verb of the main clause. In this position, the variable does not c-command the adjunct phrase, assuming the latter is adjoined to VP. However, a variable in the subject position of the main clause would c-command the adjunct phrase and, consequently, the parasitic gap. But a variable in the subject position cannot license a parasitic gap, as shown in (68):

68a. *Who left before we could greet?

68b. *Who$_i$ [IP t$_i$ *left* [*before we could greet* [e]]]?

This condition on the licensing of parasitic gaps is sometimes called the **anti-c-command condition**: a parasitic gap is licensed by a variable which does not c-command it.

Thirdly, parasitic gaps are licensed by S-structure variables only. Variables which arise as a result of QR at LF are apparently unable to license a parasitic gap:

69a. *I forgot who filed every/which article without reading

69b. *every/which article$_i$ [I forgot who filed* t$_i$ [*without reading* [e]]]

The quantified/*wh*-phrase in (69a) raises at LF, leaving a variable behind which does not c-command the parasitic gap. However, this LF variable is apparently unable to license the parasitic gap. The fact that LF variables cannot license parasitic gaps whereas S-structure variables can suggests that parasitic gaps are licensed at S-structure.

The conditions on the licensing of parasitic gaps discussed are summarized in the following descriptive generalization:

70. **Parasitic Gaps**
    A parasitic gap is licensed at S-structure by a variable which does not c-command it.

Obviously, (70) should be derivable from some general and independent principles, although it is not easy to see how. At any rate, to the extent that (70) is derivable from the principles of Binding Theory, it shows that these principles arguably apply at S-structure. If this is the case, the possibility that A'-bound pronouns receive a bound variable interpretation at LF, pointed out above, would not necessarily give rise to a violation of BC C. This is because at the level at which binding conditions apply (i.e. S-structure) the pronoun is still a pronoun (as opposed to a variable), and as such is subject to BC B, rather than BC C.

7.4.4   Summary

To the extent that R-expressions, in particular variables, have a 'local domain', it is the c-command domain of their operator, in which they are required to be A-free (Binding Condition C). A'-binding of variables (and pronouns) does not involve a relationship of reference-assignment, and therefore falls outside the scope of Binding Theory, understood as a theory of A-binding. Certain properties of parasitic gaps, and arguably also of A'-bound pronouns, suggest that the principles of Binding Theory apply at the level of S-structure.

7.5   *PRO and Control*

This section deals with the distribution and interpretation of PRO. In the subsection dealing with distribution we shall discuss the distinctive properties of the positions in which PRO typically occurs, with the purpose of identifying the condition which determines its distribution. In the subsection dealing with interpretation, we shall try to identify the factors which determine the interpretation of PRO. As will become clear, some of these factors are still largely mysterious.

7.5.1   Distribution

7.5.1.1   PRO Theorem   We have seen that PRO typically occurs in the subject position of non-finite clauses:

71a. The manager tried to blame the players
71b. *The manager$_i$ tried* [PRO$_i$ *to blame the players*]
72a. Blaming the players won't help
72b. [PRO$_i$ *Blaming the players*] *won't help*

In (71) PRO has an antecedent in the sentence, namely the subject of the root clause. In (72), however, PRO does not have an antecedent in the sentence. In a well-defined discourse context, PRO in (72) can have a specific antecedent, e.g. 'the manager'. Otherwise, PRO is said to have an arbitrary interpretation. In view of the fact that PRO typically occurs in the subject position of non-finite clauses, it should be possible to determine the nature of the principle which governs the distribution of PRO by identifying the characteristic properties of the subject position of non-finite clauses.

The characteristic property of the subject position of non-finite clauses is that it is non-Case-marked, unless the non-finite clause is introduced by a prepositional complementizer or embedded under an ECM verb:

73a. For the manager to blame the players is surprising
73b. [CP *For* [IP *the manager to blame the players*]] *is surprising*

74a. The players believe the manager to be vindictive
74b. *The players believe* [IP *the manager to be vindictive*]

75a. *For to blame the players is surprising
75b. *[CP *For* [IP PRO *to blame the players*]] *is surprising*

76a. *The players believe to be vindictive
76b. *The players believe* [IP PRO *to be vindictive*]

On the basis of these examples it could be concluded that PRO occurs in non-Case-marked positions, as shown in (71) and (72) above, and is excluded from Case-marked positions, as shown in (75) and (76). The conclusion that PRO is excluded from Case-marked positions is further supported by the fact that it cannot occur in the subject position of finite clauses, or the object position of (transitive) verbs and prepositions:

77a. *Blamed the players
77b. *PRO *blamed the players*

78a. *The manager blamed
78b. *The manager* [VP *blamed* PRO]

79a. *The manager put the blame on
79b. *The manager put the blame* [PP *on* PRO]

Thus, the preliminary indications are that an account of the distribution of PRO lies with Case Theory.

However, there are reasons to believe that an account of the distribution of PRO lies with Government Theory, rather than Case Theory. A fact about Case-marked positions is that they are also invariably governed, given that Case is assigned under government. Notice, however, that the reverse is not true: not all positions which are governed are also Case-marked. Case-marked positions form a subclass of the class of governed positions. Positions which are governed but non-Case-marked represent the real test for determining whether the distribution of PRO is regulated by Case or by Government. If PRO cannot occur in a position which is governed but non-Case-marked, the conclusion will have to be that PRO is excluded from governed positions, rather than Case-marked positions. One such position is the object position of passives:

80a. The player was sacked (by the manager)
80b. *The player*ᵢ *was sacked* tᵢ (*by the manager*)

81a. *It/there was sacked (by the manager)
81b. *It/there was [VP *sacked* PRO] (*by the manager*)

Recall (from Chapter 6) that passive verbs do not assign Case to their object – the accusative Case of the base transitive verb is 'absorbed' by the passive morpheme. Recall also that it is apparently for this reason that the object in passives obligatorily moves to the subject position. Now, if PRO is excluded from non-Case-marked positions, rather than from governed positions, there is no reason why it should not occur in the object position of passives. (81) shows that PRO cannot occur in the object position of a passive verb.

Although the object position of passives is non-Case-marked it is governed (by the passive verb). The fact that PRO cannot occur in this position suggests that PRO is probably excluded from governed positions, rather than from non-Case-marked positions. Further evidence for this conclusion can be gleaned from the following examples:

82a. *Their belief the manager to be vindictive
82b. *Their belief [IP *the manager to be vindictive*]

83a. *Their belief to be vindictive
83b. *Their belief [IP PRO *to be vindictive*]

(82) was cited in Chapter 6 as evidence that nouns, contrary to related transitive verbs, lack the ability to assign Case. The fact that (82) is ungrammatical is therefore attributed to the inability of the noun *belief* to exceptionally Case-mark the subject of the embedded non-finite clause. Note, however, that the noun governs the subject position of the embedded non-finite clause in (82), as well as in (83). The fact that PRO cannot occur in the embedded subject position in (83) indicates that PRO is excluded from governed, rather than from Case-marked, positions.

Chomsky (1981) has suggested that this property of PRO can be stated in the form of a theorem called the **PRO Theorem**:

84. PRO Theorem
   PRO must be ungoverned.

As a theorem, (84) can presumably be shown to be true on independent grounds: we should be able to show that it follows from some independent factors. We shall return to this issue below. For the moment, the ungrammatical examples where PRO is situated in a governed position can be assumed to be excluded by (84).

7.5.1.2   PRO in DP   We have seen that DP can function as the 'local domain' for an anaphor or a pronoun when it includes a subject, but apparently not when it does not include a subject. The relevant examples are reproduced here:

85a. The players heard stories about each other
85b. *The players*ᵢ heard [DP *stories about each other*ᵢ]

86a. *The players heard his stories about each other
86b. *The players*ᵢ heard [DP *his*ⱼ *stories about each other*ᵢ]

In (85) the DP containing the anaphor apparently does not have a subject, so that the anaphor can be bound by an antecedent located outside the DP. In (86), the DP containing the anaphor does include a subject, and consequently the anaphor cannot be bound by an antecedent located outside the DP. However, there is a piece of evidence, ignored above, which seems to cast doubt on this analysis. The examples below show that a pronoun is also allowed in the position of the anaphor in both contexts:

87a. The players heard stories about them
87b. *The players*ᵢ *heard* [DP *stories about them*ᵢ]
88a. The players heard his stories about them
88b. *The players*ᵢ *heard* [DP *his*ⱼ *stories about them*ᵢ]

The fact that a pronoun co-indexed with the subject of the sentence can occur in (88) is not surprising. The presence of the subject in the DP containing the pronoun *them* means that the 'local domain' of the pronoun is DP, in which the pronoun *them* is free, as expected. What is unexpected is the fact that a pronoun co-indexed with the subject of the sentence can occur in (87), where the DP apparently lacks a subject, and therefore does not qualify as the 'local domain' for the pronoun. BC A and BC B together predict that anaphors and pronouns should be in complementary distribution, a prediction which is borne out by most contexts discussed so far. (86) and (87), where the anaphor and the pronoun are apparently in free variation, rather than in complementary distribution, seem to run counter to this prediction.

However, there is a difference in interpretation between (86) and (87) which, if taken into consideration, reveals that these examples do not run counter to the otherwise general pattern of complementary distribution between anaphors and pronouns. In (86) the stories about the players are understood to be told by the players themselves, so that (86) can be paraphrased as meaning that the players heard their own stories about each other. In (87), however, the stories are understood to be told by somebody else, so that the sentence can be paraphrased as meaning that the players heard somebody else's stories about them. Now, it is plausible to assume that this somebody else (i.e. the individual who tells stories about the players) is somehow structurally present in the DP in (87), presumably in the form of a null category. Chomsky (1986a) has suggested that the null category in question is PRO, so that (87) has the representation shown in (89) below:

89. *The players*ᵢ *heard* [DP PROⱼ *stories about them*ᵢ]

According to this representation the 'local domain' of the pronoun is the DP, in which it is free as required by BC B. Note, incidently, that (89) represents an analysis for the fact (discussed in Chapter 5) that the subject of derived nominals is present in the form of an 'implicit argument' (e.g. *The* PRO *destruction of the city* [PRO *to prove a point*]). The 'implicit argument' is present in 'noun phrases' with an agentive reading in the form of a PRO. Although the noun *stories* does not have a corresponding verb from which it can be said to derive, it clearly has an external argument.

What about (85)? We could maintain the analysis outlined above for this example, whereby the DP containing the anaphor does not instantiate a (null) subject, and therefore does not qualify as the 'local domain' of the anaphor. However, on grounds of consistency it is plausible to argue that the DP in this example also instantiates a null PRO subject, on a par with its counterpart in (87/89). The fact that the storytelling in this example is done by the players themselves will then mean that PRO is co-referential with (i.e. controlled by) the subject of the sentence. The intended representation is shown in (90):

90. *The players*ᵢ *heard* [DP PROᵢ *stories about each other*ᵢ]

According to this analysis, the 'local domain' of the anaphor is DP, not the whole sentence as assumed above. The anaphor is bound in this DP, by the PRO subject of DP. The fact that PRO is co-indexed with (controlled by) the subject of the sentence means that the anaphor is also co-indexed with the subject of the sentence. This is precisely the reason for the initial impression that the anaphor is bound by the subject of the sentence.

Thus, the initial impression of a context where an anaphor and a pronoun are in free variation, rather than in the expected complementary distribution, turns out to be false, caused by the control properties of the sentences. The fact that the control properties of lexical categories play a crucial role in the representation and interpretation of sentences is made more evident by comparing the following examples with (86) and (87) above:

91a. The players told stories about each other
91b. *The players$_i$ told* [$_{DP}$ PRO *stories about each other$_i$*]

92a. The players told stories about them
92b. **The players$_i$ told* [$_{DP}$ PRO *stories about them$_i$*]

(92a) cannot have the interpretation shown in (92b), where the pronoun inside the DP is co-referential with the subject of the sentence. The ungrammatical status of this example contrasts sharply with the grammatical status of the apparently similar example in (87) above. The difference between the two examples is that in (87) the verb is *hear* and in (91) it is *tell*; otherwise, the structures are virtually identical. In situations involving control of a PRO subject of a DP, *hear* seems to be a free-control verb, in the sense that the PRO subject of its DP object can either be controlled by the subject of *hear* or by a discourse-controller. In the same context, however, *tell* seems to be an obligatory subject-control verb, so that the PRO subject of its DP object is obligatorily interpreted as co-referential with the subject of *tell*. This means that in (92), as well as in (91), PRO bears the same index as the subject of the sentence, giving rise to a situation where the pronoun in (92) is inappropriately bound inside its 'local domain'. Thus, the contrast between (87) and (92) is a reflection of the contrast in the control properties of the verbs they include.

That verbs have different control properties is a fact which exists independently of the examples discussed. For example, *persuade* is an obligatory object-control verb, whereas *ask* allows both subject- and object-control:

93a. The manager persuaded the players to leave
93b. *The manager$_i$ persuaded the players$_j$* [PRO$_j$ *to leave*]
93c. **The manager$_i$ persuaded the players$_j$* [PRO$_i$ *to leave*]

94a. The manager asked the players to resign
94b. *The manager$_i$ asked the players$_j$* [PRO$_i$ *to resign*]
94c. *The manager$_i$ asked the players$_j$* [PRO$_j$ *to resign*]

(93a) cannot have the interpretation shown in (93c), where the controller of PRO is the subject of the sentence. (94a), however, can have either of the two interpretations in (94b) and (94c). This much is well known. What is much less known is the range of factors which determine the choice of the controller. For example, if the complement *to resign* in (94) is replaced with the passive version *to be allowed to leave*, subject control becomes strongly favoured, so that the interpretation shown in (95c) becomes harder to get (if not unavailable):

95a. The manager asked the players to be allowed to leave
95b. *The manager$_i$ asked the players$_j$* [PRO$_i$ *to be allowed to leave*]
95c. **The manager$_i$ asked the players$_j$* [PRO$_j$ *to be allowed to leave*]

The verb *tell* also seems to have different control properties, depending on the nature of the complement including PRO. We have seen that *tell* imposes obligatory subject control on the PRO subject of its DP object. However, when the complement including PRO is a non-finite clause, as in (96) below, object control is strongly favoured, so that the interpretation shown in (96c) is harder to obtain (if not impossible):

96a. The manager told the players to leave
96b. *The manager_i told the players_j [PRO_j to leave]*
96c. **The manager_i told the players_j [PRO_i to leave]*

As pointed out above, the factors which determine the choice of the controller are still poorly understood. What should be clear is that the control properties of verbs play a crucial role in the interpretation of sentences, and therefore in the assignment of reference to anaphors and pronouns.

As a final point on the issue of PRO-in-DP, we need to determine the position of PRO in the structure of DP. Obviously, our decision on this matter is partly dictated by the PRO Theorem: PRO must be assigned to an ungoverned position. This has the immediate effect of ruling out Spec-DP as a possible position for PRO, on the grounds that it is accessible to government from outside. In the examples above, where DP is in the object position of the verb, Spec-DP is accessible to government by the verb. Recall that Spec positions are generally accessible to government from outside. Recall also (from Chapter 6) that Spec-DP is accessible to Case-marking by an ECM verb (e.g. *I consider* [DP *him a great athlete*]). In view of this, the position we are left with is Spec-NP, i.e. the thematic subject position where subjects of 'noun phrases' are base-generated (Chapter 6). Accordingly, a more detailed structure of (97a) is shown in (97b):

97a. The players heard stories about each other
97b. *The players heard* [DP D [NP PRO [N' *stories about each other*]]]

Notice that in Spec-NP, PRO c-commands the anaphor inside N', so that the binding relation between them is legitimate. Notice also that if Case is a property of overt DPs only, and if DP subjects move to Spec-DP for Case, it is not surprising that PRO remains in its D-structure position. However, the status of PRO with respect to the Case Requirement is not straightforward, as we will see below.

7.5.2 Interpretation

We have seen that PRO shares properties with both anaphors and pronouns. In some contexts PRO must have an antecedent in the sentence, whereas in others it may not have an antecedent in the sentence. The control properties of verbs, among other factors, play a crucial role in determining the interpretation of PRO. Here we will review other contexts which further illustrate the ambivalent nature of PRO, and then briefly discuss the issue of whether Control is reducible to Binding or should be kept separate as an independent module of the Grammar.

In addition to the fact that PRO in some (obligatory Control) contexts has an obligatory antecedent in the sentence, PRO also resembles anaphors in that it must be in the c-command domain of its antecedent:

98a. *The manager's assistants tried to blame himself
98b. **[DP *The manager's*_i *assistants*]_j *tried* [PRO_i *to blame himself*_i]]*

99a. The manager's assistants tried to blame him
99b. [DP *The manager's*_i *assistants*]_j *tried* [PRO_j *to blame him*_i]]

In (98) *The manager* in the subject position of the DP does not c-command PRO. (99) shows that pronouns, contrary to anaphors, do not have to be in the c-command domain of their antecedent. Thus in this respect PRO patterns with anaphors, rather than with pronouns.

However, in many other contexts PRO patterns with pronouns instead of with anaphors. In addition to the fact that PRO does not have to have an antecedent in the sentence in certain contexts, it can also have a 'remote' antecedent in some other contexts:

100a. The manager believes (that) it would be deceptive to blame himself
100b. *The manager$_i$ believes (that) [it would be deceptive [PRO$_i$ to blame himself$_i$]]*

PRO also resembles pronouns in that it can take a 'split' antecedent:

101a. The manager expected his assistant to accept the proposal to resign together
101b. *The manager$_i$ expected [his assistant$_i$ to accept the proposal [PRO$_i$ to resign together]*

As indicated by *together*, PRO in this example has a dual/plural interpretation, derived from two separate singular antecedents *the manager* and *his assistant*. This is a property which characterizes pronouns, but not anaphors.

It was the fact that PRO seems to share properties with both anaphors and pronouns which motivated the conclusion that it has the feature specifications [+a, +p]. Notice, however, that these feature specifications give rise to a contradiction when considered in relation to BC A and BC B. The feature [+a] implies that PRO is required (by BC A) to be bound in its GC, and the feature [+p] implies that it is required (by BC B) to be free in its GC. Chomsky (1981) has suggested that the outcome of this contradiction is that PRO never has a GC. In other words, the contradiction would not arise if PRO did not have a GC, given that Binding Conditions A and B impose restrictions on anaphors and pronouns in relation to GC. One way of guaranteeing that PRO does not have a GC is if it does not have a governor, assuming that the governor does indeed play a crucial role in defining GC. This is precisely the way in which the content of the PRO Theorem (the requirement that PRO be ungoverned) can be shown to be true. The reasoning is as follows. If PRO has a governor it will have a GC, and if PRO has a GC a contradiction will arise in relation to BC A and BC B. Therefore, PRO does not have a governor.

However, this solution has been found unsatisfactory by a number of linguists. Some of the alternative analyses offered have in common the attempt to treat PRO as a pure anaphor, with the feature specifications [+a, −p]. The ultimate aim of this attempt is to reduce Control (Theory) to Binding (Theory), a welcome simplification, if possible. However, the fact that PRO has contradictory properties, together with the fact that the control properties of verbs play a role in its interpretation, make this prospect unlikely, at least for the moment.

7.5.3 PRO and Case

One of the major issues still to be resolved is the status of PRO with respect to the Case Requirement. The fact that PRO is restricted to non-governed positions implies that it never receives Case, given that Case is assigned under government. If the Case Requirement is understood to take the form of a Case Filter which applies to overt DPs only, the fact that PRO is unmarked for Case does not raise problems. If, on the other hand, the Case Requirement is understood to hold for all argument DPs (null and overt) then PRO raises an obvious problem.

Chomsky (1986a) has suggested that PRO can be assumed to have inherent Case, where the notion 'inherent Case' is understood differently from that discussed in Chapter 6 in relation to oblique and partitive Case. The inherent Case associated with PRO is understood to take the form of a (Case) feature, on a par with other grammatical features. To the extent that this hypothesis is viable, it implies that PRO is not dependent for Case on a Case-assigner, and hence the fact that it occurs in non-Case-marked positions.

However, as Chomsky points out, 'this decision conceals a problem rather than solving it'. In Chapter 6 we saw that overt DPs also have a Case feature, encoded in D, and that the assignment of nominative Case, for example, essentially amounts to a process of 'matching' the Case features of finite I with those of the DP in Spec-IP via Spec-Head Agreement. Yet, unlike PRO, overt DPs cannot occur in a non-Case-marked subject position of a non-finite clause (see Chapter 7).

The possibility that PRO is not dependent on a Case-assigner seems initially to be inconsistent with the idea that in non-finite passives, such as in (102) below, PRO would have to be assumed to move to Spec-IP, just as overt DPs do in the same situation:

102a. The manager refused to be blamed
102b. *The manager$_i$ refused* [PRO$_i$ *to be blamed* t$_i$]

If it is generally the case that DP-movement to Spec-IP is motivated by Case, it is not clear why PRO should move in (102), on the assumption that it (already) has inherent Case. Note, however, that there are several possible arguments around this problem.

First, it could be argued that movement of PRO in (102) is motivated by EPP, rather than by the Case Requirement, although the ungrammatical status of **The manager* *expected there to be blamed* PRO gives rise to the familiar argument against an EPP-based analysis for DP-movement. Alternatively, the movement of PRO in (102) could be argued to be motivated by the PRO Theorem. PRO has to raise to Spec-IP because its D-structure position is governed. This argument entails that PRO Theorem does not hold for D-structure representations.

A third argument could be constructed along the following lines. Although PRO bears a Case feature in the sense explained above, it needs to have this feature 'matched' with the Case feature of I under Spec-Head Agreement. This argument entails that non-finite I is marked for the Case feature, although not necessarily for the other agreement features. If we assume further that PRO differs from overt DPs in that it lacks the person, number and gender features, but is specified for the Case feature, we may well be in a position to account for the differences in the distribution of PRO and overt DPs, as well as for the status of PRO in relation to the Case Requirement. The issue remains open.

7.5.4   Summary

PRO patterns with anaphors in certain contexts and with pronouns in others, depending on certain factors which are still not well understood. The distribution of PRO is restricted to non-governed positions, including the thematic subject position of DPs. The reason for this restriction is arguably to ensure that PRO does not have a GC. On the assumption that PRO has the feature specification [+a, +p], a GC for it would result in contradictory requirements imposed by BC A and BC B. Certain factors which determine the interpretation of PRO apparently have no equivalents in binding relations involving anaphors and pronouns, suggesting that Control is not likely to be reducible to Binding.

7.6   *Licensing and Full Interpretation*

7.6.1   Full Interpretation

An important term which has been used in previous chapters as well as this chapter is 'licensing'. For example, in Chapter 4 it was said that head categories license their X-bar projections, and in this chapter parasitic gaps were said to be licensed by variables with certain properties. The term 'licensing' is understood more widely to refer to relationships between elements in representations, and, ultimately, between elements in representations and the principles of Grammar which apply to them. For example, anaphoric elements can be said to be licensed by their antecedents, and the relationship between anaphoric elements and their antecedents can be said to be licensed by the principles of Binding Theory. The same is true for numerous other relationships discussed up to now.

Chomsky (1986a) has suggested that representations at the levels of PF and LF (the interface levels) are subject to an overarching principle, called the principle of **Full Interpretation**, which ensures that the elements included in these representations are properly licensed. The principle of FI can be loosely defined as follows (adapted from Chomsky (1986a)):

103. **Full Interpretation**
     '. . . every element at PF and LF. . .must receive an appropriate interpretation – must be licensed . . .'.

Chomsky goes on to explain that elements are licensed at PF by being assigned an appropriate phonetic representation. On the other hand, elements are licensed at LF by being assigned a representation which is consistent with the principles of the Grammar, understood as conditions on licensing. Among the consequences of some of the licensing conditions operating at LF is that examples such as the following are excluded:

104a. *I was in England last year* [*the man*]
104b. [*Who*] *John saw Bill*
104c. *John was here yesterday* [*walked*]

Each of these examples fails to satisfy the principle of FI because it involves an element (the one included between brackets) which is not licensed by relevant conditions of the Grammar. The presence of an element which is not licensed by a relevant condition leads to a situation where the representation is not interpretable in the intended sense.

In (104a) the argument *the man* is not licensed because it is not assigned a thematic role, i.e. because it does not satisfy the Theta Criterion. In (104b) the *wh*-phrase in brackets is not licensed because it does not bind a variable. This explanation implies the existence of a condition which requires *wh*-phrases to bind a variable at LF. The condition in question is sometimes called the **ban against vacuous quantification**, where quantification is understood in the broader sense to include *wh*-phrases, understood as quasi-quantifiers (Chapter 5). The ban in question amounts to the condition that every operator must bind a variable (for it to be licensed). Note that movement of at least *wh*-phrases in situ in the LF representation of multiple *wh*-questions, such as *Who bought what?* (chapter 5), can be said to follow from the ban against vacuous quantification. We now turn to a separate discussion of the situation in example (104c).

7.6.2 Predication

The element included between brackets in (104c) is a predicate. We have discussed two different notions of 'predicate'. One was loosely defined in Chapter 2 as referring to the material included in VP in structural representations, and the other (which originated with logicians) was said in Chapter 5 to refer to non-arguments, i.e. elements which denote events, states, and relationships of various sorts (Chapter 5). Although the element included in brackets in (104c) is a predicate in both senses of the term, the notion 'predicate' we are interested in at the moment is the second one.

Predicates are said to be licensed at LF by **predication**, i.e. by being linked to a subject of which they are predicated. The linkage can be understood in terms of the process of the assignment of the external thematic role by the predicate to the subject (Chapter 5), or in terms of a process of co-indexation between the predicate and the subject, or in terms of both. Representation (104c) is excluded on the grounds that the predicate *walked* does not have a subject to which it is appropriately linked.

The condition in question amounts to the requirement that predicates have a subject or, more generally, the requirement that clauses have a subject. Initially, this requirement looks to be none other than EPP, so that EPP can be said to follow from the more fundamental requirement that predicates must be licensed by a subject. However, the situation is not as straightforward as it may look. Recall that the EPP can either be satisfied by an argument assigned a thematic role or by an expletive, as shown in (105a,b):

105a. A unicorn is in the garden
105b. There is a unicorn in the garden

In (105a) the predicate *(is) in the garden* can be said to be predicated of the subject of the sentence *a unicorn*, in the loose sense that it 'says something about the subject' *a unicorn*. However, in (105b) the predicate cannot be said to be predicated of the subject of the sentence *there* in the intended sense. The latter is a 'semantically empty' element, and therefore cannot enter into a semantic predication relationship. It looks, therefore, as though EPP does not follow entirely from the LF-requirement that predicates be licensed via predication. EPP can be satisfied by a formal subject (any subject) whereas the latter can only be satisfied by an argument subject of which the predicate is actually predicated.

Chomsky (1986a) has suggested an LF derivation of (105b) which can be said to lead to a unification of the two requirements at the LF level. The idea is that, since expletive elements are 'semantically empty' and therefore do not play a role in the interpretation of the sentences in which they occur, they can be said to be eliminated at LF. In (105b) the expletive *there* is eliminated as a result of movement of the argument *a unicorn* to the subject position, a process sometimes called **expletive-replacement**. The resulting LF-representation is identical to the one in (105a), where *a unicorn* occupies the subject position of the sentence and is appropriately linked to the predicate. In other words, the LF representation derived by the process of expletive-replacement is one of which it can accurately be said that the predicate is predicated of the subject. Thus, although the content of the EPP does not follow from the predication requirement in the Syntax, it arguably does at LF.

Note the predicate of a sentence does not necessarily have to be of the category VP. The predicate can in principle be any of the existing categories. For example, in small clauses the predicate can be AP, PP, VP or DP (Chapter 4). In relatives, where the relative clause is said to be predicated of the head noun it modifies, the predicate is a CP. Note that, by analogy with relative CPs, adjectives are also predicated of the nouns they modify, and adverbs are predicated of the categories they modify, although in the latter cases it is not clear whether the licensing element has the status of a subject. The analysis of small clauses outlined in Chapter 4 seems to suggest that the predicate does not have to be a maximal projection either but can be a single-bar projection. For example, in *I consider* [AP *her* [A' *intelligent*]] the predicate is an A' (for a different view and a discussion of predication in general see Rothstein (1983) and Napoli (1989)).

To close the discussion of predication here, let us briefly discuss *wh*-questions in relation to the principle we have called the [+WH]-CP Principle (Chapter 4):

106a. I wonder who Mary saw
106b. *I wonder Mary saw Bill/who
107. **[+ WH]-CP Principle**
    [+ WH]-CPs must have a ([+ WH]) specifier.

(106b) is excluded by (107) since it includes a [+ WH]-CP (selected by the verb *wonder*) which does not have a *wh*-phrase in Spec-CP. In Chapter 4 it was pointed out that the restriction imposed by (107) on [+ WH]-CPs parallels the requirement imposed by EPP on clauses. Now, to the extent that the content of the EPP can be said to follow from the LF-predication requirement, and ultimately from the principle of FI, (107) can also be said to follow from the same requirement. Obviously, this would be the case if [+ WH]-CPs were assumed to be some sort of predicates which are licensed by an operator in Spec-CP (see Browning (1987) for a discussion of predication in operator-constructions).

7.6.3 Summary

Representations at PF and LF (the interface levels) are subject to an overarching condition, called Full Interpretation, which requires each element in them to be appropriately licensed. A representation is interpretable if all the elements it includes are licensed by relevant conditions. The licensing conditions at LF are basically the conditions of the Grammar which hold at this level. For example, the licensing condition on arguments is the Theta Criterion. On the other hand, the licensing condition on operators is the requirement that they bind a variable. Finally, the licensing condition on predicates is that they must have a subject.

7.7 *Conclusions and Revisions*

In this chapter we discussed the distribution of DPs as determined by their referential properties in combination with the principles of Binding Theory and, in the case of PRO, Control Theory. In addition to PRO, there are three classes of DPs: anaphors, pronouns, and R-expressions. Anaphors have the feature specifications [+ a, − p], meaning that they are pure anaphors. Pronouns have the feature specifications [− a, + p], meaning that they are pure pronouns. R-expressions have the feature specifications [−a, − p], meaning that they are neither anaphoric nor pronominal. Finally, PRO has the feature specifications [+ a, + p], meaning that it has properties in common with both anaphors and pronouns.

The class of anaphors includes reflexives, reciprocals, and DP-traces. They have in common the fact that they require an antecedent inside a well-defined 'local domain', called GC. This requirement takes the form of a binding condition, called BC A. The class of pronouns includes overt pronouns, and an additional empty category to be discussed in Chapter 9. Contrary to anaphors, pronouns impose an anti-locality condition on their antecedent, meaning that their antecedent must be located outside their GC. The binding condition which encodes this requirement is called BC B.

The class of R-expressions includes names (referring expressions) and variables. The binding condition which accounts for the properties of these expressions, called BC C, stipulates that an R-expression cannot be bound in the domain of its operator. Variables, being traces of moved operators, are invariably bound by the operator. However, this particular relation of binding, called A′-binding, falls outside the scope of Binding Theory. The latter concerns itself with A-binding relations, which are essentially relations of reference-assignment. Operators are not referential expressions, and therefore cannot enter into relations of reference-assignment.

The feature specifications of PRO reflect the fact that it patterns with anaphors in certain contexts and with pronouns in others. The hybrid character of PRO gives rise to a contradiction in relation to BCs A and B. However, given that BCs A and B make reference to GC, the contradiction would not arise if PRO did not have a GC. PRO would not have a GC if it did not have a governor. It is arguably for this reason that PRO is restricted to ungoverned positions (PRO Theorem). As for the interpretation of PRO, a number of factors seem to play a role which are still not well understood. Moreover, the involvement of these factors seems to indicate that Control, i.e. the mechanism responsible for assigning an interpretation to PRO, is not reducible to Binding (Theory).

Finally, this chapter also included a discussion of the issue of interpretation and licensing of elements in representations at LF. LF representations are subject to a general condition, called Full Interpretation, which requires that every element they include be licensed in an appropriate manner. A representation is interpretable if all the elements in it are licensed by relevant conditions.

Exercises

Exercise 1

The examples below are instances of what is sometimes called 'long-distance binding':

1. The players thought that pictures of each other were on sale
2. The players thought that each other's pictures were on sale
3. The players thought that pictures of them were on sale
4. The players thought that their pictures were on sale

Explain whether these examples raise any problems for the Theory of Binding discussed in this chapter.

Exercise 2

Consider the following examples:

1a. Whose manager does he like?
1b. *$[_{DP}$ *Whose$_i$ manager*$]_j$ *does he$_i$ like* t$_j$?
2a. Who does he like?
2b. *Who_i *does he$_i$ like* t$_i$?

The interpretations in (1b) and (2b) seem to be excluded for the same reason, having to do with Strong Crossover. However, while it is true that the *wh*-phrase in (1) has 'crossed over' the pronoun in the subject position, the pattern of indexation in (1b) does not, strictly speaking, involve a situation of Strong Crossover. Explain why, and suggest a possible analysis for (1b) which would result in subsuming it under the phenomenon of Strong Crossover. Note that (1) involves a situation of pied-piping, where the *wh*-phrase is moved as part of a larger DP phrase.

Exercise 3

The following examples look problematic for Binding Theory, as they include a reflexive which apparently does not have an antecedent in the sentence:

1. This article was written by Mary and myself
2. Mary and myself stayed away

Compare these examples with their counterparts in (3) and (4), which are ungrammatical:

3. *This article was written by Mary and himself
4. *Mary and himself stayed away

What do these examples reveal about the properties of the reflexive in (1) and (2) and its status in Binding Theory?

Exercise 4

Consider the following short dialogue:

Speaker A: I don't like you in this mood
Speaker B: I don't like me in this mood either

Speaker B's utterance seems to involve a violation of BC B – or does it?

Exercise 5

Discuss the binding properties of all the relevant elements in the following example:

1. Which players seemed to each other to be winning?

What conclusions can be drawn in relation to the levels at which Binding Conditions apply?

Further Reading

The theory of Binding discussed in this chapter is the one outlined in Chomsky (1980b; 1981) and further refined in Chomsky (1982; 1986a). Prior to these works there was a substantial amount of literature on anaphors and pronouns. Among the early works are Lakoff (1968), Dougherty (1969), Postal (1971), Jackendoff (1972), Chomsky (1973), Lasnik (1976), and Reinhart (1976).

The distinction between A-binding and A'-binding is discussed in Chomsky (1981; 1982; 1986a). The crossover phenomena were first identified in Postal (1971), and later discussed in more details in Wasow (1972; 1979). Resumptive pronouns are discussed in Chomsky (1982), and in more detail in Sells (1984) and Borer (1984a). On pronouns and bound variables see Higginbotham (1980). On parasitic gap constructions see Taraldsen (1981), Engdahl (1983; 1985), Chomsky (1982; 1986b), Kayne (1984), Bennis and Hoekstra (1984), Longobardi (1985), Browning (1987), Tellier (1988), and Frampton (1989).

The discussion of PRO and Control in this chapter is based on Chomsky (1980b; 1981;

1986a) and Manzini (1983). For more on the relationship between Binding and Control see Koster (1984) and Borer (1989). For a different view see Bresnan (1982a).

The principle of Full Interpretation is introduced in Chomsky (1986a). On predication see Williams (1980), Rothstein (1983), and Napoli (1989). On predication and licensing in *wh*-constructions see Browning (1987) and Tellier (1988).

8

Movement Theory

Contents

8.1 *Move-α*

In the course of this book we have identified a number of transformations responsible for the derivation of various kinds of constructions. So far, the list of transformations includes Topicalization, *Wh*-movement, DP-movement, Extraposition, Heavy NP Shift, Quantifier Raising, I-lowering (to V), V-raising (to I), and I-movement (to C). Note that apart from *Do*-support, all these transformations have in common the property of moving a category from one position to another. This fact suggests the possibility of reducing all these transformations to a single general principle which performs all the operations previously performed by individual transformations. The general principle in question is called **Move-α**, where alpha is a variable which ranges over all categories. Move-alpha can be simply defined as in (1):

1. **Move-α**
   Move any category anywhere.

To accommodate *Do*-support, as well as deletion operations (see below), Lasnik and Saito (1984) have suggested an even more general version of (1), called **Affect-α**, where 'affect' ranges over the operations of movement, insertion, and deletion. However, since the discussion below is mainly concerned with movement operations, we shall use the version Move-α.

Contrary to individual transformations, as defined in Chapter 3 and elsewhere, Move-alpha makes reference neither to the positions targeted by the movement operations nor to the conditions on the movement operations. Recall (from Chapter 3) that our definition of *wh*-movement included a reference to the position it targets, as well as a reference to the *Wh*-island Condition, the Complex Noun Phrase Condition, and the Cyclicity Condition. On the other hand, our definition of DP-movement (alias NP-movement) included a reference to the position it targets (i.e. an empty DP) as well as to TSC and SSC. The definitions of other transformations also included reference to the same kind of information. The incorporation of this information into the definition of transformations was necessary to prevent them from over-generating. In view of this, the fact that Move-α does not incorporate any of the information mentioned means that it will inevitably over-generate – obviously, it is not the case that you can move any category anywhere. An important fact we (are supposed to) have learned from our discussions in the previous chapters is that generally you can only move certain categories, from certain positions, to certain other positions, over a certain distance.

Thus, we need to impose appropriate conditions on Move-α to prevent it from over-generating. The task involved here is similar in principle to the task carried out in Chapter 4 in relation to the replacement of PS rules with X-bar schemata. The core properties of PS rules were factored out and stated as conditions on the structural representation of lexical items. The same can be done with conditions on transformations: the core properties of these conditions can also be factored out and stated separately as conditions on the representations derived by Move-α. This means, in essence, that we allow Move-α to over-generate in principle, but in practice we impose conditions on its output that will have the effect of excluding undesirable representations. This move is in keeping with the general attempt to replace construction-specific rules with general principles and conditions on representations.

As a matter of fact, a substantial part of this task has already been carried out with respect to the conditions on DP-movement. In the previous chapter we saw that the effects of TSC and SSC derive from BC A on the assumption that DP-traces are anaphors. The effects of TSC were also found in Chapter 6 to derive from the uniqueness requirement on the Case properties of chains. Movement of a DP from the subject position of a tensed clause to the subject position of a root clause leads to the derivation of a chain with two Case positions (an ill-formed chain). These independent conditions on representations have the effect of restricting DP-movement. Other conditions on representations also impose restrictions on DP-movement. For example, the uniqueness requirement on the thematic properties of chains restricts DP-movement of arguments to non-theta-marked positions. This has the effect of excluding (3), while allowing (2):

2a. John is certain to win
2b. *John$_i$ is certain* [t$_i$ *to win*]

3a. *John is confident to win
3b. **John* is confident* [t$_i$ *to win*]

(3) involves movement to a theta-marked position, leading to the derivation of a chain with two theta-positions (an ill-formed chain).

It is not only DP-movement that is constrained by independent conditions on representations; other movements are as well. For example, in Chapter 4 we saw that the Structure Preserving Principle (SPP) has the effect of forcing head categories to move to head positions and maximal projections to maximal (Spec) positions. The consequence is that (5) below is excluded, while (4) is allowed:

4a. Which car will John fix?
4b. [$_{CP}$ [$_{DP}$ *Which car*]$_i$ [$_{C'}$ [$_I$ *will*]$_j$ [$_{IP}$ *John* [$_{I'}$ t$_j$ [$_{VP}$ *fix* t$_i$]]]]]?

5a. *Will which car John fix?
5b. *[$_{CP}$ [$_I$ *Will*]$_j$ [$_{C'}$ [$_{DP}$ *which car*]$_i$ [$_{IP}$ *John* [$_{I'}$ t$_j$ [$_{VP}$ *fix* t$_i$]]]]]?

(5) is derived by movement of I to Spec-CP and of the *wh*-DP to C. These operations are excluded on the grounds that they give rise to representations which are inconsistent with the principles of X-bar Theory (Chapter 4). Thus, SPP restricts the set of positions which can be targeted by *wh*-movement and head-movement processes to the ones compatible with the category moved in X-bar terms. Another consequence of the constraints on representations imposed by X-bar Theory is the restriction of possible movements to substitution movements and adjunction movements, i.e. the 'structure-preserving' movements as opposed to the 'structure-building' movements.

The Spec-Head Agreement requirement (another condition on representations) imposes even more stringent conditions on the positions which can be targeted by *wh*-movement. Movement of *wh*-phrases is restricted to the Spec position of [+ WH]-CPs, with the effect that (7) below is excluded, while (6) is allowed:

6a. I wonder who Mary saw
6b. *I wonder* [$_{CP}$ *who*$_i$ [$_{C'}$ [+ WH] [$_{IP}$ *Mary saw* t$_i$]]]

7a. *I believe who Mary saw
7b. **I believe* [$_{CP}$ *who*$_i$ [$_{C'}$ [– WH] [$_{IP}$ *Mary saw* t$_i$]]]

In (6) the embedded C is [+ WH], so that it and the *wh*-phrase in Spec-CP are in Spec-Head Agreement. In (7), however, the embedded C is [– WH], so that it and the *wh*-phrase in Spec-CP are in violation of the Spec-Head Agreement requirement.

Thus, the scope of Move-α is already severely restricted by independent conditions on representations. As a matter of fact, the Grammar in its current form goes beyond imposing conditions on Move-α to providing an explanation for why its various instances take place. In Chapter 3 nothing was said in relation to why, for example, a DP object of a passive verb has to move to the subject position, and why the *wh*-phrase in a simple *wh*-question has to move to COMP (Spec-CP). In the subsequent chapters it transpired that movement of these categories to the positions indicated was motivated by certain requirements of the Grammar. DP-objects of passives move to the subject position in order to satisfy the Case Requirement, and *wh*-phrases in simple *wh*-questions move to Spec-CP so that *wh*-questions can satisfy the requirement that [+ WH]-CPs have a (*wh*-) specifier. On the other hand, quantified phrases and *wh*-phrases in situ move at LF for scope reasons or, alternatively, to satisfy the requirement that every quantified phrase bind a variable (the ban against vacuous quantification (Chapter 7)). The end result is that most movement processes are motivated: categories move because they have to.

Note, finally, that although some constraints on Move-α are imposed by conditions belonging to various modules of the Grammar, this does not necessarily have to be the case with all constraints on Move-α. It is possible that some of these constraints belong to the **Movement Theory** module itself, and function as conditions on the application of Move-α or on the representations derived by Move-α. This is the situation which will transpire in this chapter, although in the last section we will discuss attempts to derive some of these conditions from the independently motivated principles of Binding Theory. This forms part of the general endeavour to capture common patterns underlying phenomena which superficially may look different. It is important to bear in mind that, although we have been assuming that Move-α performs a (movement) operation, and will continue to do so, this does not have to be the case. It is possible to think of Move-α as a principle which establishes, via a process of co-indexation similar to the one assumed in Binding Theory, a relationship between the position occupied by the antecedent and the position occupied by the trace.

8.2 *Bounding Theory: Subjacency*

8.2.1 Island Conditions and Cyclicity

In Chapter 3 we saw that the Cyclicity Condition imposes on a sentence such as (8a) the derivation outlined in (8b):

8a. Which car did you think (that) John would fix?
8b. *Which car$_i$ did you think* [$_{CP}$ t$_i'$ [$_{C'}$ *(that)* [$_{IP}$ *John would fix* t$_i$]]]?

The Cyclicity Condition imposes a successive cyclic derivation on (instances of long) *wh*-movement, with each step targeting the nearest Spec-CP position, as shown in (8b). The latter includes two traces: the initial trace, which marks the D-structure position of the moved *wh*-phrase, and the intermediate trace, which marks the Spec-CP position used by the *wh*-phrase on its journey up to the root Spec-CP position.

Now, compare (8) to example (9) below, which involves *wh*-movement out of a *wh*-island (the trace of *when* has been ignored):

9a. *Which car do you wonder when John will fix?
9b. **Which car$_i$ do you wonder* [$_{CP}$ *when* [$_{C'}$ e [$_{IP}$ *John will fix* t$_i$]]]?

In Chapter 3, examples of this type were said to be excluded by the *Wh*-island Condition on *wh*-movement. However, there is a sense in which the *Wh*-island Condition reduces to the Cyclicity Condition. Note that the derivation outlined in (9b) involves a violation of the Cyclicity Condition, as the *wh*-phrase moves directly to the root Spec-CP rather than in successive cyclic steps. The reason why the *wh*-phrase is forced to move directly, presumably, has to do with the fact that the embedded Spec-CP position is filled with the *wh*-phrase *when*. Spec-CP is said to be an **escape hatch** used by moved *wh*-phrases in order to circumvent the Cyclicity Condition. In (8) above, the embedded Spec-CP is empty and therefore can be used as an escape hatch out of the embedded clause by the moved *wh*-phrase. However, in (9) the embedded Spec-CP is filled, and therefore cannot be used as an escape hatch by the moved *wh*-phrase to circumvent the Cyclicity Condition.

With complex 'noun phrases' involving a relative clause, it looks as though the Complex Noun Phrase Condition also reduces to the Cyclicity Condition:

10a. *Which car have you met someone who can fix?
10b. *Which car$_i$ have you met [$_{DP}$ someone [$_{CP}$ who can fix t$_i$]]]?

Recall that relative clauses usually involve an internal process of *wh*-movement, so that the Spec-CP of the relative clause in (10) is filled with a *wh*-phrase, *who*. In view of this, the object *wh*-phrase *which car* cannot make use of the Spec-CP of the relative clause as an escape hatch out of the relative clause. Consequently, it is forced to move directly to the root Spec-CP, thereby violating the Cyclicity Condition.

However, not all complex 'noun phrases' include a relative clause. The complex 'noun phrase' in (11) below includes a CP-complement of a noun:

11a. *Which car did you hear the rumour that John would fix?
11b. *Which car$_i$ did you hear [$_{DP}$ the rumour [$_{CP}$ t$'_i$ [$_{C'}$ that [$_{IP}$ John would fix t$_i$]]]]?

In this example the Spec-CP of the CP-complement is free, and therefore can be used as an escape hatch by the object *wh*-phrase in moving to the root Spec-CP, as shown in (11b). The latter, unlike (10) above, does not involve a violation of the Cyclicity Condition, and yet it is excluded. Thus, it seems that the Complex Noun Phrase Condition is not fully reducible to the Cyclicity condition after all.

Notwithstanding this conclusion, the similarities between the three conditions suggest that they probably do reduce to a single underlying condition. Chomsky (1973) has argued that they do indeed reduce to a single condition, called **Subjacency**. The definition of Subjacency we will adopt here is the following:

12. **Subjacency**
   Movement cannot cross more than one bounding node in a single step, where bounding nodes are IP and DP.

Let us see how Subjacency derives the effects of the three conditions discussed above. The derivations of the examples above are reproduced here, with bounding nodes included in a circle:

13a. *Which car$_i$ did* [⊕ *you think* [$_{CP}$ t$'_i$ [$_{C'}$ *(that)* [⊕ *John would fix* t$_i$]]]]?

13b. **Which car$_i$ do* [⊕ *you wonder* [$_{CP}$ *when* [$_{C'}$ e [⊕ *John will fix* t$_i$]]]]?

13c. **Which car$_i$ have* [⊕ *you met* [⊕ *someone* [$_{CP}$ *who* [⊕ *can fix* t$_i$]]]]?

13d. **Which car$_i$ did* [⊕ *you hear* [⊕ *the rumour* [$_{CP}$ t$'_i$ [$_{C'}$ *that* [⊕ *John would fix* t$_i$]]]]]?

Starting with the Cyclicity Condition, Subjacency forces movement of a *wh*-phrase from an embedded clause to a higher clause to operate in two steps, as shown in (13a). Each step crosses only one bounding node, IP. Movement of the *wh*-phrase to the root clause directly (in a single step) would result in crossing two IP nodes (the embedded IP and the root IP) and is therefore excluded. Moving on to the *Wh*-island Condition, we have seen that this condition reduces to the Cyclicity Condition, and therefore is also derivable from Subjacency. Because the Spec-CP of the embedded clause in (13b) is filled, the *wh*-phrase is forced to move directly to the root clause in a single step, thereby crossing two IPs (bounding nodes).

Finally, the Complex Noun Phrase Condition also reduces to Subjacency. We have seen that the cases which include a relative clause, such as (13c), reduce to the Cyclicity Condition, and therefore to Subjacency. In (13c) the *wh*-phrase is forced to move in a single step to the root clause, thereby crossing two IPs (bounding nodes). In fact, movement in this example crosses a third bounding node, which is DP. This is precisely where Subjacency differs from the Cyclicity Condition, with the consequence that Subjacency accounts for cases of complex 'noun phrases' with a CP-complement of N, whereas the Cyclicity Condition does not. Although the first step of the movement in (13d) crosses only one bounding node, the embedded IP, the second step crosses two bounding nodes, the complex DP and the root IP.

Thus, the three major conditions on *wh*-movement are indeed reducible to a single condition, namely Subjacency. As defined in (12) above, Subjacency is a condition on movement (Move-α) rather than a condition on representations derived by movement. This is somewhat inconsistent with the stated aim of replacing conditions on movement with conditions on representations derived by movement. Having said that, it is not at all clear whether Subjacency should be regarded as one or the other. It is possible to state Subjacency in such a way that it becomes a locality condition on the representation of traces in relation to their antecedent (the moved category), to the effect that a given trace cannot be separated from its antecedent by more than one bounding node. However, we will maintain the definition of Subjacency in (12) for the moment. Later in this chapter we will discuss an attempt to unify it with other conditions on representations still to be discussed. It is partly because Subjacency is sometimes regarded as a condition on movement that it is thought to belong to a separate sub-theory of Grammar called **Bounding Theory**.

8.2.2   Subjacency and LF-movement

Compare the following examples, both of which involve a complex 'noun phrase' (the declarative counterpart of both sentences is 'John was in the car that hit Bill'):

14a. *Who was John in the car that hit?
14b. *Who_i *was* [$_{IP}$ *John in* [$_{DP}$ *the car* [CP O_j [$_{C'}$ *that* [$_{IP}$ t_j *hit* t_i]]]]?

15a. Who was in the car that hit who?
15b. LF: *Who_i who_j* [$_{IP}$ t_j *was in* [$_{DP}$ *the car* [CP O_k *that* [$_{IP}$ t_k *hit* t_i]]]]?

(14) is a simple *wh*-question where movement of the *wh*-object of *hit* takes place at the S-structure. The sentence exhibits a Subjacency violation as expected, since it involves extraction out of a complex 'noun phrase' island. (15), on the other hand, is a multiple *wh*-question, where the *wh*-object of *hit* remains in situ at S-structure, and does not move to

the root Spec-CP until LF (Chapter 5). The LF-movement of the *wh*-phrase in (15), like that of its counterpart in (14), also crosses (the same) bounding nodes. Unlike (14), however, (15) does not exhibit an island effect, in the sense that it is significantly better than (14). The difference in grammatical status between examples such as (14) and (15) in English and other languages has led Huang (1982), among others, to conclude that Subjacency does not hold for LF-movement.

The lack of Subjacency effects with LF-movement apparently shows up with respect to other islands as well. The following examples involve a *wh*-island (the declarative counterpart is 'I wonder where John met Bill'):

16a. *Who do you wonder where John met?
16b. *Who_i do [_IP you wonder [_CP where [_IP John met t_i]]]?

17a. Who wonders where John met who?
17b. LF: Who_i who_j [_IP t_j wonder [_CP where [_IP John met t_i]]]?

The difference between the two examples is that in (16) extraction of the *wh*-object of *meet* takes place at the S-structure, whereas in (17) (a multiple *wh*-question) it takes place at LF. However, in both examples the movement crosses (the same) bounding nodes. As with the complex 'noun phrase' examples above, the two examples exhibit a notable difference in grammatical status, which seems to confirm the idea that Subjacency does not hold for LF-movement.

8.2.3 Summary

The effects of the Cyclicity Condition, the *Wh*-Island Condition, and the Complex Noun Phrase Condition can all be reduced to a single condition called Subjacency. The latter is considered to be a condition on Move-alpha, although it is possible to conceive of it as a condition on the output of Move-alpha. There is evidence which suggests that Subjacency does not hold for LF-movement, as sentences (multiple *wh*-questions) which include a *wh*-phrase inside an island do not seem to exhibit the island effects.

8.3 *The Empty Category Principle*

8.3.1 Subject–Object Asymmetries

Compare the following examples:

18a. ??Which car do you wonder how to fix?
18b. ??Which car_i do you wonder [_CP how [_IP PRO to fix t_i]]?
19a. *Who do you wonder how will fix the car?
19b. *Who_i do you wonder [_CP how [_IP t_i will fix the car]]?

(18) involves extraction of the *wh*-object of *fix* out of a *wh*-island, and (19) involves extraction of the *wh*-subject of the embedded clause out of the same *wh*-island. A consequence of this difference is that (18) exhibits a weaker degree of ungrammaticality (indicated by the two question marks), compared to (19). The two examples illustrate the fact that there is an **asymmetry** between objects and subjects with respect to extraction.

For reasons which we will try to identify below, objects are more easily extractable than subjects.

The observed asymmetry is not necessarily restricted to extraction out of islands. It also shows up in constructions which do not involve extraction out of an island, such as the following:

20a. Which car did you say (that) John would fix?
20b. *Which car$_i$ did you say* [$_{CP}$ t$_i'$ *(that)* [$_{IP}$ *John would fix* t$_i$]]?

21a. Who did you say (*that) would fix the car?
21b. *Who$_i$ did you say* [$_{CP}$ t$_i'$ [$_{C'}$ e [$_{IP}$ t$_i$ *would fix the car*]]]?
21c. **Who$_i$ did you say* [$_{CP}$ t$_i'$ [$_{C'}$ *that* [$_{IP}$ t$_i$ *would fix the car*]]]?

(20) shows that the object can be successfully extracted out of the embedded clause irrespective of whether the complementizer *that* is present or missing. (21a–c), on the other hand, show that a subject can only be successfully extracted out of the embedded clause if the complementizer *that* is missing. The phenomenon illustrated in (21c) is known as the **That-trace Effect**, referring to the sequence *that* followed by the trace in the (embedded) subject position (*that*-t). In an earlier framework (Chomsky and Lasnik, 1977), the *that*-trace effect cases were accounted for in terms of a special filter, called the **'That'-trace Filter**. Later on, it turned that cases of the *that*-trace effect form part of a more general pattern revealing an asymmetry between subjects and objects with respect to extraction.

The fact that the ungrammaticality of (21c) is of the stronger type is significant. Given that this example does not involve a Subjacency violation (the embedded clause is not an island), it follows that the stronger type of ungrammaticality is not due to Subjacency violations but to violations of another, different condition. This conclusion has a crucial implication for the difference in the degree of deviance between (18) and (19) above. (19) resembles (21c) in that it involves extraction of the subject and in that it exhibits the stronger type of deviance. Presumably, whatever reason is responsible for the stronger type of deviance exhibited by (21c) is also responsible for the stronger type of deviance exhibited by (19). In other words, in addition to the Subjacency violation, (19) involves a second violation of whatever condition makes it harder to extract subjects in general. Judging by the status of (18), Subjacency violations alone give rise to a weaker degree of deviance.

The explanation for the observed asymmetry between subjects and objects will presumably have to be based on differences in the structural properties of subjects and objects. One such difference is that objects are usually governed by a lexical category whereas subjects are governed by a functional (non-lexical) category, namely I (chapter 6). Let us assume that government by a lexical category is a 'stronger' form of government than government by a functional category. Let us then call the 'stronger' form of government **proper government** and define it as in (22) below. Using the notion of proper government, we can then set up a condition on traces which requires them to be properly (strongly) governed. This condition is called the **Empty Category Principle (ECP)**, and is defined as in (23):

22. **Proper Government**
    A properly governs B iff
    A governs B, and A is a lexical category.

23. **Empty Category Principle (ECP)**
    Non-pronominal empty categories must be properly governed.

ECP is usually conceived of as a condition on non-pronominal empty categories in general, for reasons which we do not need to explore here. By 'non-pronominal empty categories' we will understand here traces. ECP differs markedly from Subjacency in that it is a condition on the representation of traces derived by Move-α, rather than a condition on Move-α itself.

Let us now see how the ECP and Subjacency together account for the examples discussed above, starting with (18) and (19), reproduced here as (24) and (25):

24a. ??Which car do you wonder how to fix?
24b. ??*Which car$_i$ do you wonder* [$_{CP}$ *how* [$_{IP}$ PRO *to fix* t$_i$]]?
25a. *Who do you wonder how will fix the car?
25b. **Who$_i$ *do you wonder* [$_{CP}$ *how* [$_{IP}$ t$_i$ *will fix the car*]]?

On a general note, ECP discriminates between (traces in) the subject position and (traces in) the object position of the verb via the notion of proper government. Traces in the object position are invariably lexically governed by the verb, and therefore will always satisfy ECP. By contrast, traces in the subject position are not lexically governed, their governor (I) being a non-lexical category, and therefore will not satisfy ECP. Thus, in (24) the trace satisfies ECP by virtue of being in the object position of the verb, where it is lexically governed by the verb, and therefore properly governed. The weaker deviance of this example is due to the Subjacency violation, as explained above. In (25), however, the trace in the subject position does not satisfy ECP, as it is not lexically governed and therefore not properly governed. Thus, (25) differs from (24) in that it involves an ECP violation, in addition to the Subjacency violation. The stronger degree of deviance it exhibits is due precisely to the ECP violation, and is not necessarily related to the Subjacency violation it also involves.

Let us now turn to (20) and (21), reproduced below as (26) and (27) respectively:

26a. Which car did you think (that) John would fix?
26b. *Which car$_i$ did you think* [$_{CP}$ t$_i'$ *(that)* [$_{IP}$ *John would fix* t$_i$]]?

27a. Who did you think (*that) would fix the car?
27b. **Who$_i$ *did you think* [$_{CP}$ t$_i'$ [$_{C'}$ *that* [$_{IP}$ t$_i$ *would fix the car*]]]?
27c. *Who$_i$ did you think* [$_{CP}$ t$_i'$ [$_{C'}$ e [$_{IP}$ t$_i$ *would fix the car*]]]?

In (26) the trace is located in the object position of the verb *fix*, where it is lexically governed by the verb, and therefore properly governed. In (27b) the trace is located in the subject position, where it is not lexically governed, and therefore not properly governed. The sentence is therefore ungrammatical as predicted, with a stronger type of violation. (27c), however, is problematic. The trace in the subject position is apparently not properly governed, and yet the sentence is impeccably grammatical. Thus something special needs to be said about this example, if the analysis in terms of ECP is to be maintained. Obviously, an explanation for the sharp contrast between (27b) and (27c) will have to rely on the fact that (27b) includes the complementizer *that*, whereas (27c) does not.

The impeccable status of (27c) implies that an additional form of proper government needs to be recognized alongside lexical government. The additional form of proper government needed is called **antecedent-government** (i.e. government by an antecedent), and is defined as in (28) below. (29) is the revised definition of proper government:

28. **Antecedent-Government**
    A antecedent-governs B iff
    (i)   A and B are co-indexed.
    (ii) A c-commands B.
    (iii) A is not separated from B by a barrier.

29. **Proper Government**

A properly governs B iff

(i) A governs B and A is a lexical category; *or*

(ii) A antecedent-governs B.

The definition of antecedent-government is **conjunctive**, meaning that for a given category to satisfy antecedent-government all the conditions listed in (i), (ii), and (iii) have to be satisfied. The definition of proper government in (29), however, is **disjunctive**, meaning that only one of the two conditions, (i) and (ii), needs to be satisfied for proper government to hold.

Let us now see how our revised definition of proper government accounts for the data discussed so far. Clause (i) of the definition of proper government is our initial definition of proper government, which accounts for all the cases above, except (27c). The latter is the example which motivated the introduction of clause (ii) in the definition of proper government. The trace in the subject position in this example now satisfies proper government via antecedent-government by the intermediate trace. The latter satisfies all three conditions listed in (28), and therefore qualifies as antecedent-governor for the initial trace. Condition (iii) referring to 'barrier' is the one responsible for the contrast between (27b) and (27c). The idea is that the presence of the complementizer *that* renders C′ a barrier to antecedent-government, so that in (27b) the intermediate trace does not antecedent-govern the initial trace even though it is co-indexed with and c-commands the initial trace. In other words, the intermediate trace in (27b) does not qualify as antecedent-governor for the initial trace because the intermediate trace does not satisfy condition (iii) of the definition of antecedent-government. In (27c) C′ is not a barrier because C is not filled with the complementizer *that*.

8.3.2   Adjunct-traces: That-deletion and Gamma-marking

We have noticed an asymmetry between subjects and objects with respect to extraction: subjects are less easily extractable than objects. It is not surprising to know that adjuncts pattern with subjects in this respect, rather than with objects. This is because, like subjects, adjuncts are not governed by a lexical head, so that traces in adjunct positions, like their counterparts in subject positions, can only satisfy ECP via antecedent-government. Example (30a) below cannot have the interpretation shown in (30b), and (31a) cannot have the interpretation shown in (31b) (the possible interpretation of these examples whereby the adjunct *wh*-phrase *how* modifies the matrix verb, in which case it is locally extracted from the root clause, is ignored because it is irrelevant to the discussion):

30a. How do you wonder whether John fixed the car?

30b. *How_i do you wonder [$_{CP}$ whether [$_{IP}$ John fixed the car t_i]]?

31a. How have you met someone who could fix the car?

31b. *How_i have you met [$_{DP}$ someone [$_{CP}$ who [$_{IP}$ could fix the car t_i]]]?

(30b) includes a *wh*-island, and (31b) includes a complex 'noun phrase' island. The stronger nature of the violation shown by these examples means that the initial trace is not antecedent-government. For the moment we will assume that this is because the antecedent of the trace is 'too far away' from the trace to antecedent-govern it. To be a little more precise, an antecedent is 'too far away' if it is not included in the same clause (CP) as the trace. Another way of putting it is to say that CP is a barrier to antecedent-government, so that condition (iii) in the definition of proper government above is not satisfied by the antecedent in (30b) and (31b).

With this in mind consider example (32) below, in comparison to (33), reproduced from above:

32a. How did you think (that) John would fix the car?
32b. *How$_i$ did you think* [$_{CP}$ t$'_i$ *that* [$_{IP}$ *John would fix the car* t$_i$]]?
32c. *How$_i$ did you think* [$_{CP}$ t$'_i$ e [$_{IP}$ *John would fix the car* t$_i$]]?

33a. Who did you think (*that) would fix the car?
33b. **How$_i$ did you think* [$_{CP}$ t$'_i$ [$_{C'}$ *that* [$_{IP}$ t$_i$ *would fix the car*]]]?
33c. *Who$_i$ did you think* [$_{CP}$ t$'_i$ [$_{C'}$ e [$_{IP}$ t$_i$ *would fix the car*]]]?

(32a) can have the interpretation shown in (32b,c), where the adjunct *wh*-phrase *how* modifies the embedded verb. This shows that the adjunct *wh*-phrase can be extracted out of the embedded clause irrespective of whether the complementizer *that* is present, as in (32b), or absent, as in (32c). In this respect adjunct extraction differs from subject extraction, as the latter is sensitive to the presence/absence of the complementizer (33a–c). Recall that we excluded (33b) on the grounds that the presence of the complementizer renders C' a barrier to antecedent-government of the initial trace by the intermediate trace. Notice, however, that this explanation predicts (32b) to be on a par with (33b), i.e. the presence of the complementizer in (32b) should block antecedent-government of the initial adjunct trace by the intermediate trace, just as it does in (33b). Thus, more needs to be said to account for the contrast between (32b) and (33b), which is sometimes said to show that adjunct extraction differs from subject extraction in that it does not give rise to the *that*-trace effect.

To account for this contrast, Lasnik and Saito (1984) have suggested an analysis which makes a crucial distinction between the levels at which argument traces and adjunct traces are licensed with respect to ECP, where licensing takes the form of the assignment of the feature [+ γ]: a trace is licensed with respect to ECP if it bears the feature-specification [+ γ]. Argument traces, such as subject and object traces, must be licensed (i.e. must satisfy ECP) at S-structure, whereas adjunct traces need not be licensed (need not satisfy ECP) until LF. Put differently, argument traces must be properly governed at S-structure, whereas adjunct traces do not have to be properly governed at S-structure, although they must be properly governed at LF. The underlying idea is that all traces must satisfy ECP at LF, by virtue of bearing the feature-specification [+ γ].

Let us now see how this analysis accounts for the contrast between (32b) and (33b), reproduced below with their respective S-structure and LF-representations:

34a. How did you think (that) John would fix the car?
34b. S-structure (γ-marking does not apply):
   How$_i$ did you think [$_{CP}$ t$'_i$ [$_{C'}$ *that* [$_{IP}$ *John would fix the car* t$_i$]]]?
34c. LF (*that*-deletion):
   How$_i$ did you think [$_{CP}$ t$'_i$ [$_{C'}$ e [$_{IP}$ *John would fix the car* t$_i$]]]?
$$[+ \gamma]$$

35a. *Who did you think that would fix the car?
35b. S-structure (γ-marking applies):
   **Who$_i$ did you say* [$_{CP}$ t$'_i$ [$_{C'}$ *that* [$_{IP}$ t$_i$ *would fix the car*]]]?
$$[- \gamma]$$
35c. LF (*that*-deletion):
   **Who$_i$ did you say* [$_{CP}$ t$'_i$ [$_{C'}$ e [$_{IP}$ t$_i$ *would fix the car*]]]?
$$[- \gamma]$$

Starting with (35), the trace is an argument (subject) trace, and therefore must satisfy proper government at S-structure. However, in (S-structure) (35b) the subject trace is not antecedent-governed by the intermediate trace, owing to the presence of the complementiser *that*. Consequently, the trace is assigned the [– γ] feature which seals its fate with respect to ECP in a negative way. Thus, the explanation for (35) remains much as it was earlier. Moving on to (34), the trace involved is an adjunct-trace, and therefore does not have to satisfy ECP until LF. Consequently, although at S-structure (34b) the adjunct-trace is not properly governed, the mechanism of γ-marking does not apply to it because it is a non-argument trace. Lasnik and Saito suggest that at the LF level the complementizer *that* deletes (Affect-α), on the grounds that it is 'semantically empty' and does not play a role in interpretation (Chapter 7). Once the complementizer is deleted, C' ceases to be a barrier to antecedent-government of the initial by the intermediate trace. Consequently, the initial trace is assigned the feature [+ γ], thereby satisfying ECP. Obviously, the mechanism of *that*-deletion at LF is available to (35) as well. However, because (35) involves an argument trace, and because the fate of argument traces is sealed at S-structure with respect to ECP, *that*-deletion would not result in rescuing (35) at LF – the argument trace is already assigned the negative value of the [γ] feature.

8.3.3 Intermediate Traces: Trace-deletion and Theta-government

So far, the discussion has been restricted to initial traces, that is, traces located in the D-structure position of the extracted category. However, ECP as formulated above applies to all traces, including intermediate traces. In this section we will discuss the status of intermediate traces with respect to ECP.

Consider the contrast between the following examples, noted by Lasnik and Saito (1984):

36a. *How do you wonder whether John said Mary solved the problem?
36b. *How$_i$ do you wonder* [$_{CP}$ *whether* [$_{IP}$ *John said* [$_{CP}$ t$'_i$ e [$_{IP}$ *Mary solved the problem* t$_i$]]]]?
37a. ??Who do you wonder whether John said solved the problem?
37b. ??*Who$_i$ do you wonder* [$_{CP}$ *whether* [$_{IP}$ *John said* [$_{CP}$ t$'_i$ e [$_{IP}$ t$_i$ *solved the problem*]]]]?

The extracted *wh*-phrase is an adjunct in (36) and an argument (subject) in (37). In both examples the initial trace is antecedent-governed by the intermediate trace, and yet (36) is notably worse than (37). Presumably, (36) involves an ECP violation, in addition to the Subjacency violation, whereas (37) involves only a Subjacency violation, induced by the presence of *whether*. Lasnik and Saito argue that, given that the initial trace is properly governed in the two situations, the 'offending trace' must be the intermediate trace.

The solution Lasnik and Saito offer is as follows, assuming that intermediate traces are also subject to ECP. Starting with (37), because the initial trace is an argument it receives the [+ γ] feature at S-structure, by virtue of being antecedent-governed by the inter-mediate trace. Having done its job, the intermediate trace can then delete at LF. Note that, unlike initial traces, intermediate traces do not have the status of variables at LF (they do not translate logically into variables) and therefore do not contribute to the interpretation of sentences. Now, since the intermediate trace is the 'offending trace', meaning the one that does not satisfy proper government, its deletion at LF eliminates the problem (i.e. ECP violation). In (36) the initial trace is an adjunct, and therefore need not satisfy proper government until LF. For this, the initial trace is crucially dependent on the intermediate trace, given that adjunct-traces can only satisfy proper government via antecedent-government. The consequence is that, unlike its counterpart in (37), the intermediate trace in (36) cannot delete at LF. Since the intermediate trace is the 'offending trace', it is the one responsible for the ungrammaticality of (36).

Presumably, the 'offence' of the intermediate trace is that it is not properly governed.

The antecedent of this trace (i.e. the *wh*-phrase itself) is 'too far away', given the assumption that antecedent-government is a local relation confined to a clause. How about lexical government? According to the definition of proper government adopted so far, the intermediate trace in (36) and (37) should be able to satisfy proper government via lexical government by the verb *say*. The configuration involved is shown in (38):

38. ... *said* [$_{CP}$ t_i' [$_{C'}$ e [$_{IP}$ ...

We have been assuming all along that specifiers are usually accessible to government from outside, so that in (38) the verb lexically governs the intermediate trace in Spec-CP. This implies that the intermediate trace is properly governed, contrary to what was concluded on the basis of the contrast between (36) and (37). It seems that the definition of proper government has to be revised once more, to ensure that in configuration (38) the verb does not properly govern the intermediate trace. The revision needs to be undertaken to maintain the analysis outlined for (36) and (37), which is predicated on the conclusion that the intermediate trace (the 'offending trace') is not properly governed.

Instead of lexical government the relation needed is one which does not result in the proper government of the trace in (38), while still guaranteeing that verbs generally properly govern their object. Recall that objects usually satisfy proper government, and are usually easier to extract. The difference between the trace in (38) and an object of a verb is that the object is assigned a thematic role by the verb, whereas in (38) the trace is not assigned a thematic role by the verb, although it is governed by the verb. Let us then substitute the notion of **theta-government**, defined as in (39) below, for the notion of lexical government in the definition of proper government. (40) is the revised definition of proper government:

39. **Theta-government**
    A theta-governs B iff A is an X^0 category that theta-marks B.

40. **Proper Government**
    A properly governs B iff
    (i) A theta-governs B; or
    (ii) A antecedent-governs B.

The previous definition of proper government allowed a lexical category, such as the verb in (38), to properly govern the specifier of an XP simply by virtue of (lexically) governing it. The new definition incorporating the requirement of theta-government does not have this specific consequence. For a lexical category to properly govern another category, it has to both govern it and theta-mark it. Thus a verb will always properly govern its object by virtue of governing it and theta-marking it. The verb in configuration (38), however, does not properly govern the trace in Spec-CP, although it (merely) governs it. This is because the verb does not theta-mark Spec-CP. We therefore obtain the desired result, which is to prevent the ('offending') intermediate trace in (36) and (37), with the configuration in (38), from being properly governed by the verb.

Before we move on to discuss DP-traces, a word about an outstanding problem which arises from the assumption that antecedent-government is confined to CP. Consider example (41a) with the interpretation shown in (41b):

41a. How did you think John would fix the car?
41b. *How$_i$ did you think* [$_{CP}$ t_i' [$_{IP}$ *John would fix the car* t_i]]]?

The initial adjunct-trace satisfies the ECP at LF by virtue of being antecedent-governed by the intermediate trace. The problem raised by (41b) relates to the status of the intermediate trace with respect to ECP. Note, first of all, that this trace cannot delete at LF, as the initial trace is dependent on it for antecedent-government, as explained above. On the other hand, the verb does not properly govern the intermediate trace simply because the verb does not theta-govern the intermediate trace. Finally, the *wh*-phrase does not antecedent-govern the intermediate trace, on the grounds that the *wh*-phrase is 'too far away'. The consequence is that the intermediate trace in (42) is not properly governed, and yet the sentence does not exhibit any violation effect.

The issue concerning this example boils down to finding an appropriate definition for the expression 'too far away'. Let us assume as a working hypothesis that an antecedent is 'too far away' if it is separated from its trace by another *wh*-phrase. Thus, in *wh*-islands, for example, the antecedent is 'too far away' from the initial trace, as a distinct *wh*-phrase usually intervenes between the two elements in this situation. This will ensure that the intermediate ('offending') trace in (36) and (37) above is not antecedent-governed by the moved *wh*-phrase. In (41b), however, the *wh*-phrase is not 'too far away' from the intermediate trace, as no other *wh*-phrase intervenes between the moved *wh*-phrase and the intermediate trace. The role of intervening *wh*-phrases in breaking chain-links (i.e. antecedent-government) will be discussed in more detail later in this chapter.

8.3.4 DP-traces: CP-reduction and Improper Movement

So far, we have only been concerned with traces of *wh*-phrases. Given that ECP does not discriminate between types of trace, i.e. it does not refer to a specific class of traces to the exclusion of others, it is expected to hold for all types of trace. In this subsection we shall discuss the status of DP-traces with respect to ECP.

Because DP-movement is in most parts a local operation (recall that DP-traces are anaphors), DP-traces invariably satisfy ECP via antecedent-government. In certain cases the DP-trace is also theta-governed:

42a. The vase was broken (by John)
42b. *The vase$_i$ was* [$_{VP}$ *broken* t$_i$] (*by John*)
43a. The vase broke
43b. *The vase$_i$ I* [$_{VP}$ *broke* t$_i$]
44a. John is believed to have resigned
44b. *John$_i$ is believed* [$_{IP}$ t$_i$ *to* [$_{VP}$ *have resigned*]]

In all three examples the DP-trace is antecedent-governed by the moved DP. In (42) and (43) the DP-trace is also theta-governed by the passive verb and ergative verb, respectively. In (44), however, the trace in the embedded subject position is not theta-governed, although it is (merely) governed by the root ECM verb. Recall (from Chapter 7) that the government relation between the ECM verb and the embedded subject is necessary in ECM constructions for the purposes of Exceptional Case Marking, hence the conclusion that non-finite clauses embedded under an ECM verb are structurally realized as IP, rather than CP.

The situation with respect to DP-traces in raising constructions needs clarification. Consider (45b–d) below as alternative derivations for (45a):

45a. Mary seems to be happy
45b. *Mary$_i$ seems* [$_{CP}$ [$_{C'}$ e [$_{IP}$ t$_i$ *to be happy*]]]
45c. *Mary$_i$ seems* [$_{CP}$ t$_i'$ [$_{C'}$ e [$_{IP}$ t$_i$ *to be happy*]]]
45d. *Mary$_i$ seems* [$_{IP}$ t$_i$ *to be happy*]

(45b) does not include an intermediate trace in the embedded Spec-CP, implying that DP-movement operates directly out of the embedded clause. The trace, being a subject trace, is not theta-governed, and therefore can only satisfy ECP via antecedent-government. If CP is a barrier to antecedent-government, then obviously the trace is not antecedent-governed by the moved DP. If, on the other hand, CP is not a barrier to antecedent-government, as concluded above, then antecedent-government holds in (45b). Note, however, that derivation (45b) is independently excluded by BC A, in combination with the assumption that DP-traces are anaphors. The fact that the antecedent is located in the root clause implies that the GC of the DP-trace is the root clause. However, the DP-trace does not have a governor in the root clause, as the presence of CP prevents the root verb from governing the embedded subject position.

Moving on to (45c), this derivation includes a trace in the embedded Spec-CP, implying that DP-movement operates via this position. This kind of movement, i.e. movement from an A-position to an A′-position and then to an A-position again (A → A′ → A), is sometimes called 'improper movement'. The impropriety involved can be understood to relate to the fact that this kind of movement gives rise to an unusual chain, as well as a situation where the initial anaphoric trace is A′-bound by the intermediate trace. Although this relationship between the initial trace and the intermediate trace helps the initial trace satisfy ECP (via antecedent-government), it does not help it satisfy BC A. Thus, derivation (45c) is excluded for the same reason as (45b), among other reasons we have not discussed.

We are then left with derivation (45d). The latter involves a representation which differs from the others in that it lacks a CP. The consequence is that the trace in the embedded subject position is governed by the root verb, so that the GC of the trace is the root clause. The trace is bound in the root clause, thereby satisfying BC A. As for its status with respect to ECP, although the trace is not theta-governed by the root verb (because it is not theta-marked by the root verb), it is antecedent-governed by the moved DP. Thus, like ECM constructions, raising constructions also involve a process of CP-reduction affecting the embedded non-finite clause.

8.3.5   The ECP and LF-movement (Superiority Effects)

Compare the following examples, which are instances of multiple *wh*-questions:

46a. Who saw what?
46b. S-str: $[_{CP}$ *Who*$_i$ $[_{C'}$ e $[_{IP}$ t$_i$ I $[_{VP}$ *see what*$]]]]$?
46c. LF: $[_{CP}$ *what*$_j$ *Who*$_i$ $[_{C'}$ e $[_{IP}$ t$_i$ I $[_{VP}$ *see* t$_j$$]]]]$?

47a. *What did who see?
47b. *S-str: $[_{CP}$ *What*$_j$ $[_{C'}$ *did* $[_{IP}$ *who* I $[_{VP}$ *see* t$_j$$]]]]$?
47c. *LF: $[_{CP}$ *who*$_i$ *What*$_j$ $[_{C'}$ *did* $[_{IP}$ t$_i$ I $[_{VP}$ *see* t$_j$$]]]]$?

In (46) the subject *wh*-phrase moves to Spec-CP at S-structure and the object *wh*-phrase remains in situ. Movement of the object *wh*-phrase to Spec-CP does not take place until LF. In (47) the reverse situation is found, so that the object *wh*-phrase moves to Spec-CP at S-structure, and the subject *wh*-phrase does not undergo this movement until LF. The contrast between the two examples is a further illustration of the subject–object asymmetry with respect to extraction, this time at the LF level. An object *wh*-phrase can move (at LF) to a Spec-CP already filled by another *wh*-phrase (46), whereas a subject *wh*-phrase cannot (47). These phenomena are sometimes called **Superiority Effects**.

As with overt extraction, adjunct *wh*-phrases pattern with subject *wh*-phrases with respect to covert extraction:

48a. Why did you say what?
48b. S-str: $[_{CP}$ *Why*$_i$ $[_{C'}$ *did* $[_{IP}$ *you* I $[_{VP}$ *say what*$_j$$]$ t$_i$$]]]$?
48c. LF: $[_{CP}$ *what*$_j$ *Why*$_i$ $[_{C'}$ *did* $[_{IP}$ *you* I $[_{VP}$ *say* t$_j$$]$ t$_i$$]]]$?

49a. *What did you say why?

49b. *S-str: [CP *What*ⱼ [C′ *did* [IP *you* I [VP *say* tⱼ] *why*ᵢ]]]?

49c. *LF: [CP *why*ᵢ *What*ⱼ [C′ *did* [IP *you* I [VP *say* tⱼ] tᵢ]]]?

(48) shows that an object *wh*-phrase can move to a Spec-CP position already filled by another *wh*-phrase, and (49) shows that an adjunct *wh*-phrase (like a subject *wh*-phrase) cannot move to a Spec-CP position already filled by another *wh*-phrase. Thus, adjunct *wh*-phrases pattern with subject *wh*-phrases with respect to (covert) LF-movement, just as they do with respect to (overt) S-structure movement. Presumably, an account of this asymmetry between object *wh*-phrases, on the one hand, and subject and adjunct *wh*-phrases, on the other, with respect to LF-movement is expected to operate on the same lines as the parallel asymmetry with respect to S-structure movement. Recall that the difference between the two types of *wh*-phrase is that object *wh*-phrases can satisfy proper government via antecedent-government or theta-government or both, whereas subject and adjunct *wh*-phrases can only satisfy proper government via antecedent-government.

A possible account of the observed asymmetry relies partly on the **COMP-indexing** rule suggested in Aoun *et al.* (1981), and adapted in (50):

50. **COMP-indexing**
    [COMP . . . XPᵢ . . .] → [COMP . . . XPᵢ . . .] iff COMP dominates only i-indexed elements.

For the moment, we shall ignore the condition relating to indexing associated with the rule. We shall understand (50) to mean, simply, that COMP acquires the index of the first category that moves to it. Obviously, (50) was based on the (earlier) structure of the clause, where COMP was the only node in the pre-IP domain (Chapters 2 and 3). In the current structure, COMP in (50) can be understood to refer to Spec-CP, the position occupied by moved *wh*-phrases.

Given (50), the LF representations of examples (46) and (47) above have the patterns of indexation shown in (51) and (52), respectively:

51a. Who saw what?

51b. S-str: [CP [Spec *Who*ᵢ]ᵢ [C′ e [IP tᵢ I [VP *see what*ⱼ]]]]?

51c. LF: [CP [Spec *what*ⱼ *Who*ᵢ]ᵢ [C′ e [IP tᵢ I [VP *see* tⱼ]]]]?

52a. *What did who see?

52b. *S-str. [CP [Spec *What*ᵢ]ᵢ [C′ *did* [IP *who*ᵢ I [VP *see* tᵢ]]]]?

52c. *LF: [CP [Spec *who*ⱼ *What*ᵢ]ᵢ [C′ *did* [IP tⱼ I [VP *see* tᵢ]]]]?

Because it is the subject *wh*-phrase which moves first (at S-structure) to Spec-CP in (51), Spec-CP acquires the index of the subject *wh*-phrase. Assuming that the antecedent-government relation holds between Spec-CP (a position) and a trace at the LF level, the subject *wh*-trace in (51c) is antecedent-governed by Spec-CP, thereby satisfying ECP. The object *wh*-trace, however, is not antecedent-governed by Spec-CP, simply because Spec-CP does not bear the index of the object *wh*-phrase. However, being in the object position of the verb *see*, the object *wh*-trace satisfies ECP via theta-government. Turning now to (52), Spec-CP acquires the index of the object *wh*-phrase since it is the object *wh*-phrase which moves to it first (at S-structure). The consequence of this situation is that the subject *wh*-trace in (52c) is not antecedent-governed by Spec-CP, and therefore is excluded by ECP. In contrast, the object *wh*-phrase is both antecedent-governed by Spec-CP and theta-governed by the verb. In other words, because Spec-CP acquires the index of the object *wh*-phrase, rather than that of the subject *wh*-phrase, the trace of the subject *wh*-phrase is deprived of the only mechanism whereby it can satisfy ECP, namely antecedent-government by Spec-CP.

More generally, the ability of an object *wh*-phrase to move to a Spec-CP position already filled with another *wh*-phrase is due to the fact that its trace is not crucially dependent on antecedent-government to satisfy ECP: it can always satisfy ECP via theta-government. On the other hand, the inability of a subject *wh*-phrase to move to a Spec-CP position already filled by another *wh*-phrase, and therefore bearing a different index, is due to the fact that its trace is crucially dependent on antecedent-government to satisfy ECP. The same account extends to examples (48) and (49), where the contrast is between the trace of an adjunct *wh*-phrase which is crucially dependent on antecedent-government to satisfy ECP and the trace of an object *wh*-phrase which is not. Thus, the comparatively privileged status of the traces of object *wh*-phrases with respect to ECP, i.e. the fact that they can satisfy ECP either via antecedent-government or theta-government or both, is responsible for the observed asymmetry with respect to LF-movement, just as it was shown above to be responsible for the parallel asymmetry with respect to overt *wh*-movement.

The analysis outlined makes an interesting prediction. Multiple *wh*-questions which involve a subject *wh*-phrase and an adjunct *wh*-phrase are expected to be impossible, irrespective of which of the two categories moves to Spec-CP first. This is because in this situation the traces of both *wh*-phrases are dependent on antecedent-government to satisfy ECP, and since Spec-CP can bear the index of only one of them (the first to move it) the trace of the other *wh*-phrase will always fail to satisfy ECP. The following examples show that the prediction is borne out:

53a. *Who disappeared why?
53b. *S-str: [$_{CP}$ [$_{Spec}$ *Who*$_i$]$_i$ [$_{C'}$ e [$_{IP}$ t$_i$ I [$_{VP}$ *disappear*] *why*$_j$]]]?
53c. *LF: [$_{CP}$ [$_{Spec}$ *why*$_j$ *Who*$_i$]$_i$ [$_{C'}$ e [$_{IP}$ t$_i$ I [$_{VP}$ *disappear*] t$_j$]]]?

54a. *Why did who disappear?
54b. *S-str: [$_{CP}$ [$_{Spec}$ *Why*$_j$]$_j$ [$_{C'}$ *did* [$_{IP}$ *who*$_i$ I [$_{VP}$ *disappear*] t$_j$]]]?
54c. *LF: [$_{CP}$ [$_{Spec}$ *who*$_i$ *Why*$_j$]$_j$ [$_{C'}$ *did* [$_{IP}$ t$_i$ I [$_{VP}$ *disappear*] t$_j$]]]?

In (53) the trace of the subject is antecedent-governed by the co-indexed Spec-CP, and therefore satisfies ECP. However, the trace of the adjunct *wh*-phrase is not antecedent-governed, and therefore does not satisfy ECP. In (54) it is the trace of the adjunct *wh*-phrase which satisfies ECP via antecedent-government by Spec-CP. The trace of the subject *wh*-phrase in this example is not antecedent-governed, and therefore does not satisfy ECP.

8.3.6 Summary

There is an asymmetry with respect to extraction (both overt and covert) between subjects and adjuncts, on the one hand, and objects of verbs, on the other. The difference is that objects are governed and theta-marked by a lexical category, whereas subjects and adjuncts are not. The principle of the Grammar which regulates the distribution of traces (ECP) makes reference to the notion of government by a theta-assigning lexical category, as well as to government by an antecedent subject to certain conditions. Antecedent-government accounts for the fact that, although extraction of subjects and adjuncts is more restricted than extraction of objects, it is not excluded altogether.

8.4   *Unifying Subjacency and Government: The Barriers Framework*

Subjacency and ECP were said above to be two separate conditions, the former being a condition on movement and the latter a condition on the representation of traces. The difference is reflected in their respective definitions. The definition of Subjacency does not make reference to government, whereas the definition of ECP relies crucially on the notion of government: proper government is a 'stronger' form of government. It is desirable to have a unified approach to government (ECP) and movement (Subjacency), such that Subjacency would make reference to the same structural relations as government. One such approach is outlined in Chomsky (1986b) and is often called the **Barriers** framework. In this section we shall discuss the general characteristics of this framework, simplifying to a considerable degree an otherwise fairly complex system of ideas and relations. Note, as a guiding principle, that the term 'government' is understood in the discussion below to include both head-government and antecedent-government, and can mean either depending on the issue being discussed.

8.4.1   Defining Barriers

Central to the Barriers framework, as its name suggests, is the notion 'barrier'. The intuitive idea underlying it is that a given maximal projection may not be a barrier to government inherently, but may become a barrier as a result of being in the proximity of another maximal projection.

To see how, consider the following familiar examples:

55a. *I believe* [$_{IP}$ *her to be clever*]
55b. *I consider* [$_{DP}$ *him a great athlete*]
55c. *I find* [$_{AP}$ *him crazy*]
55d. *I want* [$_{PP}$ *them out of my room now*]
55e. *They made* [$_{VP}$ *us leave immediately*]

These examples illustrate the fact, pointed out in various parts of this book, that specifiers of XPs are generally accessible to government from outside. In all five examples, the subject of the embedded XP is governed (and assigned Case) by the root verb. This means that maximal projections are usually not barriers to government from outside, so that IP, DP, AP, PP, and VP in (55a–e), respectively, are not barriers. It is plausible to assume that this is true of CP as well, as we shall see below — indeed, of all maximal projections.

With this in mind, consider now the following, equally familiar examples:

56a. John decided to leave
56b. *John decided* [$_{CP}$ e [$_{IP}$ PRO *to leave*]]

In this example the root verb *decide* does not govern PRO in the subject position of the embedded clause (recall that PRO can only occur in non-governed positions). In view of this, the question which arises is the following: why is PRO not governed in (56) despite the fact that, as we saw above, neither CP nor IP is a barrier to government from outside? The difference between (55e) and (56) lies in that in (56) the subject is separated from the root verb by both IP and CP, whereas in (55a) the subject is separated from the root verb only by IP.

Capitalizing on this difference, let us try to work out why government of the subject is blocked in (56) but not in (55a) and, by extension, other examples in (55). In (55a) the embedded IP is governed by the root verb, which is a lexical category, whereas in (56) the embedded IP is governed by C, which is a non-lexical category. Using the terminology discussed in the previous section, IP is theta-governed (by the verb) in (55a), but not in (56). In the latter example, IP is governed, if at all, by a functional category, namely C. Let us call the relation of theta-government L-marking, and define it as in (57) below. (58) is the definition of theta-government reproduced here for reference:

57. **L-marking**
    A L-marks B iff A theta-governs B.

58. **Theta-government**
    A theta-governs B iff A is an X^0 category that theta-marks B.

The IP in (55a) is L-marked, because it is theta-governed by the root verb, whereas its counterpart in (56) is not, because it is not theta-governed. The governor of IP in (56) is C which (is a non-lexical category and therefore) does not theta-mark IP.

With this in mind, let us now assume that maximal projections which are L-marked are never barriers. Accordingly, IP in (55a) is not a barrier, given that it is L-marked (by the root verb), and hence the root verb can govern across IP. It is tempting to assume the reverse: that maximal projections which are not L-marked are invariably barriers. This would mean with respect to (56) that IP is a barrier, and hence that the root verb does not govern Spec-IP. CP in this configuration is not a barrier, as it is L-marked by the root verb. However, there are familiar reasons to believe that IP alone is never a barrier to government, even when it is non-L-marked. Consider the following example, bearing in mind that antecedent-government is a form of government:

59a. How did John fix the car?
59b. [CP *How*ᵢ [C' *did* [IP *John fix the car* tᵢ]]]?

The moved adjunct-phrase *how* antecedent-governs its trace across IP, implying that IP is not a barrier to government. Note that this is the case even though IP is not L-marked.

Rather than concluding from (59) that it is not the case that maximal projections which are not L-marked are barriers, let us assume instead that IP is an exception – Chomsky calls IP a 'defective' category. Let us assume further that IP is an exception only in a partial way. More precisely, although IP is never a barrier when it is not L-marked, it can cause a maximal projection which immediately dominates it to be a barrier. To put it in more mundane terms, although IP has the capacity to be a barrier, it never takes the responsibility of blocking government, but is always happy to pass it on to the maximal projection immediately dominating it. We now have two distinct notions of 'barrier': inherent barriers, i.e. maximal projections which are barriers by virtue of being non-L-marked, and barriers by inheritance, i.e. maximal projections which are barriers by virtue of immediately dominating IP or a maximal projection which is a barrier. Accordingly, 'barrier' can be defined as in (60):

60. **Barrier**
    A is a barrier (for B) iff:
     i) A is not L-marked; or
     ii) A immediately dominates IP; or
     iii) A immediately dominates a non-L-marked category.

Notice that if it were not for the 'defective' nature of IP, we would not need clause (ii) in (60). IP differs from the other categories in that it is never a barrier inherently, even when it is not L-marked.

Let us now see how (60) accounts for the examples above. (55a) and (56) are reproduced here:

61a. *I believe* [IP *her to be clever*]
61b. *John tried* [CP e [IP PRO *to leave*]

In (61a) IP is not a barrier, both because, inherently, it never is anyway and, redundantly, because it is L-marked by the root verb. Thus, the verb governs and assigns Case to the subject of the embedded clause. In (61b) IP is also not inherently a barrier, and neither is CP, since CP is L-marked by the root verb. However, because CP immediately dominates IP, and because IP usually transmits barrierhood to the maximal projection immediately dominating it, CP inherits barrierhood from IP and becomes a barrier itself (by inheritance). In other words, CP is a barrier by virtue of clause (ii) in the definition of barrier above. This is an example of situations where a given category which is not inherently a barrier may become one by virtue of being in the vicinity of certain categories. Thus, in (61b) the root verb does not govern PRO in the subject position of the embedded clause.

The relation of inheritance between CP and IP is basically intended to capture the generalization that the relation of government (both head-government and antecedent-government) can hold across each of these categories individually but not across both of them together. The fact that (antecedent-) government can hold across IP and CP individually but not across both of them together is demonstrated in the following example, with the interpretation whereby the adjunct *wh*-phrase modifies the embedded verb:

63a. How did you say (that) John solved the problem?
63b. *How$_i$ did you say* [CP t$_i'$ *(that)* [IP *John solved the problem* t$_i$]]?
63c. **How$_i$ did you say* [CP *(that)* [IP *John solved the problem* t$_i$]]?

In (63b) the intermediate trace antecedent-governs the initial trace across IP, and the moved *wh*-phrase antecedent-governs the intermediate trace across CP. In (63c), however, where movement of the *wh*-phrase applies directly, the antecedent does not govern its initial trace because CP and IP both intervene between them, resulting in a situation where CP inherits barrierhood from IP. This means that the system derives the cyclicity effects of Subjacency with respect to movement. In (63c) CP is a barrier both to (antecedent) government (ECP) and to movement (Subjacency). This is the sense in which a given maximal projection can be a barrier to both government and movement in the current system.

8.4.2 Barriers and Adjunction

Consider the following, simple example:

64a. Who did John meet?
64b. *Who$_i$ did* [IP *John* I [VP *meet* t$_i$]]?

In this structure IP is not a barrier, for the reasons mentioned. However, VP is the archetypal example of an inherent barrier, since its governor, i.e. I, is a functional category which does not L-mark it. Moreover, since IP immediately dominates VP, IP inherits barrierhood from VP, so that (64) includes two barriers between the antecedent and the trace. Thus, although (64b) does not involve an ECP violation, as the trace is theta-governed, it does involve a Subjacency violation, since movement of the *wh*-phrase crosses two barriers. More thus needs to be said about the derivation of (64a) to make it consistent with the system outlined above.

Compare (64a) to (65b) below, which involves an adjunct *wh*-phrase instead of an object *wh*-phrase:

65a. How did John fix the car?
65b. *How*$_i$ *did* [$_{IP}$ *John* I [$_{VP}$ [$_{VP}$ *fix the car*] t$_i$]]?

65c.

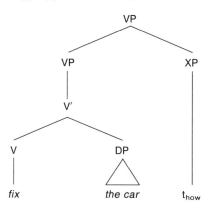

The trace of the adjunct *wh*-phrase is right-adjoined to VP, as shown in (65c). Recall (from Chapter 4) that adjuncts have a special status with respect to the categories they adjoin to: an adjunct is both a sister to and a daughter of the category it is adjoined to. Using different terminology, although adjuncts are constituent members of the categories they are adjoined to, they are not full members. Thus, V and DP in (65c) are full members of VP, but the adjoined category is not – we shall call the adjoined category in (65) an 'associate member' of VP, for clarity.

Let us now assume that maximal projections are barriers only for their full members (associate members are governed by different regulations). It follows that VP in (65) is not a barrier for the adjoined trace, simply because the adjoined trace is not a full member of VP. This accounts for the fact that this trace is antecedent-governed by the moved adjunct *wh*-phrase. With this in mind, let us go back to (64a), where the *wh*-phrase is a full member of VP, included inside V' in the object position. Suppose now that the object *wh*-phrase in this example exploits the associate-membership status temporarily, as an escape hatch out of VP. In other words, suppose that, in moving out of VP, the object *wh*-phrase adjoins to VP first, so that the derivation of (64a) is as in (66b):

66a. Who did John meet?
66b. *Who*$_i$ *did* [$_{IP}$ *John* I [$_{VP}$ t$_i'$ [$_{VP}$ *meet* t$_i$]]]?

Because the intermediate trace in (66b) is not a full member of VP, the latter is not a barrier for it. The consequence is that no barrier intervenes between the intermediate trace and the initial trace and between the antecedent and the intermediate trace, so that (66b) satisfies both ECP and Subjacency. The essence of the analysis outlined in (66b) is that it is always possible to circumvent the barrierhood of a maximal projection simply by adjoining to it. Adjunction creates a structure where an intermediate trace is neither in nor out, or, perhaps, both in and out.

In situations of long extraction, adjunction to VP takes place in both the embedded clause and the root clause, so that example (67a) has the derivation shown in (67b):

67a. Who did you say (that) John met?
67b. *Who*$_i$ *did* [$_{IP}$ *you* I [$_{VP}$ t$_i'''$ [$_{VP}$ *say* [$_{CP}$ t$_i''$ [$_{IP}$ *John* I [$_{VP}$ t$_i'$ [$_{VP}$ *met* t$_i$]]]]]]]?

Just as the moved object *wh*-phrase has to adjoin to the embedded VP containing it to circumvent its barrierhood, it also has to adjoin to the root VP, for the same reason. In the meantime, the *wh*-phrase moves to the embedded Spec-CP, to avoid crossing IP and CP together, for the reasons mentioned above. Note, however, that for the analysis outlined in (67b) to work, adjunction to both IP and CP has to be banned. This is because if adjunction to these categories were possible, their barrierhood could be circumvented simply by adjoining to them, and movement through Spec-CP would become unnecessary.

The need to ban adjunction to IP and CP is more evident with examples involving extraction out of a *wh*-island, such as (68a) below with the interpretation shown in (68b):

68a. *How do you wonder whether John fixed the car?
68b. *How$_i$ do [$_{IP}$ *you* I [$_{VP}$ t$_i'$ [$_{VP}$ *wonder* [$_{CP}$ *whether* [$_{IP}$ *John* I [$_{VP}$ [$_{VP}$ *fixed the car*] t$_i$]]]]]?

This example involves extraction of an adjunct out of a *wh*-island, a process which usually gives rise to a strong ECP-violation, in addition to a Subjacency violation. This means that one of the traces in (68b) is not (antecedent-) governed, owing to some intervening barrier. The 'offending trace' here is the initial trace which is separated from the intermediate trace by IP and CP together, a situation which always results in CP becoming a barrier by inheritance from IP. This analysis is crucially dependent on the inability of the *wh*-phrase to move to the embedded Spec-CP to circumvent the barrier-hood which results from crossing IP and CP together. Now, if the *wh*-phrase were able to adjoin to IP and CP, the barrierhood which otherwise results from crossing them together would be circumvented. Consequently, we would not have an explanation of the ungrammatical status of (68).

As a matter of fact, not only adjunction to IP and CP has to be banned but also adjunction to DP. The latter is needed to account for complex 'noun phrase' island violations of the type illustrated (69a) below, with the interpretation shown in (69b):

69a. *Who have you seen the car which was driving?
69b. *Who$_i$ have [$_{IP}$ *you* I [$_{VP}$ t$_i'$ [$_{VP}$ *seen* [$_{DP}$ *the car* [$_{CP}$ *which$_j$* [$_{IP}$ t$_i$ *was driving* t$_j$]]]]]]?

This example involves two barriers between the intermediate trace adjoined to the root VP and the initial trace in the subject position of the relative clause. CP is a barrier both by inheritance from IP and also by being non-L-marked. Recall that relative CPs are adjuncts, and therefore not theta-marked by the noun they modify. DP is also a barrier, by inheritance from the relative CP it immediately dominates. Now, for this explanation to be maintained, not only adjunction to IP and CP should be banned but also adjunction to DP. If the *wh*-movement in (69) were to be allowed to adjoin to all these three maximal projections, no barrier would be involved, and consequently we would not have an explanation for its ungrammaticality.

8.4.3 Subjacency Violations: Degrees of Deviance

In addition to an attempt to unify government and Subjacency, the Barriers system also incorporates an attempt to relate the degree of ungrammaticality in cases of Subjacency violations to the number of barriers crossed in a movement derivation. The expectation is that movement which crosses only one barrier should give rise to a less severe degree of deviance than movement which crosses two barriers, and so on. In other words, the more barriers are crossed, the more degraded the status of the sentence becomes.

We have seen that Subjacency violations typically give rise to weaker effects than ECP violations. What we have not seen yet is that among the class of Subjacency violations itself there are varying degrees of deviance. Subjacency violations involving *wh*-islands are felt to be weaker than Subjacency violations involving complex 'noun phrase' islands with relative clauses. Thus, (70) below, for example, is felt to be less bad (one question mark) than (71) (two question marks):

70a. ?Which car don't you know how to fix?
70b. ?*Which car$_i$ don't* [$_{IP}$ *you* I [$_{VP}$ t$_i$ [$_{VP}$ *know* [$_{CP}$ *how* [$_{IP}$ PRO *to* [$_{VP}$ t$_i$ [$_{VP}$ *fix* t$_i$]]]]]]]?
71a. ??Which car have you met someone who can fix?
71b. ??*Which car$_i$ have* [$_{IP}$ *you* I [$_{VP}$ t$_i$ [$_{VP}$ *met* [$_{DP}$ *someone* [$_{CP}$ *who$_j$* [$_{IP}$ t$_j$ *can* [$_{VP}$ t$_i$ [$_{VP}$ *fix* t$_i$]]]]]]]]?

Recall that *wh*-island violations, such as (70), involve a single barrier, and complex 'noun phrase' island violations, such as (71), involve two barriers. The single barrier in (70) is CP, which inherits barrierhood from IP. The two barriers in (71) are the (adjunct) relative CP and DP, the former by not being L-marked and the latter by inheritance from CP. Thus the varying degrees of deviance exhibited by (70) and (71) reflect the varying number of barriers each of them involves.

In Chapter 7 we briefly discussed another island for extraction called the adjunct-island, illustrated in (72) below. (73) illustrates a fourth island for extraction, known as the **subject-island**. Together, these two islands are sometimes referred to as cases of **Conditions on Extraction Domains** (CED), after Huang (1982) (the declarative counter-parts are *They disappeared without greeting John* and *Reading this book would be fun*):

72a. ??Who did they disappear without greeting?
72b. ??*Who$_i$ did* [$_{IP}$ *they* I [$_{VP}$ [$_{VP}$ *disappear*] [$_{PP}$ *without* [$_{CP}$ t$_i$ [$_{IP}$ PRO I [$_{VP}$ t$_i$ [$_{VP}$ *greeting* t$_i$]]]]]]]?
73a. ??This is the book which reading would be fun
73b. ??. . .[$_{CP}$ *which$_i$* [$_{IP}$ [$_{CP}$ t$_i$ [$_{IP}$ PRO I [$_{VP}$ t$_i$ [$_{VP}$ *reading* t$_i$]]]]]]. . .

In (72) the *wh*-phrase is extracted out of the PP adjunct, which we will assume here to be adjoined to VP, although this may not be entirely clear. (73) involves extraction out of a clausal (CP) subject to the Spec-CP position of the relative clause modifying the noun *book*. Since the movement here takes place inside the relative CP, only the relative CP is represented in (73b). The two examples show a similar degree of deviance as the complex 'noun phrase' case discussed above. Therefore, they are both expected to involve two barriers each. The two barriers in (72) are the PP adjunct and the IP immediately dominating it, the former by virtue of being non-L-marked (adjuncts are usually non-L-marked) and the latter by inheritance from PP. The two barriers in (73) are the clausal subject CP and the IP of the relative clause immediately dominating it, the former inherently and the latter by inheritance from the relative CP.

8.4.4   Head-movement: The Head Movement Constraint (HMC)

Compare the following examples:

74a. How tall will John be?
74b. [$_{CP}$ *How tall$_j$* [$_{C'}$ *will$_i$* [$_{IP}$ *John* [$_{I'}$ t$_i$ [$_{VP}$ *be* t$_j$]]]]]?
75a. How tall is John?
75b. [$_{CP}$ *How tall$_j$* [$_{C'}$ *is$_i$* [$_{IP}$ *John* [$_{I'}$ t$_i$ [$_{VP}$ t$_i$ t$_j$]]]]]?
76a. *How tall be John will?
76b. *[$_{CP}$ *How tall$_i$* [$_{C'}$ *be$_i$* [$_{IP}$ *John* [$_{I'}$ *will* [$_{VP}$ t$_i$ t$_j$]]]]]?

(74) involves I-to-C movement, and (75) involves V-to-I and I-to-C movements. (76) shows that the verb (*be*) cannot move directly from inside VP to C. As shown in (74), movement of the verb to C has to go through I. Note that the argument that movement of the verb has to operate through I because the inflectional elements of I need to be supported does not hold for (76). This is because in (76) I is occupied by a Modal, which normally provides support for the I elements, and prevents *Do*-support from being triggered (Chapter 3).

The constraint on head-movement illustrated in the examples above can be formulated in a number of different ways. (77) below is adapted from Chomsky (1986b):

77. **Head Movement Constraint (HMC)**
    Movement of an X^0 category A is restricted to the position of a head B that governs the maximal projection of A.

The head category which governs the maximal projection of the verb (i.e. VP) is I, and the head category which governs the maximal projection of I (i.e. IP) is C. According to the HMC, movement of the verb is restricted to I, so that if the verb moves directly to C without going through I, a violation of the HMC arises. Thus, movement of the Modal (I) to C in (74), and movement of the verb first to I (V-to-I) and then to C (I-to-C) in (75) are all consistent with HMC. However, movement of the verb directly to C in (76) is not consistent with HMC. Let us now see how the constraint encoded in HMC follows from the Barriers system.

Starting with (76), recall that VP is usually a barrier, unless the moved category is adjoined to it. Let us assume now that only maximal projections can adjoin to maximal projections, and only head categories can adjoin to head categories, a restriction which follows from the Structure Preserving Hypothesis (Chapter 4). It follows that the verb in (76), being a head category, cannot adjoin to VP to circumvent its barrierhood, and therefore has to move across it. The consequence is that VP is a barrier for the movement of the verb, causing IP to inherit barrierhood from it. Thus (76) involves two barriers, hence its ungrammatical status. Notice, however, that the barrierhood of VP should block movement of the verb in (75) as well, but apparently does not.

To account for the ability of the verb to move to I across VP and its inability to move directly to C across both VP and IP, Chomsky relies on the assumption that I generally theta-marks, and therefore theta-governs, VP. According to the definition of L-marking given above (A L-marks B iff A theta-governs B), this means that VP is not a barrier. Consequently, movement of the verb to I in (75) becomes legitimate. Notice, however, that movement of the verb directly to C in (76) also becomes legitimate. The difference between (75) and (76) is that in (76) I is filled with a non-lexical category, i.e. the Modal, whereas in (75) I is filled with (the trace of) the verb, which we will assume here to be a lexical category. In view of this, we need a definition of L-marking which makes reference to lexical categories:

78. **L-marking**
    A L-marks B iff A is a lexical category that theta-governs B.

Chomsky's analysis relies on the idea that I by itself is not an L-marking category, even though it theta-governs VP. I becomes an L-marking category after it hosts a lexical category, such as the verb *be*. Thus in (75), where I hosts the verb, I L-marks VP, so that VP is not a barrier. In (76), however, I does not host a lexical category, since it is filled by the Modal (a non-lexical category). Consequently, I in (76) does not qualify as an L-marking category according to definition (78). Thus, VP in (76) is a barrier, and hence blocks movement of the verb.

8.4.5 Summary

The Barriers system attempts to achieve two major goals. The first goal is to unify government (head-government and antecedent-government) and movement (Subjacency), so that a given category with certain properties would count as a barrier for both government and movement. The second goal is to relate the degree of deviance to the number of bars crossed in a given movement operation, with the consequence that the more barriers are crossed, the more degraded the status of the sentence is expected to become. The Barriers system also accounts for movement of head categories, otherwise regulated by a special constraint called HMC.

8.5 Unifying Antecedent-Government and Binding: Relativized Minimality and Generalized Binding

In this section we will discuss the possibility of unifying (antecedent-) government and Binding. First, we will discuss an approach, outlined in Rizzi (1990) and known as **Relativized Minimality**, which reveals a significant parallelism between (antecedent-) government and binding. Although Rizzi does not actually undertake the task of unifying the two, he clearly points out the parallelism between them: 'The analogies with the theory of binding look more than superficial, and suggest the possibility of a partial unification of government and binding . . . an important issue that I will not address here' (p. 8). In the second part of this section we shall discuss another approach, outlined in Aoun (1985) and (1986) and known as **Generalized Binding**, which does actually incorporate an attempt to unify (antecedent-) government and binding.

8.5.1 Relativized Minimality

8.5.1.1 Defining Relativized Minimality   Rizzi starts by making the important observation that the phenomena of adjunct-extraction out of *wh*-islands, super-raising, and violations of HMC have an underlying common denominator. The three phenomena are illustrated in the examples below, respectively:

79a. *How do you wonder why John fixed the car?
79b. *How_i do you wonder [$_{CP}$ why [$_{IP}$ John fixed the car t_i]]?

80a. *John seems it is likely to solve the problem
80b. *$John_i$ seems [$_{IP}$ it is likely [$_{IP}$ t_i to solve the problem]]?

81a. *How tall be John will?
81b. *[$_{CP}$ How tall [$_{C'}$ be_i [$_{IP}$ John [$_{I'}$ will [$_{VP}$ t_i]]]]?

In each of these cases an element of the same type as the antecedent (the moved category) intervenes between the antecedent and its trace. In (79) the *wh*-phrase *why* intervenes between the moved adjunct *wh*-phrase *how* and its trace in the embedded clause. In (81) the DP *it* in the Spec-IP of the first embedded clause intervenes between the moved DP *John* in the root clause and its trace in the second embedded clause. Finally, in (81) the X^0 category *will* (I) intervenes between the moved X^0 category *be* and its trace under V.

The fact that an intervening element seems to interfere with the relation between an antecedent and its trace suggests the involvement of a Minimality effect. The antecedent fails to antecedent-govern its trace because an element of the same type as the antecedent (a potential antecedent) intervenes between the two of them, and consequently qualifies as a closer antecedent-governor of the trace. The notion 'the same type' in this observation is crucial. Consider the following examples:

82a. How did you think (that) John fixed the car?
82b. *How*$_i$ *did* [$_{IP}$ *you think* [$_{CP}$ *(that)* [$_{IP}$ *John fixed the car* t$_i$]]]?
83a. Will John fix the car?
83b. *Will*$_i$ [$_{IP}$ *John* [$_{I'}$ t$_i$ [$_{VP}$ *fix the car*]]]?

In (82) two subjects intervene between the *wh*-phrase and its trace. Yet they do not block the antecedent-government relation between the *wh*-phrase and its trace. This is because the two subjects are not of the same type as the antecedent. While the subjects are A-Specifiers, meaning they occupy a Spec position which is an A-position (Spec-IP), the *wh*-phrase is an A'-Specifier, meaning it occupies a Spec position which is an A'-position (Spec-CP). (83) shows that a subject does not block antecedent-government of an X^0 trace by its antecedent either, because the subject is not of the same type as the moved X^0 category.

Because antecedent-trace relations seem to be sensitive to the peculiar properties of antecedents and intervening categories, Rizzi has argued that the version of the Minimality Condition required must be a **relativized** one, rather than the **rigid** version adopted so far (Chapter 6). The latter is rigid in the sense that it does not distinguish between the types of category which can function as minimal intervening governors. The required definition of Minimality must be relativized in the sense that only a category of the same type as the antecedent can serve as a minimal governor for the trace of the antecedent. Rizzi then formulates a relativized version of Minimality which includes both head-government and antecedent-government. The adapted version reproduced in (84) below, however, is restricted to antecedent-government, as head-government is not crucially relevant to the ensuing discussion. (85) is the definition of antecedent-government incorporating Relativized Minimality:

84. **Relativized Minimality (RM)**
    A antecedent-governs B only if there is no C such that
    (i) C is a typical potential antecedent-governor for B.
    (ii) C c-commands B and does not m-command A.

85. **Antecedent-government**
    A antecedent-governs B iff
    (i) A and B are co-indexed.
    (ii) A c-commands B.
    (iii) No barrier intervenes.
    (iv) Relativized Minimality is respected.

Clause (ii) of the definition of Relativized Minimality defines the notion 'intervene'. An intervening element is one which c-commands the trace and is c-commanded by the antecedent. Clause (i), on the other hand, defines the relativized aspect of Minimality. A typical potential governor for the trace of an A'-Specifier (antecedent) is another A'-Specifier, and a typical potential governor for the trace of an A-Specifier (antecedent) is another A-Specifier. Finally, a typical potential governor for the trace of X^0 category is another X^0 category.

Let us now return to examples (79), (80), and (81). In (79), antecedent-government of the *wh*-trace by the antecedent *how* is blocked by the *wh*-phrase *when*. The latter intervenes between the antecedent and the trace in the sense defined above, and is of the same type as the antecedent, i.e. an A'-Specifier. In (80) antecedent-government of the DP-trace by its antecedent *John* is blocked by the intervening A-specifier *it*. Finally, in (81), antecedent-government of the trace by the X^0 antecedent *have* is blocked by the intervening X^0 category [$_I$ *will*]. Thus all three examples are excluded on the grounds that the antecedent-trace relations they involve do not 'respect' the Relativized Minimality Condition of antecedent-government. In the grammatical example (82) no A'-specifier intervenes between the *wh*-trace and its antecedent *how*, and therefore no Relativized Minimality effect is involved. Similarly, in (83) no X^0 intervenes between the X^0-trace and its antecedent *have*, and therefore no Relativized Minimality effect is involved.

8.5.1.2 *Relativized Minimality and Binding: Discussion*   It is interesting to see that the super-raising example above, reproduced below, lends itself to an alternative account in terms of Binding Theory (Chapter 7):

86a. *John seems it is likely to solve the problem
86b. *$John_i$ seems [$_{IP}$ *it is likely* [$_{IP}$ t_i *to solve the problem*]]

The DP-trace, being an anaphor, is not bound in the (c-command) domain of the nearest subject *it*, so that (86) is excluded by BC A. According to this analysis, (86) is an instance of SSC, although it may also involve a violation of a condition on the output of Move-α. The fact that an intervening subject in (86) interferes with the relationship between the antecedent and its trace is part of a more general pattern which includes overt anaphors, e.g. *The players expected* [*the manager to blame each other*]. Thus, as far as (86) is concerned, the Relativized Minimality effect reduces to a Minimality effect on binding, i.e. to SSC, which defines the binding domain of anaphoric elements as the domain of the nearest subject.

On a more general level, apart from cases of HMC, the other cases isolated by Relativized Minimality, at least superficially, involve typical patterns of SSC, so much so that Relativized Minimality can be paraphrased as saying that a trace should be bound in the (c-command) domain of the nearest subject (specifier) to it. In Chapter 7, it was pointed out that the similarities between the 'local domain' of variables, defined by their operator, and the 'local domain' of anaphors, defined by a subject, were close enough to warrant a search for a unified notion of 'local domain' for both of them. Suppose we paraphrase BC C (or add a new binding condition) to the effect that a variable must be A'-bound (but A-free) in the (c-command) domain of the nearest subject (operator), just as BC A basically says that an anaphor must be A-bound in the (c-command) domain of the nearest subject. The question, then, is what counts as a subject for which DP-type. This is where Relativized Minimality comes in. Among the major insights of Relativized Minimality is that not just any specifier counts as a subject for any DP-type. For a DP-trace (anaphor) only an A-specifier counts as the subject, and for a variable (*wh*-trace) only an A'-specifier counts as a subject.

Before we move on to see how this synthesized version of Binding Theory accounts for the Relativized Minimality cases, let us first try to formalize the notion of a relativized (potential) antecedent. It is possible to do this by exploiting standard assumptions about indexation and the way it determines binding relations. Two categories are co-indexed if they bear identical features. For example, in *John suspects themselves, John* and *themselves* cannot be co-indexed because they do not bear the same number feature, so that *John* cannot serve as an antecedent for (cannot bind) the anaphor. In Chapter 4 and subsequent chapters we have seen that *wh*-phrases are specified for the feature [+ WH], while non-*wh*-phrases are specified for the feature [− WH]. Assuming that traces bear the features of their antecedents, so that variables are [+ WH] and DP-traces are [−WH], it follows that only a [+ WH] phrase can serve as an antecedent for a variable.

Obviously, not all features are relevant to both A- and A′ binding relations. The feature [+/–WH], for example, is not relevant to A-binding relations, which essentially concern reference-assignment (Chapter 7). On the other hand, the person, gender, and number features are crucially relevant to A-binding relations, as they play a role in determining (restricting) reference. Now, since the nearest subject to an anaphor is the one which A-binds the anaphor, and since the nearest operator to a variable is the one that A′-binds the variable, it follows that only an A-specifier will count as the nearest subject for the A-binding of a DP-trace, and only an A′-specifier (an operator) will count as the nearest subject for the A′-binding of a variable. Thus the notion of relativized antecedent follows from the features of the categories involved, in combination with standard assumptions about indexation and the way it determines binding relations.

Now, in (86) the DP-trace is not bound in the (c-command) domain of the nearest subject (A-specifier), which is *it*, and therefore is in violation of BC A, as explained above. The other case of Relativized Minimality involving a *wh*-phrase and a variable is reproduced in (87) below, together with (88):

87a. *How do you wonder why John fixed the car?
87b. *How_i *do you wonder* [CP why_j [IP *John fixed the car* t_i]]?
88a. How did you think (that) John would fix the car?
88b. *How_i *did you think* [CP t_i (*that*) [IP *John would fix the car* t_i]]?

In (87) the variable (*wh*-trace) is not A′-bound in the (c-command) domain of the nearest subject (A′-specifier), which is *why*. Therefore, the variable in (87) is in violation of a binding condition which requires a variable to be bound in the domain of the nearest subject (A′-specifier) to it. In (88), however, the variable is A′-bound within the domain of the nearest subject (A′-specifier), which could be either the intermediate trace or the moved *wh*-phrase itself. The subject of the embedded clause (an A-specifier) does not qualify as a subject for the A′-binding of the variable because it does not bear the relevant feature ([+WH]).

Thus it seems that a binding account for the Relativized Minimality cases involving DP-traces and adjunct-variables is possible. As far as other cases are concerned, in particular adjunct-traces, the analysis outlined in terms of binding seems to break down. The following example involves extraction of an object *wh*-phrase out of a *wh*-island, and therefore exhibits only a weaker (Subjacency) violation:

89a. ?Which car do you wonder how John will fix?
89b. ?*Which car_i *do you wonder* [CP how_j [IP *John will fix* t_i]]?

This example involves a pattern of indexation identical to the one involved in the Relativized Minimality cases above ([wh_i . . . wh_j . . . x_i]), where the variable is also not A′-bound in the (c-command) domain of the nearest subject (A′-specifier). Unless there is an independent explanation for why violation of the same principle gives rise to milder deviance when the variable involved is an argument, but to a stronger violation when the variable is a non-argument, (89) and related cases remain problematic.

In the system developed by Rizzi, examples such as (89) are accounted for in terms of the idea that argument variables, assumed to bear referential indices, can have long-distance antecedents. On the other hand, non-argument (adjunct) variables, assumed not to bear referential indices, cannot have long-distance antecedents, and therefore need a local antecedent. In the system outlined above, both types of variable are assumed to need a local antecedent, by virtue of the condition which requires variables to be bound in the domain of the nearest A′-specifier, and hence (89) is problematic.

At any rate, the parallelism between the Relativized Minimality cases and the SSC cases are intriguing enough to warrant an attempt to reduce antecedent-government relations to a generalized theory of binding which subsumes both A-binding and A'-binding relations. We now turn to an approach which incorporates precisely such an attempt. It will become clear that some of the ideas mentioned above in relation to the A'-binding of variables form the basis of this approach.

8.5.2 Generalized Binding

Aoun (1986) begins by arguing that, contrary to appearances, variables, like anaphors (and pronouns), are indeed subject to SSC and NIC (Chapter 7). Examples which suggest that variables are not subject to these two conditions are (90) and (91):

90a. Who did you say (that) Mary saw?
90b. *Who$_i$ did you say* [$_{CP}$ *(that)* [$_{IP}$ *Mary saw* t$_i$]]?

91a. Who did you say solved the problem?
91b. *Who$_i$ did you say* [$_{CP}$ [$_{IP}$ t$_i$ *solved the problem*]]?

In (90) the variable is A'-bound by the antecedent across the subject of the embedded clause, and indeed across the subject of the root clause as well. In (91) the variable is located in a nominative island, from which anaphors are generally excluded (Chapter 7).

Aoun argues that a close look at other examples reveals that variables are indeed subject to SSC and NIC. The examples he discusses with respect to SSC relate to extraction out of 'noun phrases' in French and Italian which, unfortunately, we cannot discuss here. On the other hand, the examples he discusses with respect to NIC are the familiar ones in (92–4):

92a. *Who do you wonder how solved the problem?
92b. **Who do you wonder* [$_{CP}$ *how* [$_{IP}$ t$_i$ *solved the problem*]]?

93a. *Who do you think that saw Bill?
93b. **Who$_i$ do you think* [$_{CP}$ *that* [$_{IP}$ t$_i$ *saw Bill*]]?

94a. *It is unclear what who saw
94b. *LF: *It is unclear* [$_{CP}$ *who$_j$ what$_i$* [$_{IP}$ t$_j$ *saw* t$_i$]]

All three examples involve a variable in a nominative island. Ignoring the fact that all three also involve material in the pre-IP domain of the embedded clause, they at least superficially show that variables are subject to some form of NIC. As a matter of fact, the *that*-trace effect example (93) was previously treated as a residual case of NIC (Chomsky, 1981), indicating its connection to NIC cases.

To the extent that this conclusion is warranted, it indicates that the distribution of variables with respect to their A'-antecedent is governed by the same conditions of Binding Theory which govern the distribution of anaphors. This in turn indicates that the theory of A-binding should be generalized to include A'-binding relations, with the rather attractive consequence that the effects of antecedent-government (more generally, ECP) are derivable from a generalized binding theory. Aoun suggests replacing the conditions of A-binding discussed in chapter 7 with the generalized conditions of X-binding in (95) below:

95. **Generalized Binding Conditions**
    A. An anaphor must be X-bound in its GC.
    B. A pronoun must be X-free in its GC.

C. A name (R-expression) must be A-free (where X = A or A').

96. **Governing Category**
    B is the GC for A iff B is the minimal maximal projection containing A, a governor for A, and a SUBJECT accessible to A.

97. **Accessibility**
    A is accessible to B iff B is in the c-command domain of A, and co-indexing of (A,B) would not violate any grammatical principle (e.g. BC C)

A SUBJECT (read 'big subject') can be either a (normal) subject (a specifier of IP), or Agr under I. (95–7) are intended to account for all the elements which enter into binding relations, but the discussion here will be restricted to variables.

Two important assumptions play a crucial role in the theory of Generalized Binding. First, variables are subject to both BC A and BC C. They are subject to BC A because they are anaphoric in nature, and, like anaphors, they require an antecedent in the sentence. They are subject to BC C because they are variables, by virtue of being A'-bound. The second assumption is that it is CP (S' in the structure used by Aoun), rather than IP (S), which counts as the GC for variables. This is clearly shown in examples such as (98):

98a. Who left?
98b. [$_{CP}$ *Who*$_i$ [$_{IP}$ t$_i$ Agr *left*]]?

If variables must have an antecedent inside their GC, then the GC of the variable in (98) must be CP, rather than IP.

A consequence of the assumption that variables are subject to both conditions A and C is that variables in non-subject positions in embedded domains have the whole sentence as the GC. Example (99) is reproduced from above:

99a. Who did you say (that) Mary saw?
99b. *Who*$_i$ *did you say* [$_{CP}$ [$_{IP}$ *Mary* Agr *saw* t$_i$]]?

The definition of GC above specifies that GC must include an accessible SUBJECT, and the definition of accessibility specifies that co-indexation between the SUBJECT and the variable must not violate any condition. Now, if the variable in (99) were to be co-indexed with Agr, then by transitivity the variable would also be co-indexed with the subject *Mary*. This is because the subject and Agr are co-indexed for independent reasons (Spec-Head Agreement). Consequently, the variable in (99) would be A-bound by *Mary*, in violation of BC C. Thus, the variable in (99) does not have an accessible SUBJECT in the embedded clause, and therefore the embedded clause cannot be its GC. Its GC is the whole sentence, where it is A'-bound by the antecedent *wh*-phrase.

In contrast to variables in non-subject positions, variables in the subject position of an embedded clause can have an accessible SUBJECT in the embedded clause, and consequently be A'-bound in it:

100a. Who did you think solved the problem?
100b. *Who*$_i$ *did you think* [$_{CP}$ t$_i'$ [$_{IP}$ t$_i$ Agr *solved the problem*]]?

Co-indexation between the variable and Agr in this example would not give rise to a violation of BC C. This is because Agr cannot be an A-binder, as it does not occupy an A-position. Therefore, Agr qualifies as an accessible SUBJECT for the variable trace, and the embedded clause as its GC. The variable is A'-bound in the embedded clause by the intermediate trace, as required by BC A.

Let us now see how the theory accounts for the NIC cases above, reproduced here:

101a. *Who do you wonder how solved the problem?

101b. *Who_i do you wonder [$_{CP}$ how [$_{IP}$ t_i solved the problem]]?

102a. *Who do you think that saw Bill?

102b. *Who_i do you think [$_{CP}$ that [$_{IP}$ t_i saw Bill]]?

103a. *It is unclear what who saw

103b. *LF: It is unclear [$_{CP}$ who_j $what_i$ [$_{IP}$ t_j saw t_i]]

Recall from earlier that Superiority cases such as (105) are accounted for in terms of the COMP Indexing mechanism, reproduced here:

104. **COMP-indexing**

[COMP . . . XP_i. . .] → [COMP . . . XP_i . . .] iff COMP dominates only i-indexed elements.

By virtue of this mechanism, Spec-CP in (103) acquires the index of the object *wh*-phrase *what* moved to it at S-structure. Consequently, movement of the subject *wh*-phrase *who* to Spec-CP at LF results in a situation where its trace is not antecedent-governed (A'-bound) by Spec-CP. This is the reason (103) is ruled out.

(104) also accounts for the cases in (101) and (102), with the LF representations shown in (105) below:

105a. *Who_i do you wonder [$_{CP}$ [Spec $how_j]_j$ [$_{IP}$ t_i solved the problem]]]?

105b. *Who_i do you think [$_{CP}$ t_i that [$_{IP}$ t_i saw Bill]]?

105c. *It is unclear [$_{CP}$ [Spec who_j $what_i]_i$ [$_{IP}$ t_j saw $_j$]]

Note that Spec-CP in (105c) bears the index of the object *wh*-phrase which moves to it first, as pointed out above. Consequently, the variable in the subject position is not A'-bound in its GC (embedded CP). The situation in (105a) is identical to the one in (105c). Spec-CP bears the index of the adjunct *wh*-phrase *how* moved to it first (at S-structure), resulting in a situation where the variable trace in the subject position is not A'-bound in its GC (the embedded CP), and is therefore in violation of BC A. As for (105b), the complementizer *that* is assumed to be a non-index-bearing element, so that its presence in CP prevents the COMP-indexing mechanism from applying – COMP-indexing does not apply if COMP (CP) dominates a non-i-indexed element such as *that*. Consequently, the variable in the subject position is left without an A'-antecedent in the embedded clause, in violation of BC A.

It should be clear that Generalized Binding Theory can successfully handle various cases that have otherwise been analysed in terms of special government-based requirements on variables. The theory extends to other cases not discussed here, with minimal additional assumptions. The element that seems to be missing from it, in the form presented, is the Minimality effect on A'-binding relations discussed above in relation to Relativized Minimality – i.e. the fact that a closer A'-specifier disrupts the A'-binding relation between an antecedent and a variable. However, the Minimality effect on A'-binding relations has been extensively investigated in Aoun and Li (1991). It turns out that not only *wh*-phrases but various other types of intervening A'-specifier give rise to a Minimality effect on A'-binding relations. The conclusions which emerge confirm the suspicion that dependency relations involving variables and their operators are ultimately binding relations, to be accounted for in terms of a generalized theory of binding.

8.5.3   Summary

The cases which fall within the scope of Relativized Minimality, apart from the X^0 ones, reveal an interesting parallelism between antecedent-government and binding. The parallelism suggests that dependency relations involving traces and their antecedents are fundamentally similar to dependency relations involving overt anaphors and their antecedents, and therefore that perhaps they all should be accounted for in terms of a generalized theory of binding. To the extent that this is feasible, the conditions on Move-α and the conditions on antecedent-trace relations derived by Move-α are ultimately binding conditions, and therefore belong to the domain of Binding Theory. This is the fundamental tenet of the theory of Generalized Binding briefly outlined in this section.

8.6   *Conclusions and Revisions*

We started this chapter by observing that most of the transformational rules discussed in the previous chapters had in common the property of moving a given category from one position to another. This observation raised the possibility of reducing all these transformational rules to a single general principle called Move-α. The transformational rules which insert or delete material in representations could be accommodated by adopting an even more general version of Move-α called Affect-α. The attempt to replace the transformational rules by a general principle is part of the broader attempt to replace construction-specific rules by general principles.

Since our definitions of transformations included references to landing sites, and conditions on the application of the transformations designed to prevent them from overgenerating, we were faced with the prospect that Move-α would over-generate. We then realized that the scope of Move-α was already severely restricted by various conditions on representations belonging to different modules of the Grammar. Some other conditions could simply be factored out of the definitions of transformations themselves, and stated either as conditions on the application of Move-α or as conditions on representations derived by Move-α.

Two major conditions have been identified and discussed, Subjacency and ECP. Subjacency is a condition on (the application of) Move-α, and is itself a general version of a number of individual conditions previously thought to be unrelated. ECP, on the other hand, is a condition on the representation of traces. These two conditions were initially said to be independent of each other, and to belong to separate modules. However, we have seen that it is possible to design a system (e.g. the Barriers system) where the two conditions could be merged, and make reference to the same notions and structural relations.

In the last section of the chapter we discussed two approaches to antecedent-trace relations; one reveals a significant and inviting parallelism between government and binding (Relativized Minimality) and the other literally reduces the conditions of government on antecedent-trace relations to binding conditions (Generalized Binding). To the extent that the latter approach is viable, it shows that phenomena which superficially may look different are related at a deep and abstract level, and that the common patterns underlying them can be captured in terms of simple and general principles with broader scope.

Exercises

Exercise 1

Complex 'noun phrase' islands involving a CP-complement of a noun are said to give rise to a weaker Subjacency violation of the type found with *wh*-island violations (one question mark):

1. ?Which car did you hear the rumour that John fixed?
2. ?Which problem do you suspect the claim that John solved?

This means that, like *wh*-islands, they are expected to involve only one barrier, as shown in (3) and (4) below, with the interpretation whereby the adjunct *wh*-phrase *how* modifies the embedded verb *fix/solve*:

3. *How did you hear the rumour that John fixed the car?
4. *How do you resent the claim that John solved the problem?

Explain, first, why (3) and (4) show that the island in question must involve at least one barrier, and, secondly, whether examples (1–4) receive a satisfactory explanation in the Barriers framework.

Exercise 2

Relative clauses are sometimes said not to exhibit the *that*-trace effect (1), contrary to embedded declarative clauses (2):

1. The car *(that) hit the boy has been found
2. The car (that) you said (*that) hit the boy has been found

Try to find an explanation for why this is the case, taking into consideration the fact that the occurrence of *that* is obligatory with relative clauses such as (1). You may also want to take into consideration the discussion of relative clauses in Chapter 3, where it is pointed out that, although the *that* which occurs in relative clauses looks the same as the one which occurs in embedded clauses, it may have different properties.

Exercise 3

Among the instances of Move-α we have not discussed in this chapter is Topicalization. On the basis of the following examples, determine whether Topicalization and traces of topicalized categories are subject to the same conditions as other instances of Move-α and their traces:

1. This problem, I can solve
2. ?This problem, I wonder whether I can solve
3. ??This problem, I know someone who can solve
4. *This problem, I think that is difficult (to solve)

Exercise 4

The examples below illustrate a phenomenon, called **Left Dislocation**, which is closely related to Topicalization:

1. This problem, I can solve it
2. This problem, I wonder whether I can solve it
3. This problem, I know someone who can solve it
4. This problem, I think that it is difficult (to solve)

Outline an analysis for Left Dislocation on the basis of these examples, explaining in what respects it differs from Topicalization, if at all.

Exercise 5

Outline a derivation for each of the two examples below, and evaluate the status of the movement and traces they involve with respect to Subjacency and the ECP:

1. Who was John killed by?
2. Which city did you witness the destruction of?

Further Reading

The attempt to unify some of the earlier constraints on movement, in particular the A-over-A condition and some of Ross's island constraints, appeared in Chomsky (1973). Subjacency, and more generally the issue of bounded v. unbounded movement, has generated a large amount of literature which is hard to represent in terms of a few selected references. The claim that Subjacency does not hold of LF-movement is made in Huang (1982) and Lasnik and Saito (1984; 1992). For a different view on the unbounded nature of LF-movement see Nishigauchi (1986), Pesetsky (1987), and Fiengo *et al.* (1988).

Although subject-object asymmetries with respect to movement had been noted in earlier work, their formal treatment in terms of ECP appears in Chomsky (1981) and Belletti and Rizzi (1981). The mechanisms of gamma-marking and trace-deletion are discussed in Lasnik and Saito (1984; 1992), as noted in the main text, as well as in Chomsky (1986b). An attempt to extend the ECP to LF-movement is made in Kayne (1984). An early discussion of the Superiority effects in English multiple *wh*-questions appears in Chomsky (1973). On this issue see also Jaeggli (1980), Aoun *et al.* (1981), and Pesetsky (1987).

The original sources relating to the Barriers system, Relativized Minimality, and Generalized Binding are as mentioned in the main text. On the Head Movement Constraint see Travis (1984), Koopman (1984), Chomsky (1986b), and Baker (1988).

9

Parameters and Cross-Linguistic Variation

Contents

9.1 *Language Variation and Parameters*

9.1.1 Introduction

A theory of language has to address two major issues. The first issue relates to the fact that languages, despite their superficial differences, are identical at a deep and abstract level. In the theory outlined in this book, this property of human languages is accounted for by postulating the existence of a set of abstract principles common to all languages, by virtue of being genetically determined. These principles are collectively referred to as Universal Grammar (UG). In the previous chapters we identified a number of such principles on the basis of an analysis of a wide array of facts in the English language. Although the investigation has been restricted to one language, some of the principles isolated and tested for validity are sufficiently deep and general to allow us to make a preliminary claim as to their universal character. Obviously, these principles of UG are open to further testing against data from other languages, which may either confirm their universal character (possibly in a modified form) or reveal their language-specific character, or even force their rejection altogether. In this chapter we will test the validity of some of these principles of UG against data from a relatively broad range of related and unrelated languages.

The second issue that a theory of language has to address is the converse of the first. Despite the fact that languages are identical at a deep and abstract level, they exhibit some significant differences at the surface level. A close examination of the cross-linguistic (and cross-dialectal) differences reveals that they are not arbitrary, and in most parts not isolated either. The patterns revealed by cross-linguistic differences seem to suggest that variation is restricted, presumably by a predetermined set of constraints. The task of a theory of language is, then, to discover the nature of these constraints and how they relate to the system of principles we call UG. This is one of the major issues we will be concerned with in this chapter.

In the theory outlined in this book (the Principles and Parameters Theory), linguistic variation is accounted for in terms of **parameters**. A parameter is understood as a restricted set of options (or values) associated with a given principle or category. Choice of one option/value yields a given pattern, and choice of a different option/value yields a different pattern. The metaphor often used to explain parameters is an (old-fashioned) light switch with two options – on and off – each of which yields a different state of affairs. Whether the values of parameters are binary or *n*-ary is an interesting question which has received attention in the literature, although a clear answer to it remains elusive. In this chapter we will discuss parameters which lend themselves to a binary division of values, and others which do not.

Parameters are said to be set (or fixed) on the basis of the properties of surface PF-strings, the only representations directly available (visible) to the language learner. It is unlikely that languages differ with respect to the properties of the (invisible) LF level. At this level, sentences with similar meanings from different languages are expected to have identical representations in the relevant respects. In this chapter, we will discuss constructions where a certain key constituent occupies different positions in different languages in S-structure (and PF) representations but occupies the same position in all languages in LF representations.

An interesting question relating to the issue of parameters is whether they are associated with the principles of UG (Chomsky, 1986a), or with individual categories in their lexical entries (Borer, 1984c), although one does not necessarily preclude the other. In order to be able to evaluate these two views empirically, and in order to gain a perspective over the types of parameter suggested in the literature, we will start by briefly discussing three different parameters as representative examples. The first parameter is called the **Head (or Directionality) Parameter**, and is intended to account for differences among languages relating to the order of complements with respect to their heads. The second parameter is sometimes called the **Subjacency Parameter**, and is intended to account for differences among languages relating to bounding nodes. The third parameter, which we will call here the ***Wh*-movement Parameter**, is intended to account for differences among languages relating to whether a *wh*-phrase in a simple *wh*-question is left in situ at S-structure or fronted to Spec-CP.

9.1.2 The Head/Directionality Parameter

Languages differ as to whether they have the order Verb–Object (VO), as in English, or the order Object–Verb (OV), as in German:

1a. Mary sagt, daß Hans den Ball kaufte
    Mary says that Hans the ball bought
    'Mary says that Hans bought the ball'
1b. . . . *daß Hans* [VP [DP *den Ball*] [V *kaufte*]]

Chomsky (1986a) has suggested that the difference between English-type languages and German-type languages illustrated in (1) can be accounted for in terms of the parameter shown in (2) below, understood to be associated with X-bar Theory. The Head Parameter has two values: Head-first (or Head-initial) and Head-last (or Head-final). The first value yields the order shown in (3a), found in English-type languages, and the second value yields the order shown in (3b), found in German-type languages. Accordingly, the difference between English and German responsible for the observed difference in word order reduces to the assumption that English selects value (i) whereas German selects value (ii) of the Head Parameter.

2. **Head Parameter**
   (i) Head-first
   (ii) Head-last

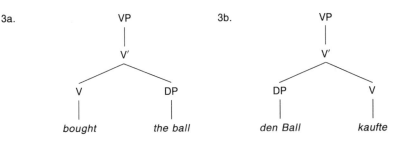

The idea that a language selects a given value of the Head Parameter arguably implies that all head categories in the language are expected to select their complement in the same direction. This expectation seems to be fulfilled by the functional category I in both languages. In English, where heads select their complement to the right, I precedes VP. In German, where heads select their complement to the left, I follows VP. That German I follows VP is shown in (4a) by the order of the finite auxiliary in relation to the non-finite main verb, assuming that the auxiliary occupies I.

4a. . . . .daß   Hans   den Ball   gekauft   hat
       that   Hans   the ball   bought   has
   '. . .that Hans has bought the ball.'

4b.

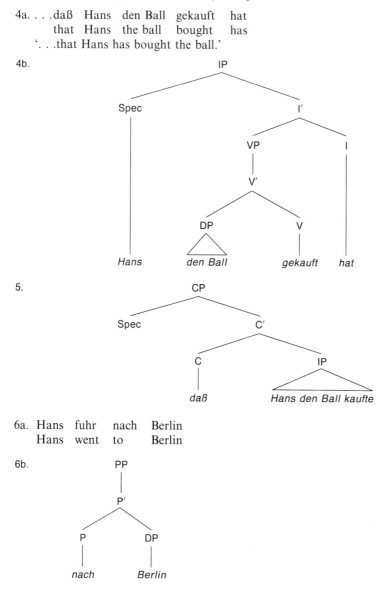

6a. Hans   fuhr   nach   Berlin
    Hans   went   to   Berlin

However, not all head categories in German select their complement in the same direction as V and I. Note that the order of the complementizer in relation to IP in (4a) is the same as in English, suggesting that C selects its IP-complement to the right in German, as shown in (5, 6a, 6b) show that prepositions in German also resemble their counterparts in English in that they select their complement to the right. Languages which are consistently head-final are expected to have **postpositions**, rather than prepositions. Thus German is not consistently head-final, but is instead a mixed language, where certain categories are head-final and others head-initial. English, however, is a consistently head-initial language, where all categories select their complement to the right.

The observed properties of word order in German show that categories in the same language may select different values of a given parameter. This seems to confirm the view that parameters are associated with individual categories, as part of the set of idiosyncratic properties specified in their lexical entries. Just as individual categories differ with respect to whether they select a complement and whether they assign Case to the complement they select, they also differ with respect to the direction in which they select their complement. There have been attempts in the literature to derive the effects of the Head Parameter from parametrized restrictions on the directionality of the assignment of thematic roles and/or Case (e.g. Koopman, 1984; Travis, 1984). The idea is that if a given category chooses to assign its internal thematic role and/or Case to the right, its complement will appear to its right (Head-initial), and if a given category chooses to assign its internal thematic role and/or Case to the left, its complement will appear to its left. The functional (non-lexical) categories I and C can be brought into line with lexical categories by assuming that they, too, assign a thematic role and/or Case to their respective complements. As we shall see below, these assumptions can be usefully implemented to account for certain word order differences between languages.

9.1.3   The Subjacency Parameter

Consider the following example from Italian, discussed in Rizzi (1982) together with others:

7a. tuo fratello,   a cui   mi   domando che   storie abbiano raccontato
    your brother   to whom   myself   I-ask   which sories   they-have told
    ?'your brother, to whom I wonder which stories they told'
7b. . . .[$_{CP}$ *a cui*$_i$ [$_{IP}$ *mi domando* [$_{CP}$ *che storie*$_j$ [$_{IP}$ *abbiano raccontato* t$_j$ t$_i$]]]]

This example involves extraction out of a *wh*-island, which is expected to give rise to a (weaker) Subjacency violation, as it usually does in English (Chapter 8). However, contrary to its English counterpart shown in the gloss, the Italian example (7a) does not exhibit a Subjacency violation. Apparently, extraction out of a *wh*-island does not give rise to a Subjacency violation in Italian.

Initially, this difference between English and Italian may seem to suggest that Subjacency is after all a language-specific principle. However, Rizzi argues that such a conclusion would be inaccurate, as extraction out of other islands does indeed give rise to a Subjacency violation in Italian. Example (8) below includes a complex 'noun phrase' island:

8a. ??Tuo fratello a cui   temo   la possibilità che   abbiano raccontato
     your   brother to whom I-fear the possibility that   they-have told
     tutto
     everything
     ??'your brother, to whom I fear the possibility that they have told everything'
8b. . . .[$_{CP}$ *a cui*$_i$ [$_{IP}$ *temo* [$_{DP}$ *la possibilità* [$_{CP}$ t$_i$ *che* [$_{IP}$ *abbiano racontato* t$_i$ *tutto*]]]]]

The fact that extraction out of a complex 'noun phrase' island gives rise to a Subjacency violation, as it does in English, shows clearly that Subjacency is not likely to be a language-specific condition on movement. An adequate account of the difference between Italian and English would have to be based on the assumption that Subjacency constrains movement in both English and Italian.

On this basis, Rizzi has suggested that Italian differs from English with respect to which nodes (categories) count as bounding nodes. In English the bounding nodes are IP and DP (Chapter 8), whereas in Italian the bounding nodes are CP and DP. The underlying idea is that while Subjacency specifies that movement cannot cross two bounding nodes together, it does not specify which categories count as bounding nodes, so that languages can differ as to which categories they choose as bounding nodes. English chooses IP and DP, whereas Italian chooses CP and DP.

Let us now see how this suggestion accounts for the data above. In example (7) *wh*-movement crosses two IPs but only one CP. Because IP does not count as a bounding node in Italian, no Subjacency violation arises. On the other hand, because IP counts as a bounding node in English, a Subjacency violation arises in the English equivalent example. In (8), *wh*-movement crosses one CP, one DP, and one IP together. As such, the movement is bound to give rise to a Subjacency violation in both Italian and English, and hence Italian and English are similar with respect to extraction out of complex 'noun phrase' islands.

It may seem initially that the Subjacency Parameter is hard to classify in terms of whether it is associated with a principle of UG (Subjacency) or with relevant individual categories. However, to the extent that the formulation of Subjacency does not offer a choice between potential bounding nodes, the Subjacency Parameter can be said to be associated with the relevant individual categories. It is plausible to assume that the Subjacency Parameter is associated with a given category in the form of a binary choice between whether it is a bounding or a non-bounding node. The choice between these two values is then decided on the basis of the data available to the learner.

9.1.4   The *Wh*-movement Parameter

Consider example (9) below from Japanese, discussed in Lasnik and Saito (1992), in comparison with the English examples in (10) (TOP: 'topic marker', ACC: 'accusative Case marker', and Q: 'question marker'):

9a. John-wa   nani-o   kaimasita   ka?
    John-TOP   *what*-ACC   *bought*   Q
    'What did John buy?'
9b. [CP [IP *John-wa* [VP [DP *nani-o*] [V *kaimasita*]]] *ka*]?
9c. *for which thing* x, *John bought* x

10a. What did John buy?
10b. *John bought what?
10c. *for which thing* x, *John bought* x

Note, first of all, that Japanese is a consistently head-final language, so that the *wh*-phrase in (9) *nani-o* occupies the object position situated to the left of the verb [OV], and the question marker *ka* occupies the C position situated to the right of IP [IP C]. Example (9) shows that in Japanese simple (i.e. non-multiple) *wh*-questions, the *wh*-phrase remains in situ, meaning that it does not have to undergo *wh*-movement at S-structure (overt movement). As a matter of fact, Lasnik and Saito argue that Japanese lacks overt *wh*-movement altogether. This situation is the opposite of that found in English, where the *wh*-phrase has to undergo overt *wh*-movement in simple *wh*-questions (Chapter 4). (10a) above is a *wh*-question, whereas (10b) does not have a *wh*-question reading.

Next to English and Japanese, which represent the opposite ends of a continuum, there exist languages where overt movement of the *wh*-phrase is possible but not obligatory. French is an example of this type of language:

11a. Qui as-tu vu?
 who have-you seen
 'Who have you seen?'
11b. Tu as vu qui?
 you have seen who
 'Who have you seen?'
11c. *for which person* x, *you saw* x

The two examples are synonymous, and both qualify as *wh*-questions in French. In (11a) the *wh*-phrase is fronted to Spec-CP, triggering SAI, so that this example is identical in word order to its English counterpart in (10a) above. In (11b), however, the *wh*-phrase remains in situ, and the sentence has the word order of the English example (10b) above. Yet, while (11b) is a possible *wh*-question in French, (10b) is not a possible *wh*-question in English.

In Chapter 4 we accounted for the contrast between (10a) and (10b) and between (12a) and (12b) below in terms of the condition in (13):

12a. *I wonder* [CP *who* [C' [+ WH] [IP *Mary saw*]]]
12b. **I wonder* [CP e [C' [+ WH] [IP *Mary saw who/Bill*]]]
13. [+ WH]-CPs must have a ([+ WH])-specifier.

(13) is a sort of extended extended projection principle. Just as ([+ FINITE]) IPs must have an (overt) specifier at S-structure, [+ WH]-CPs must also have an (overt) specifier at S-structure, with the parallelism between the two possibly following from predication, and ultimately Full Interpretation (Chapter 7). The fact that the specifier must be a *wh*-phrase, i.e. must be specified for the feature [+WH], follows from Spec-Head Agreement, just as the fact that a *wh*-phrase can only be moved to the Spec position of a [+ WH]-CP (**I believe who Mary saw*) also follows from Spec-Head Agreement. In (12a,b) the embedded CP is [+WH], an obligatory property of clauses selected by the verb *wonder*. (12b) is excluded by (13), as the embedded CP lacks a specifier. The analysis extends to the contrast between (10a) and (10b), on the assumption that root (non-selected) *wh*-interrogatives are also specified for the feature [+WH]. The latter is a property of all *wh*-interrogatives, and possibly also *yes/no* interrogatives (Chapter 4). (10b), understood to have the feature [+WH] (indicated by the question mark), is excluded by (13), on a par with (12b). Note that multiple *wh*-questions such as *Who said what?* are also consistent with (13), on the assumption that the subject *wh*-phrase is in Spec-CP at S-structure: In English *wh*-phrases are licensed in situ by the presence of a *wh*-phrase in Spec-CP.

Obviously, (13) apparently does not hold for S-structure representations of Japanese *wh*-questions such as (9) and French *wh*-questions such as (11b). As far as Japanese is concerned, (13) apparently does not hold for the structure representations of selected [+ WH]-CPs either. This is shown in the following examples, discussed in Lasnik and Saito (1992) (NOM: 'nominative Case marker'):

14a. Mary-ga John-ga hon-o katta to kiite iru koto
 Mary-NOM *John*-NOM *book*-ACC *bought* COMP *heard* *fact*
 'the fact that Mary heard that John bought a book'

14b. Mary-ga   John-ga   nani-o   katta   ka kiite iru   koto
  Mary-NOM *John*-NOM *what*-ACC *bought* Q *heard* *fact*
 'the fact that Mary heard what John bought'

15a. *Mary-ga   John-ga   hon-o   katta   to   siritagatte iru koto
  Mary-NOM *John*-NOM *book*-ACC *bought* COMP *want-to-know fact*
 lit. 'the fact that Mary wants to know that John bought a book'

15b. Mary-ga   John-ga   nani-o   katta   ka siritagatte iru   koto
  Mary-NOM *John*-NOM *what*-ACC *bought* Q *want-to-know* *fact*
 'the fact that Mary wants to know what John bought'

As Lasnik and Saito point out, the verb *kiite iru* 'heard' in (14) allows for a [+ WH]-CP complement, and the verb *siritagatte iru* 'want-to-know' in (15) requires a [+ WH]-CP complement. However, in neither (14b) nor (15b) does the *wh*-phrase occupy the Spec position of the selected [+ WH]-CP.

The problem we are facing in relation to (13) is somewhat similar to the problem discussed above with respect to Subjacency. The facts of Japanese and French *wh*-interrogatives seem to suggest that (13) is perhaps not a requirement which holds of all languages. Note, however, that this is true only as far as the S-structure representations of *wh*-interrogatives are concerned. Presumably, *wh*-phrases in situ in Japanese and French *wh*-interrogatives raise to the Spec position of the [+ WH]-CP at LF, so that at this level their LF representations are identical to those of their English counterparts. *Wh*-phrases in situ raise to Spec-CP at LF for the same reason that *wh*-phrases in situ in English multiple *wh*-questions also raise to Spec-CP at LF (Chapter 5). Thus *wh*-interrogatives in Japanese (and French) also satisfy (13), but at LF instead of at S-structure.

It could be concluded, along with Lasnik and Saito, that (13) (or a similar requirement) holds for *wh*-interrogatives in both types of language, and that the parametric difference between English-type languages and Japanese-type languages reduces to the fact that the former satisfy (13) at S-structure whereas the latter satisfy it at LF. French-type languages, on the other hand, can either satisfy it at S-structure or at LF, at least as far as root *wh*-interrogatives are concerned.

This parameter, unlike the previous ones, cannot be said to be associated with a given category, in this case C. Note that it is unlikely that Japanese *wh*-interrogatives, for example, differ from their counterparts in English in that they lack the feature [+ WH] under C. This is because the presence of this feature is necessary to characterize the clauses in question as *wh*-interrogative, and therefore to be distinguished from declarative and other clauses. Moreover, the presence of the feature [+ /– WH] in selected clauses is necessary to account for the difference in the selectional properties of verbs, as shown by the Japanese examples in (14) and (15) above, and parallel examples in Chinese discussed in Huang (1982).

9.1.5 Summary

Differences among languages can be accounted for in terms of parameters, which are a set of well-defined options each of which gives rise to a specific pattern. It is not clear whether parameters are associated with general principles of the Grammar or with particular categories. Parametric differences relating to the order of complements with respect to their heads suggest that they must be associated with individual categories, as categories in the same language may choose different options. This view is arguably also supported by parametric differences relating to the choice of a bounding node. However, parametric differences relating to the choice between moving *wh*-phrases at S-structure, not moving them at S-structure, or either, seem to suggest otherwise.

9.2 The Pro-Drop Parameter and Null Arguments

In this section we shall discuss differences between languages relating to the ability or inability to instantiate null arguments in the subject position of finite clauses and the object position of transitive verbs. We will see that the parameter responsible for some of the differences discussed, called the **Pro-drop Parameter**, must be seen to be associated with particular individual categories.

9.2.1 Null Subjects

Consider the following examples from Italian:

16a. Lui ha telefonato
    he has telephoned
    'He has phoned'
16b. Ha telefonato
    has telephoned
    *'(He) has phoned'
17a. Gianni ha detto che lui ha telefonato
    Gianni has said that he has telephoned
    'Gianni said that he has phoned'
17b. Gianni ha detto che ha telefonato
    Gianni has said that has telephoned
    'Gianni said that *(he) has phoned'

In Italian finite clauses, both root (16) and embedded (17), the appearance of the subject pronoun is optional, contrary to what is found in English, as shown in the gloss. Italian is said to allow subject pronouns to drop, and therefore is a **pro-drop** language, whereas English does not allow subject pronouns to drop, and therefore is a **non-pro-drop** language. The problem raised by examples (16b) and (17b) is similar to the problem we faced above in relation to the requirement that *wh*-questions have a specifier. Superficially, (16b) and (17b) seem to suggest that it is not the case that (finite) clauses must have a subject in all languages, implying that EPP is perhaps specific to English and similar languages.

Before we address this issue, let us first try to discover why Italian allows subject pronouns to drop but English does not. Initially, the answer to this question seems straightforward. Italian allows subject pronouns to drop because their content can be recovered from the subject Agr morpheme on the verb. As shown in (18) below, Italian has rich Agr inflection, so that each member of the conjugation paradigm is clearly distinguishable from the others:

18a. (io) mangio   'I eat'
18b. (tu) mangi   'you eat'
18c. (lui/lei) mangia   'he/she eats'
18d. (noi) mangiamo   'we eat'
18e. (voi) mangiate   'you eat'
18f. (essi) mangiano   'they eat'

The agreement features overtly encoded in the Agr element of I make the presence of subject pronouns with identical agreement features redundant. In comparison, Agr in

English is poor (abstract), so that the feature-content of a dropped subject pronoun cannot be recovered from it, and hence English, contrary to Italian, is not a pro-drop language. It seems that pro-drop of subject pronouns is allowed only in situations where the feature-content of the dropped pronoun is recoverable from an overt Agr element.

Let us now return to the issue relating to the EPP. Rizzi (1982) has suggested that, contrary to appearances, examples with a dropped subject pronoun do have a subject, realised as a null category. Assuming this to be the case, the question is what the nature of this null category is. In Chapter 7 it was pointed out that the repertoire of null categories lacked a member corresponding to the fourth logical combination [– a, + p], i.e. a pure pronominal category which would correspond to overt pronouns. Rizzi has argued that this is precisely the null category instantiated in the subject position of the root clause in (16b) and the embedded clause in (17b), above, given that the 'missing' subject in these examples has the interpretation of a pure pronominal. The null category in question is represented as **pro** (read 'small/little *pro*', as opposed to the big PRO), so that (16b) and (17b) have the representations shown in (19a) and (19b) below, respectively:

19a. *pro* ha telefonato
19b. *Gianni ha detto* [CP *che* [IP pro *ha telefonato*]]

In (19a) *pro* has an antecedent in the discourse context, and in (19b) it can either have an antecedent in the discourse context or be co-referential with the subject of the root clause *Gianni*.

Having identified the nature of the null category in null subject sentences, we now need to determine the conditions under which it appears. This step is necessary to account for the difference between Italian and English, i.e. to explain why *pro* cannot occur in the subject position of finite clauses in English:

20a. **pro* has phoned
20b. *John said that *pro* has phoned

Presumably, the explanation would have to depend on the conclusion, reached above, that the option of allowing null subjects is crucially dependent on the presence of an overt (rich) Agr category under I capable of identifying the feature-content of the null subject. This conclusion can be stated in the form of a licensing condition on the appearance of *pro*, along the lines of (21):

21. **Condition on the licensing of pro**
    pro is licensed by an overt Agr category co-indexed with it.

Co-indexation between Agr under I and *pro* in Spec-IP is part of the Spec-Head Agreement relation characteristic of finite clauses. Because the Agr category in English is largely abstract (poor) it cannot license *pro*, hence the fact that English does not allow null subjects.

9.2.2   Free Inversion and the Absence of *That*-trace Effects

It has been observed that languages which allow null subjects also tend (i) to allow subjects to appear freely in the postverbal position (**Free Inversion**) and (ii) not to show *that*-trace effects (e.g. Taraldsen, 1981; Rizzi, 1982). The following examples are from Italian:

22a. Ha telefonato Gianni
    has telephoned Gianni
    'Gianni has phoned'

22b. Hai detto che ha telefonato Gianni
    have said that has telephoned Gianni
    'You have said that Gianni has phoned'

23a. Chi hai detto che ha telefonato?
    who have said that has telephoned
    'Who have you said (*that) has phoned?'

23b. *Chi*$_i$ *hai detto* [$_{CP}$ t$'_i$ [$_{C'}$ *che* [$_{IP}$ t$_i$ *ha telefonato*]]]?

In (22a,b) the subject *Gianni* appears following the verb *telefonato*, an option which in English is excluded with intransitive (non-unaccusative) verbs such as *phone*. Inversion of the subject in Italian is 'free' in the sense that it is possible with all types of verb, transitive, intransitive and unaccusative. In (23) the subject is extracted out of an embedded clause introduced by the complementizer *che* 'that', a situation which invariably gives rise to ungrammaticality in English. In Chapter 8 we saw that the so-called *that*-trace effect found in English equivalents of (23) is standardly treated as involving a violation of ECP.

It seems to be generally the case that the phenomenon of null subjects and the phenomena illustrated in (22) and (23) cluster together, such that the former implies the latter two. If a language allows null subjects, e.g. Italian, it will also allow free inversion of subjects, and will not exhibit the *that*-trace effect. Conversely, if a language does not allow null subjects, e.g. English, it will not allow free inversion of subjects and will exhibit the *that*-trace effect. A proper analysis of the phenomena illustrated in (22) and (23) would therefore have to link them to the phenomenon of null subjects. One such analysis is outlined in Rizzi (1982) and Chomsky (1982).

Starting with free inversion of subjects, Rizzi has suggested the analysis outlined in (24):

24a. D-str: [$_{IP}$ *Gianni* I [$_{VP}$ *ha telefonato*]]
24b. S-str: [$_{IP}$ pro I [$_{VP}$ [$_{VP}$ *ha telefonato*] *Gianni*]]

At D-structure the subject is situated in Spec-IP, the canonical subject position. Move-α then applies to move the subject and right-adjoin to VP (the postverbal subject position). The movement involved is a lowering one, in the sense that the landing site of the moved subject (the VP-adjoined position) does not c-command the initial (D-structure) position of the subject (Spec-IP). In view of this, the null category left behind in the subject position in (24b) cannot be a trace, because a trace would not satisfy the ECP. The null category in question is *pro*, which, being a pronominal null category, is not subject to ECP (Chapter 8). As in null subject sentences, *pro* in (24b) is properly licensed by the overt Agr category under I. Now, because the subject position vacated by an inverted subject can only be occupied by *pro*, the phenomenon of free inversion of subjects is made dependent on the existence of the null subject phenomenon. Thus, languages which allow null (i.e. *pro*) subjects are expected to allow free inversion of subjects. Conversely, languages which do not allow null subjects are expected not to allow free inversion of subjects.

Sentences which exhibit the absence of the *that*-trace effect are argued to have the (roundabout) derivation outlined in (25) below:

25a. D-structure:
    hai detto [$_{CP}$ *che* [$_{IP}$ *chi* I [$_{VP}$ *ha telefonato*]]]
25b. Free inversion:
    hai detto [$_{CP}$ *che* [$_{IP}$ pro I [$_{VP}$ [$_{VP}$ *ha telefonato*] *chi*]]]
25c. *Wh*-movement
    Chi$_i$ *hai detto* [$_{CP}$ t$'_i$ *che* [$_{IP}$ pro I [$_{VP}$ [$_{VP}$ *ha telefonato*] t$_i$]]]

The core idea of the analysis is that extracted subjects undergo free inversion prior to their extraction. In other words, the derivation of sentences such as (23) involves two steps. The first step consists of movement of the *wh*-subject to the postverbal position (free inversion). The second step consists of *wh*-movement of the *wh*-subject from the VP-adjoined postverbal position. The theoretical basis of the analysis includes the assumptions that, first, traces can satisfy ECP via lexical government (and not necessarily theta- or antecedent- government) and, secondly, that the VP-adjoined position is lexically governed by the verb. The consequence is that a trace in the VP-adjoined position, (25c), would satisfy ECP. In contrast, a trace in the subject position would not satisfy ECP, for the same reason as in English. The presence of the complementizer *che* 'that' blocks antecedent-government of the trace in Spec-IP by the intermediate trace in Spec-CP, giving rise to an ECP violation. Thus, according to the analysis outlined in (25) above, the lack of the *that*-trace effect in Italian and the ECP violation which arises from it are only apparent (not real).

It should be clear in what sense the analysis outlined in (25) relates the phenomenon of the (apparent) absence of the *that*-trace effect to the null subject property. The absence of the *that*-trace effect is dependent on the possibility of free inversion of the subject in the sense that for a subject to be extracted out of a clause introduced by *che* 'that' the subject has to move to the postverbal VP-adjoined position first. As we have seen, free inversion of subjects is in turn dependent on null subjects: for a subject to be able to invert, Agr has to be sufficiently rich to license *pro* in the Spec-IP position vacated by the inverted subject. For a detailed discussion of displaced subjects in relation to *pro*, see Shlonsky (1987).

9.2.3   Null Objects

9.2.3.1   Identified Null Objects   In addition to the agreement relation between the subject and the Agr category of finite I, some languages also display an overt agreement relation between the object and an Agr category attached to the verb (**object agreement**). One such language is Chichewa, although in Chichewa object agreement seems to be optional. The following examples are cited in Baker (1988) (SP: 'subject agreement prefix', OP: 'object agreement prefix', ASP: 'aspect'):

26a. Mikango yanu i- na- thamangits -a   mbuzi zathu
     lions   *your* SP-PAST-*chase*   -ASP *goats* *our*
     'Your lions chased our goats'

26b. Mikango yanu i-na-zi-   thamangits -a   mbuzi zathu
     lions   *your* SP-PAST-OP- *chase*   -ASP *goats* *our*
     'Your lions chased our goats'

(26a) includes only one Agr morpheme, which agrees with the subject of the sentence. (26b), however, includes two distinct Agr morphemes; one agrees with the subject of the sentence and the other with the object of the verb. To distinguish between the two types of agreement morpheme, we shall refer to the subject Agr morpheme as AgrS and to the object agreement morpheme as AgrO. Pending a detailed discussion of the theoretical status of AgrO (compared to AgrS) below, we will assume for the moment that, while AgrS is base-generated under I, as we have been assuming, AgrO is base-generated attached to the verb.

The relevance of object agreement to the issue of null arguments lies in that languages which have overt (rich) object agreement inflection allow null objects with a pronominal interpretation, just as languages with overt subject agreement inflection, e.g. Italian, were shown above to allow null subjects with a pronominal interpretation. For example, the object in the Chichewa example (26b) above can be dropped, in which case the 'missing' object has a pronominal interpretation:

27a. Mikango yanu i-na-zi-   thamangits -a
      lions   your SP-PAST-OP- *chase*   -ASP
      'Your lions chased them (the goats)'
27b. *Mikango yanu i-na-* [$_{VP}$ [$_V$ zi$_i$-*thamangits-a*] pro$_i$]

Note that just as the presence of a (null) subject in Italian null subject sentences is required by EPP, the presence of a (null) object in (27) is required by PP and the Theta Criterion, given the transitive nature of the verb. The null object in (27) is a *pro* whose feature-content is identified by the AgrO morpheme attached to the verb and with which it is co-indexed.

There is thus a complete parallelism between Italian null subjects and Chichewa null objects: they are both made possible by the presence of a co-indexed overt Agr morpheme. As a matter of fact, the parallelism goes further than this. Bresnan and Mchombo (1987) show that when the AgrO morpheme is present in Chichewa sentences, an overt object is free to appear in positions other than the object position immediately following the verb. This property of objects in Chichewa is arguably the equivalent of the free-inversion property of overt subjects in Italian and other null subject languages. It is plausible to attribute the freedom of ordering objects in the relevant Chichewa examples to the same reason responsible for the freedom of ordering subjects in Italian.

9.2.3.2 Arbitrary Null Objects   Unlike Chichewa, Italian and English do not have overt object agreement inflection. As such, they are not expected to allow null objects, just as languages which do not have overt subject agreement inflection, e.g. English, were shown above not to allow null subjects. On the assumption that the null object would be *pro*, as in Chichewa null object sentences, its occurrence would not be licensed by an overt AgrO morpheme. With this in mind, consider the following examples from Italian discussed in Rizzi (1986a):

28a. Questo conduce la gente a concludere quanto segue
      this   leads   the people to-conclude what   follows
      'This leads people to conclude what follows'
28b. Questo conduce la gente a [PRO concludere quanto segue]
      this   leads   people   [PRO to-conclude what   follows]
29a. Questo conduce a concludere   quanto segue
      this   leads   to conclude what   follows
      *'This leads to conclude what follows'
29b. *Questo conduce e$_i$ a [PRO$_i$ concludere quanto segue]*

The verb *conduce* 'leads' has an overt object in (28), but not in (29). The absence of an overt object seems not to give rise to ungrammaticality in Italian, although it does in English equivalent examples shown in the gloss. Rizzi shows that the Italian example in (29) must be assumed to instantiate a null object, represented in (29b) by the symbol *e*. The presence of the null object is needed to explain the fact that PRO is understood to have the implicit object of the root verb as an antecedent (a controller). Assuming that control is essentially a relation between two A-positions (Chapter 7), the Italian example in (29) must be concluded to instantiate a null object.

Further evidence for the presence of a null object in sentences of the type illustrated in (29) can be gleaned from examples such as (30) below:

30a. La buona musica reconcilia con se stessi
    the good music reconciles with themselves
    '*Good music reconciles with oneself.'
30b. *La buona musica reconcilia* e_i *con se stessi*$_i$

For the reflexive anaphor *se stessi* in this example to satisfy BC A, it has to have a binder in the sentence. Moreover, the binder of the reflexive anaphor is understood to be the object of the verb *reconcilia* 'reconcile'. The subject *la buona musica* cannot be the antecedent, as it is singular while the reflexive anaphor is plural. Together, these facts show that (30) must include a null object, represented in (30b) as *e*. Note that the English equivalent of (30) is also ungrammatical (*Good music reconciles *(one) with oneself*), confirming the difference between English and Italian in this respect. Italian apparently allows null objects whereas English does not.

Assuming that the null category in question is *pro* (PRO is excluded as the object position is governed), it seems that the prediction spelled out above is only partially fulfilled. The prediction is fulfilled in English, where the lack of overt object agreement seems to result in the lack of null objects. However, the prediction is not completely fulfilled in Italian, which seems to allow null objects even though it resembles English in that it lacks overt object agreement. Technically, the problem is that *pro* seems to occur in an environment where it is not licensed, given the condition on the licensing of *pro* above in (21). It seems that we need to reformulate the licensing condition on *pro* to accomodate the facts of Italian. A good indication as to the nature of the revision required relates to the fact that null objects in Italian, contrary to their counterparts in the Chichewa example with overt object agreement, have a generic/arbitrary interpretation. The null object in the Italian examples above is understood to mean 'people in general' or 'one'.

Whether the null object has a specific interpretation, as in the Chichewa example, or an arbitrary one, as in the Italian examples, depends on the presence or absence of overt object agreement. The specific interpretation associated with null objects in the Chichewa example is the consequence of the restrictions on the reference of *pro* imposed by the AgrO morpheme. On the other hand, the generic/arbitrary interpretation associated with null objects in Italian is the consequence of the absence of restrictions on the reference of *pro*, which are in turn due to the absence of an overt AgrO morpheme. To a large extent, the mechanism responsible for the assignment of an interpretation to *pro* is parallel to (or the same as) the mechanism responsible for the assignment of an interpretation to PRO (Chapter 7). PRO has a specific interpretation when it has an antecedent in the sentence, as in *John$_i$ tried* [PRO$_i$ *to leave*], and an arbitrary interpretation when it does not have an antecedent in the sentence, as in *It is difficult* [PRO$_i$ *to predict their next move*].

Two conclusions can be drawn from the comparison just made between null objects in Chichewa and Italian. First, it seems that a distinction needs to be made between the mechanism responsible for the formal licensing of *pro* and the mechanism responsible for the assignment of an interpretation (reference) to *pro*. This is indicated by the likelihood that the mechanism responsible for the assignment of an interpretation to *pro* is the same as the one responsible for the assignment of an interpretation to PRO – i.e. a mechanism which applies to null categories in general and is not necessarily specific to *pro*. Secondly, overt object agreement inflection seems to relate to the interpretation of *pro* rather than to its formal licensing. This is shown by the fact that *pro* can be licensed even in the absence of overt object agreement inflection, as in Italian null object sentences, and that the effect that overt object agreement inflection has on *pro* is simply to restrict its interpretation to a specific reference. Rizzi (1986a) has suggested a theory of *pro* which makes a clear distinction between its formal licensing and its interpretation. (31) and (32) below are adapted from this theory:

31. **_Pro_-drop Parameter**

   pro is governed by a designated X^0 (formal licensing).

32. **Identification Convention**

   pro has the feature complex specified on X^0; otherwise, it has arbitrary features.

(31) is a licensing schema, where 'designated head' is a head which, as a lexical property, can license *pro* under government. The consequence of associating the licensing of *pro* with specific categories is that the class of designated heads may vary from one language to another. In Italian, for example, it includes finite I and V, given that *pro* is allowed in both the subject position of finite clauses and the object position of a specific class of verbs. In English, however, the class of designated heads has zero-members, as *pro* is allowed neither in the subject position of finite clauses nor in the object position of any verb. (32) is the convention which specifies the conditions under which *pro* has a given interpretation, which is presumably part of a more general convention on the identification of null categories. *pro* has a specific interpretation in situations where its licensing head incorporates an overt Agr morpheme, and an arbitrary/generic interpretation when its licensing head does not incorporate such an element.

According to the theory outlined in (31) and (32), the fact that English does not allow null arguments is not so much due to the absence of overt (subject and object) agreement inflection. Recall that Italian allows null objects even though it lacks overt object agreement inflection. Rather, it is due to the assumption that English lacks categories which can license *pro* as a lexical property. It is this lexical property which accounts for the parametric distinction between English on the one hand and Italian and Chichewa on the other. Rizzi concludes that in English sentences such as *This leads to the following conclusion,* the internal thematic role of the verb *lead* is saturated in the Lexicon, and therefore does not project onto a structural position in the Syntax (Chapter 5). Because this process takes place in the Lexicon, no violation of PP or the Theta Criterion arises.

As a final remark, it is possible that there is a link between verbs which enter into this lexical process and verbs with 'typical' objects such as *eat* and *drink*. The ability of the object of these verbs to drop has traditionally been attributed to the fact that its reference can somehow be derived from the meaning of the verb itself. For example, *John ate* is usually understood (out of unusual contexts) to mean that John ate something edible (food), and not, for example, 'marbles'. Having said that, it is not clear how the object of *lead* is 'typical' in a similar sense.

9.2.3.3 Null Operator Objects   Italian is not unique among members of the Romance family in allowing null objects. European Portuguese has also been reported to allow null objects. (33a,b) below and other examples from European Portuguese below are discussed in Huang (1984) and Raposo (1986):

33a. Joana viu-os   na televisão   ontem
     Joana saw-them on television   yesterday
     'Joana saw them on television yesterday'

33b. Joana viu na televisão   ontem
     Joana saw on television   yesterday
     'Joana saw *(them) on television yesterday'

Unlike (33a), (33b) lacks an overt object for the verb *viu* 'saw'. Superficially, it looks as though European Portuguese resembles Italian in this respect, and that the analysis outlined above for Italian null objects can perhaps be extended to European Portuguese examples such as (33b). However, there are reasons to believe that European Portuguese null objects are different in nature from their counterparts in Italian.

First of all, null objects in European Portuguese tend not to have a generic/arbitrary interpretation, contrary to their counterparts in Italian. Null objects in European Portuguese tend to be understood as refering to an individual (or entity) understood in the discourse context, sometimes referred to as **zero-topic**. Secondly, null objects in European Portuguese cannot co-occur with a (fronted) *wh*-phrase in the same sentence, again contrary to their counterparts in Italian. This is shown in example (34) below, compared to the Italian example in (35) discussed in Rizzi (1986a):

34a.*Para qual dos filhos é que Maria comprou?
    for which of-his children is that Maria bought
    'For which of his children did Maria buy it?'
34b.[$_{CP}$ *para qual dos filhos* [$_{C'}$ *é que Maria comprou* e_i]]?

35a. Quale musica riconcilia con se stessi?
    which music reconciles with themselves
    'Which music reconciles one with oneself?'
35b.[$_{CP}$ *Quale musica* [$_{C'}$ *riconcilia* e_i *con se stessi*]]?

The fact that null objects in European Portuguese cannot co-occur with a *wh*-phrase, shown in (34), is interesting in so far as it gives an indication of the nature of the null category. If the null category is assumed to be a null *wh*-operator of the type found in English relatives such as *the book* [$_{CP}$ O_i [$_{IP}$ *I bought* t_i]], (Chapter 3) the fact that it cannot co-occur with a *wh*-phrase would then follow from the general constraint that at S-structure only one *wh*-phrase can be in Spec-CP. On the other hand, the fact that null objects in Italian can co-occur with a *wh*-phrase, as shown in (35), confirms that null objects in this language are not null *wh*-operators.

The conclusion that null objects in European Portuguese are null *wh*-phrases which move to the relevant Spec-CP is supported by a number of other facts discussed in Huang (1984) and Raposo (1986). Here we shall mention only two of them. First, when the null object is situated inside an island a Subjacency effect arises. In Chapter 3 we used this test to detect the presence of null *wh*-phrases in English relatives without an overt *wh*-phrase. The context for (36) below is a 'conversation . . . about some important documents':

36a. ??Eu informei a policia da possibilidade de o Manel ter guardado no cofre da sala de jantar
    '*I informed the police of the possibility that Manel had kept in the safe of the dining room'
36b. ??*Eu informei a policia da* [$_{DP}$ *possibilidade de* [$_{CP}$ [$_{IP}$ *O Manel ter guardado* e_i *no cofre da sala de jantar*]]]

The null object in this example, marked by *e* with an index in the object position of the verb *guardado* 'kept', is included inside a complex 'noun phrase' island. The fact that the sentence exhibits a Subjacency violation shows that the null object moves out of the island, and therefore is a null *wh*-operator.

Secondly, when a null object is co-indexed with a c-commanding subject, a kind of strong crossover effect arises (Chapter 7). Thus (37a) below cannot have the interpretation shown in (37b):

37a. Joao disse que Pedro viu
    Joao said that Pedro saw
37b.*$Joao_i$ *disse que Pedro viu* e_i

The situation in this example is identical to the situation found in English strong crossover cases such as Who_i *does* he_i *like* t_i, indicating that the null object is a null *wh*-

phrase which moves to Spec-CP, crossing over the subject and leaving behind a variable situated to the right of a co-indexed A-specifier (Chapter 7).

There are thus good reasons to conclude that null objects in European Portuguese differ from their counterparts in Italian. In European Portuguese they are null *wh*-phrases which move to an appropriate Spec-CP in the Syntax. On the other hand, in Italian they are realized as *pro* which receives an arbitrary interpretation for lack of identification. Null objects in European Portuguese do not fall under the scope of the pro-drop parameter. Recall that null *wh*-phrases are also allowed in English, although in English their occurrence is much more restricted to contexts where the null *wh*-operator has an antecedent (an identifier) in the sentence. In relatives, for example, the null *wh*-phrase is co-indexed with the head of the relative clause (Chapter 3). European Portuguese, together with Chinese and others, belongs to a group of languages which have been described as 'context-oriented', where null categories, for example, can rely on antecedents understood in the context and not necessarily present in the sentence. For a discussion of the difference between these languages and non-'context-oriented' languages such as English, see Huang (1984).

9.2.4 Summary

It seems that there is not necessarily a link between overt (rich) Agr inflection and null arguments. Null arguments can be found, in the form of syntactically 'active' null categories, in contexts which are not related to overt agreement inflection. The role of overt agreement inflection seems to restrict the reference of a given null argument, rather than to license it in formal terms. The licensing of null arguments seems to depend on the properties of individual categories selecting the argument. Two types of null argument have been identified. One type is realized as a pronominal null category and the other as a null *wh*-phrase. The former falls under the scope of the pro-drop parameter, whereas the latter falls under the scope of a more general parameter distinguishing between 'context-oriented' languages, and non 'context-orientated' languages. For different views on the pro-drop parameter, sometimes also called the **Null Subject Parameter**, see the papers in Jaeggli and Safir (1989).

9.3   *Some Word Order Parameters*

We have seen that languages may differ with respect to the directionality in which heads select their complement, and that these differences may be attested in the same language. In this section we shall discuss other major differences in word order, and the nature of the parameters underlying them. First, we will discuss the **V2 (Verb Second)** phenomenon, whereby in some languages the finite verb is required to be in the 'second position' in root clauses. In other languages, the finite verb is required to be in the 'second position' in both root and embedded clauses. We shall then discuss the **VSO** phenomenon, whereby in some languages the most natural position, or the only position, for the subject is the one immediately following the finite verb. As we will see below, some studies have argued that the process which underlies the V2 phenomenon and that which underlies the VSO phenomenon are the same. Other studies, one of which will be discussed below, have argued that the two phenomena are not necessarily linked, at least as far as some VSO languages are concerned.

9.3.1   The V2 Parameter

9.3.1.1 V2 in Root Clauses   We have seen that in German embedded clauses the verb normally follows its object, and a finite auxiliary follows the main verb. Examples (38) and (39) are reproduced from above:

38a.... daß   Hans   den Ball   kaufte
       that   Hans   the ball   bought
38b.[CP *daß* [IP *Hans* [VP [DP *den Ball*] [V *kaufte*]]]

39a.... daß   Hans   den Ball   gekauft   hat
       that   Hans   the ball   bought   has
39b.[CP *daß* [IP *Hans* [VP [DP *den Ball*] [V *gekauft*]] [I *hat*]]]]

These facts were accounted for by assuming that in German V and I select their complements to the left, contrary to C, which selects its IP-complement to the right. With this in mind, consider now the following examples, both of which are root sentences:

40a.Hans   kaufte   den Ball
     Hans   bought   the ball
40b.*Hans den Ball   kaufte
     Hans   the ball   bought
41a.Hans   hat den Ball   gekauft
     Hans   has the ball   bought
41b.*Hans den Ball   gekauft   hat
     Hans   the ball   bought   has

In (40a) the verb precedes its object, instead of following it. (40b) shows that the [OV] order characteristic of embedded clauses is in fact excluded in root sentences such as (40a). On the other hand, in (41a) the order of the verb and its object is consistent with the order found in embedded clauses. In this example, it is the order of the finite auxiliary which is inconsistent with the [V AUX] order characteristic of embedded clauses. (41b) shows that the latter order is in fact excluded in root sentences such as (41a).

The differences in word order between embedded and root clauses apparently presents us with a dilemma. We either abandon the conclusion that the underlying order in German is [OV] and [VP I], or maintain this conclusion and explain the differences in word order between the two clauses in terms of some peculiar property of root clauses. Note that whatever the nature of this peculiar property, it is unlikely to be that root clauses differ from the embedded ones in that root clauses have the underlying orders [VO] and [I VP]. Such a hypothesis would be *ad hoc* (non-explanatory) and, in addition, empirically inaccurate. As clearly shown in (41a), the OV order is indeed found in root clauses as well. A closer look at the examples in (40a,b) and (41a,b) leads to the observation that the finite verb is required immediately to follow the first constituent of the sentence, and that the ungrammatical status of (40b) and (41b) is possibly due to the fact that these examples do not observe this restriction on the order of the finite verb. This observation is confirmed by the following examples:

42a. Gestern   kaufte   Hans   den Ball
    Yesterday   bought   Hans   the ball
42b.*Gestern   Hans   den Ball   kaufte
    Yesterday   Hans   the ball   bought

43a. Im Park   hat Hans   den Ball   gekauft
     In the park   has Hans   the ball   bought

43b. *Im Park   Hans   den Ball   gekauft   hat
      In the park   Hans   the ball   bought   has

43c. *Im Park   Hans   hat den Ball   gekauft
      In the park   Hans   has the ball   bought

In the grammatical examples (42a) and (43a) the finite verb immediately follows the first constituent, whereas in the ungrammatical examples (42b) and (43b,c) it does not. Thus, finite verbs in root clauses seem to be subject to a constraint which restricts them to the 'second position', standardly known as the **V2 Constraint**. Our next step is to identify the nature of the 'second position' in question.

Examples (42a) and (43a) indicate that the 'second position' must be in the pre-IP domain, given that the finite verb precedes the subject (Spec-IP). The status of the finite verb as a head category implies, by virtue of SPH (Chapter 4), that the 'second position' is C, the only head position in the pre-IP domain. On the other hand, the status of the category in the 'first position' as a maximal projection implies that the 'first position' is Spec-CP. Presumably, the finite verb and the XP in the 'first position' reach C and Spec-CP respectively, via movement from IP-internal positions. In view of this, the word order properties of root clauses cannot be said to reflect the underlying order of heads, in particular V and I, with respect to their complements. Thus the fact that the finite auxiliary in (43a), for example, does not follow the main verb cannot be said to argue against the conclusion, reached on the basis of the order in embedded clauses, that I follows its VP-complement. Rather, the order of I in relation to VP and the order of V in relation to its complement can be said to be the same in both embedded and root clauses, and the peculiar word order properties of the root clause can be said to be derived by movement of the finite verb to C (the 'second position') and the movement of an XP constituent to Spec-CP (the 'first position').

Accordingly, (44a) below, for example, has the derivation outlined in (44b) (movement of the finite verb from VP (rightward) to I has been ignored). The finite verb moves from I (leftward) to C, the 'second position' referred to by the V2 Constraint. Like the finite verb, the DP in Spec-CP also moves from a position inside IP, namely the object position of the verb. The process responsible for this movement is often called (somewhat misleadingly) Topicalization (Chapter 2). Presumably, the V2 Constraint applies to all root clauses, so that in example (40a), with the deceptive superficial order SVO, the subject is actually in Spec-CP and the (finite) verb is in C.

The essentials of the analysis outlined are based on early work by Bierwisch (1963), progressing through Koster (1975), Thiersch (1978), and den Besten (1983), among others. Its major aspect is that it maintains a uniform view with respect to the underlying order of constituents in both embedded and root clauses. The word order differences between embedded and root clauses are the consequence of the application of V-movement to C and Topicalization to Spec-CP in root clauses. On the other hand, the application of these movements in root clauses is the consequence of a constraint on word order which holds for root clauses but not necessarily for embedded clauses. The V2 Constraint requires the finite verb in root clauses to be in C, which in German is to the left of IP, hence the 'second position' effect.

44a. Den Ball   hat   Hans   gekauft
     the   ball   has   Hans   bought

44b.

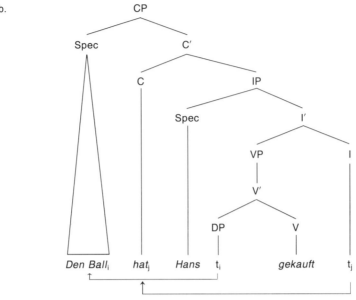

The reason why the V2 Constraint does not hold for embedded clauses receives a plausible explanation on the basis of the hypothesis that the 'second position' is C. Because embedded clauses tend to have their C position filled with a complementizer, the verb cannot move to it (den Besten, 1983). Interestingly, when the complementizer is missing from the complement class of a restricted class of verbs (Grewendorf, 1988), called 'bridge verbs', the V2 effect can be observed in embedded clauses as well. The following examples are cited in Vikner (1990):

45a. Er sagt, daß die Kinder diesen Film gesehen haben
He says that the children this film seen have

45b. Er sagt, diesen Film haben die Kinder gesehen
He says this film have the children seen

45c. *Er sagt, daß diesen Film haben die Kinder gesehen
He says that this film have the children seen

In (45a) the complementizer *daß* is present and the embedded clause does not exhibit the V2 effect. In (45b) the complementizer is missing, and consequently the embedded clause exhibits the V2 effect. (45c) is excluded because it exhibits the V2 effect in the presence of the complementizer. These examples show that the V2 effect is in complementary distribution with the complementizer, confirming the idea that the 'second position' is indeed C.

The question we still need to address is the following: why does the finite verb have to move to C in (root) clauses? Note that the answer to this question will effectively amount to an explanation of the parametric difference between V2 languages such as German and non-V2 languages such as English. Various hypotheses have been suggested in the literature, which have in common the idea that C in V2 languages, when not filled by a complementizer, has a special property which forces the finite verb to move to it (Koopman, 1984; Travis, 1984; Holmberg, 1986; Platzack, 1986a,b; Haegeman, 1986). Some of these hypotheses relate the parametric distinction in question to Case, the idea being that in V2 languages nominative Case is assigned (to the subject in Spec-IP) via government from C, rather than via Spec-Head Agreement with I. Furthermore, for C to be able to assign nominative Case it has to be 'lexically supported', where the category providing lexical support is the verb. Note that if the assignment of nominative Case by C is further assumed to operate under the linear condition of adjacency (Chapter 6), the fact that C in German selects its IP-complement to the right, instead of to the left, should also follow. The reverse order [IP C] would result in a linear order where (the category in) C is not adjacent to the subject in Spec-IP (check for yourself!).

9.3.1.2 *V2 in Embedded Clauses* We have seen that V2 is allowed in the complement clause of a restricted class of verbs in German, in situations where the C position is not filled by a complementizer. However, there are V2 languages (in the Germanic family) which allow embedded V2 even in the presence of a complementizer. Examples of such languages are Yiddish and Icelandic, illustrated respectively in the following examples (Vikner, 1990):

46a. *. . . az   dos yingl oyfn   veg   vet zen a kats
            that the boy on-the way will see a cat
46b. . . . az   dos yingl vet oyfn   veg   zen a kats
            that the boy will on-the way see a cat

47a. *. . . to   Helgi aldrei hevur hitt Maríu
            that Helga never has   met Maria
47b. . . . to   Helgi hevur aldrei hitt Maríu
            that Helga has   never met Maria

Yiddish and Icelandic have the underlying orders [VO] and [I VP], like English. The order of adverbs such as 'on the way' in (46a,b) and 'often' in (47a,b) is used as a diagnostic for the V2 effect. Clauses are judged to exhibit the V2 effect when the finite verb precedes the adverb, and not to exhibit the V2 effect when the finite verb follows the adverb. Accordingly, the grammatical examples (46b) and (47b) exhibit the V2 effect, whereas the ungrammatical ones (46a) and (47a) do not. Together, these examples show that Yiddish and Icelandic exhibit the V2 effect in embedded clauses. Moreover, the V2 effect holds in the presence of a complementizer, contrary to what is found in German. Obviously, this particular fact raises a problem for the analysis whereby the 'second position' is assumed to be C. Two major hypotheses have been suggested in the literature to deal with this problem, which we shall discuss here briefly.

The first hypothesis rests on two assumptions. First, the 'second position' is I, rather than C, in both root and embedded clauses. Secondly, Spec-IP is/can be an A'-position occupied by topicalized categories (e.g. Santorini, 1989; Diesing, 1990; Rögnvaldsson and Thráinsson, 1990). According to this hypothesis, (46b) and (47b) above have S-structure representations along the lines shown in (48a) and (48b) below, respectively:

48a. [$_{CP}$ *az* [$_{IP}$ *dos yingl* [$_{I'}$ *vet*$_i$ [$_{ADV}$ *oyfn veg*] [$_{VP}$ t$_i$ *zen a kats*]]]]

        that   the boy   will   on-the-way   see a cat
48b. [$_{CP}$ *to* [$_{IP}$ *Helgi* [$_{I'}$ *hevur*$_i$ [$_{ADV}$ *aldrei*] [$_{VP}$ t$_i$ *hitt Maríu*]]]]

        that Helga   has   never   met Maria

On the other hand, examples (49a) and (50a) below, where the category in the 'first position' is not the subject, have representations along the lines shown in (49b) and (50b). In the Yiddish example (49), the 'first position' (i.e. Spec-IP) is occupied by the adverb 'tomorrow', possibly topicalized from a clause-final position, and in the Icelandic example (50) Spec-IP is occupied by the object of the verb:

49a. . . . az   morgn   vet dos yingl oyfn   veg   zen a kats
          that tomorrow   will the boy   on-the way   see a cat
49b. [$_{CP}$ *az* [$_{IP}$ *morgn* [$_{I'}$ *vet*$_i$ [$_{VP}$ *dos yingl* [$_{ADV}$ *oyfn*] [$_{V'}$ t$_i$ *zen a kats*]]]]

50a. . . . az   Maríu hevur Helgi aldrei hitt
          that Mariu has   Helga never met
50b. [$_{CP}$ *az* [$_{IP}$ *Maríu*$_j$ [$_{I'}$ *hevur*$_i$ [$_{VP}$ *Helgi* [$_{ADV}$ *aldrei*] [$_{V'}$ t$_i$ *hitt* t$_j$]]]]]

In both examples the subject is in Spec-VP (Chapter 7), where it presumably receives its Case via government from some appropriately located category. It should be clear how this analysis solves the problem raised by V2 in the presence of a complementizer. By assuming that the 'second position' is I, rather than C, co-occurrence of V2 and the complementizer not only ceases to be problematic but even becomes expected.

The second hypothesis rests on the assumption that the 'second position' in embedded V2 clauses is the head of an additional projection XP intervening between CP and IP, with properties similar to those of CP (Holmberg, 1986). Here, we will call the projection in question XP, so that examples (49a) and (50a) above have representations along the following lines, respectively:

51a. [$_{CP}$ *az* [$_{XP}$ *dos yingl*$_i$ [$_{C'}$ *vet*$_i$ [$_{IP}$ t$_j$ [$_{ADV}$ *oyfn*] [$_{I'}$ t$_i$ [$_{VP}$ t$_i$ *zen a kats*]]]]]]
51b. [$_{CP}$ *az* [$_{XP}$ *Helgi*$_j$ [$_{C'}$ *hevur*$_i$ [$_{IP}$ t$_j$ [$_{ADV}$ *aldrei*] [$_{I'}$ t$_i$ [$_{VP}$ t$_i$ *hitt Maríu*]]]]]]

The possibility of embedded V2 in the presence of a complementizer in Yiddish and Icelandic is reduced, in the context of this analysis, to the presence of an additional projection whose head functions as the 'second position' and its Spec as the 'first position'.

9.3.1.3   Residual V2   Studies on the V2 phenomenon have mostly concentrated on providing an answer to the question: Why does the finite verb have to move to the 'second position'? Note, however, that this question represents only part of the picture. The other part relates to the following question: Why does the 'first position' invariably have to be filled by a topicalized category in declarative V2 clauses? The German examples below lack a topicalized constituent, and consequently cannot be construed as declarative sentences, although they can be construed as *yes/no* questions:

52a. *Kickte Hans   den Ball
     kicked   Hans   the ball
52b. *Hat Hans   den Ball gekickt
     has Hans   the ball   kicked

The fact that these examples cannot be construed as declarative sentences is due to the 'first position' being empty, even though the 'second position' is appropriately filled by the finite verb, judging by the order of the constituents. The ungrammatical status of (52a,b) cannot be attributed to a violation of the V2 Constraint, if the latter is understood as the requirement that the finite verb be in C.

Once the second question raised above is taken into consideration a third question becomes obvious: Which of the two categories involved in V2 (the finite verb and the topicalized XP) pulls the other to the pre-IP domain? A possible answer to this question can be gleaned from the facts of English. For reasons which will become clear shortly,

English is sometimes called a 'residual V2 language'. English is obviously not a V2 language in the sense that German and other Germanic languages are. This is trivially shown by the order of constituents in the following examples:

53a. Mary often reads the Socialist Worker
53b. To John Mary gave a book

The counterparts of these sentences with similar word orders are ungrammatical in V2 languages, for the simple reason that the finite verb does not occupy the 'second position'. However, English does exhibit what looks like the V2 effect in root *wh*-questions. Movement of *wh*-phrases to root Spec-CP in English (root *wh*-subjects excepted) general-ly triggers movement of the finite auxiliary to C (SAI, Chapter 3):

54a. Why has John left early?
54b. *Why John has left early?

55a. *I wonder why has John left early
55b. I wonder why John left early

The ungrammatical status of (55a), where the *wh*-question is in an embedded domain, is the reason why SAI was said to be a 'root phenomenon' (Chapter 3). If by V2 we understand the obligatory presence of the finite verb in C, there is a sense in which English can be said to exhibit the V2 phenomenon in *wh*-questions.

As a matter of fact, the V2 effect is not necessarily restricted to *wh*-questions in English. It also arises in sentences involving topicalization of a constituent with a negative content:

56a. Never have I seen anything like that
56b. *Never I have seen anything like that

57a. The committee has resolved that under no circumstances should he be allowed to continue in his work
57b. ??The committee has resolved that under no circumstances he should be allowed to continue in his work

These examples show that, like preposed *wh*-phrases, topicalized 'negative' elements in English also trigger SAI, giving rise to an effect which to all intents and purposes is similar to the V2 effect. Note that (57) exhibits the V2 effect in the presence of the complementizer *that*, similar to the V2 effect in embedded clauses found in Yiddish and Icelandic. Assuming that the subject in this example occupies Spec-IP, the inversion effect lends support to the idea that there is an additional projection between CP and IP in embedded clauses, with properties similar to those of CP (Tsimpli, 1990).

To the extent that SAI can be considered a manifestation of the V2 effect, it is clear, as far as English is concerned, that the V2 effect is triggered by the presence of an operator (a *wh*-phrase or a negative topicalized category) in Spec-CP. Note that this generalization can be maintained if the non-negative topicalized elements in examples such as (58b) above are assumed not to occupy Spec-CP (Chapter 3), contrary to their negative counterparts. If the conclusion that the V2 effect arises only when Spec-CP is filled (by an operator) were to extend to languages with a generalized V2 effect, the parametric distinction between these languages and languages with limited V2 would hinge on an answer to the second question raised above (Why does the 'first position' (Spec-CP) have to be filled with an operator in declarative sentences?), rather than on the first question (Why does the 'second position' (C) have to be filled with a finite verb?). Movement of the finite verb to the 'second position' when Spec-CP is filled by an operator is not an exclusive property of V2 languages, but, rather, a property of all languages. In other words, the V2 effect, understood as the obligatory movement of the finite verb to C, seems to be a by-product of the actual parameter underlying the V2 phenomenon, rather than its core property.

9.3.2 VSO Languages

VSO languages can be loosely characterized as the languages where the most natural order of the subject is in the position immediately following the inflected verb, preceding the object and other VP-material. Having said that, there are significant differences between VSO languages regarding the order of the subject. Some VSO languages, such as Standard Arabic, seem to allow the SVO order in addition to their characteristic VSO order. Others, however, such as Welsh, apparently do not allow the SVO order in neutral sentences. We shall discuss two major hypotheses concerning the parametric distinction between these languages and SVO languages such as English. The first hypothesis, which we shall call the **V-to-C Analysis**, will be discussed in relation to Welsh. The second hypothesis, which we shall call the **Subject-inside-VP Analysis**, will be discussed in relation to Standard Arabic.

9.3.2.1 The V-to-C Analysis   The following are representative examples of two types of VSO sentence in Welsh, discussed in Sproat (1985a):

58a. Gwelodd Siôn ddraig
     Saw   Siôn dragon
     'Siôn saw a dragon'
58b. Gwnaeth Siôn weld draig
     did   Siôn see   dragon
     'Siôn saw a dragon'

The two sentences are synonymous, although they differ slightly in their constituent structures. (58a) has a simple structure, where the I elements appear on the main verb. (58b) is said to have a **periphrastic** structure, where the main verb is uninflected, and the I elements appear on an auxiliary verb with properties not unlike those of the English '*do*-support'. The two sentences display the VSO order in the sense that the subject immediately follows the finite verb, although in (58b) the subject precedes the non-finite main verb.

    Some of the early work on VSO languages concentrated on the question of whether or not they instantiate a VP like SVO languages. Presumably, the question was motivated by the fact that the VP constituents, i.e. the verb and its complements, are discontinuous in VSO languages, with the subject intervening between them. Starting with Emonds (1980), the focus of attention shifted to trying to work out how the VSO order is derived from a structure where the verb and its complements form a VP and are adjacent at D-structure. Underlying this attempt is the assumption that all languages have a unique underlying sentence structure, and that word order differences are merely surface phenomena, in that they are the result of movement processes which apply in some languages but not in others.

    The essence of Emonds' proposal is that the VS(XP) order in VSO languages such as Welsh is derived by movement of the verb to C (via I), from a structure which is identical to that of English in relevant respects. Accordingly, (58a) above, for example, has the derivation shown in (59):

59. [$_{CP}$ [$_{C'}$ *Gwelodd*$_i$ [$_{IP}$ *Siôn* [$_{I'}$ t$_i$ [$_{VP}$ t$_i$ *ddraig*]]]]]

In other words, the [V S (XP)] order in VSO languages is derived by the same process responsible for the derivation of the word order [WhP V S (XP)] in English *wh*-questions such as *Why is John unhappy?* The difference is that, while movement of the finite verb to C in English is triggered by the presence of an operator in Spec-CP, in VSO languages such as Welsh it apparently applies irrespectively. Thus, according to this analysis VSO languages are basically V2 languages, in that their finite verbs invariably move to C.

Sproat (1985a) attributes this property of VSO languages to a parametrized restriction on the directionality of nominative Case-assignment by I. In Welsh I can only assign nominative Case rightward, so that for I to be able to do so it has to move to C, located to the left of the subject. Movement of the verb to C along with I, on the other hand, is needed to 'lexically support' I, either for purely morphological reasons (the I elements being morphologically dependent) or in order to enable it to assign Case. When 'support' for I is provided by a dummy auxiliary, as in (58b) above, movement of the main verb becomes unnecessary. Strictly SVO languages such as English differ in that I can assign nominative either to the right or to the left. The parametric difference between VSO and SVO languages, therefore, reduces to a parametrized restriction on the directionality of Case-assignment by I. Recall from above that a similar parameter has been invoked to account for the difference between V2 languages and non-V2 languages, emphasizing the parallelism between the V2 phenomenon and the VSO phenomenon.

The analysis outlined and the parallelism with V2 languages is supported by two important properties of Welsh. First, finite clauses do not allow the SVO order. In sentences such as (60) below, where the subject precedes the finite verb, the subject is topicalized, and has a contrastive focus reading rather than a neutral reading (Jones and Thomas, 1977):

60. Mair   a   fydd   yn aros am John
    Mair   PRT will-be   in wait for John
    'It is Mair who will be waiting for John'

The status of the pre-verbal subject as a topic/focus category occupying Spec-CP is also indicated by the presence of the particle *a* which appears in relatives and other operator-movement constructions as well. The analysis outlined above, whereby the finite verb moves to C, predicts that if the subject precedes the finite verb the subject will have the status of an operator, as it would occupy Spec-CP.

The other property of Welsh which supports the analysis outlined above relates to the fact that (embedded) non-finite clauses, contrary to their finite counterparts, allow the SVO order; in fact, they require it (Awbery, 1976):

61. Dymunai Wyn i   Ifor ddarllen y   llyfr
    wanted   Wyn for Ifor to-read the book
    'Wyn wanted (for) Ifor to read the book'

Note that the subject in this clause is preceded by the preposition 'for', which has the function of assigning Case to the subject in the absence of a finite I. As Sproat points out, this state of affairs is expected on the assumption that in finite clauses the complex [V + I] moves to C to be in a position from which it can assign Case to the subject. For a detailed theoretical study of the Syntax of Welsh, see Rouveret (1992).

9.3.2.2 The Subject-inside-VP Analysis   As pointed out above, Standard Arabic belongs to the group of VSO languages which allow the SVO order, in addition to their characteristic VSO order:

62a. raʔa-a   l -ʔawlaadu   Zaydan
    saw -3MS the -boys   Zayd
    'The boys saw Zayd'

62b. l-ʔawlaadu   raʔa-w   Zaydan
    the-boys   saw -3MP   Zayd
    'The boys saw Zayd'

The two sentences, though synonymous, differ in one important respect. In the VSO example (62a), the subject does not agree in number with (the AgrS category of) the verbal complex: the subject is plural, whereas the AgrS element is singular. In the SVO example (62b), however, the subject agrees with the (AgrS category of) the verbal complex.

Capitalizing on this difference in agreement between post-verbal and pre-verbal subjects, Koopman and Sportiche (1991) and Mohammad (1989) have argued that agreement in number between the subject and the (AgrS category of) I in the SVO order implies that the subject is in Spec-Head Agreement with I, and therefore occupies Spec-IP. On the other hand, the lack of agreement in number between the subject and (the AgrS category of) I in the VSO order implies that the subject is not in Spec-Head Agreement with I, and therefore does not occupy Spec-IP. They have suggested that in the VSO order the subject remains inside VP, where it is base-generated (the Subject-inside-VP Hypothesis (Chapter 6)). Accordingly, (62a) and (62b) have representations along the following lines, respectively:

63a. [$_{IP}$ e [$_{I'}$ *raʔaa*$_i$ [$_{VP}$ *l-ʔawlaadu* [$_{V'}$ t$_i$ *Zaydan*]]]]

63b. [$_{IP}$ *l-ʔawlaadu*$_j$ [$_{I'}$ *raʔaw*$_i$ [$_{VP}$ t$_j$ [$_{V'}$ t$_i$ *Zaydan*]]]]

In both examples the verb raises to I. The difference in the order of the subject is attributed to the idea that in (63a) the subject remains in its D-structure position, where it is assigned nominative Case under government by I. The fact that in this structure the subject is not in Spec-Head Agreement with I accounts for the lack of agreement in number between them. In (63b), however, the subject moves to Spec-IP, where it is assigned nominative Case under Spec-Head Agreement with I. The fact that the subject in this structure is in Spec-Head Agreement with I accounts for the agreement in number between them.

Note that under a strict interpretation of EPP, whereby a subject is required in the Spec-IP position, (63a) may be problematic on the assumption that Spec-IP remains empty. However, the Spec-IP position can plausibly be assumed to be filled by an expletive *pro*, so that VSO sentences in Arabic would in a sense be parallel to English sentences such as *There is a unicorn in the garden*. Like its overt English counterpart *it*, the expletive *pro* in Standard Arabic has the (default) third-person singular features, and therefore can be said to be in Spec-Head Agreement with I. Mohammad (1989) has argued that the presence of an expletive subject in VSO clauses can be detected in situations where they are embedded under the complementizer *ʔanna* 'that':

64. dhanan -tu   ʔanna -hu raʔa-a   l-ʔawlaadu   Zaydan
    believed -1S   that   -it ṣaw-3MS the-boys   Zayd
    'I believed that the boys saw Zayd'

The complementizer *ʔanna*, which usually assigns accusative Case to the pre-verbal subject, has the peculiar property of forcing the expletive subject to be 'lexicalized'. In (64) the expletive subject appears as a clitic on the complementizer.

According to the analysis outlined, the parametric difference between VSO (or mixed) languages such as Standard Arabic and SVO languages such as English is that in the former I can assign nominative both under government and under Spec-Head Agreement, whereas in the latter I can only assign Case under Spec-Head Agreement. In Standard Arabic, I assigns nominative under government in the VSO order, and under Spec-Head Agreement in the SVO order. The lack of the option of nominative-Case-assignment under government in strictly SVO languages such as English is the reason they do not allow the VSO order in declarative sentences as freely as do mixed languages such as Standard Arabic. For a different view on the structure of Arabic SVO and VSO sentences, see Benmamoun (1992).

9.3.3 Summary

V2 languages fall into two major groups. In one group the V2 Constraint holds mainly for root clauses, and in another group the V2 Constraint holds for both root and embedded clauses in a parallel way. The first group suggests that the 'second position' is C otherwise occupied by the complementizer, as the finite verb and the complementizer are in complementary distribution in relation to the 'second position'. The second group, however, where V2 clauses co-occur freely with the complementizer, suggests that the 'second position' is not the C position occupied by the complementizer. English is a 'residual V2 language' in the sense that the finite verb is required to be in the 'second position' in *wh*-questions and sentences with topicalized negative elements. Some VSO languages seem to lend themselves to an analysis which groups them together with V2 languages, while others seem to suggest a different analysis. Most of the parameters suggested in the literature to account for V2 and VSO languages seem to rely, at least partly, on the notion of 'directionality'.

9.4 *Incorporation Phenomena*

In this section we shall outline the broad aspects of a syntactic approach to the derivation of complex predicates developed in Baker (1988), sometimes called **Incorporation Theory**. Baker's approach should be considered in relation to previous analyses which have argued that the derivation of complex predicates takes place in the Lexicon in terms of special rules, rather than in the Syntax in terms of the general principle Move-α. One of the main arguments for a lexical analysis has been that the derivation of complex predicates results in changes of the grammatical functions of certain related 'noun phrases'. Baker argues that these changes can be accounted for in terms of the syntactic approach of Incorporation. Unfortunately, the limits of space mean that a complete presentation of Baker's impressive and voluminous book is impossible.

9.4.1 Incorporation Theory (Noun Incorporation)

Compare the following examples from Mohawk (Postal, 1979) (N: 'neuter agreement', SUF: 'nominal inflection suffix'):

65a. Ka-rakv　　ne　　sawatis　hrao-*nuhs*　-a?
　　 3N-*be-white* Det　*John*　　 3M-　*house*　-SUF
　　 'John's house is white'
65b. Hrao-*nuhs*-rakv　　ne　　sawatis
　　 3M-　*house-be-white* Det　*John*
　　 'John's house is white'

The two sentences are synonymous, but differ with respect to the position of the noun *nuhs* 'house'. In (65a) the noun is situated inside the 'noun phrase' complement of the stative verb *-rakv* 'be white', where it agrees with the possessor subject of the 'noun phrase'. In (65b), however, the noun appears **incorporated** into the verbal complex, and is situated between the verb and the AgrO morpheme. A major consequence of the incorporation of the noun relates to a change of object agreement. In (65a) the verb carries the neuter AgrO morpheme, implying that it agrees with the 'noun phrase' 'John's house' headed by the neuter noun 'house'. In the incorporation example (65b), however, the verb carries the masculine AgrO morpheme, implying that it agrees with the possessor of 'house', namely 'John'. Assuming, as is standardly the case, that object agreement is a manifestation of direct-objecthood (object agreement is usually restricted to the direct object), it seems that the possessor in (65b) acquires the status of a direct object as a result of the incorporation of the noun into the verb. Thus the incorporation of the noun into the verb apparently results in a change of the grammatical function of the possessor of the incorporated noun from being the subject of the noun phrase to becoming the direct object of the verb.

In the discussion of passives and ergatives/unaccusatives (Chapter 6), we saw that a change in the grammatical function of a given noun phrase can be the result of syntactic movement. The internal argument of passives and unaccusatives acquires the status of a subject as a result of moving to the subject position in the Syntax. Note, however, that the situation with respect to the possessor in N-incorporation constructions is different. The possessor cannot be said to acquire the status of the direct object of the verb as a result of moving to a base-generated empty object position. Such a movement is excluded by PP in conjunction with the Theta Criterion (Chapter 5). The situation of the possessor in (65b) is more akin to that of ECM subjects (Chapter 6). The ECM subject acquires the status of 'object of the verb' in so far as it is governed (and assigned) Case by the ECM verb. Structurally, though, it occupies the subject position of the embedded clause, and thematically it is the subject of the embedded verb. The same argument can be made for the possessor in (65b) above. The possessor in this example has the status of 'object of the verb' in so far as it is governed by the verb. Structurally, though, it occupies the subject position of the 'noun phrase'.

Thus the change in the grammatical function of the possessor does not necessarily exclude a syntactic analysis for N-incorporation. Baker argues that there is evidence which indicates that N-incorporation must be syntactic rather than lexical. Before we discuss the evidence, let us first outline Baker's syntactic analysis for N-incorporation and the effect it has on the possessor. At the heart of Baker's theory of incorporation is the hypothesis stated in (66):

66. **Uniformity of Theta Assignment Hypothesis (UTAH)**
    Identical thematic relationships between items are represented by identical structural relationships between those items at the level of D-structure.

The effects of UTAH can be simply illustrated in terms of a passive sentence such as *The ball was kicked (by John)* in comparison to its active counterpart *John kicked the ball*. In both sentences *the ball* is the internal argument of the verb *kick*. By virtue of UTAH, *the ball* must bear the same structural relationship to the verb at D-structure in both sentences, so that in the passive sentence it should be in the object position of the verb at D-structure just as it is in the active sentence. This is basically the reasoning behind the standard analysis of passives (Chapter 5). With respect to N-incorporation examples such as (65b) above, UTAH implies that the noun 'house' occupies the same position as its non-incorporated counterpart in (65a) at D-structure, i.e. a position inside the 'noun phrase'. The incorporation of N into the verb, therefore, must take place at the post-D-structure level, presumably in the mapping from D-structure onto S-structure. Accord-

67.

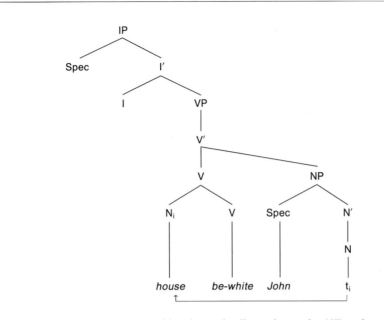

ingly, (65b) has a derivation roughly along the lines shown in (67), where the 'noun phrase' is assigned an NP, rather than a DP, structure (note that the 'noun phrase' is the internal argument of the stative verb 'be-white'). N-incorporation into V is an instance of head-to-head movement, whereby the head N of NP moves and head-adjoins to V. The moved N antecedent-governs its trace inside NP, presumably for the same reason that the verb in V-to-I and I-to-V movements antecedent-governs its trace (Chapter 8).

To account for the effect of N-incorporation on the possessor (Spec-NP), Baker has suggested the following statement, which he calls (somewhat misleadingly) a corollary:

68. Government Transparency Corollary (GTC)

A lexical category which has an item incorporated into it governs everything which the incorporated item governed in its original structural position.

Assuming that N governs Spec-NP, the verb in (67) governs the possessor in Spec-NP by virtue of the fact that it has N incorporated into it. Baker argues that, if object agreement is understood to be a reflection of a government relation between the verb and the 'noun phrase' it agrees with, the government relation between the verb and the possessor which results from N-incorporation in (65b/67) accounts for the object agreement relationship between the verb and the possessor and, consequently, for the observation that the possessor acquires the status of the direct object of the verb.

A major argument for a syntactic analysis of N-incorporation relates to the generalization that only internal arguments of verbs, most typically patients of transitive verbs, can incorporate (Mithun, 1984, 1986). In contrast, typical subject arguments tend not to incorporate. This is shown in the following examples from Mohawk (Postal, 1979) (PRE: 'nominal inflection prefix'):

69a. Yao-wir -aʔa   ye -   nuhweʔ -s   ne ka -nuhs -aʔ
    PRE-*baby*-SUF   3FS/3N-*like*   -ASP *the* PRE -*house* -SUF
    'The baby likes the house'
69b. Yao -wir -aʔa   ye-   *nuhs* -nuhweʔ -s
    PRE -baby-SUF   3FS/3N-*house*-like   -ASP
    Lit. 'The baby house-likes'

69c. *Ye-   *wir-*   nuhwe?-s ne ka   -nuhs -a?
    3FS/3N -baby- like   PRE -house -SUF
    Lit. 'Baby-likes the house'
69d. [IP [NP t_i] I [VP V + [N]$_i$ . . .]]

(69b) involves N-incorporation out of the object position, and (69c) involves N-corporation out of the subject position. Baker argues that the noted restriction on N-incorporation is syntactic in essence, in the sense that it reflects the restrictions on movements imposed by HMC/ECP. Incorporation of a noun from the subject position (Spec-IP) into the verb, outlined in (69d), is a lowering movement, and therefore results in a situation where the incorporated head does not antecedent-govern its trace (for lack of c-command).

Another major argument for a HMC/ECP-based analysis of N-incorporation relates to another generalization about N-incorporation, namely that objects of prepositions, unlike direct objects of verbs, do not incorporate. This is shown in the following examples from Niuean (Seiter, 1980) (ABS: 'absolutive Case marker'):

70a. Ne tutala a au ke he tau *tagata*
    PAST-*talk* ABS-I *to* PL-*person*
    'I was talking to (the) people'
70b. *Ne tutala *tagata* a au (ke he)
    PAST-*talk-person* ABS-I (*to*)
    Lit. 'I was people-talking (to)'
70c. V + N$_i$ [PP P [NP [N t_i]]]

On the assumption that N-incorporation is a head-to-head movement process, (70b) falls under the scope of HMC/ECP. As shown in (70c), movement of N to V across P gives rise to a violation of HMC/ECP: the incorporated noun does not antecedent-govern its trace inside PP, owing to the intervening P, which creates a Minimality effect.

Before we move on to discuss other instances of incorporation, a word about N-incorporation and Case Theory. In the Mohawk example (65b) above, with the structure shown in (67), the verb is unaccusative, and therefore does not assign Case to the 'noun phrase' in the object position (Chapter 6). The question then is: How does the 'noun phrase' satisfy the Case Requirement? Baker's answer is that the 'noun phrase' satisfies the Case Requirement via the incorporation of its head N into the verb. The idea is that there are various ways a 'noun phrase' can satisfy the Case Requirement, which relate to the various types of existing Case; inherent Case, structural Case, etc. Incorporation of the head N of the 'noun phrase' into the verb is another way in which a given 'noun phrase' can satisfy the Case Requirement. Thus, although the verb in (65b) does not assign Case, its 'noun phrase' complement satisfies the Case Requirement by virtue of the incorporation of its head N into the verb. As a matter of fact, Baker outlines a well-developed, and in many respects novel, approach to Case, spelling out its relevance to the PF and LF levels. Unfortunately, we cannot go into the details of this approach here for lack of space.

9.4.2   Verb Incorporation: Morphological Causatives

Compare the following examples from Chichewa (Trithart, 1977):

71a. Mtsikana ana-chit-its-a   kuti   mtsuku   u-*gw*-e
    girl   AGR-*do-make*-ASP *that*   *water-pot* AGR-*fall*-ASP
    'The girl made the water-pot fall'

71b. Mtsikana anau-*gw*-ets-a   mtsuko
     girl   AGR-*fall-make*-ASP *water-pot*
     'The girl made the water-pot fall'

The two examples are synonymous, and are instances of different types of **causative construction**. In (71a) the **causativized** verb *gw* 'fall' appears in the embedded clause and is inflected separately from the **causative verb** *ets* 'make' of the root clause. Thus, (71a) is identical to the type of the bi-clausal causative construction found in English, as shown in the gloss. In (71b), however, the causativized verb appears incorporated into the causative verb and is inflected together with it. (71b) is an instance of so-called **morphological causatives**, which superficially seem to be mono-clausal (rather than bi-clausal) in structure.

As with N-incorporation, V-incorporation in (71b) results in an apparent change in the grammatical function of the subject of the incorporated category. The 'noun phrase' 'the water-pot', situated in the subject position of the embedded clause in (71a), exhibits the properties of a direct object in the incorporation example (71b). This is shown by the fact that it can trigger object agreement with the verb and can become the subject when the verb is in the passive form (unfortunately, in (72a) and numerous other examples below, the features of the AgrO morpheme (OP) are not spelled out in the source):

72a. Mphunzitsi a-na-wa-lemb-ets-a   ana
     teacher   SP-PAST-OP-*write*-CAUS-ASP *children*
     'The teacher made the children write'
72b. Ana   a-na-lemb-ets-edw-a   ndi mphunzitsi
     children SP-PAST-*write*-CAUS-PASS-ASP *by   teacher*
     'The children were made to write by the teacher'

In (72a) the verbal complex includes an object agreement morpheme which agrees with the **causee** 'children'. In (72b) the causee appears in the subject position and the verb is in the passive form. Note that passives in Chichewa, as in many other languages, are not periphrastic, in the sense that they do not consist of a passive participle and an auxiliary verb. Morphological passives are marked simply by a passive morpheme attached to the root verb.

Baker argues that morphological causatives such as (71b), though superficially mono-clausal, have a bi-clausal structure identical to that of the causative construction in (71a). Note that this assumption is forced by UTAH, given that the two constructions in (71a) and (71b) are thematic paraphrases of each other. The fact that the embedded causativized verb in (71b) appears incorporated into the root causative verb is the result of a syntactic head-to-head movement process. The intended derivation is roughly as outlined in (73). The causativized verb *fall* moves in a successive cyclic way consistent with the requirements of HMC/ECP. Baker argues that this V-movement process creates, by virtue of GTC, an ECM-like structure, where the root verb governs and assigns Case to the subject of the embedded clause (the causee). This accounts for the direct object-like properties of the causee illustrated in (72a,b) above, on a par with ECM subjects in general.

In the causative examples discussed so far the causativized verb is intransitive. Languages which have morphological causatives display a striking degree of similarity with respect to causativization of intransitive verbs, in so far as the thematic subject of the causativized verb invariably has direct object-like properties. However, when the causativized verb is transitive, languages tend to differ as to whether the thematic subject or the thematic object of the causative verb has direct-object-like properties. Baker illustrates this difference in terms of two different dialects of Chichewa, the dialect described in Trithart (1977) (Chichewa-B) and another dialect (Chichewa-A).

73.

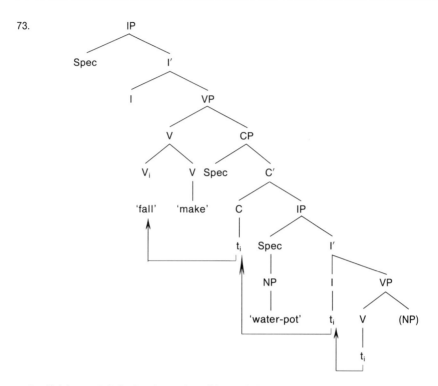

In Chichewa-B it is the thematic subject of the causativized verb (the causee) which has direct-object-like properties, as shown by the fact that it can trigger object agreement (74b) and that it can move to the subject position when the verb is in the passive form (74c):

74a. Catherine a-na-kolol-*ets*-a   mwana wake chimanga
     Catherine SP-PAST-*harvest*-CAUS-ASP *child   her   corn*
     'Catherine made her child harvest the corn'
74b. Catherine a-na-mu-kolol-*ets*-a   mwana wake chimanga
     Catherine SP-PAST-OP-*harvest*-CAUS-ASP *child   her   corn*
     'Catherine made her child harvest the corn'
74c. Mnyamata a-na-kolol-*ets*-edw-a   chimanga ndi Catherine
     boy   SP-PAST-*harvest*-CAUS-PASS-ASP *corn   by Catherine*
     'The boy was made to harvest the corn by Catherine'

That the thematic object of the causativized verb has none of these direct object-like properties is shown by the fact that it can neither trigger object agreement (75a) nor move to the subject position when the verb is in the passive form (75b):

75a. *Catherine a-na-chi-kolol-*ets*-a   mwana wake chimanga
     Catherine SP-PAST-OP-*harvest*-CAUS-ASP *child   her   corn*
     'Catherine made her child harvest the corn'
75b. *Chimanga chi-na-kolol-*ets*-edw-a   mwana wake ndi Catherine
     corn   SP-PAST-*harvest*-CAUS-PASS-ASP *child   her   by Catherine*
     'The corn was made to be harvested by her child by Catherine'

Baker argues that, since these causatives of transitive verbs resemble causatives of intransitive verbs, in that the subject of the causativized verb has direct-object-like properties, they have the derivation outlined in (73) above. The thematic object of the causativized verb, located inside the embedded VP, is not accessible to exceptional Case-marking by the derived verb, and hence it does not have direct-object-like properties. In contrast, the subject of the causativized verb is accessible to exceptional Case-marking from the root verb, and hence it has direct object-like properties.

However, in Chichewa-A and other languages (Gibson, 1980), it is the thematic object of the causativized verb which has direct-object-like properties, rather than the thematic subject. This is shown in the following examples from Chichewa-A by the fact that it can trigger object agreement with the derived verb (76b), and that it can move to the subject position when the derived verb is in the passive form:

76a. Anyani a-na-meny-*ets*-a   ana   kwa buluzi
     baboons SP-PAST-*hit*-CAUS-ASP *children to*   *lizard*
     'The baboons made the lizard hit the children'
76b. Anyani a-na-wa-meny-*ets*-a   ana   kwa buluzi
     baboons SP-PAST-OP-*hit*-CAUS-ASP *children to*   *lizard*
     'The baboons made the lizard hit the children'
76c. Ana   a-na-meny-*ets*-edw-a   kwa buluzi (ndi anyani)
     children SP-PAST-*hit*-CAUS-PASS-ASP *to*   *lizard by*   *baboons*
     'The children were made to be hit by the lizard (by the baboons)'

That the thematic subject of the causativized verb (the causee) has none of these properties is shown by the fact that it can neither trigger object agreement (77a) nor move to the subject position when the derived verb is in the passive form (77b):

77a. *Anyani a-na-zi-meny-*ets*-a   ana   kwa mbuzi
     baboons SP-PAST-OP-*hit*-CAUS-ASP *children to*   *goats*
     'The baboons made the goats hit the children'
77b. *Buluzi a-na-meny-*ets*-edw-a   ana   (ndi anyani)
     lizard   SP-PAST-*hit*-CAUS-PASS-ASP *children by*   *baboons*
     'The lizard was made to hit the boys (by the baboons)'

(76a) differs from its Chichewa-B counterpart (74a) in that in (76a) the thematic object precedes the thematic subject of the causativized verb in word order, and the thematic subject is preceded by the preposition 'to'. In (74a), however, the reverse order is found, so that the subject precedes the object of the causativized verb and neither the subject nor the object is preceded by a preposition.

Given that Chichewa-A-type causatives of transitive verbs differ from Chichewa-B-type causatives of transitive verbs, Baker agues that the former must have a different derivation, though the same structure. The derivation in question is roughly as outlined in (78). Prior to the incorporation of the causativized verb into the root causative verb, the VP containing the causativized verb and its thematic object moves to the Spec position of the embedded CP. The consequence of this movement is that the thematic object of the causativized verb, located in Spec-CP, becomes accessible to exceptional Case-marking from the derived root verb, and hence shows direct-object-like properties. The other consequence of VP-movement to Spec-CP is that the causee, located in the subject position of IP, is not accessible to exceptional Case-marking from the derived root verb, and hence does not have direct-object-like properties. The preposition 'to', shown in (76a), is inserted by a special mechanism for the purpose of assigning Case to the causee.

Thus the difference between the two types of causative of transitive verbs relates to whether or not the VP containing the causativized verb moves to Spec-CP prior to the incorporation of the causativized verb into the causative verb. In addition to the

78.

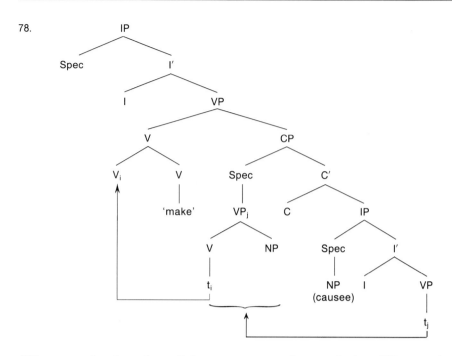

differences pointed out here, Baker goes on to point out further differences between languages with respect to the grammatical functions of the arguments of the causativized verb, explaining them in terms of parameters relating to the Case properties of individual verbs in various languages.

9.4.3 Preposition Incorporation: Applicatives

Compare the following examples from Chichewa:

79a. Mbidzi zi-na-perek-a   msampha *kwa* nkhandwe
    zebras SP-PAST-*hand*-ASP *trap* *to* *fox*
    'The zebras handed the trap to the fox'
79b. Mbidzi zi-na-perek-*er*-a   nkhandwe msampha
    zebras SP-PAST-*hand-to*-ASP *fox*   *trap*
    'The zebras handed the fox the trap'

In (79a) the indirect object (goal) appears inside a PP headed by the preposition 'to' and following the direct object (theme). In (79b), however, the goal argument appears adjacent to the verb, and preceding the theme argument. Moreover, the preposition 'to' is absent and the verb shows an extra morpheme known as the **applied morpheme**. It should be clear that the **applicative construction** in (79b) is the equivalent of the Dative Shift construction in English, as shown in the gloss (Chapters 5 and 6).

The two examples in (79a,b) are thematic paraphrases of each other, where the arguments bear the same thematic relationships to the verb. In view of this, UTAH requires that they have identical D-structures and that, consequently, surface differences between them must be the result of rules applying at the post-D-structure level. Baker argues that the applicative construction (79b) is derived by a process of P-incorporation into the verb, roughly along the lines shown in (80). The fact that PP is ordered before the theme argument does not necessarily follow from UTAH, nor, for that matter, from

80.

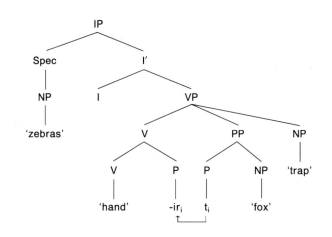

HMC/ECP. The order in (80) could be forced in terms of the idea that Case-assignment by the complex verb (derived by P-incorporation) to the complement of P, called the **applied object**, is subject to adjacency. A crucial assumption in Baker's system, not mentioned so far, is that traces of incorporated categories cannot act on behalf of their antecedent as far as Case-assignment is concerned. Thus the trace of the incorporated preposition in (80) does not assign Case to the applied object; rather, it is the derived complex verb which does so.

Baker argues that it is this property of applicatives which accounts for the general fact that applied objects invariably display direct-object-like properties (Marantz, 1984). In Chichewa this is shown by the fact that the applied object can trigger object agreement with the verb (81a), and can move to the subject position when the verb is in the passive form (81b):

81a. Amayi a-ku-mu-umb-ir-a   mtsuko   mwana
     woman SP-PRES-OP-*mould-for*-ASP *water-pot child*
     'The woman is moulding the water-pot for the child'
81b. Mbidzi zi-na-gul-ir-idw-a   nsapato (ndi kalulu)
     zebras SP-PAST-*buy-for*-PASS-ASP *shoes by   hare*
     'The zebras were bought shoes (by the hare)'

The reason why the applied object in (81a) appears following the basic object (theme argument), rather than preceding it as in (79b) above, is probably due to the fact, discussed earlier in this chapter, that when the AgrO morpheme is present in Chichewa sentences the object tends to have more freedom of ordering (Bresnan and Mchombo, 1987). (79b) differs from (81a) in that it does not include an AgrO morpheme, and hence the applied object is restricted to the position immediately following the applicative verb.

Another property of Chichewa applicatives is that the basic object (the theme argument), contrary to the applied object, does not show direct-object-like properties. Thus it can neither trigger object agreement on the verb (82a) nor move to the subject position when the verb is in the passive form (82b):

82a. *Amayi a-na-u-umbir-a   mwana mtsuko
     woman SP-PAST-OP-*mould-for*-ASP *child   water-pot*
     'The woman is moulding the water-pot for the child'
82b. *Nsapato zi-na-gul-ir-idw-a   mbidzi (ndi kalulu)
     shoes   SP-PAST-*buy-for*-PASS-ASP *zebras by   hare*
     'Shoes were bought for the zebras (by the hare)'

The properties of applicatives in Chichewa are clearly similar to the properties of Dative Shift constructions in English (Chapters 5 and 6). Presumably, the reason why the basic object does not have direct-object-like properties is because it does not receive the ('primary') structural accusative Case of the verb. However, this is not a general property of all basic objects in applicatives across languages, as Baker points out. Just as there are dialects of British English where the basic object in Dative Shift constructions shows direct object-like properties on a par with the applied object, so that *Mary was given a book* and *A book was given Mary* are both acceptable, there are languages where the basic object of applicatives also shows direct-object-like properties. Baker accounts for these differences in terms of parameters relating to the Case properties of verbs in various languages, on a par with his account for similar differences in causatives.

Note finally that, contrary to the cases of N and V incorporation discussed above, there is no morphological relationship between the preposition in (79a) and the applied morpheme in (79a). In the N and V incorporation cases, the same (recognizable) root appears in both the incorporation examples and their non-incorporation paraphrases. However, the preposition in (79a) does not seem to be morphologically related to the applied morpheme in (79b). Baker argues that this difference simply reflects the fact that the preposition in (79b) is an affix, whereas the one in (79a) is not. Because the preposition in (79b) is an affix, it is forced to attach to the verb by virtue of an interaction between its morphological selectional properties and the following condition:

83. **Stray Affix Filter**
    *X if X is a lexical item whose morphological subcategorization frame is not satisfied at S-structure.

The preposition in (59a) is not an affix, and therefore is not forced to incorporate into the verb, and hence (59a), unlike (59b), is not an applicative construction.

V-incorporation in morphological causatives could also be attributed to the same reason. In morphological causatives the causative verb tends to be an affix with morphological selectional properties which require it to attach to a verb root. Because lowering processes are generally excluded in Baker's system, it is the causativized verb which moves up to the causative verb in the root clause, rather than the other way round. It should be emphasized, however, that not all cases of incorporation in Baker's system are attributed to (83). For example, causatives in Romance are known to have properties similar to those of morphological causatives, in so far as the causative and the causativized verbs must be adjacent, with the causee preceded by the preposition 'to' in causatives of transitive verbs (e.g. Aissen, 1979; Comrie, 1976; Kayne, 1975). Yet one would be hard-pressed to call the causative verb in Romance an affix, as it has the properties of an independent word. Likewise, in the cases of N-incorporation discussed above, the incorporating noun is not an affix but a root, so that the complexes derived by the incorporation of these nouns into the verb are like those of compounds.

9.4.4   Summary

N-incorporation, morphological causatives, and applicatives, among other phenomena not discussed here, seem amenable to a syntactic analysis in terms of head-to-head movement (Incorporation), in so far as the domains of incorporation parallel those of Move-α. The apparent changes in the grammatical functions of certain 'noun phrases' triggered by incorporation processes can be attributed to a rearrangement in government relations which follows from the process of incorporation, rather than to a change in the structural positions of those 'noun phrases'.

9.5 I-Lowering and V-Raising: The Split INFL Hypothesis

This section is concerned with certain cross-linguistic differences relating to word order. The focus of the discussion will be the order of the verb (both finite and non-finite) in relation to VP-adverbs and negation elements in English and French. A comparison of the relevant facts in the two languages will reveal that the structure of the sentence adopted so far needs a radical revision, affecting mainly the constituent elements of I. The discussion in this chapter is mainly based on Chomsky (1991c) and Pollock (1989).

9.5.1 Weak versus Strong AgrS and Economy

In Chapters 3 and 4 we saw that English instantiates both I-lowering to V (Affix-hopping) and V-raising to I, the former with main verbs and the latter with auxiliary verbs:

84a. John often kisses Mary
84b. [$_{IP}$ *John* [$_{I'}$ t$_i$ [$_{VP}$ *often* [$_{VP}$ *kiss*+[I]$_i$ *Mary*]]]]

85a. *John kisses often Mary
85b. *[$_{IP}$ *John* [$_{I'}$ I+[*kiss*]$_i$ [$_{VP}$ *often* [$_{VP}$ t$_i$ *Mary*]]]]

86a. John has completely lost his mind
86b. [$_{IP}$ *John* [$_{I'}$ I+[$_V$ *have*] [$_{VP}$ *completely* [$_{VP}$ t$_i$ *lost his mind*]]]]

87a. *John completely has lost his mind
87b. *[$_{IP}$ *John* [$_{I'}$ t$_i$ [$_{VP}$ *completely* [$_{VP}$ *have*+[I]$_i$ *lost his mind*]]]]

(84) and (85) show that only I-lowering is possible with main verbs, and (86) and (87) show that only V-raising is possible with auxiliary verbs. Now, compare the English examples in (84–87) to their French counterparts below:

88a. *Jean souvent embrasse Marie
    Jean often kisses Marie
88b. *[$_{IP}$ *Jean* [$_{I'}$ t$_i$ [$_{VP}$ *souvent* [$_{VP}$ *embrasser*+[I]$_i$ *Marie*]]]]

89a. Jean embrasse souvent Marie
    Jean kisses often Marie
89b. [$_{IP}$ *Jean* [$_{I'}$ I+[$_V$ *embrasser*]$_i$ [$_{VP}$ *souvent* [$_{VP}$ t$_i$ *Marie*]]]]

90a. Jean a complètement perdu la tête
    Jean has completely lost his head
90b. [$_{IP}$ *Jean* [$_{I'}$ I+[$_V$ *avoir*]$_i$ [$_{VP}$ *complètement* [$_{VP}$ t$_i$ *perdu la tête*]]]]

91a. *Jean complètement a perdu la tête
    Jean completely has lost the head
91b. *[$_{IP}$ *Jean* [$_{I'}$ t$_i$ [$_{VP}$ *complètement* [$_{VP}$ *avoir*+[I]$_i$ *perdu la tête*]]]]

(88) and (89) show that the situation with main verbs in French is the reverse of that found in English. While in English main verbs do not raise to I, in French they do so obligatorily. (90) and (91) show that there is no contrast between French and English with

respect to auxiliary verbs. Auxiliary verbs obligatorily move to I in both languages. Examples (88–91) also show that there is no contrast between main verbs and auxiliary verbs in finite clauses.

To account for the contrast between main verbs in English and French, and the similar behaviour of auxiliary verbs in the two languages, Pollock (1989) capitalizes on the difference in categorial nature between the complex heads derived by V-raising to I and I-lowering to V, together with an assumption bearing on the nature of AgrS in the two languages. V-raising to I results in the derivation of a complex I, given that I is the host (i.e. the category adjoined to). However, I-lowering to V results in the derivation of a complex V, given that in this case V is the host (Chapter 4). The two complex head structures are shown in (92a) and (92b).

92a. I-lowering

$[_V V + [I]]$

92b. V-raising

$[_I [V] + I]$

The assumption bearing on the nature of AgrS in the two languages is as follows. In English AgrS (or I) is 'opaque', possibly on account of its largely abstract nature. The 'opaque' nature of English I has the effect of 'confining' categories adjoined to it, in such a way that they cannot transmit their lexical properties to their arguments. In contrast, French AgrS (or I) is 'transparent', possibly on account of its comparatively less abstract nature (the plural paradigm). The 'transparent' nature of French I means that it does not confine lexical categories adjoined to it, contrary to its English counterpart. Let us now see how these assumptions account for the data above, starting with English.

Example (85) involves movement and adjunction of the main verb to I. Because English I is 'opaque' the main verb is confined, and consequently cannot transmit its thematic roles to its arguments. Thus this example is excluded on the grounds that the arguments of the verb fail to be assigned a thematic role, and therefore fail to satisfy the Theta-Criterion. On a more general level, main verbs in English cannot raise to I because if they do so they will be confined inside an 'opaque' I which will prevent them from transmitting thematic roles to their arguments. In contrast, the process of I-lowering, involved in the derivation of (84), does not result in the confinement of V, as V itself is the host in this situation (92a). Consequently, V can assign its thematic roles to its arguments. Example (86) involves movement of an auxiliary verb to I, deriving a complex I in which the auxiliary verb is confined. However, because auxiliary verbs do not assign thematic roles (they do not take arguments), their confinement inside the English 'opaque' I does not give rise to a similar violation. This is precisely the reason why auxiliary verbs can move to I, contrary to main verbs. What remains to be explained is example (87), that is why I-lowering is not possible with auxiliary verbs. We shall return to this point below. Let us now discuss parallel examples in French.

Recall that French differs from English in that its I is 'transparent'. Consequently, although the head complex derived by V-movement to I is the one shown in (92b), I does not prevent the verb from transmitting its thematic roles to its arguments. It is for this reason that movement of main verbs to I is possible in French, accounting for example (89). Note that, since French I is 'transparent' anyway, we expect auxiliary verbs to be able to move to I as well, as shown in (90). What we still need to account for is the fact that I-lowering is excluded with both main verbs and auxiliary verbs, as shown in (88) and (91).

This is related to the fact that I-lowering is also excluded with auxiliary verbs in English. The generalization which underlies these facts is that V-raising is obligatory whenever it is possible. Because V-raising is possible with main verbs in French, and because it is possible with auxiliary verbs in both French and English, it is obligatory.

To explain this generalization, let us have a closer look at the S-structure representation of the English example (84), reproduced here:

93a. John often kisses Mary
93b. $[_{IP}$ *John* $[_{I'}$ t_i $[_{VP}$ *often* $[_{VP}$ *kiss* $+ [I]_i$ *Mary*]]]]

Chomsky (1991c) remarks that this representation involves an ill-formed chain, where the trace of the lowered I is not c-commanded, and therefore not antecedent-governed, by I. Since head-traces can only satisfy the ECP via antecedent-government, (93) technically involves an ECP violation, although the sentence is grammatical. Assuming that ECP holds at LF (Chapter 8), Chomsky suggests that the derivation of (85) involves an additional head-movement step at LF, whereby the complex $[V + I]$ raises to I, resulting in the elimination of the 'offending' trace in I. The derived LF-representation is roughly as shown in (94):

94. $[_{IP}$ *John* $[_{I'}$ $[kiss + I]_i$ $[_{VP}$ *often* $[_{VP}$ t_i *Mary*]]]]

The head-movement process which applies at LF is basically 'corrective' in nature, in the sense that it is intended to 'correct' chains that would otherwise not satisfy the conditions on chain formation (ECP) applying at LF.

Let us now return to the examples where I-lowering gives rise to ungrammaticality, using the French example for illustration:

95a. *Jean souvent embrasse Marie
    Jean   often   kisses   Marie
95b. *S-str: $[_{IP}$ *Jean* $[_{I'}$ t_i $[_{VP}$ *souvent* $[_{VP}$ *embrasser* $+ [I]_i$ *Marie*]]]]

95c. LF: $[_{IP}$ *Jean* $[_{I'}$ $[embrasser + I]_i$ $[_{VP}$ *souvent* $[_{VP}$ t_i *Marie*]]]]

Like the S-structure of (84) above, (95b) involves an ill-formed chain, where the trace is not antecedent-governed by the lowered I. Initially, this may seem to be the reason for the ungrammatical status of (95a). However, it could be argued that, since ECP is 'checked' at LF, the derivation of (95a) can be assumed to involve an additional head-movement process at LF, on a par with that of (84), so that the LF-representation of (95) is as in (95c). If this derivation were possible, the ungrammatical status of (95a) would remain mysterious. Therefore, the derivation outlined in (95b,c) has to be excluded, while maintaining the parallel derivation for the English example (85).

Chomsky has suggested a condition on derivations called the 'least effort' condition, understood as part of an overarching principle of **economy of derivation**. The interpretation of this condition relevant to the present discussion is that 'shorter derivations are always chosen over longer ones'. This is to say that, in a situation where more than one derivation is possible for a given sentence, the one which involves less (movement) steps is chosen over the others. Recall that the grammatical version of (95a) (*Jean embrasse souvent Marie*) is derived by V-movement to I (overt raising), I in French being 'transparent'. The chain derived by this movement is well-formed, and therefore no 'corrective' head-movement is required at LF. In contrast, the derivation of (95a) with a well formed chain requires a 'corrective' movement at LF, shown in (95c), and therefore involves one extra movement step. For this reason, this derivation is excluded by the 'least effort' condition, in favour of the derivation which involves overt V-raising, and no subsequent 'corrective' movement at LF.

On a more general level, a derivation which involves overt lowering inevitably involves raising at LF, whereas a derivation which involves overt raising does not. Thus, if overt raising is possible, as is generally the case in French, any alternative derivation which involves overt lowering (and subsequent raising at LF) will be excluded in favour of one which involves legitimate overt raising (and no subsequent raising at LF). The explanation in terms of the 'least effort' condition extends to the impossibility of lowering with auxiliary verbs in both English and French. Because overt raising is always possible with auxiliary verbs, it is obligatory by the 'least effort' condition.

According to the analysis outlined, the parametric difference between English-type languages, sometimes called 'lowering languages', and French-type languages, sometimes called 'raising languages', reduces to a difference in the properties of I, more precisely AgrS. Because English AgrS is 'opaque', main verbs cannot move to it, although auxiliary verbs can, and because French AgrS is 'transparent' both main verbs and auxiliaries can move to it. On the other hand, because main verbs in French and auxiliary verbs in French and English can overtly move to I, they have to move overtly to I by virtue of the 'least effort' condition – the alternative derivation which makes use of overt lowering would involve more steps. Chomsky uses the term 'weak' (instead of 'opaque') for English AgrS, and the term 'strong' (instead of 'transparent') for French AgrS.

9.5.2   Negation: The Neg Phrase

9.5.2.1   Negation in English   Consider the following examples:

96a. John does not like his teacher
96b. $[_{IP}$ *John* $[_{I'}$ $[do]$ + I *not* $[_{VP}$ *like his teacher*$]]]$

97a. *John not likes his teacher
97b. *$[_{IP}$ *John* $[_{I'}$ t_i *not* $[_{VP}$ *like* + $[I]_i$ *his teacher*$]]]$
＿＿＿＿＿＿＿↑

98a. *John likes not his teacher
98b. *$[_{IP}$ *John* $[_{I'}$ $[like]_i$ + I *not* $[_{VP}$ t_i *his teacher*$]]]]$
↑＿＿＿＿＿＿＿

These examples illustrate the fact that the presence of the negative element (Neg) *not* in English sentences with main verbs forces the application of '*Do*-support' (Chapter 3). Somehow, Neg prevents the inflectional elements of I from attaching to the verb, irrespective of whether I lowers to V, as in (97), or V raises to I, as in (98). While (98) can be said to be independently excluded by the fact that main verbs in English never raise to I anyway, it is not clear why (97), where I lowers to V, should be excluded.

So far we have been assuming that Neg is base-generated under I. However, it is not clear whether *not* is an inflectional element of the same order as Tense and AgrS. From a morphological point of view, *not* (at least in its non-contracted form) is an autonomous category, not dependent on a verb as the Tense and AgrS elements tend to be. The strongest evidence for the independence of *not* from I, however, relates to its syntactic behaviour. Pollock (1989) remarks that the blocking effect that *not* has on the process which associates the I elements with the verb (Affix-hopping/I-lowering) seems to suggest that *not* is a head category with its own X-bar projections. On the basis of this observation, among others, Pollock suggests the structure shown in (99) for negative clauses. Given that superficially *not* intervenes between the I elements, 'supported' by the auxiliary *do*, and the main verb, it is natural to assume that NegP is located between I and

99.

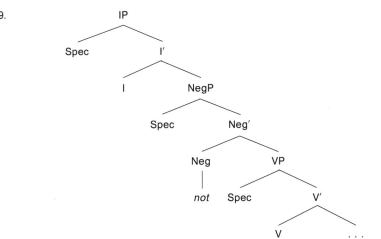

VP. While the head Neg is filled by *not*, it can be assumed either that Spec-NegP is empty or that it does not project at all, specifiers being generally optional unless required to be present by a specific principle.

How does the revised structure (99) explain the fact that Neg prevents the I elements from attaching to the main verb in English? Recall that in affirmative sentences the I elements attach to the main verb via I-lowering to V. Recall also that this movement creates an ill-formed chain, which is subsequently 'corrected' by raising the complex [V + I] to I at LF. Applying this derivation to a negative sentence such as (96) above would yield the following LF representation :

100. [$_{IP}$ *John* [$_{I'}$ [*like* + I]$_i$ [$_{NegP}$ *not* [$_{VP}$ t$_i$ *John*]]]]

Notice that movement of the complex [V + I] to I skips over a distinct head category, Neg, inducing a violation of HMC/ECP – the antecedent is 'too far away' from its trace to antecedent-govern it, owing to the presence of the intervening Neg, which creates a Minimality effect (Chapter 8). Thus a derivation for negative sentences such as *John does not like his teacher* similar to the derivation of its affirmative counterpart *John likes his teacher* is not possible, on the grounds that the 'corrective' head movement process of the complex [V + I] to I at LF gives rise to a violation of HMC/ECP.

In view of this situation, English makes use of the rule of *Do*-support to salvage negative sentences with main verbs. The rule applies at S-structure (or in the mapping from S-structure to PF) and inserts *do* to 'support' the inflectional elements of I which otherwise remain 'stranded' (Chapter 3). *Do*-support is a language-specific rule used as a last resort to save negative sentences which cannot otherwise be derived by a UG-determined process. According to Chomsky (1991c), the use of language-specific rules such as *Do*-support is subject to the 'least effort' condition, such that these rules only apply if UG-determined processes, e.g. head-movement, are blocked. This view of language-specific rules makes it possible to rule out sentences such as **John does like his teacher* with a non-emphatic reading. Because non-emphatic affirmative sentences such as *John likes his teacher* can be derived in terms of head-movement processes, as we have seen, the application of *Do*-support in these sentences is excluded by the 'least effort' condition.

9.5.2.2   Negation   and   Object-agreement   in   French   Compare   the   English   negative
sentences above to their French counterparts below:

101a. Les enfants (n')   aiment   pas   Jean
     the children Neg *like*   Neg *Jean*
101b. [$_{IP}$ *Les enfants* [$_{I'}$ (*n'*) [*aimer*]$_i$ + I *pas* [$_{VP}$ t$_i$ *Jean*]]]

102a. *Les enfants (ne)   pas   aiment   Jean
     the   *children* Neg Neg *like*   *Jean*
102b. *[$_{IP}$ *Les enfants* [$_{I'}$ t$_i$ *ne pas* [$_{VP}$ *aimer* + [I]$_i$ *Jean*]]]

In Standard French, negation in finite clauses is marked with both the pre-verbal element
ne and the post-verbal element *pas*. In Colloquial French, however, the pre-verbal Neg
element tends to be dropped fairly frequently in most contexts, resulting in a situation
where negation is marked with just the post-verbal Neg element *pas*. Contrary to what is
found in English, the presence of Neg in French sentences with a main verb does not
prevent the I elements from attaching to the verb via V-raising to I, as shown in (101).
(102) is derived by I-lowering to V, a step which invariably gives rise to ungrammaticality
in French for the reasons discussed above. Assuming that the French equivalent of the
English *not* is *pas*, it seems that the main verb in French can move across Neg, as shown in
(101b), without giving rise to a HMC/ECP violation, contrary to what is found in
English. To explain why, we need to examine the order of the verb with respect to Neg
and VP-adverbs in non-finite clauses.
     Consider the following examples:

103a. Ne   pas   paraître   triste . . .
     Neg Neg *to-appear   sad*
103b. **Ne paraître pas triste* . . .

104. *Paraître   souvent   triste* . . .
     to-appear   often   sad

The ungrammatical example (103b), where the order is [V *pas*], shows that non-finite
verbs, contrary to their finite counterparts, do not move beyond Neg to I. As shown in
(103a), where the order is [*pas* V], non-finite verbs are confined to a position lower than
Neg. On the other hand, (104), where the order is [V ADV], shows that non-finite verbs
do move outside VP, to a position higher than the VP-adjoined position occupied by the
adverb. When compared to (103a,b), example (104) seems to indicate the presence of an
additional position in the sentence structure which is lower than Neg, as indicated by the
order [Neg V] (103a), and higher than VP, as indicated by the order [V ADV] (104).
     Pollock has suggested that the position in question is Agr, which Chomsky assumes to
be AgrO, rather than AgrS. We have seen that there are languages, such as Chichewa,
which instantiate an overt AgrO morpheme, just as there are languages, such as Italian,
which instantiate an overt AgrS morpheme. The latter fact was invoked in Chapter 4 to
justify the assumption that languages which do not have an overt AgrS category, such as
English, have an abstract counterpart. The argument extends to AgrO in a natural way,
so that languages which do not have an overt AgrO category, such as English, have an
abstract counterpart. As far as French is concerned, there is evidence internal to the
language for the existence of an AgrO category. The evidence relates to the agreement of
participles with preposed objects, discussed in Kayne (1987) in relation to examples such
as the following:

105a. Paul les   a   repeintes
    Paul them (F.PL.) *has repainted* (F.PL.)
105b. Combien de tables   a   Paul   repeintes?
    how-many   tables (F.PL.) *has Paul   repainted* (F.PL.)?

In (105a) the participle agrees with the preposed pronoun in number and gender, and in (105b) it agrees with the moved *wh*-phrase in the same features. To all intents and purposes, this agreement relation between the participle and the object is similar to the agreement relation between the verb and the object discussed above in relation to Chichewa, although the contexts in which object agreement is overtly manifested in French are more restricted. Assuming that all sentences instantiate an AgrO category with its own X-bar projections, and assuming that this category is located immediately above VP, the structure of the sentence (affirmative and negative) is now as shown in (106). Recall that we are assuming that the French counterpart of the English *not* is *pas*, hence the decision to locate it under Neg. The particle *ne* in Standard French can be assumed to occupy Spec-NegP. When the verb moves to I in finite clauses, *ne* cliticizes onto it. Cliticization of the particle *ne* onto the verb under I can be thought of as a phonological process which takes place at PF.

106.

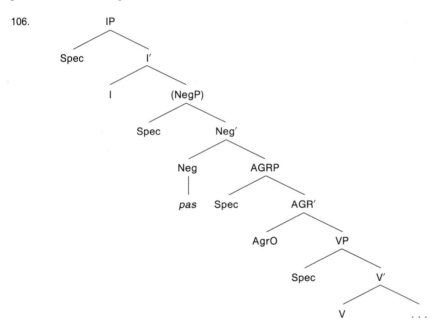

Let us now see how structure (106) accounts for word order in French finite and non-finite clauses, both affirmative and negative. Starting with (104), the order [ADV V] is derived by movement of the verb to AgrO, a process sometimes known as 'short V-movement', with the effect shown in (107):

107. [$_{IP}$ PRO I [$_{AgrOP}$ AgrO + [$_V$ *paraître*]$_i$ [$_{VP}$ *souvent* [$_{VP}$ t$_i$ *triste*]]]]

Moving on (backwards) to (103b), its ungrammatical status suggests that the verb cannot move beyond Neg, to I, in non-finite clauses. This can be attributed to the possibility that non-finite I, like English finite I, and unlike French finite I, is 'weak'. Movement of a main verb to non-finite I in French therefore results in a Theta-Criterion violation along the lines outlined above in relation to main verbs in English finite clauses. The situation in the finite sentence (101), however, is slightly more complicated. A more detailed representation of its S-structure is as follows:

108. [$_{IP}$ *Les enfants* [$_{I'}$ [[*aimer*] + AgrO]$_i$ + I] [$_{NegP}$ *pas* [$_{AgrP}$ t$_{AgrO}$ [$_{VP}$ t$_v$ *Jean*]]]]]

The subscripts associated with the traces are intended to indicate the categorial nature of the trace, crucial to the explanation to be outlined. Recall that movement and adjunction to a head category results in the derivation of a complex structure of the host head category. Thus movement of the verb to AgrO results in the derivation of a complex AgrO category, movement of [[V] + AgrO] to I results in the derivation of a complex I, and so on. Moreover, when the complex [[V] + AgrO] moves to a higher position, the trace left behind is categorially AgrO, when the verb moves to AgrO the trace it leaves behind is categorially V, and so on.

Given the assumption that French finite I is 'strong', the presence of the main verb under I in (108) is legitimate. What is apparently illegitimate is the fact that in moving to I from AgrO, the head-complex has skipped over Neg, a situation which should give rise to an HMC/ECP violation. The 'offending trace' t$_{AgrO}$ fails to be antecedent-governed by the head-complex in I, because of the intervening Neg. Chomsky suggests that the S-structure representation (108) would become legitimate with respect to HMC/ECP if the 'offending trace' were to delete at LF. Underlying this suggestion is the idea that (traces of) elements which do not play a role in the interpretation of sentences, e.g. (traces of) AgrO, are deletable at LF, but (traces of) categories which play a role in determining meaning, e.g. (traces of) verbs, are not deletable at LF. Thus, the reason main verbs can move across Neg in French, according to the analysis outlined, is the availability of the mechanism of trace-deletion at LF. Assuming this to be the case, we now face the following question: Why cannot the same mechanism be used to salvage derivations of ungrammatical negative sentences in English such as (109) below?

109a. *John not likes his teacher
109b. S-str: [$_{IP}$ *Mary* [$_{I'}$ t$_I$ [$_{NegP}$ *not* [$_{AgrP}$ t$_{AgrO}$ [$_{VP}$ *like* + [I] *John*]]]]]

109c. LF: [$_{IP}$ *Mary* [$_{I'}$ [*like* + [I]] [$_{NegP}$ *not* [$_{AgrP}$ t$_V$ [$_{VP}$ t$_V$ *John*]]]]]

Recall that, with main verbs in English, I lowers to V in the Syntax, deriving the S-structure (109b). Since this structure involves an ill-formed chain, a raising process applies at LF, deriving the LF-representation (109c). The difference between overt V-raising and V-raising at LF is that the latter is not an adjunction movement but a substitution one. Because AgrO has already been adjoined to V in the lowering process, raising of the complex [V + [I]] to AgrO at LF is not, strictly speaking, adjunction to AgrO, since AgrO is not there any more. Instead, the LF-movement of the complex [V + [I]] to AgrO results in a substitution of the trace occupying it. Recall that the prime motivation of raising at LF is to eliminate 'offending traces'. It follows from this situation that the trace left subsequent to movement of the complex [V + [I]] to I, across Neg, is a verb trace (not an AgrO trace), as shown in (109c). Because the trace in question is that of a category, i.e. the verb, which plays a role in determining meaning, it cannot delete at LF. It is for this reason that the trace-deletion strategy does not salvage English negative sentences such as (109a).

On a general level, because the derivation of French (negative) sentences involves straightforward overt raising, the trace in AgrO is invariably of the nature t$_{AgrO}$, and therefore deletable at LF. On the other hand, because the derivation of English (negative) sentences involves overt lowering and subsequent raising at LF, the trace in AgrO in the

LF-representation is of the nature t_V, and therefore not deletable. Since this trace is the 'offending trace', an HMC/ECP violation is involved.

9.5.3 AgrS, AgrO, and Structural Case

9.5.3.1 AgrS and Tense The move to dissociate Neg from I and assign it the status of a head category in its own right removes one of the major anomalies of the I category with respect to the principles of X-bar Theory. In the previous structure of the sentence, the 'dual headedness' of I, as dominating inflectional categories as well as non-inflectional ones, was inconsistent with the one-to-one relation between categories and projections implicit in X-bar Theory. In the previous section, we discussed empirical reasons which indicate that Neg behaves syntactically like an independent head category, rather than like a member of the category I. Similarly, the postulation of an AgrO category which projects its own X-bar structure is motivated on both theoretical and empirical grounds, the latter having to do with 'short movement' evident in French non-finite clauses.

The structure of the sentence which has emerged from these major revisions is one where I dominates AgrS and Tense only. However, it could be argued that the 'dual headedness' problem is not entirely eliminated, as I still dominates two arguably distinct categories: AgrS and Tense. The logic of the argument of dismantling the I category, sometimes referred to as the **Split INFL Hypothesis**, seems logically to lead to a situation where AgrS and Tense are also each assigned an autonomous categorial status. This means that AgrS heads a maximal projection of its own (AgrSP), and Tense a maximal projection of its own (T(ense)P). Accepting the logic of the argument, the question arises as to how these two categories are ordered with respect to each other: is AgrS higher than T or vice versa?

Belletti (1990) has argued that the order of AgrS and T in finite verbal complexes in Italian suggests that AgrS is higher than T:

110a. Legg-eva-no
      read-T(imperfect)-AgrS (1pl.)
      'They read'
110b. Parl-er-o
      speak-T(future)-AgrS(1s.)
      'I will speak.'

In both examples the T morpheme is closer to the verb root than the AgrS morpheme, suggesting that the verb adjoins to T first, forming with it the complex [[V] + T], which then adjoins to AgrS to derive the surface complex [[[V] + T] + AgrS]. Note that, by virtue of HMC/ECP, which prevents a head from moving across another head, the fact that V attaches to T first implies that T is lower than AgrS. Accordingly, the structure of the sentence as in (111). Although (111) is based on the order of inflectional morphemes in Italian, it is plausible to assume that other languages such as English instantiate the same order and, therefore, the same structure of the sentence. Negative clauses instantiate NegP in addition to the categories in (111), although as far as NegP is concerned there seems to be a certain degree of variation among languages as to its hierarchical position (Belletti, 1990).

9.5.3.2 Structural Accusative and Spec-Head Agreement In Chapter 6 a distinction was made between two types of Case, inherent and structural. Inherent Case is determined at D-structure, and involves a thematic relationship between the assigner and the assignee. Structural Case, on the other hand, is determined at S-structure, and does not necessarily

111.

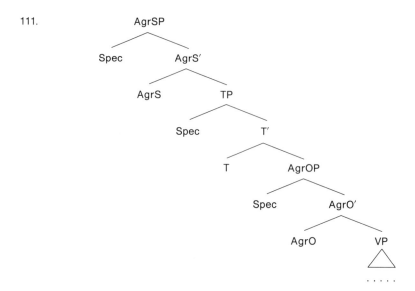

involve a thematic relationship between the assigner and the assignee. The structural Cases are nominative, accusative, and possibly also genitive, assigned to subjects of 'noun phrases' via Spec-Head Agreement with (the Agr category of) D. Restricting ourselves to nominative and accusative, the former was said to be assigned under Spec-Head Agreement with (the AgrS category of) I, and the latter under government by a transitive verb. It is desirable to have a unified approach to structural Case, such that all structural Cases are assigned under the same condition, Spec-Head Agreement. This unified approach was not possible in the context of the previous structure of the sentence, as it did not include an AgrO category parallel to the AgrS category. However, now that the structure of the sentence has been revised to included an AgrO category, accusative Case can also be said to be assigned under Spec-Head Agreement with AgrO, just as nominative Case is assigned under Spec-Head Agreement with AgrS.

In the context of the new structure, both agreement in features and structural Case can in fact be considered to be (overt) manifestations of Spec-Head relations. This means that a given DP which agrees with AgrS and bears nominative Case is a DP which is (structurally) in a Spec-Head relation with AgrS, and a DP which agrees with AgrO and receives structural accusative is a DP which is in a Spec-Head relation with AgrO. In Chapter 6 it was pointed out that nominative Case was not, strictly speaking, assigned. Case is encoded in the form of a feature in both (the D head of) DP and AgrS, and nominative Case-assignment basically amounts to an agreement relation between AgrS and the DP in Spec-IP (now Spec-AgrSP) which includes other agreement features such as person, gender, and number. The same point can now be made about direct objects in relation to AgrO, so that accusative Case is not actually assigned, but simply reveals that the object and AgrO are (structurally) in a Spec-Head relation.

A radical implication of the idea that structural accusative is a manifestation of a Spec-Head Agreement relation, which we are not going to pursue here, is that (transitive) verbs do not assign structural accusative, contrary to traditional belief. The implication which we shall try to pursue here briefly is that DPs bearing structural accusative must be in the Spec position of AgrOP at some level of representation, presumably, the level where the Case features are 'checked'. This is true not only for direct objects but also for ECM subjects, so that in a sentence like *I believe John to be clever*, the ECM subject must be in Spec-AgrOP at some level of representation; effectively, raising-to-object. Presumably

DPs reach this position as a result of DP-movement from their thematic (D-structure) position, similar to the movement of the subject from Spec-VP (the thematic subject position) to Spec-IP (now Spec-AgrSP). On the assumption that the VP-internal thematic object position and the ECM subject position are non-Case-marked, and that Spec-AgrOP, like Spec-AgrSP, is an A-position, the chain derived is an A-chain where the head occupies the Case-marked position and the root the theta-marked position. What we need to do next is reconcile the idea that direct objects 'receive' Case in Spec-AgrOP with the idea that, in English, main verbs, and consequently their direct objects, do not leave VP at S-structure (*John (often) kisses (*often) Mary*). Note with respect to structure (111) that, if the direct object is in Spec-AgrOP, the verb must be higher than at least AgrO for the English VO order to be derived.

The inconsistency between the assumption that structural accusative is 'assigned' under Spec-Head Agreement with AgrO and the fact that main verbs in English do not move out of VP at S-structure will arguably disappear if it is assumed that the Case Requirement does not have to be satisfied at S-structure, but at LF, as would be plausible in the context of the Visibility Hypothesis (Chapter 6). Thus the main verb and its direct object remain inside VP at S-structure, and the I elements lower to V, as we have seen. Recall that the [V + I] complex raises out of VP at LF to 'correct' the chain derived by lowering of the I elements to V. It is plausible to assume that at this level the direct object also raises to Spec-AgrOP where it is 'assigned' structural accusative or, more accurately, where its accusative Case feature is 'checked' against the accusative Case feature of AgrO. This would make it possible to exclude examples such as **John saw she* in terms of Spec-Head Agreement (the Case features of the DP object and AgrO are different), on a par with Standard English examples such as **The children knows John*. In languages which have overt V-raising, such as French, the direct object can also be said to raise to Spec-AgrOP at S-structure. There seems to be a correlation between (overt) V-raising and (overt) object-raising (Object Shift), which has been noted and discussed by Holmberg (1986) with respect to Germanic languages (see also Vikner, 1990).

9.5.3.3 *Summary* Differences between languages in the order of the verb in relation to VP-adverbs and Neg elements can be accounted for in terms of a parameter relating to the 'strength' and 'weakness' of AgrS. In English-type languages AgrS is 'weak', and therefore the verb cannot move to it, whereas in French-type languages AgrS is 'strong', and consequently the verb must move to it. Derivations are guided by an overarching principle of economy, which has the effect of forcing the choice of 'economical' derivations over the less 'economical' ones. The investigation of the way V-movement processes interact with I-elements, together with certain theoretical considerations, has led to a major revision of the structure of the sentence, such that each of the categories previously thought to belong under I projects its own X-bar structure (the Split INFL Hypothesis).

9.6 Conclusions and Revisions

In this chapter we have addressed the question of how the theory outlined in this book, the Principles and Parameters Theory, accounts for the fact that languages, though similar at a deep and abstract level, show systematic variation affecting various aspects of their grammars. That languages are indeed similar at an abstract level has been demonstrated in this chapter by showing that certain abstract principles reached in the previous chapters on the basis of an in-depth study of English do indeed hold for other languages, although in some cases this may not seem to be the case initially.

We have seen that in the Principles and Parameters Theory, cross-linguistic variation is accounted for in terms of parameters, which are basically sets of well-defined options each of which yields a different pattern. For example, differences in the order of complements in relation to their heads are accounted for in terms of a binary set of options relating to left- and right- selection, and the difference between languages which front *wh*-phrases and languages which do not are accounted for in terms of another binary set of options relating to *wh*-movement. Various other aspects of cross-linguistic variation can be accounted for in terms of relevant sets of options, although in some cases it is not clear exactly how the options (the parameter) should be defined.

A substantial number of parameters discussed in this chapter seem to indicate that parameters are associated with individual categories, rather than with the general principles of UG. Moreover, most of the differences seem to be determined by the properties of the members of the closed-class system (functional categories), long recognized as the elements which harbour language-particular characteristics.

Further Reading

This chapter, unlike the previous ones, cites a number of major bibliographical sources in the main text. Further reading relating to the various issues discussed can be pursued through the major relevant sources cited. This section will be used to cite references relating to other syntactic issues involving parameters which, unfortunately, could not be discussed owing to limitations on space.

One of the major issues, often referred to in the literature as **Configurationality**, deals with the difference between languages which allow a relative or considerable freedom of ordering constituents and languages with rigid word order. Among the relevant references are Mohanan (1982), Hale (1983), Jelinek (1984), Saito and Hoji (1983), Saito (1985), Horvath (1986), E-Kiss (1987), Maracz (1989), and papers in Kenesei (1985; 1987).

A related issue is often referred to in the literature as **Scrambling**, a term introduced in Ross (1967) to account for languages with 'free word order'. For a general discussion of scrambling and the various theories put forward to deal with it, see the introduction to Grewendorf and Stenerfeld (1990), a volume which includes articles and references on scrambling, though mainly in relation to the Germanic languages.

The distribution and behaviour of **Clitics** (morphologically dependent pronouns) has received considereable attention in the literature. On clitics in the Romance languages see Kayne (1975; 1984; 1989), Jaeggli (1981), Rizzi (1982; 1986b), among others. On clitics in the Semitic languages see Aoun (1982), Borer (1984c), among others.

A substantial amount of recent work on **Diachronic Syntax** (Historical Linguistics) is guided by the idea that diachronic variation involves a process of (re)setting relevant parameters. In this context see Lightfoot (1979; 1981; 1991), Adamson *et al.* (1990), Pearce (1990), and references cited therein.

Recent work on **First-Language (L1) Development** has also been guided by the idea that acquisition involves a process of fixing parameters (Chomsky, 1981; 1986a). The implications for research on first-language development of the shift towards a theory based on principles and parameters are discussed in Williams (1987). Among the recent volumes which include papers written from this perspective are Roeper and Williams (1987), Frazier and De Villiers (1990), and Weissenborn *et al.* (1992). Among the major issues currently debated is whether the early stages of acquisition involve a full structure of the sentence (the Continuity Hypothesis) or a reduced structure which subsequently matures into a full structure (the Maturation Hypothesis). For different views on this issue see Pierce (1989), Radford (1990), and Tsimpli (1992). Overviews on research on first-language development can be found in Goodluck (1991) and Atkinson (1992).

A parallel development has taken place in research on **Second-Language (L2) Development**. Among the volumes which include papers on this subject are Flynn and O'Neil (1988), Pankhurst *et al.* (1988), and Gass and Schachter (1989). See also Flynn (1987) and White (1989). For a different view, see Smith and Tsimpli (1991) and Tsimpli and Roussou (1991).

Research on **Sign Language** has also recently produced valuable contributions to our understanding of human languages and to the development of the principles and parameters theory. Among the volumes which include relevant papers are Edmondson and Karlsson (1990), Fischer and Siple (1990), Lucas (1990). See also Lillo-Martin (1991) and references cited therein.

There is substantial literature on **Linguistic Aphasiology (Neuro(psycho)linguistics)**, in particular agrammatism in Broca's aphasia. For an overview of the major issues and references see Caplan (1987) and the introduction to Menn and Obler (1990). For analyses of agrammatic speech in the context of the Principles and Parameters theory, see Grodzinsky (1990) and references cited therein. For an attempt to raise the issue relating to the status of parameters in Agrammatism, see Ouhalla (1993).

Bibliography

Abney, S. (1987). *The English Noun Phrase in its Sentential Aspect*. Doctoral dissertation, MIT, Cambridge, Mass.

Adamson, S., Law, V., Vincent, N., and Wright, W. (eds) (1990). *Papers from the Fifth International Conference on English Historical Linguistics*. Amsterdam: Benjamins.

Aissen, J. (1979). *The Syntax of Causative Constructions*. New York: Garland Press.

Akmajian, A., and Heny, F. W. (1975). *An Introduction to the Principles of Transformational Grammar*. Cambridge, Mass.: MIT Press.

—— Steele, S., and Wasow, T. (1979). 'The Category AUX in Universal Grammar', *Linguistic Inquiry* 10, 1–64.

Allwood, J., Andersson, L. G., and Dahl, Ö. (1977). *Logic in Linguistics*. Cambridge: Cambridge University Press.

Aoun, J. (1982). *The Formal Nature of Anaphoric Relations*. Doctoral dissertation, MIT, Cambridge, Mass.

—— (1985). *A Grammar of Anaphora*. Cambridge, Mass.: MIT Press.

—— (1986). *Generalized Binding*. Dordrecht: Foris.

—— Hornstein, N., and Sportiche, D. (1981). 'Some Aspects of Wide Scope Quantification', *Journal of Linguistic Research* 1, 69–95.

—— and Li, Y. A. (1991). 'The Interaction of Operators', in R. Freidin (ed.), *Principles and Parammeters in Comparative Grammar*. Cambridge, Mass.: MIT Press, 163–81.

—— and Sportiche, D. (1983). 'On the Formal Theory of Government', *Linguistic Review* 2, 211–36.

Aronoff, M. (1976). *Word Formation in Generative Grammar*. Cambridge, Mass.: MIT Press.

Atkinson, M. (1992). *Children's Syntax: An Introduction to Principles and Parameters Theory*. Oxford: Blackwell.

Authier, J.-M. (1988). 'Null Object Constructions in Kinande', *Natural Language and Linguistic Theory* 6, 19–37.

—— (1989). 'Two Types of Empty Operator', *Linguistic Inquiry* 20, 117–25.

Awbery, G. (1976). *The Syntax of Welsh*. Cambridge: Cambridge University Press.

Baker, C. L. (1970). 'Notes on the Description of English Questions: The Role of an Abstract Question Morpheme', *Foundations of Language* 6, 197–219.

—— (1978). *Introduction to Generative-Transformational Syntax*. Englewood Cliffs, NJ: Prentice-Hall.

Baker, M. C. (1988). *Incorporation: A Theory of Grammatical Function Changing*. Chicago: University of Chicago Press.

—— Johnson, K., and Roberts, I. (1989). 'Passive Arguments Raised', *Linguistic Inquiry* 20, 219–51.

Baltin, M. (1983). 'Extraposition: Bounding versus Government-Binding', *Linguistic Inquiry* 14, 155–62.

Baltin, M. (1984). 'Extraposition Rules and Discontinuous Constituents', *Linguistic Inquiry* 15, 157–63.

Belletti, A. (1988). 'The Case of Unaccusatives', *Linguistic Inquiry* 19, 1–34.

—— (1990). *Generalized Verb Movement*. Turin: Rosenberg & Sellier.

—— and Rizzi, L. (1981). 'The Syntax of *Ne*', *The Linguistic Review* 1, 117–54.

Benmamoun, E. (1992). *Functional and Inflectional Morphology: Problems of Projection, Representation and Derivation*. Doctoral dissertation, University of Southern California, Los Angeles.

Bennis. H., and Hoekstra, T. (1984). 'Gaps and Parasitic Gaps', *Linguistic Review* 4, 29–87.

den Besten, H. (1983). 'On the Interaction of Root Transformations and Lexical Deletive Rules', in W. Abraham (ed.), *On the Formal Syntax of Wesgermania*. Amsterdam: Benjamins, 47–131.

Bierwisch, M. (1963). *Grammatik des deutschen Verbs*. Berlin: Akademie.

Borer, H. (1984a). 'Restrictive Relatives in Modern Hebrew', *Natural Language and Linguistic Theory* 2, 219–60.

—— (1984b). 'The Projection Principle and Rules of Morphology', in C. Jones and P. Sells (eds), *Proceedings of the Fourteenth Annual Meeting of NELS*. Amherst: University of Massachusetts, 16–33.

—— (1984c). *Parametric Syntax: Case Studies in Semitic and Romance Languages*. Dordrecht: Foris.

—— (1986). 'I – Subjects', *Linguistic Inquiry* 17, 375–416.

—— (1989). 'Anaphoric AGR', in O. Jaeggli and K. Safir (eds), *The Null Subject Parameter*. Dordrecht: Kluwer.

Brame, M. (1981). 'The General Theory of Binding and Fusion', *Linguistic Analysis* 7, 277–325.

—— (1982). 'The Head Selector Theory of Lexical Specifications and the Nonexistence of Coarse Categories', *Linguistic Analysis* 10, 321–5.

Bresnan, J. W. (1970). On Complementizers: Toward a Syntactic Theory of Complement Types', *Foundations of Language* 6, 297–321.

—— (1972). *Theory of Complementation in English*. Doctoral dissertation, MIT, Cambridge, Mass.

—— (1976). 'Non-arguments for Raising', *Linguistic Inquiry* 7, 485–501.

—— (1982a). 'Control and Complementation', *Linguistic Inquiry* 13, 343–434.

—— (1982b). *The Mental Representation of Grammatical Relations*. Cambridge, Mass.: MIT Press.

—— and Mchombo, S. (1987). 'Topic, Pronoun and Agreement in Chichewa', *Language* 63, 741–82.

Bromberger, S., and Halle, M. (1991). 'Why Phonology is Different', in A. Kasher (ed.), *The Chomsky Turn*. Oxford: Blackwell, 56–77.

Browning, M. (1987). *Null Operator Constructions*. Doctoral dissertation, MIT, Cambridge, Mass.

Burzio, L. (1986). *Italian Syntax: A Government-Binding Approach*. Dordrecht: Reidel.

Caplan, D. (1987). *Neurolinguistics and Linguistic Aphasiology: An Introduction*. Cambridge: Cambridge University Press.

Chomsky, N. (1957). *Syntactic Structures*. The Hague: Mouton.

—— (1965). *Aspects of the Theory of Syntax*. Cambridge: Cambridge University Press.

—— (1966). *Cartesian Linguistics*. New York: Harper & Row.

—— (1968). *Language and Mind*. New York: Harcourt, Brace & World. (Extended edition, 1972.)

—— (1970). 'Remarks on Nominalizations', in R. Jacobs and P. S. Rosenbaum (eds), *Readings in English Transformational Grammar*. Waltham, Mass.; Ginn.

—— (1972). *Studies on Semantics in Generative Grammar*. The Hague: Mouton.

—— (1973). 'Conditions on Transformations', in S. R. Anderson and P. Kiparsky (eds), *A Festschrift for Morris Halle*. New York: Holt, Rinehart & Winston.

—— (1975a). *Logical Structure of Linguistic Theory*. New York: Plenum.

—— (1975b). *Reflections on Language*. New York: Pantheon.

—— (1977a). *Essays on Form and Interpretation*. New York: North-Holland.

—— (1977b). 'On *Wh*-Movement', in P. Culicover, T. Wasow, and A. Akmajian (eds), *Formal Syntax*. New York: Academic Press.

—— (1980a). *Rules and Representations*. New York: Columbia University Press.

—— (1980b). 'On Binding', *Linguistic Inquiry* 11, 1–46. Reprinted in F. Heny (ed.), *Binding and Filtering*. London: Croom Helm.

—— (1981). *Lectures on Government and Binding*. Dordrecht: Foris.

—— (1982). *Some Concepts and Consequences of the Theory of Government and Binding*. Cambridge, Mass.: MIT Press.

—— (1986a). *Knowledge of Language: Its Nature, Origin and Use*. New York: Praeger.

—— (1986b). *Barriers*. Cambridge, Mass.: MIT Press.

—— (1987a). 'Transformational Grammar: Past, Present and Future', in *Generative Grammar: Its Basis, Development and Prospects*: special issue, *Studies in English Language and Literature*. Kyoto University of Foreign Studies, 33–80.

—— (1987b). *Language in a Psycholinguistic Setting*: special issue of *Sophia Linguistica: Working Papers in Linguistics* 22. Tokyo: Sophia University.

—— (1988). *Language and Problems of Knowledge: The Managua Lectures*. Cambridge, Mass.: MIT Press.

—— (1991a). Linguistics and Adjacent Fields: A Personal View. In A. Kasher (ed.), *The Chomskyan Turn*. Oxford: Blackwell, 3–25.

—— (1991b). 'Linguistics and Cognitive Science: Problems and Mysteries', in A. Kasher (ed.), *The Chomskyan Turn*. Oxford: Blackwell, 26–55.

—— (1991c). 'Some Notes on Economy of Representation and Derivation', in R. Freidin (ed.), *Principles and Parameters in Comparative Grammar*. Cambridge, Mass.: MIT Press, 417–54.

—— Huybregts, R., and van Riemsdijk, H. (1982). *The Generative Enterprise*. Dordrecht: Foris.

—— and Lasnik, H. (1977). 'Filters and Control', *Linguistic Inquiry* 8, 425–504.

Comrie, B. (1976). 'The Syntax of Causative Constructions: Cross-Language Similarities and Divergences', in M. Shibatani (ed.), *The Grammar of Causative Constructions*. New York: Academic Press.

Culicover, P. W., and Wilkins, W. (1984). *Locality in Linguistic Theory*. New York: Academic Press.

Curtiss, S. (1977). *Genie: A Psycholinguistic Study of a Modern-Day 'Wild Child'*. New York: Academic Press.

—— (1981). 'Dissociations between Language and Cognition: Cases and Implications', *Journal of Autism and Developmental Disorders* II.1.

—— (1982). 'Developmental Dissociations of Language and Cognition', in L. K. Obler and L. Menn (eds), *Exceptional Language and Linguistics*. New York: Academic Press, 285–312.

—— (1988). 'Abnormal Language Acquisition and Grammar: Evidence for the Modularity of Language', in L. Hyman and C. Li (eds), *Language, Speech and Mind: Studies in Honour of Victoria A. Fromkin*. London: Routledge & Kegan Paul, 81–102.

Czepulch, H. (1982). 'Case History and the Dative Alternation', *Linguistic Review* 2, 1–38.

Diesing, M. (1990). 'Verb Movement and the Subject Position in Yiddish', *Natural Language and Linguistic Theory* 8, 41–79.

Di Sciullo, A.-M., and Williams, E. (1987). *On the Definition of Word*. Cambridge, Mass.: MIT Press.

Dougherty, R. (1969). 'An Interpretive Theory of Pronominal Reference', *Foundations of Language* 5, 488–508.

Durand, J. (1990). *Generative and Non-linear Phonology*. London: Longman.

Edmondson, W. H., and Karlsson, F. (eds) (1990). *Papers from the Fourth International Symposium on Sign Language Research*. Hamburg: Signum.

Emonds, J. E. (1970). *Root and Structure Preserving Transformations*. Doctoral dissertation, MIT, Cambridge, Mass.

—— (1976). *A Transformational Approach to English Syntax: Root, Structure Preserving and Local Transformations*. New York: Academic Press.

Emonds, J. E. (1978). 'The Verbal Complex V′–V in French', *Linguistic Inquiry* 21, 49–77.

—— (1980). 'Word Order in Generative Grammar', *Journal of Linguistic Research* 1, 33–54.

Engdahl, E. (1983). 'Parasitic Gaps', *Linguistics and Philosophy* 6, 5–34.

—— (1985) 'Parasitic Gaps, Resumptive Pronouns and Subject Extractions', *Linguistics* 23, 3–44.

Fabb, N. (1984). *Syntactic Affixation*. Doctoral dissertation, MIT, Cambridge, Mass.

Fassi Fehri, A. (1980). 'Some Complement Phenomena in Arabic, the Complementizer Phrase Hypothesis, and the Non-accessibility Condition', Analyse/Théorie, 54–114. Université de Paris VIII, Vincennes.

Fiengo, R. W. (1977). 'On Trace Theory', *Linguistic Inquiry* 8, 35–61.

—— Huang, C.-T., Lasnik, H., and Reinhart, T. (1988). 'The Syntax of *Wh*-in-situ', *Proceedings of the Seventh West Coast Conference on Formal Linguistics*, 81–98.

Fischer, S., and Siple, P. (1990). *Theoretical Issues in Sign Language Research*, i. Chicago: University of Chicago Press.

Flynn, S. (1987). *A Parameter-Setting Model of L2 Acquisition*. Dordrecht: Reidel.

—— and O'Neil, W. (eds) (1988). *Linguistic Theory in Second Language Acquisition*. Dordrecht: Kluwer.

Fodor, J. D. (1982). *Semantics: Theories of Meaning in Generative Grammar*. Brighton: Harvester Press.

Fodor, J. A. (1983). *The Modularity of Mind*. Cambridge, Mass.: MIT Press.

Frampton, J. (1989). 'Parasitic Gaps and the Theory of *Wh*-Chains', *Linguistic Inquiry* 21, 49–77.

Frazier, L., and de Villiers, J. (eds) (1990). *Language Acquisition and Language Processing*. Dordrecht: Reidel.

Freidin, R. (1975). 'The Analysis of Passives', *Language* 51, 384–405.

—— (1978). 'Cyclicity and the Theory of Grammar', *Linguistic Inquiry* 9, 519–49.

Fromkin, V., and Rodman, R. (1988). *An Introduction to Language*, 4th edn. New York: Holt, Rinehart & Winston.

Gass, S. M., and Schachter, J. (1989). *Linguistic Perspectives on Second Language Acquisition*. Cambridge: Cambridge University Press.

Gibson, J. (1980). *Clause Union in Chamorro and in Universal Grammar*. Doctoral dissertation, University of California, San Diego.

Giorgi, A., and Longobardi, G. (1991). *The Syntax of Noun Phrases: Configuration, Parameters and Empty Categories*. Cambridge: Cambridge University Press.

Goldsmith, J. A. (1990). *Autosegmental and Metrical Phonology*. Oxford: Blackwell.

Goodluck, H. (1991). *Language Acquisition: A Linguistic Introduction*. Oxford: Blackwell.

Green, M. G. (1974). *Semantics and Syntactic Regularity*. Bloomington: Indiana University Press.

Grewendorf, G. (1988). *Aspekte der deutschen Syntax*. Tubingen: Narr.

—— and Stenerfeld, W. (eds) (1990). *Scrambling and Barriers*. Amsterdam: Benjamins.

Grimshaw, J. (1981). 'Form, Function and the Language Acquisition Device', in C. L. Baker and J. McCarthy (eds), *The Logical Problem of Language Acquisition*. Cambridge, Mass.: MIT Press.

—— (1990). *Argument Structure*. Cambridge, Mass.: MIT Press.

Grodzinsky, Y. (1990). *Theoretical Perspectives on Language Deficits*. Cambridge, Mass.: MIT Press.

Gruber, J. S. (1965). *Studies in Lexical Relations*. Doctoral dissertation, MIT, Cambridge, Mass.

—— (1976). *Lexical Structures in Syntax and Semantics*. Amsterdam: North-Holland.

Guéron, J. (1980). 'On the Syntax and Semantics of PP Extraposition', *Linguistic Inquiry* 11, 637–78.

—— and May, R. (1984). 'Extraposition and Logical Form', *Linguistic Inquiry* 15, 1–31.

Haegeman, L. (1986). 'INFL, COMP and Nominative Case Assignment in Flemish Infinitivals', in P. Muysken and H. van Riemsdijk (eds), *Features and Projections*. Dordrecht: Foris, 123–37.

—— (1991). *Introduction to Government and Binding Theory*. Oxford: Blackwell.

Hale, K. (1983). 'Walpiri and the Grammar of Non-Configurational Languages', *Language and Linguistic Theory* 1, 1–43.

Heny, F., and Richards, B. (1983). *Linguistic Categories: Auxiliaries and Related Puzzles*. Dordrecht: Reidel.

Higginbotham, J. (1980). 'Pronouns and Bound Variables', *Linguistic Inquiry* 11, 679–708.

—— (1985). 'On Semantics', *Linguistic Inquiry* 16, 547–93.

—— and May, R. (1981). 'Questions, Quantifiers and Crossing', *Linguistic Review* 7, 129–67.

Holmberg, A. (1986). *Word Order and Syntactic Features in the Scandinavian Languages and English*. Doctoral dissertation, University of Stockholm.

Hornstein, M., and Weinberg, A. (1981). 'Case Theory and Preposition Stranding', *Linguistic Inquiry* 12, 55–99.

Horrocks, G., and Stavrou, M. (1987). 'Bounding Theory and Greek Syntax: Evidence for *Wh*-movement in NP', *Journal of Linguistics* 23, 79–108.

Horvath, J. (1986). *Aspects of the Theory of Grammar and the Syntax of Hungarian*. Dordrecht: Foris.

Huang, C.-T., J. (1982). *Logical Relations in Chinese and the Theory of Grammar*. Doctoral dissertation, MIT, Cambridge, Mass.

—— (1984). 'On the Distribution and Reference of Empty Pronouns', *Linguistic Inquiry* 15, 531–74.

Hudson, R. A. (1987). 'Zwicky on Heads', *Journal of Linguistics* 23, 109–32.

Hyman, L. M. (1975). *Phonology: Theory and Analysis*. New York: Holt, Rinehart & Winston.

Jackendoff, R. S. (1972). *Semantic Interpretation in Generative Grammar*. Cambridge, Mass.: MIT Press.

—— (1977). *X-bar Syntax: A Study of Phrase Structure*. Cambridge, Mass.: MIT Press.

—— (1975). 'Morphological and Semantic Regularities in the Lexicon', *Language* 51, 639–71.

—— (1990). 'On Larson's Treatment of the Double Object Construction', *Linguistic Inquiry* 18, 369–411.

Jaeggli, O. (1980). *On Some Phonologically Null Elements in Syntax*. Doctoral dissertation, MIT, Cambridge, Mass.

—— (1981). *Topics in Romance Syntax*. Dordrecht: Foris.

—— (1986). 'Passive', *Linguistic Inquiry* 17, 587–633.

—— and Safir, K. (eds) (1989). *The Null Subject Parameter*. Dordrecht: Reidel.

Jelinek, E. (1984). 'Empty Categories, Case and Configurationality', *Natural Language and Linguistic Theory* 2, 39–76.

Jones, M., and Thomas, A. (1977). *The Welsh Language*. Cardiff: University of Wales Publications.

Kaye, J. (1989). *Phonology: A Cognitive View*. Hillsdale, NJ: Erlbaum.

—— and Lowenstamm, J. (1986). 'Compensatory Lengthening in Tiberian Hebrew', in L. Wetzels and E. Sezer (eds), *Studies in Compensatory Lengthening*. Dordrecht: Foris.

Kayne, R. S. (1975). *French Syntax*. Cambridge, Mass.: MIT Press.

—— (1984). *Connectedness and Binary Branching*. Dordrecht: Foris.

—— (1987). 'Facets of Romance Past Participle Agreement', MS, MIT, Cambridge, Mass.

—— (1989). 'Null Subjects and Clitic Climbing', in O. Jaeggli and K. Safir (eds), *The Null Subject Parameter*. Dordrecht: Reidel.

Kempson, R. (1977). *Semantic Theory*. Cambridge: Cambridge University Press.

Kenesi, I. (ed.) (1985). *Approaches to Hungarian*, i. Szeged: University Press.

—— (ed.) (1987). *Approaches to Hungarian*, ii. Szeged: University Press.

Kenstowicz, M. J., and Kisseberth, C. (1979). *Generative Phonology: Description and Theory*. New York: Academic Press.

Keyser, S. J., and Roeper, T. (1984). 'On the Middle and Ergative Constructions in English', *Linguistic Inquiry* 15, 381–416.

E-Kiss, K. (1987). *Configurationality in Hungarian*. Dordrecht: Reidel.

Klima, E. (1964). 'Negation in English', in J. A. Fodor and J. J. Katz (eds), *Readings in the Philosophy of Language*. Englewood Cliffs, NJ: Prentice-Hall.

Kitagawa, Y. (1986). *Subjects in Japanese and English*. Doctoral dissertation, University of Massachusetts, Amherst.

Koopman, H. (1984). *The Syntax of Verbs*. Dordrecht: Foris.

—— (1987). 'On the Absence of Case Chains in Bambara', MS, UCLA, Los Angeles.

—— and Sportiche, D. (1991). 'The Position of Subjects', *Lingua* 85, special issue on VSO languages, ed. J. McCloskey.

Koster, J. (1975). 'Dutch as an SOV Language', *Linguistic Analysis* 1, 111–36.

—— (1984). 'On Binding and Control', *Linguistic Inquiry* 15, 417–59.

Kuno, S., and Robinson, J. (1972). 'Multiple *Wh*-questions', *Linguistic Inquiry* 3, 463–87.

Kuroda, S.-Y. (1988). 'Whether We Agree or Not: A Comparative Syntax of English and Japanese', in W. Poser (ed.), *Papers on the Second International Workshop on Japanese Syntax*. CSLI, Stanford University.

Lakoff, G. (1968). 'Pronouns and Reference', distributed by the Indiana University Linguistics Club, Bloomington.

Larson, R. K. (1988). 'On the Double Object Construction', *Linguistic Inquiry* 19, 335–91.

—— (1991). 'Double Objects Revisited: Reply to Jackendoff', *Linguistic Inquiry* 21, 589–632.

Lasnik, H. (1976). 'Some Thoughts on Coreference', *Linguistic Analysis* 2, 1–22.

—— and Saito, M. (1984). 'On the Nature of Proper Government', *Linguistic Inquiry* 14, 235–89.

—— —— (1992). *Move-alpha*. Cambridge, Mass.: MIT Press.

Lees, R. (1963). *The Grammar of English Nominalizations*. The Hague: Mouton.

Levin, B., and Rappaport, M. (1986). 'The Formation of Adjectival Passives', *Linguistic Inquiry* 17, 623–62.

Lightfoot, D. (1976). 'The Theoretical Implications of Subject Raising', *Foundations of Language* 14, 257–86.

—— (1977). 'On Traces and Conditions on Rules', in O. Culicover, T. Wasow, and A. Akmajian (eds), *Formal Syntax*. New York: Academic Press.

—— (1979). *Principles of Diachronic Syntax*. Cambridge: Cambridge University Press.

—— (1981). 'Explaining Syntactic Change', in N. Hornstein and D. Lightfoot, *Explanation in Linguistics*. London: Longman, 209–39.

—— (1991). *How to Set Parameters*. Cambridge, Mass.: MIT Press.

Lillo-Martin, D. C. (1991). *Universal Grammar and American Sign Language: Setting the Null Argument Parameters*. Dordrecht: Kluwer.

Longobardi, G. (1985). 'Connectedness, Scope and C-Command', *Linguistic Inquiry* 16, 163–92.

Lucas, C. (ed.) (1990). *Sign Language Research: Theoretical Issues*. Washington, DC: Gallaudet University Press.

Manzini, H. R. (1983). 'On Control and Control Theory', *Linguistic Inquiry* 14, 421–46.

Maracz, L. (1989). *Asymmetries in Hungarian*. Doctoral dissertation, University of Groningen.

Marantz, A. (1984). *On the Nature of Grammatical Relations*. Cambridge, Mass.: MIT Press.

Mathews, G. H. (1964). *Hidatsa Syntax*. The Hague: Mouton.

May, R. (1977). *The Grammar of Quantification*. Doctoral dissertation, MIT, Cambridge, Mass.

—— (1985). *Logical Form: Its Structure and Derivation*. Cambridge, Mass.: MIT Press.

Menn, L., and Obler, L. K. (1990). *Agrammatic Aphasia: A Cross-Language Narrative Sourcebook*. Amsterdam: Benjamins.

Mithun, M. (1984). 'The Evolution of Noun Incorporation', *Language* 60, 847–95.

—— (1986). 'On the Nature of Noun Incorporation', *Language* 62, 32–8.

Mohammad, M. A. (1989). *The Sentential Structure of Arabic*. Doctoral dissertation, University of Southern California, Los Angeles.

Mohanan, K. P. (1982). 'Grammatical Relations and Clause Structure in Malayalam', in J. Bresnan (ed.), *The Mental Representation of Grammatical Relations*. Cambridge, Mass.: MIT Press.

Muysken, P. C. and van Riemsdijk, H. C. (1985). 'Projecting Features and Feature Projections', in P. Muysken and H. van Riemsdijk (eds), *Features and Projections*. Dordrecht: Foris.

Napoli, J. D. (1989). *Predication Theory*. Cambridge: Cambridge University Press.

Newmeyer, F. (1980). *Linguistic Theory in America*. New York: Academic Press.

—— (1983). *Grammatical Theory: Its Limits and Its Possibilities*. Chicago: University of Chicago Press.

—— (1991). 'Rules and Principles in the Historical Development of Generative Syntax', in A. Kasher, *The Chomskyan Turn*. Oxford: Blackwell, 200–30.

Nishigauchi, T. (1986). *Quantification in Syntax*. Doctoral dissertation, University of Massachusetts, Amherst.

Oehrle, R. (1976). *The Grammatical Status of the English Dative Shift Alternation*. Doctoral dissertation, MIT, Cambridge, Mass.

Ouhalla, J. (1993). 'Functional Categories, Agrammatism and Language Acquisition', *Linguistische Berichte* 143, 3–36.

Pankhurst, J., Sharwood-Smith, M., and van Buren, P. (eds) (1988). *Learnability and Second Languages*. Dordrecht: Foris.

Pearce, E. (1990). *Parameters in Old French Syntax: Infinitival Complements*. Dordrecht: Kluwer.

Perlmutter, D. M. (1971). *Deep and Surface Structure Constraints in Syntax*. New York: Holt, Rinehart & Winston.

—— (1978). 'Impersonal Passives and the Unaccusative Hypothesis', in *Proceedings of the Fourth Annual Meeting of the Berkeley Linguistics Society*. Berkeley: University of California, 157–89.

—— (ed.) (1983). *Studies in Relational Grammar*, i. Chicago: University of Chicago Press.

—— and Rosen, C. (eds) (1984). *Studies in Relational Grammar*, ii. Chicago: University of Chicago Press.

Pesetsky, D. (1982). *Paths and Categories*. Doctoral dissertation, MIT, Cambridge, Mass.

—— (1987). '*Wh*-in-situ: Movement and Unselective Binding', in E. Reuland and A. G. B. ter Meulen (eds), *The Representation of Indefiniteness*. Cambridge, Mass.: MIT Press.

Pierce, A. (1989). *On the Emergence of Syntax: a Crosslinguistic Study*. Doctoral dissertation, MIT, Cambridge, Mass.

Platzack, C. (1986a). 'The Position of the Finite Verb in Swedish', in H. Haider and M. Prinzhorn (eds), *Verb Second Phenomena in Germanic Languages*. Dordrecht: Foris, 27–47.

—— (1986b). 'COMP, INFL and Germanic Word Order', in L. Hellan and K. Christensen (eds), *Topics in Scandinavian Syntax*. Dordrecht: Reidel, 185–234.

Pollock, J.-Y. (1989). 'Verb Movement, UG and the Structure of IP', *Linguistic Inquiry* 20, 365–424.

Postal, P. M. (1966). 'On So-called "Pronouns" in English', in F. P. Dineen (ed.), *Report on the 17th Annual Round Table Meeting in Linguistics and Language Studies*. Washington, DC: Georgetown University Press.

—— (1971). *Cross-over Phenomena*. New York: Holt, Rinehart and Winston.

—— (1974). *On Raising*. Cambridge, Mass.: MIT Press.

—— (1979). *Some Syntactic Rules of Mohawk*. New York: Garland Press.

—— and Pullum, G. K. (1982). 'The Contraction Debate', *Linguistic Inquiry* 13, 211–22.

Quirk, R., Greenbaum, S., Leech, G., and Svartvik, J. (1985). *A Comprehensive Grammar of the English Language*. London: Longman.

Radford, A. (1988). *Transformational Grammar: A First Course*. Cambridge: Cambridge University Press.

—— (1990). *Syntactic Theory and the Acquisition of English Syntax*. Oxford: Blackwell.

Raposo, E. (1986). 'On the Null Object in European Portuguese', in O. Jaeggli and C. Silva-Corvalan (eds), *Studies in Romance Linguistics*. Dordrecht: Foris, 373–90.

Reinhart, T. (1976). *The Syntactic Domain of Anaphora*. Doctoral dissertation, MIT, Cambridge, Mass.

—— (1979). 'Syntactic Domains for Semantic Rules', in F. Guenthner and S. J. Schmidt (eds), *Formal Semantics and Pragmatics for Natural Languages*. Dordrecht: Reidel.

—— (1983). *Anaphora and Semantic Interpretation*. London: Croom Helm.

van Riemsdijk, H. (1978). *A Case Study in Syntactic Markedness: The Binding Nature of Prepositional Phrases*. Dordrecht: Foris.

—— and Williams, E. (1986). *Introduction to the Theory of Grammar*. Cambridge, Mass.: MIT Press.

Rizzi, L. (1982). *Issues in Italian Syntax*. Dordrecht: Foris.
—— (1986a). 'Null Objects in Italian and the Theory of *pro*', *Linguistic Inquiry* 17, 501–58.
—— (1986b). 'On the Status of Subject Clitics in Romance', in O. Jaeggli and C. Silva-Corvalan (eds), *Studies in Romance Linguistics*. Dordrecht: Foris, 391–419.
—— (1990). *Relativized Minimality*. Cambridge, Mass.: MIT Press.
Roberts, I. (1987). *The Representation of Implicit and Dethematized Subjects*. Dordrecht: Foris.
Roeper, T., and Williams, E. (1987). *Parameter Setting*. Dordrecht: Reidel.
Rögnvaldsson, E., and Thráinsson, H. (1990). 'On Icelandic Word Order Once More', in J. Maling and A. Zaenen (eds), *Modern Icelandic Syntax*. San Diego, Calif.: Academic Press, 3–40.
Rosenbaum, P. S. (1967). *The Grammar of English Predicate Complement Constructions*. Cambridge, Mass.: MIT Press.
Ross, J. R. (1967). *Constraints on Variables in Syntax*. Doctoral dissertation, MIT, Cambridge, Mass.
—— (1986). *Infinite Syntax!* Norwood, NJ: Ablex.
Rothstein, S. (1983). *The Syntactic Forms of Predication*. Doctoral dissertation, MIT, Cambridge, Mass.
Rouveret, A. (1992). *Principes généraux et variation typologique: une syntaxe du gallois*. Paris: CNRS.
—— and Vergnaud, J.-R. (1980). 'Specifying Reference to the Subject', *Linguistic Inquiry* 11, 97–202.
Saito, M. (1985). *Some Asymmetries in Japanese and their Theoretical Implications*. Doctoral dissertation, MIT, Cambridge, Mass.
—— and Hoji, H. (1983). 'Weak Crossover and Move Alpha in Japanese', *Natural Language and Linguistic Theory* 1, 245–59.
Santorini, B. (1990). *The Generalization of the Verb–Second Constraint in the History of Yiddish*. Doctoral dissertation, University of Pennsylvania.
Scalise, S. (1984). *Generative Morphology*. Dordrecht: Foris.
Seiter, W. (1980). *Studies in Niuean Syntax*. New York: Garland.
Selkirk, E. (1982). *The Syntax of Words*. Cambridge, Mass.: MIT Press.
Sells, P. (1984). *Syntax and Semantics of Resumptive Pronouns*. Doctoral dissertation, University of Massachusetts, Amherst.
Shlonsky, U. (1987). *Null and Displaced Subjects*. Doctoral dissertation, MIT, Cambridge, Mass.
Smith, N. V. (1989). *The Twitter Machine: Reflections on Language*. Oxford: Blackwell.
—— and Wilson, D. (1979). *Modern Linguistics: The Results of Chomsky's Revolution*. Harmondsworth, Middlesex: Penguin.
—— and Tsimpli, I. M. (1991). 'Linguistic Modularity? A Case Study of a "Savant" Linguist', *Lingua* 84, 315–51.
Spencer, A. (1991). *Morphological Theory*. Oxford: Blackwell.
Sperber, D., and Wilson, D. (1986). *Relevance: Communication and Cognition*. Oxford: Blackwell.
Sportiche, D. (1988). 'A Theory of Floating Quantifiers and its Corollaries for Constituent Structure', *Linguistic Inquiry* 19, 425–49.
Sproat, R. (1985a). 'Welsh Syntax and VSO Structure', *Natural Language and Linguistic Theory* 3, 173–216.
—— (1985b). *On Deriving the Lexicon*. Doctoral dissertation, MIT, Cambridge, Mass.
Steele, S. (1981). *An Encyclopedia of AUX*. Cambridge, Mass.: MIT Press.
Stowell, T. (1981). *Origins of Phrase Structure*. Doctoral dissertation, MIT, Cambridge, Mass.
Szabolci, A. (1987). 'Functional Categories in the Noun Phrase', in Kenesei (1985).
Taraldsen, K. T. (1981). 'The Theoretical Interpretation of a Class of Marked Extractions', in A. Belletti, L. Brandi, and L. Rizzi (eds), *Theory of Markedness in Generative Grammar*. Pisa: Scuola Normale Superiore.
Tellier, C. (1988). *Universal Licensing: Implications for Parasitic Gap Constructions*. Doctoral dissertation, McGill University, Montreal.
Thiersch, G. (1978). *Topics in German Syntax*. Doctoral dissertation, MIT, Cambridge, Mass.

Travis, L. (1984). *Parameters and the Effects of Word Order Variation*. Doctoral dissertation, MIT, Cambridge, Mass.

Trithart, M. (1977). *Relational Grammar and Chichewa Subjectivization*. Doctoral dissertation, University of California at Los Angeles.

Tsimpli, I. M. (1990). 'The Clause Structure and Word Order of Modern Greek', *UCL Working Papers in Linguistics* 2, 226–59.

—— (1992). *Functional Categories and Maturation: The Prefunctional Stage of Language Acquisition*. Doctoral dissertation, University College London.

—— and Roussou, A. (1991). 'Parameter-Resetting in L2?', *UCL Working Papers in Linguistics* 3, 149–70.

Vergnaud, J.-R. (1982), *Dépendances et niveaux de représentation en syntaxe*. Doctorat d'état, Université de Paris VII.

Vikner, S. (1990). *Verb Movement and Licensing of NP-Positions in the Germanic Languages*. Doctoral dissertation, Université de Genève.

Wasow, T. (1972). *Anaphoric Relations in English*. Doctoral dissertation, MIT, Cambridge, Mass.

—— (1977). 'Transformations and the Lexicon', in P. Culicover, T. Wasow, and A. Akmajian (eds), *Formal Syntax*. New York: Academic Press.

—— (1979). *Anaphora in Generative Grammar*. Ghent: E. Story-Scientia.

Weissenborn, J., Goodluck, J., and Roeper, T. (eds) (1992). *Studies in Theoretical Psycholinguistics: Papers from the Berlin Workshop*. Hillsdale, NJ: Erlbaum.

White, L. (1989). *Universal Grammar and Second Language Acquisition*. Amsterdam: Benjamins.

Williams, E. S. (1980). 'Predication', *Linguistic Inquiry* 11, 203–38.

—— (1981). 'Argument Structure and Morphology', *Linguistic Review* 1, 81–114.

—— (1982). 'Another Argument that Passive is Transformational', *Linguistic Inquiry* 13, 160–3.

—— (1983). 'Against Small Clauses', *Linguistic Inquiry* 14, 287–308.

—— (1987). Introduction to Roeper and Williams (1987).

Yamada, L. (1990). *A Case for the Modularity of Language*. Cambridge, Mass.: MIT Press.

Zubizarreta, M.-L. (1987). *Levels of Representation in the Lexicon and in the Syntax*. Dordrecht: Foris.

Subject Index

References are to page numbers. For those authors mentioned in the main text, see separate Author Index.

Author Index